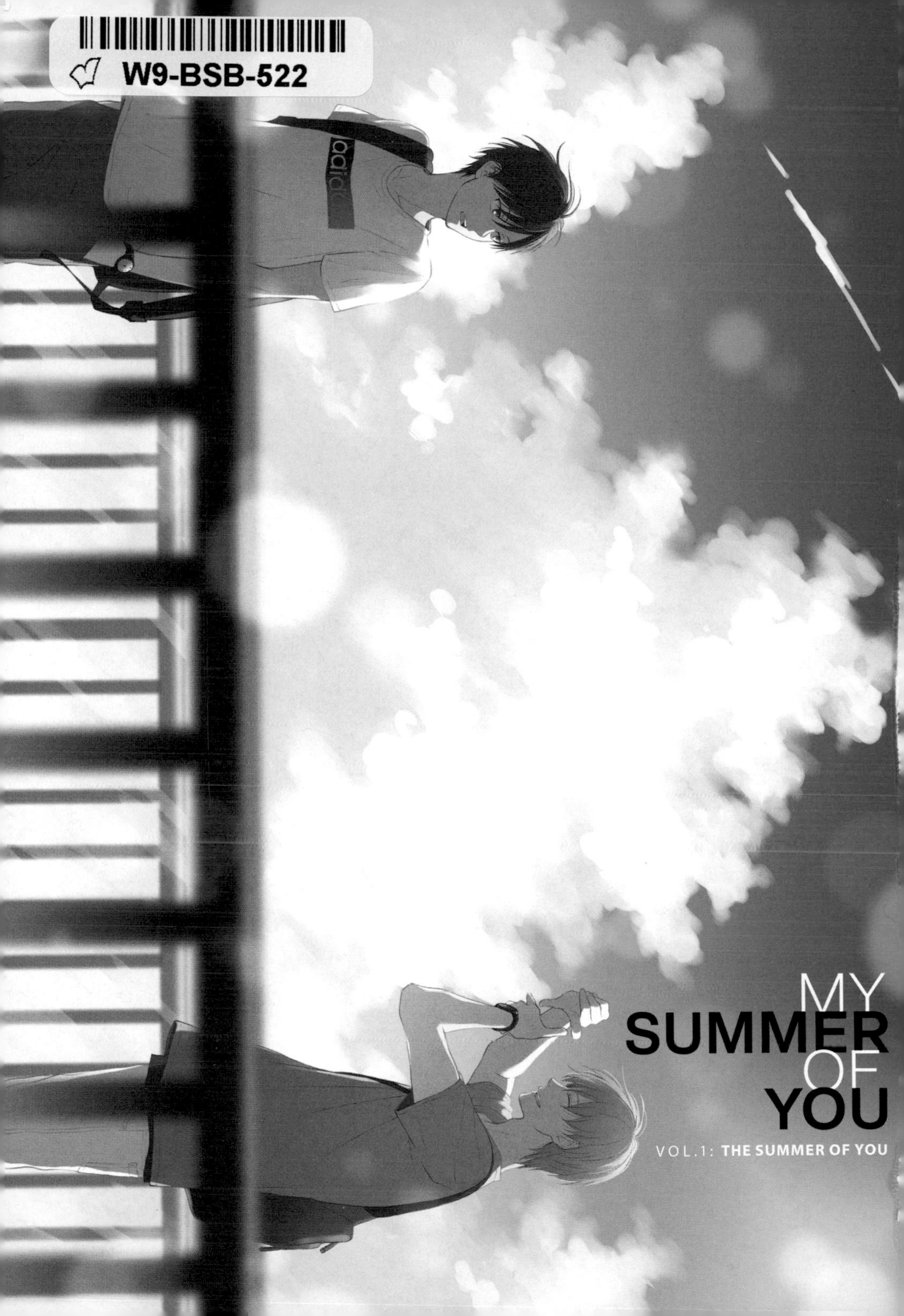

MY SUMMER OF YOU

VOL.1: THE SUMMER OF YOU

MY **SUMMER** OF **YOU**

VOL.1: **THE SUMMER OF YOU**

CONTENTS

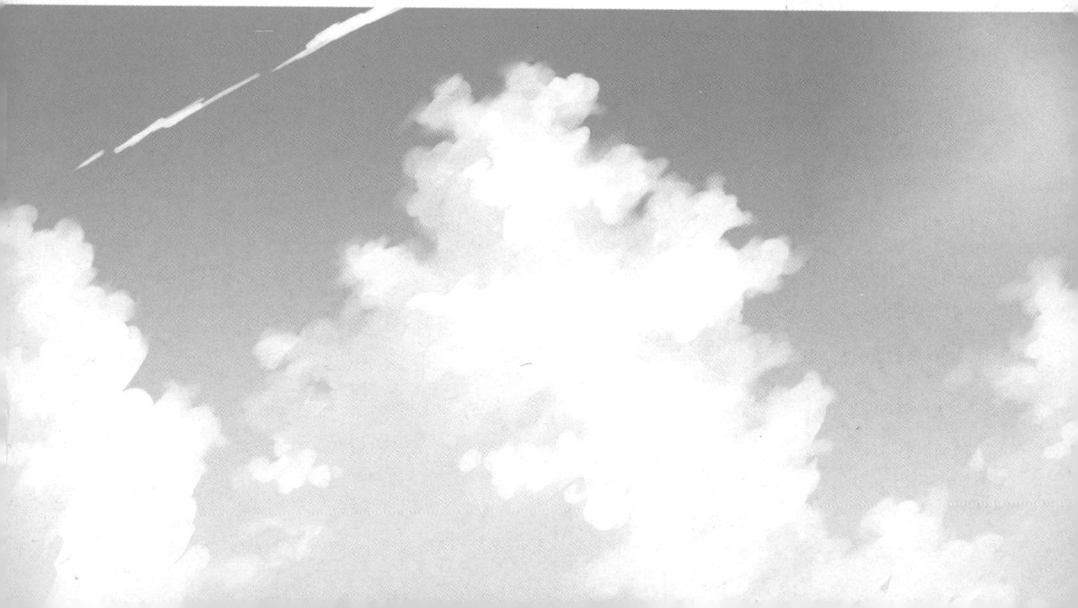

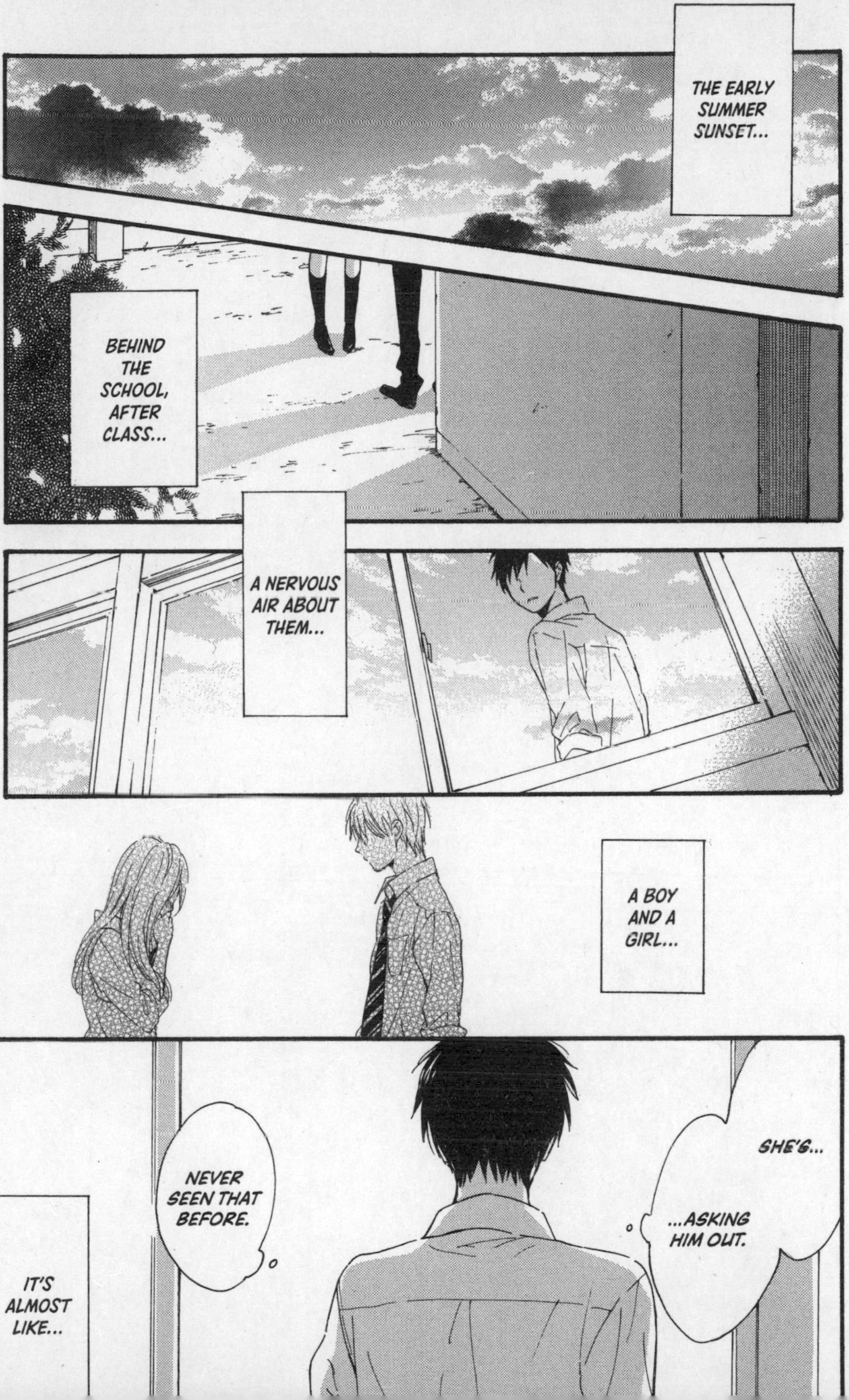
THE EARLY SUMMER SUNSET...
BEHIND THE SCHOOL, AFTER CLASS...
A NERVOUS AIR ABOUT THEM...
A BOY AND A GIRL...
SHE'S...
...ASKING HIM OUT.
NEVER SEEN THAT BEFORE.
IT'S ALMOST LIKE...

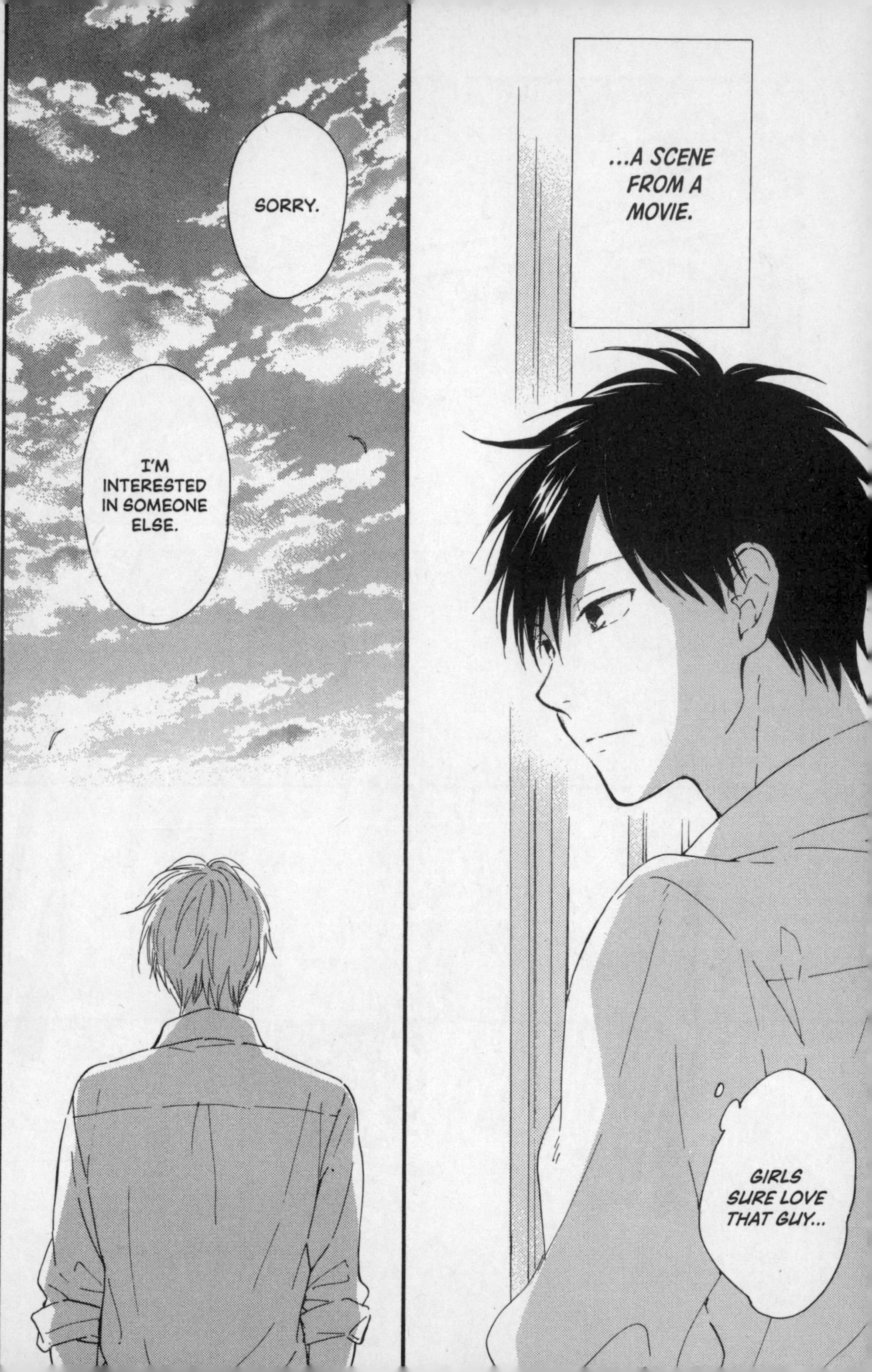
...A SCENE FROM A MOVIE.
GIRLS SURE LOVE THAT GUY...
SORRY.
I'M INTERESTED IN SOMEONE ELSE.

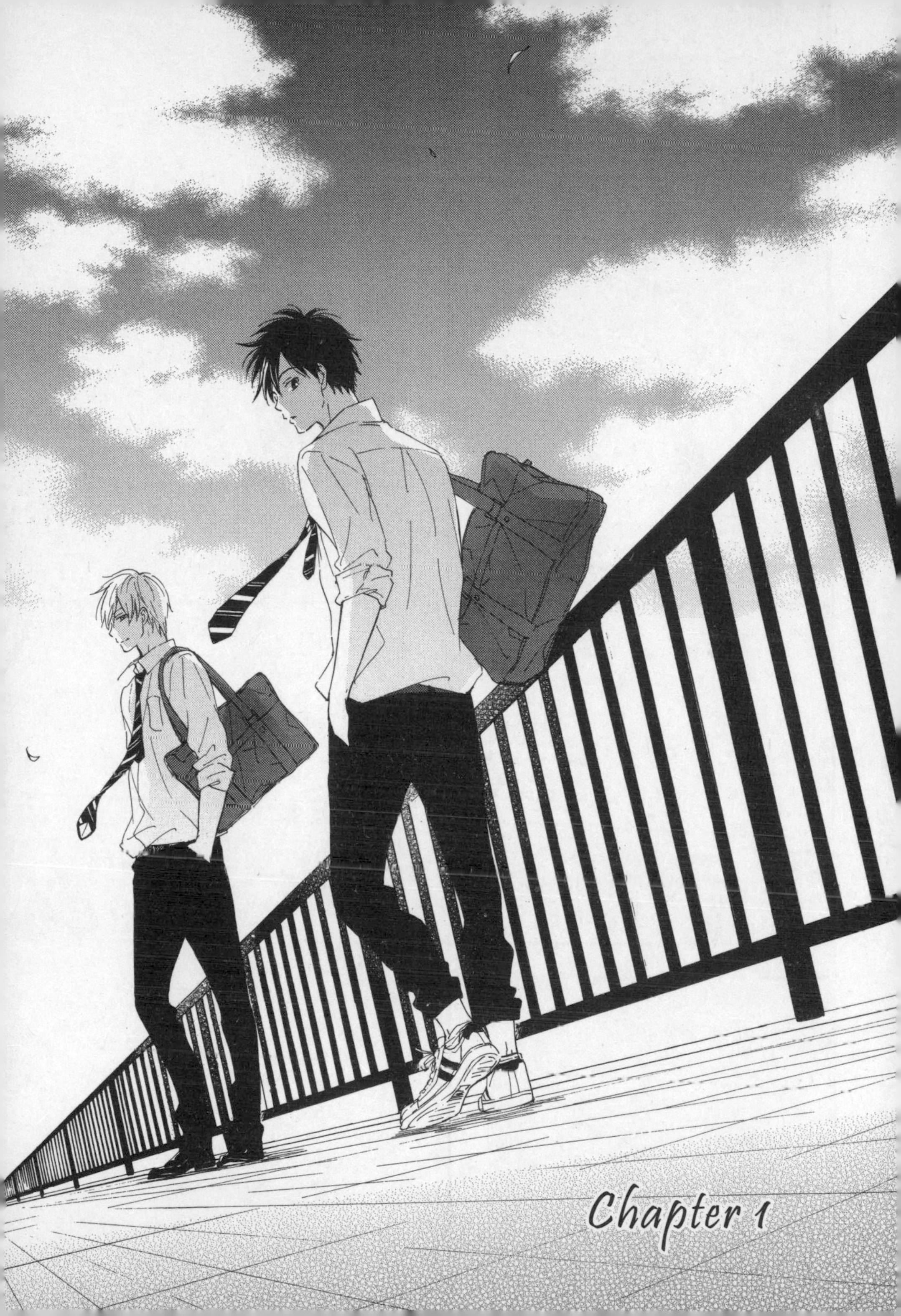
Chapter 1

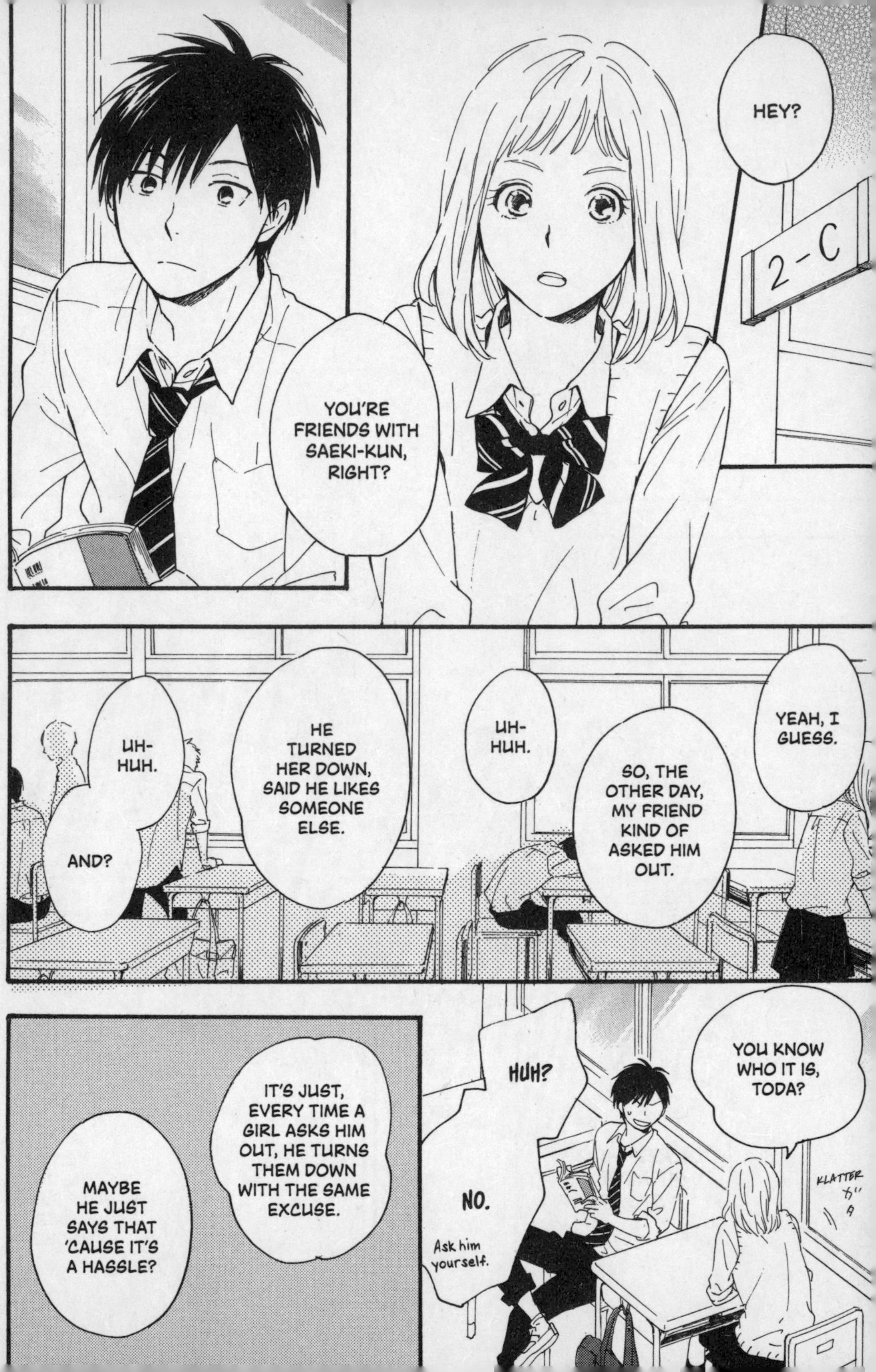
HEY?
2-C
YOU'RE FRIENDS WITH SAEKI-KUN, RIGHT?
YEAH, I GUESS.
SO, THE OTHER DAY, MY FRIEND KIND OF ASKED HIM OUT.
UH-HUH.
HE TURNED HER DOWN, SAID HE LIKES SOMEONE ELSE.
UH-HUH.
AND?
YOU KNOW WHO IT IS, TODA?
KLATTER
HUH?
NO.
Ask him yourself.
IT'S JUST, EVERY TIME A GIRL ASKS HIM OUT, HE TURNS THEM DOWN WITH THE SAME EXCUSE.
MAYBE HE JUST SAYS THAT 'CAUSE IT'S A HASSLE?

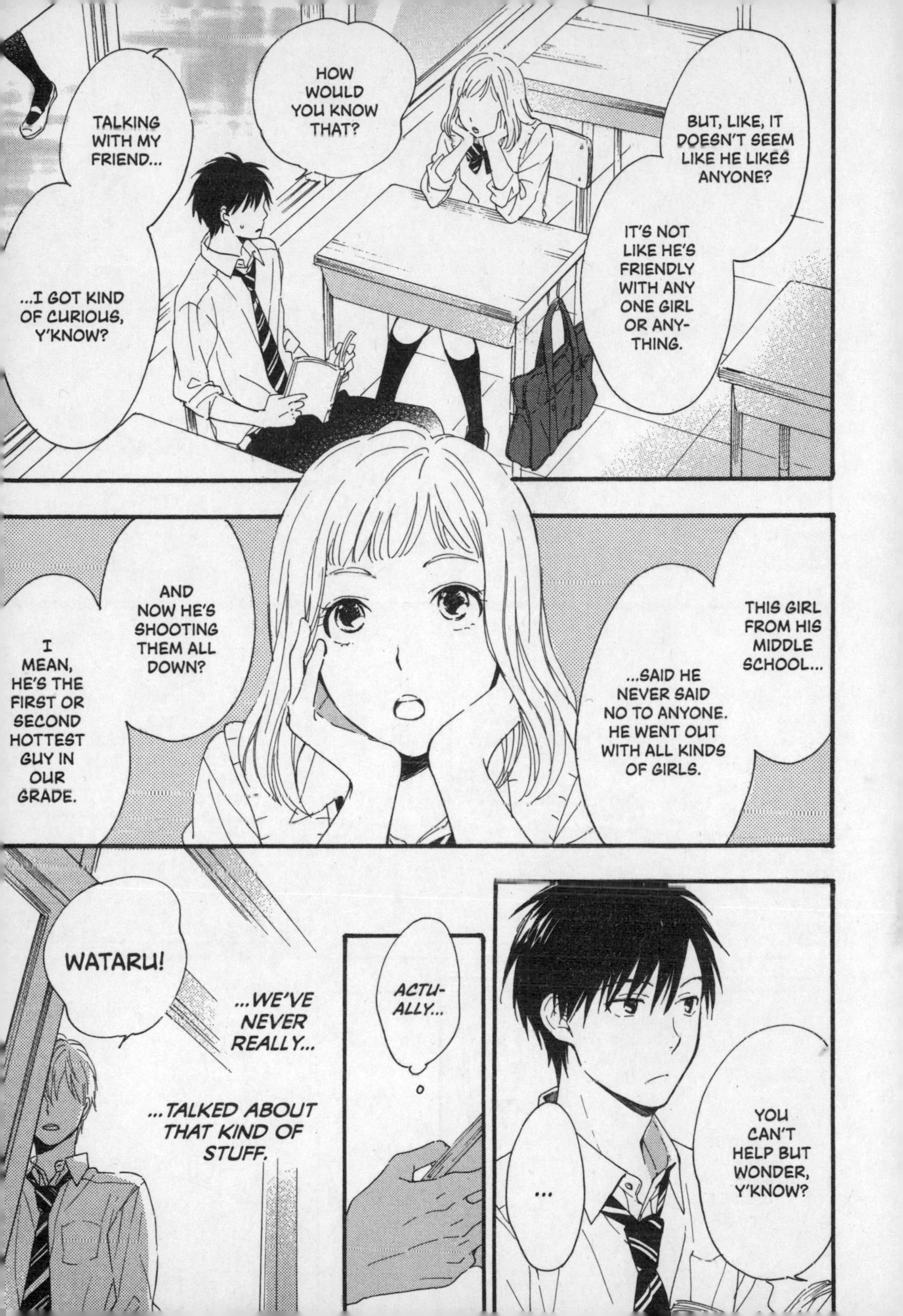
BUT, LIKE, IT DOESN'T SEEM LIKE HE LIKES ANYONE?
IT'S NOT LIKE HE'S FRIENDLY WITH ANY ONE GIRL OR ANY-THING.
HOW WOULD YOU KNOW THAT?
TALKING WITH MY FRIEND...
...I GOT KIND OF CURIOUS, Y'KNOW?
THIS GIRL FROM HIS MIDDLE SCHOOL...
...SAID HE NEVER SAID NO TO ANYONE. HE WENT OUT WITH ALL KINDS OF GIRLS.
AND NOW HE'S SHOOTING THEM ALL DOWN?
I MEAN, HE'S THE FIRST OR SECOND HOTTEST GUY IN OUR GRADE.
YOU CAN'T HELP BUT WONDER, Y'KNOW?
...
ACTU-ALLY...
...WE'VE NEVER REALLY...
...TALKED ABOUT THAT KIND OF STUFF.
WATARU!

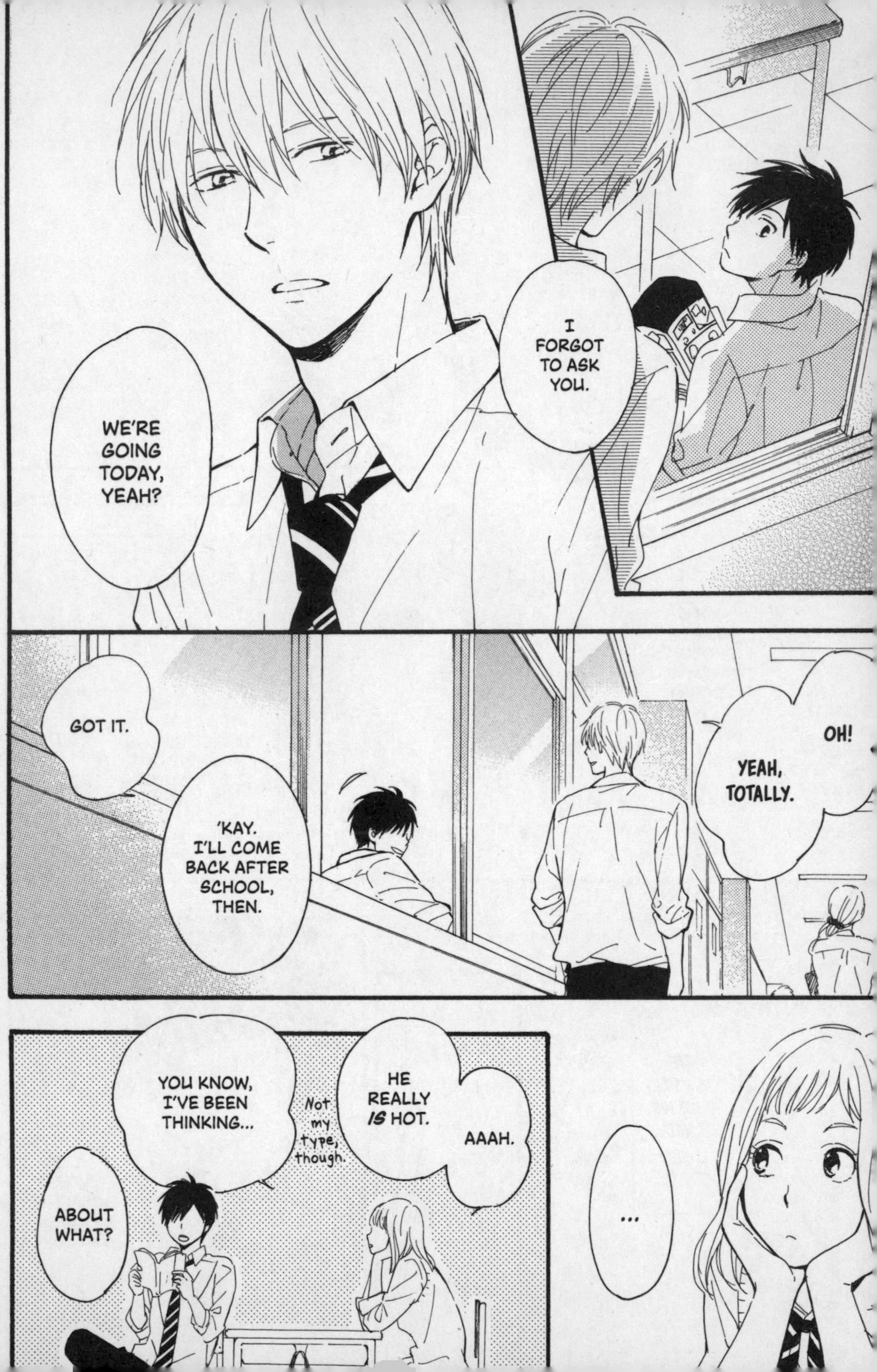
I FORGOT TO ASK YOU.
WE'RE GOING TODAY, YEAH?
OH! YEAH, TOTALLY.
GOT IT.
'KAY. I'LL COME BACK AFTER SCHOOL, THEN.
...
HE REALLY *IS* HOT.
AAAH.
Not my type, though.
YOU KNOW, I'VE BEEN THINKING...
ABOUT WHAT?

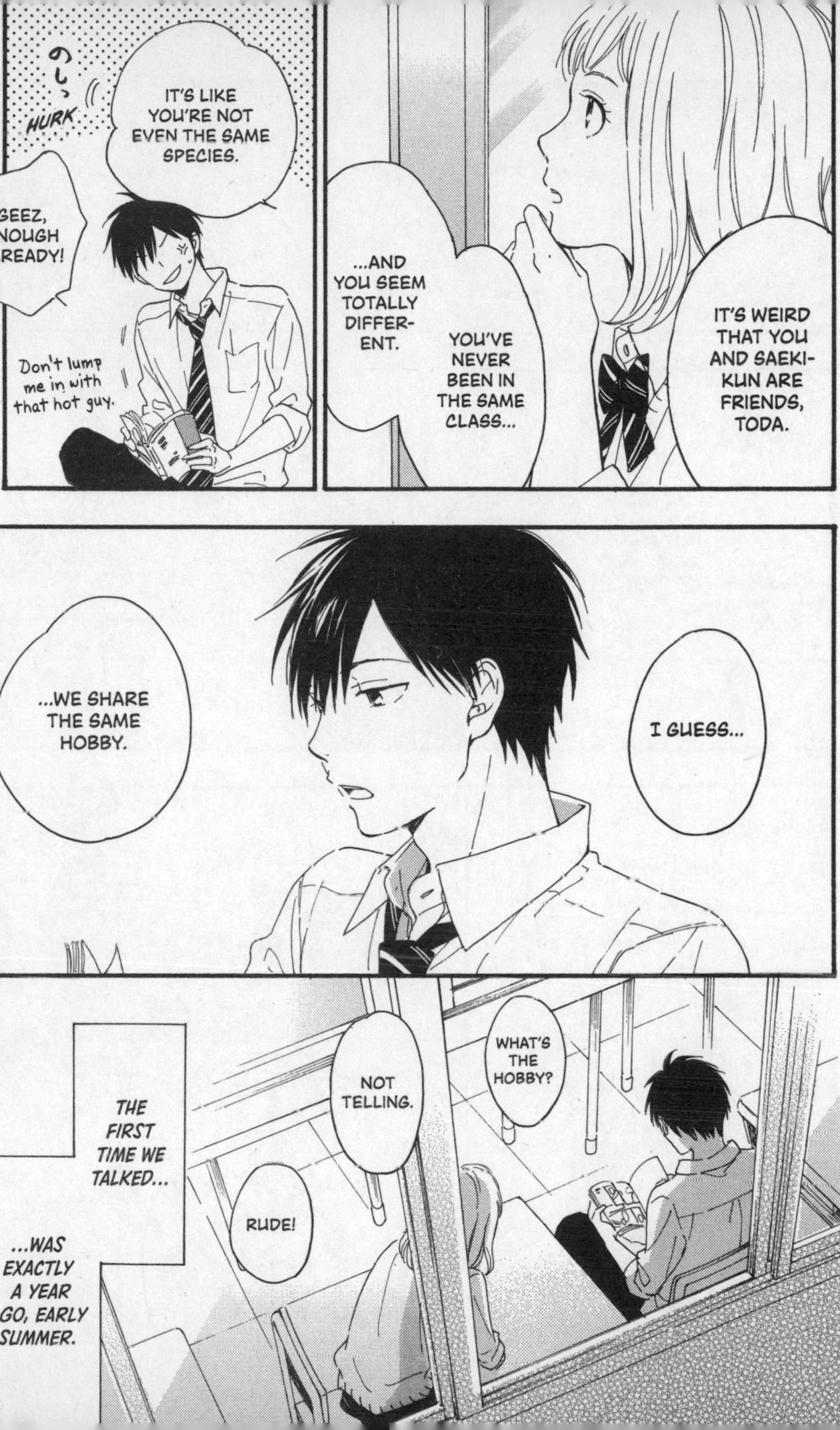
IT'S WEIRD THAT YOU AND SAEKI-KUN ARE FRIENDS, TODA.
YOU'VE NEVER BEEN IN THE SAME CLASS...
...AND YOU SEEM TOTALLY DIFFER-ENT.
IT'S LIKE YOU'RE NOT EVEN THE SAME SPECIES.
のしっ
HURK
GEEZ, ENOUGH ALREADY!
Don't lump me in with that hot guy.
I GUESS...
...WE SHARE THE SAME HOBBY.
WHAT'S THE HOBBY?
NOT TELLING.
RUDE!
THE FIRST TIME WE TALKED...
...WAS EXACTLY A YEAR AGO, EARLY SUMMER.

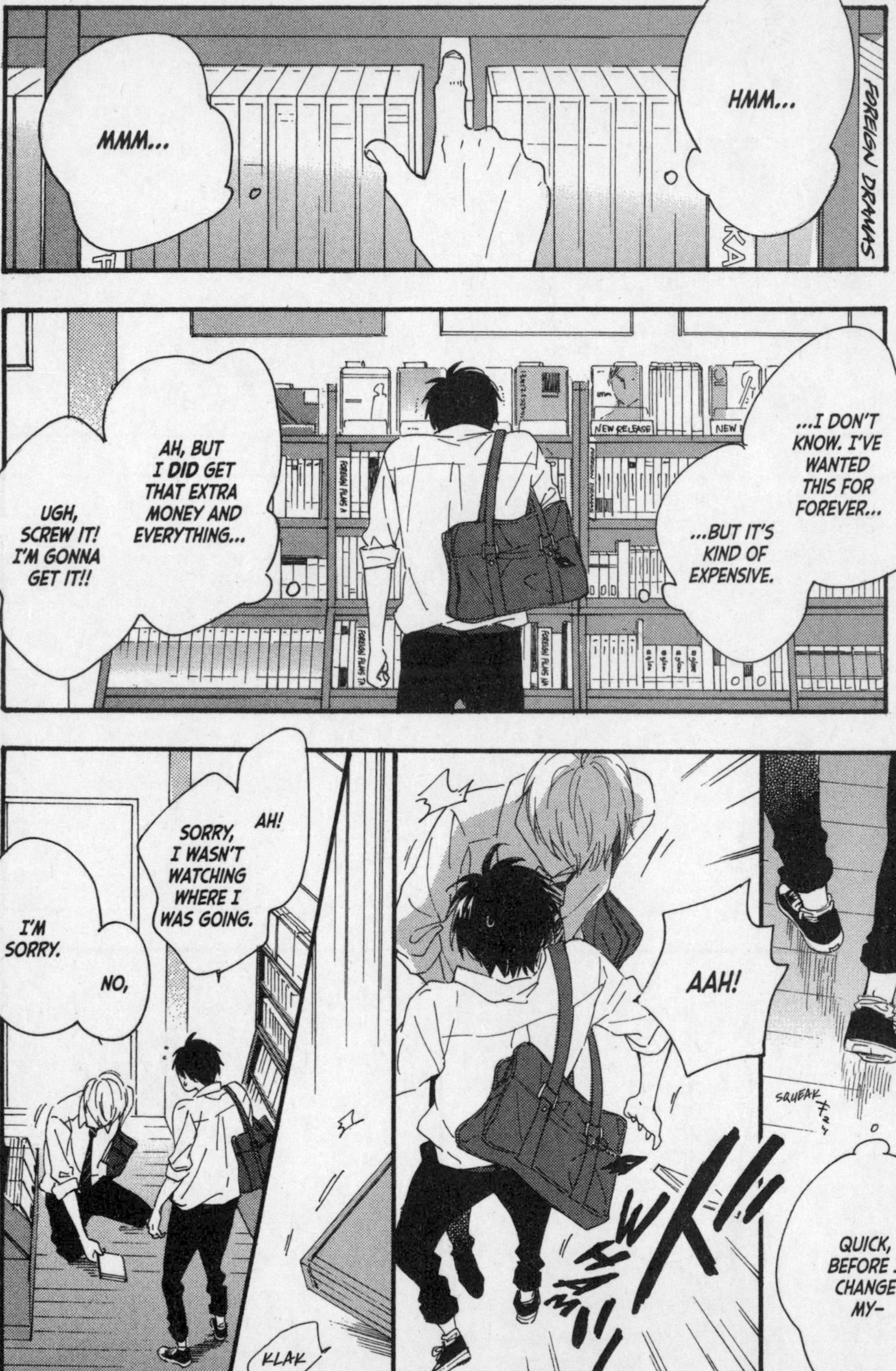
HMM...
FOREIGN DRAMAS
MMM...
NEW RELEASE
...I DON'T KNOW. I'VE WANTED THIS FOR FOREVER...
...BUT IT'S KIND OF EXPENSIVE.
AH, BUT I DID GET THAT EXTRA MONEY AND EVERYTHING...
UGH, SCREW IT! I'M GONNA GET IT!!
SQUEAK
QUICK, BEFORE I CHANGE MY—
AAH!
WHAM!!
KLAK
AH!
SORRY, I WASN'T WATCHING WHERE I WAS GOING.
NO,
I'M SORRY.

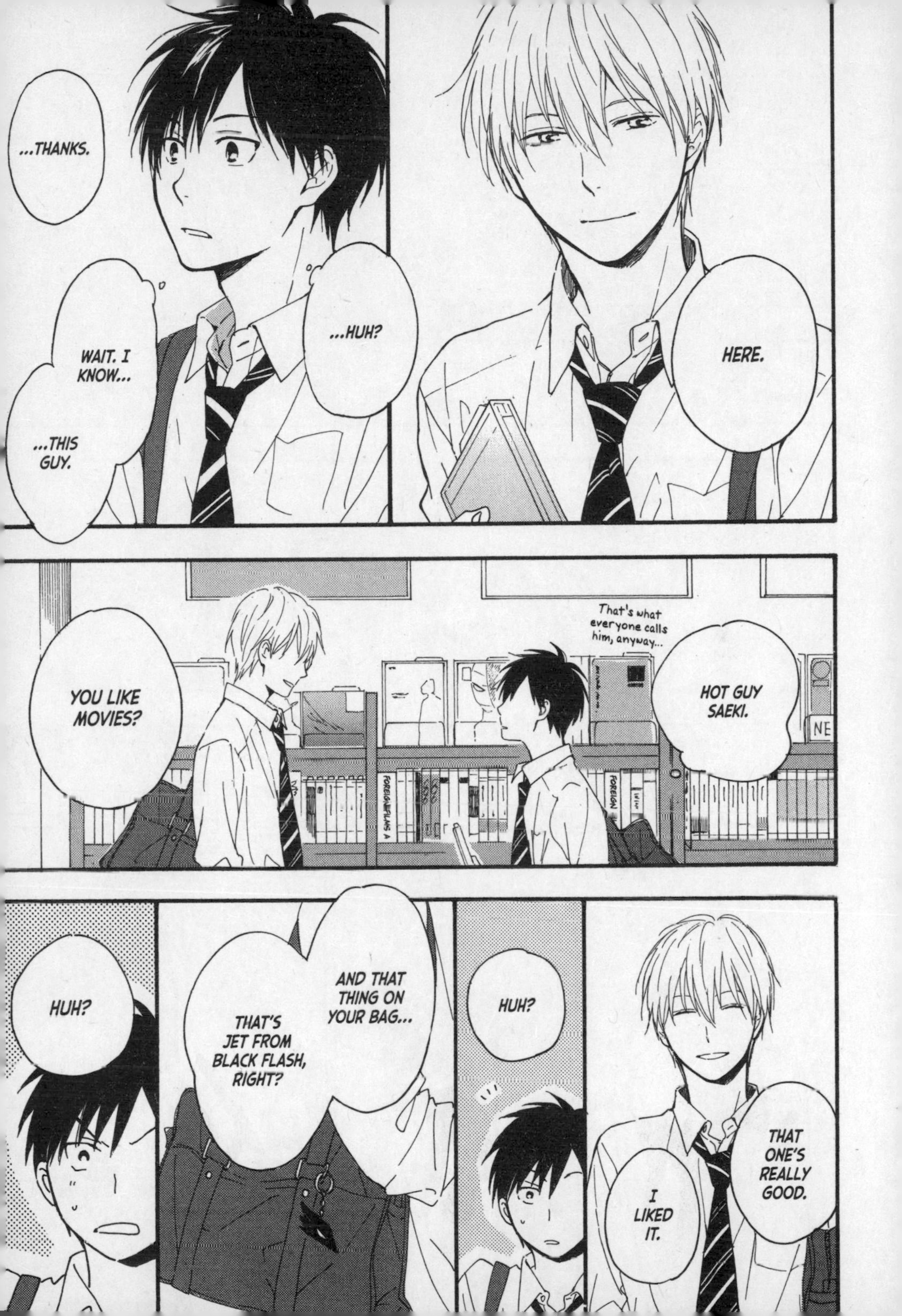
HERE.
...HUH?
...THANKS.
WAIT. I KNOW...
...THIS GUY.
HOT GUY SAEKI.
That's what everyone calls him, anyway...
YOU LIKE MOVIES?
THAT ONE'S REALLY GOOD.
I LIKED IT.
HUH?
AND THAT THING ON YOUR BAG...
THAT'S JET FROM BLACK FLASH, RIGHT?
HUH?
FOREIGN
FOREIGN FILMS A
NE

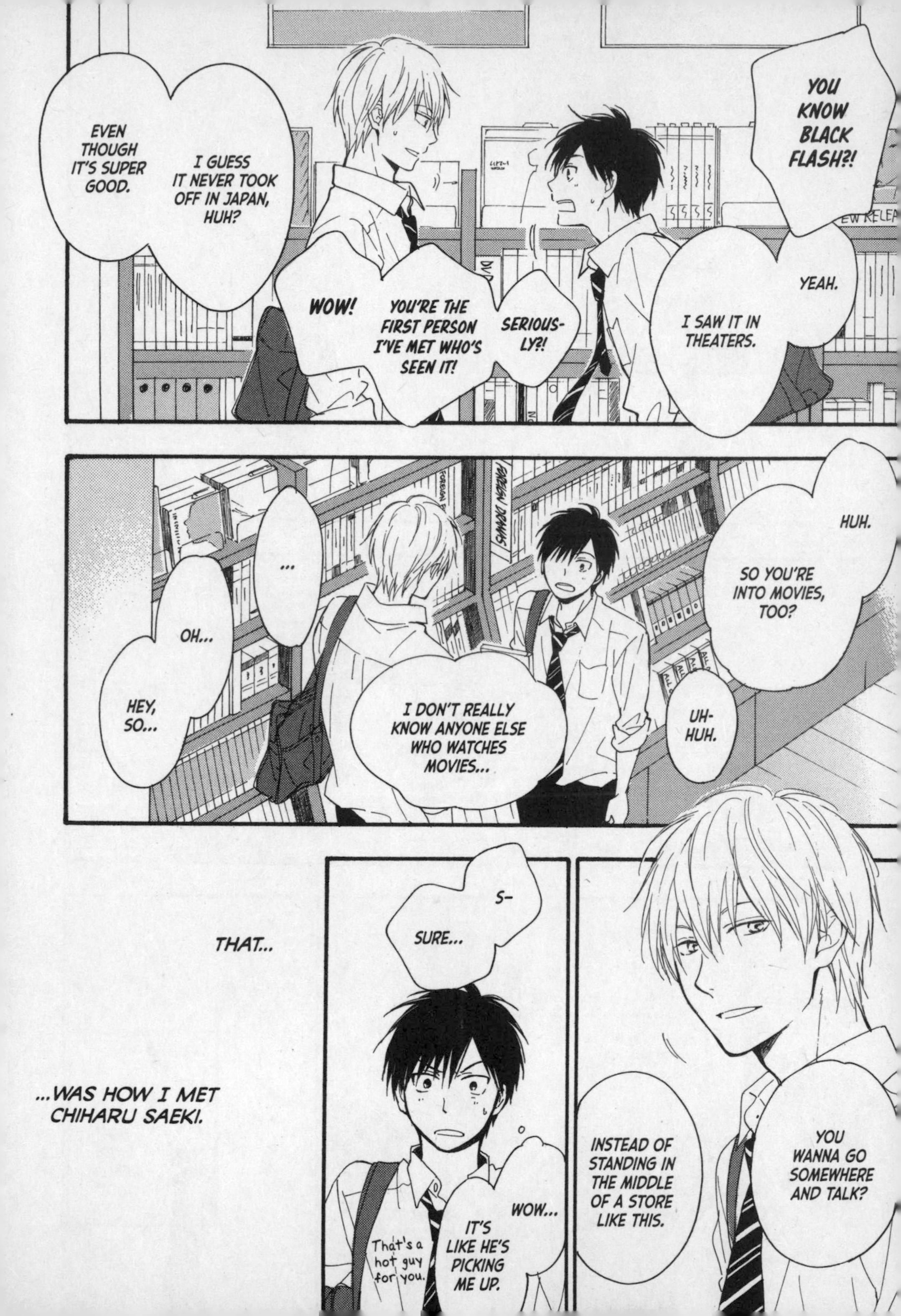
YOU KNOW BLACK FLASH?!
YEAH.
I SAW IT IN THEATERS.
SERIOUS-LY?!
WOW!
YOU'RE THE FIRST PERSON I'VE MET WHO'S SEEN IT!
I GUESS IT NEVER TOOK OFF IN JAPAN, HUH?
EVEN THOUGH IT'S SUPER GOOD.
HUH.
SO YOU'RE INTO MOVIES, TOO?
UH-HUH.
FOREIGN DRAMAS
I DON'T REALLY KNOW ANYONE ELSE WHO WATCHES MOVIES...
...
OH...
HEY, SO...
YOU WANNA GO SOMEWHERE AND TALK?
INSTEAD OF STANDING IN THE MIDDLE OF A STORE LIKE THIS.
S-
SURE...
WOW...
IT'S LIKE HE'S PICKING ME UP.
That's a hot guy for you.
THAT...
...WAS HOW I MET CHIHARU SAEKI.

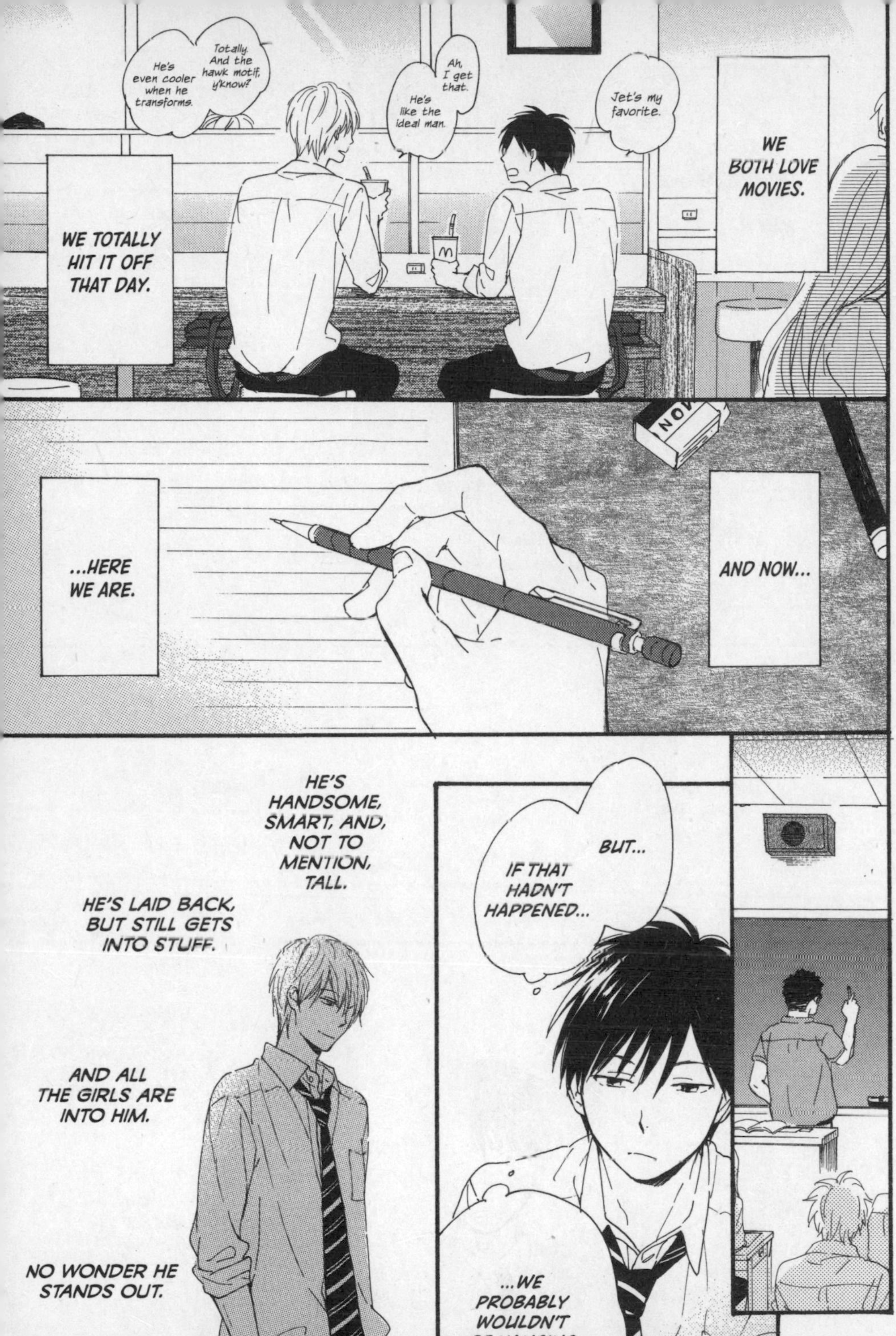
WE BOTH LOVE MOVIES.
Jet's my favorite.
Ah, I get that.
He's like the ideal man.
Totally. And the hawk motif, y'know?
He's even cooler when he transforms.
WE TOTALLY HIT IT OFF THAT DAY.
AND NOW...
...HERE WE ARE.
BUT...
IF THAT HADN'T HAPPENED...
...WE PROBABLY WOULDN'T BE HANGING OUT NOW.
HE'S HANDSOME, SMART, AND, NOT TO MENTION, TALL.
HE'S LAID BACK, BUT STILL GETS INTO STUFF.
AND ALL THE GIRLS ARE INTO HIM.
NO WONDER HE STANDS OUT.

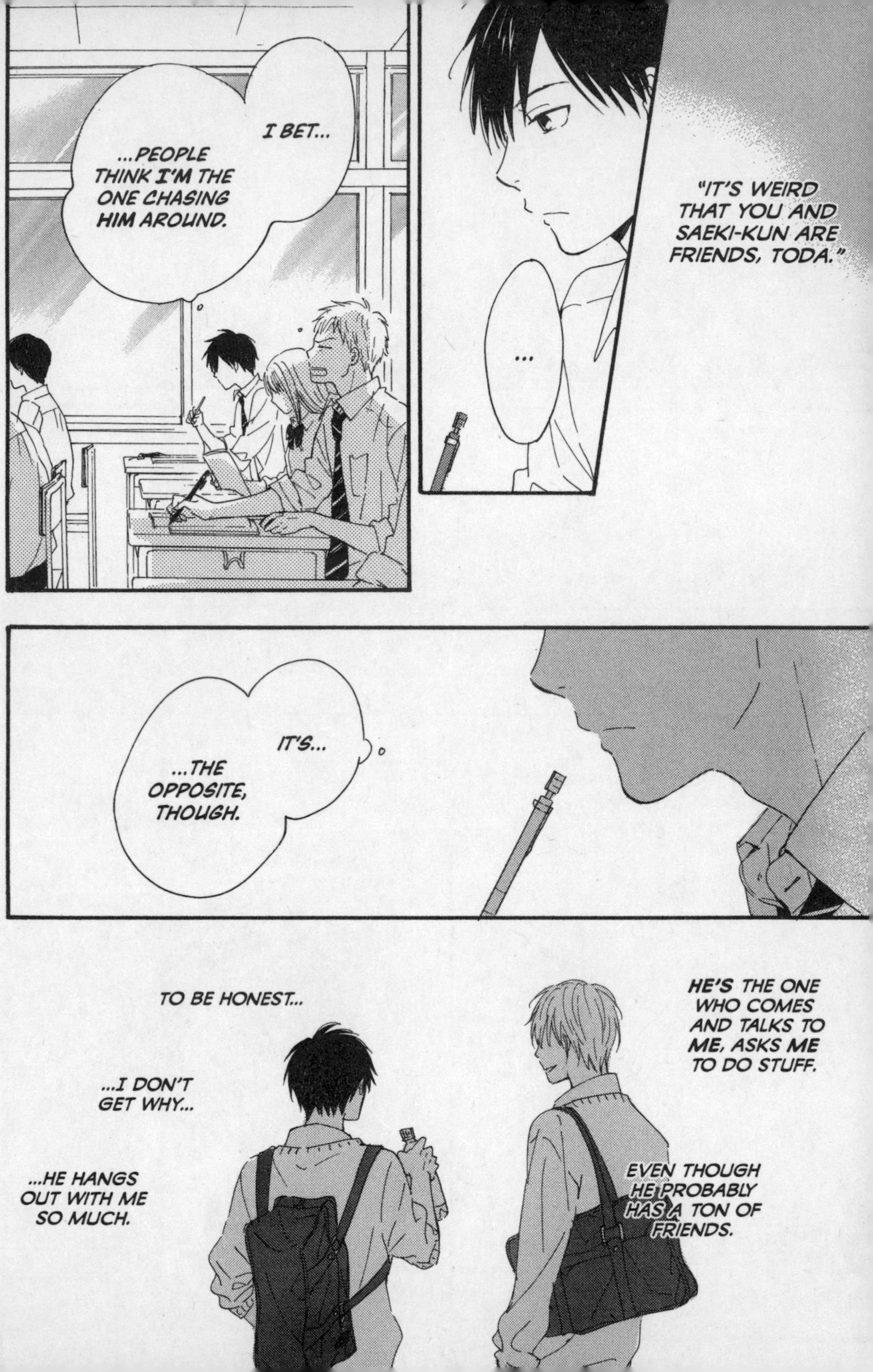
"IT'S WEIRD THAT YOU AND SAEKI-KUN ARE FRIENDS, TODA."
...
I BET...
...PEOPLE THINK I'M THE ONE CHASING HIM AROUND.
IT'S...
...THE OPPOSITE, THOUGH.
HE'S THE ONE WHO COMES AND TALKS TO ME, ASKS ME TO DO STUFF.
EVEN THOUGH HE PROBABLY HAS A TON OF FRIENDS.
TO BE HONEST...
...I DON'T GET WHY...
...HE HANGS OUT WITH ME SO MUCH.

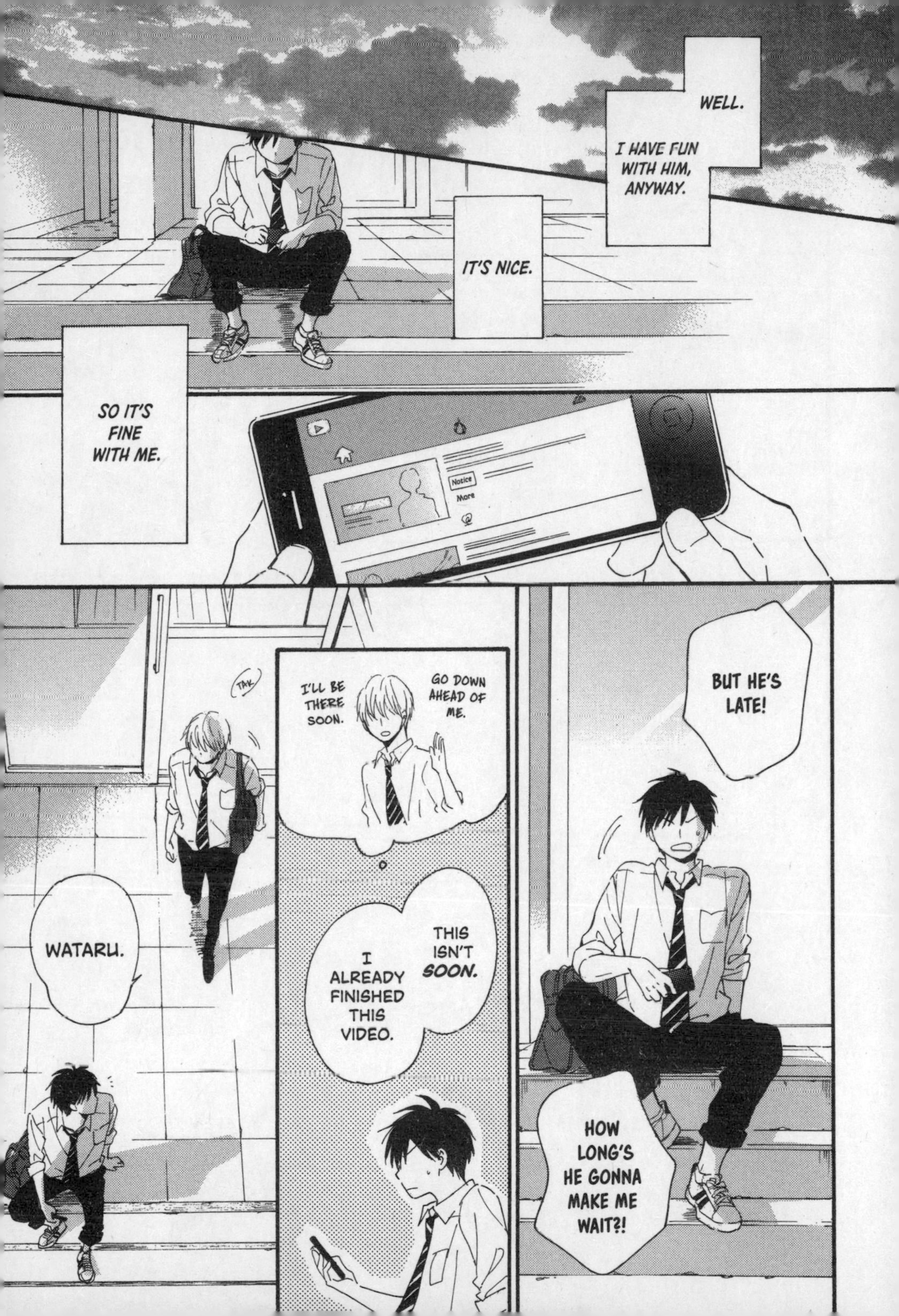
WELL.
I HAVE FUN WITH HIM, ANYWAY.
IT'S NICE.
SO IT'S FINE WITH ME.
Notice
More
BUT HE'S LATE!
HOW LONG'S HE GONNA MAKE ME WAIT?!
GO DOWN AHEAD OF ME.
I'LL BE THERE SOON.
THIS ISN'T SOON.
I ALREADY FINISHED THIS VIDEO.
TAK
WATARU.

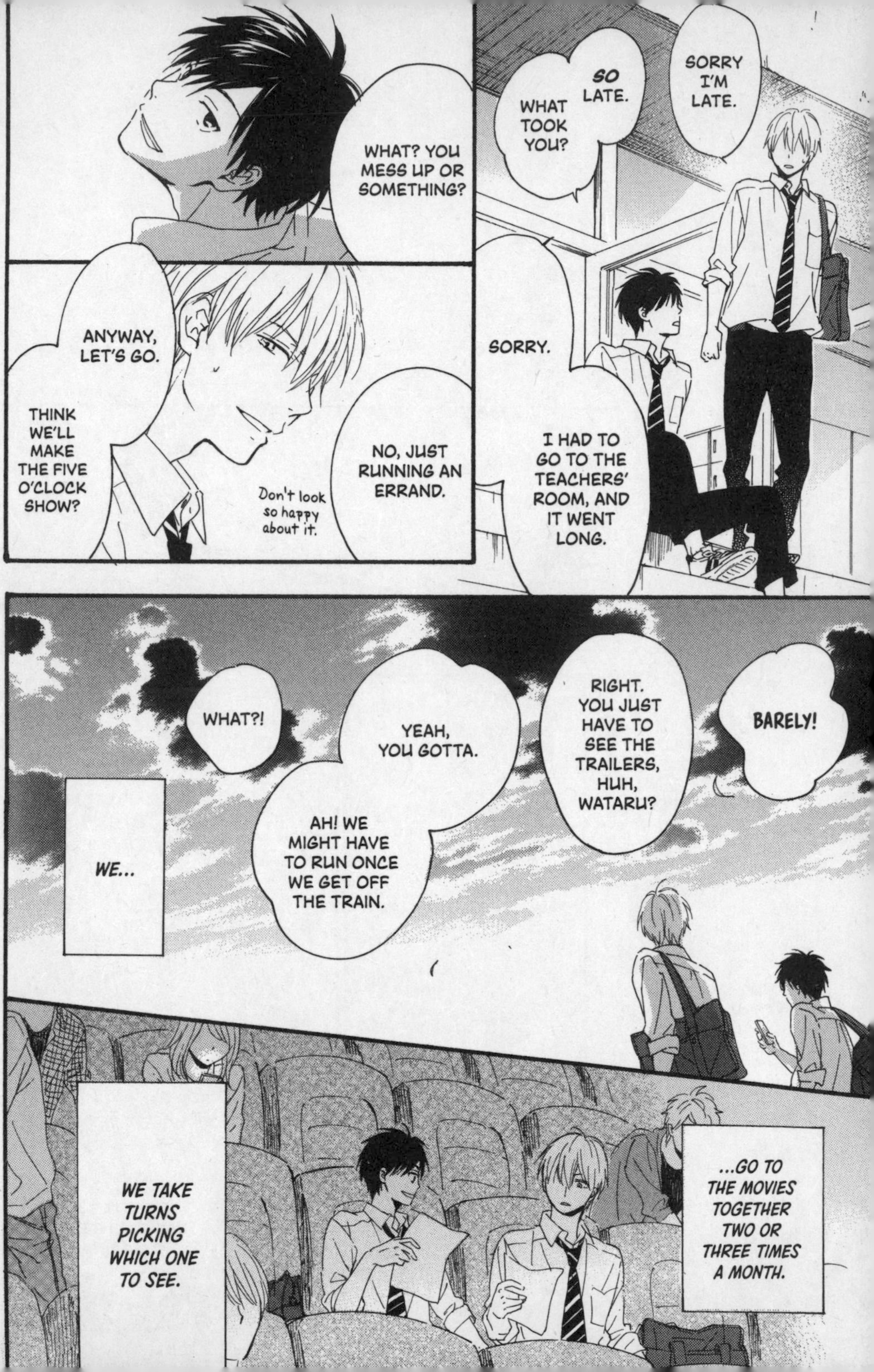
SORRY I'M LATE.
SO LATE. WHAT TOOK YOU?
SORRY.
I HAD TO GO TO THE TEACHERS' ROOM, AND IT WENT LONG.
WHAT? YOU MESS UP OR SOMETHING?
NO, JUST RUNNING AN ERRAND.
Don't look so happy about it.
ANYWAY, LET'S GO.
THINK WE'LL MAKE THE FIVE O'CLOCK SHOW?
BARELY!
RIGHT. YOU JUST HAVE TO SEE THE TRAILERS, HUH, WATARU?
YEAH, YOU GOTTA.
AH! WE MIGHT HAVE TO RUN ONCE WE GET OFF THE TRAIN.
WHAT?!
WE...
...GO TO THE MOVIES TOGETHER TWO OR THREE TIMES A MONTH.
WE TAKE TURNS PICKING WHICH ONE TO SEE.

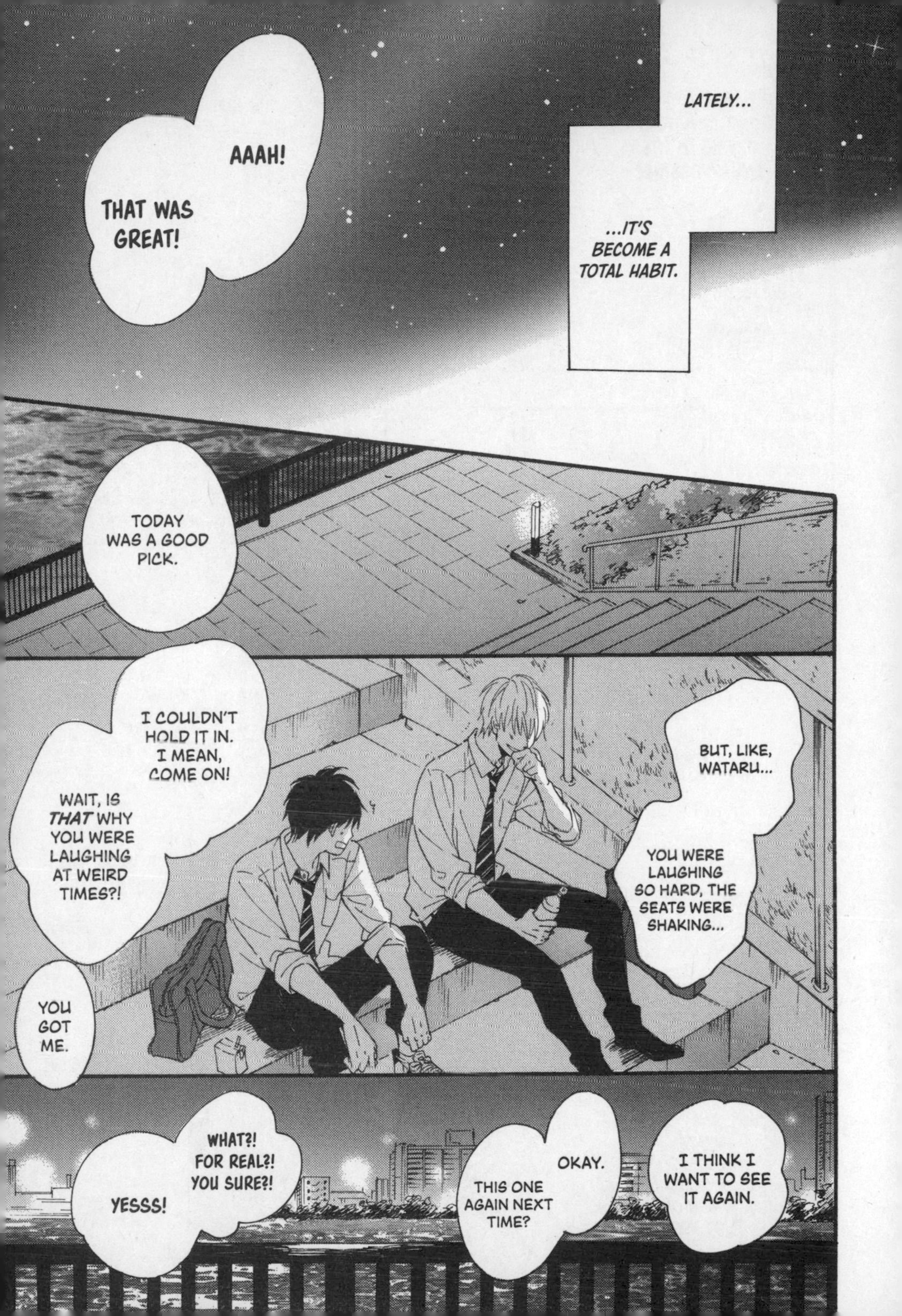
LATELY...
...IT'S BECOME A TOTAL HABIT.
AAAH!
THAT WAS GREAT!
TODAY WAS A GOOD PICK.
BUT, LIKE, WATARU...
YOU WERE LAUGHING SO HARD, THE SEATS WERE SHAKING...
I COULDN'T HOLD IT IN. I MEAN, COME ON!
WAIT, IS *THAT* WHY YOU WERE LAUGHING AT WEIRD TIMES?!
YOU GOT ME.
I THINK I WANT TO SEE IT AGAIN.
OKAY.
THIS ONE AGAIN NEXT TIME?
WHAT?! FOR REAL?! YOU SURE?!
YESSS!

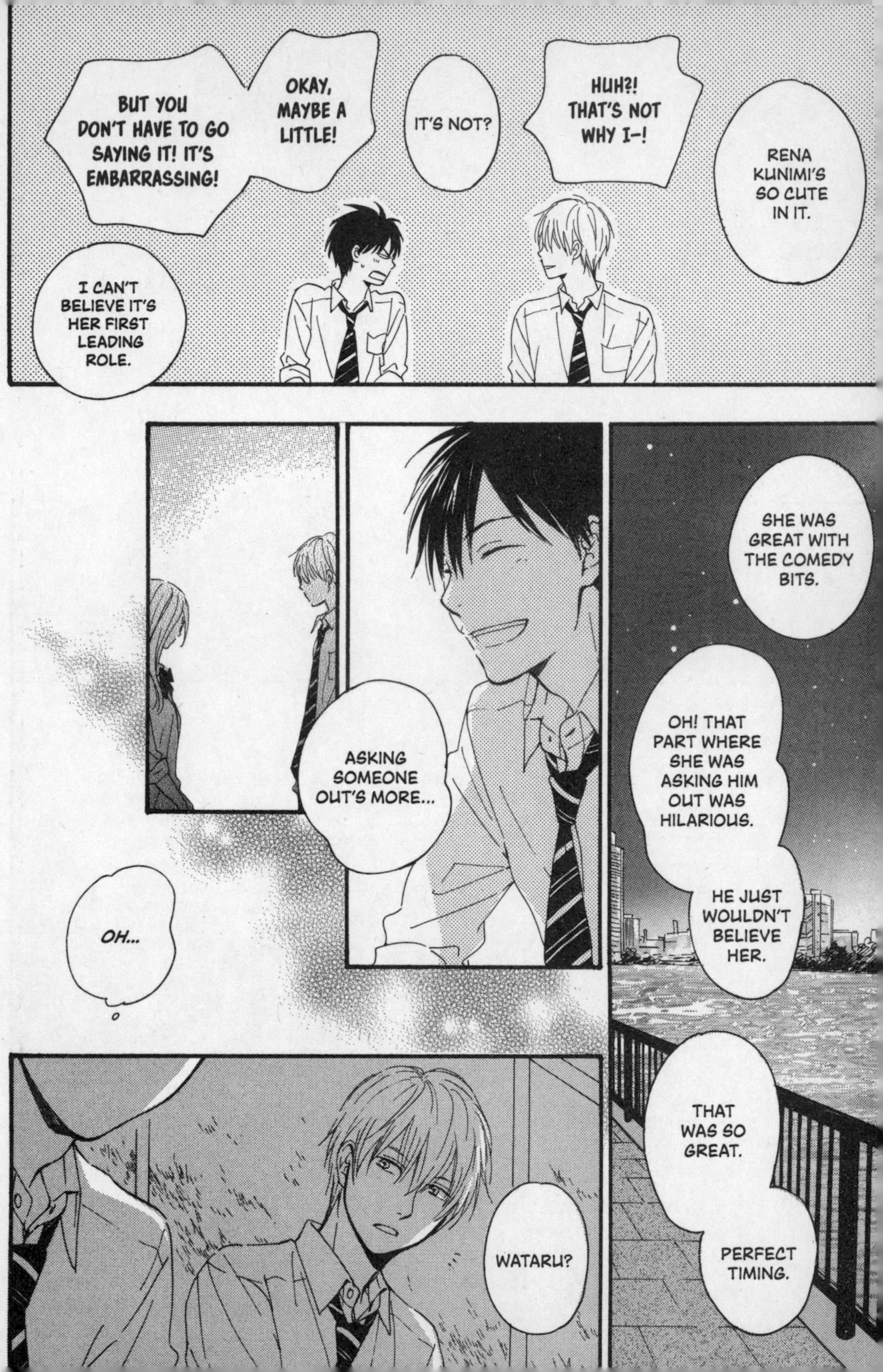
RENA KUNIMI'S SO CUTE IN IT.
HUH?! THAT'S NOT WHY I-!
IT'S NOT?
OKAY, MAYBE A LITTLE!
BUT YOU DON'T HAVE TO GO SAYING IT! IT'S EMBARRASSING!
I CAN'T BELIEVE IT'S HER FIRST LEADING ROLE.
SHE WAS GREAT WITH THE COMEDY BITS.
OH! THAT PART WHERE SHE WAS ASKING HIM OUT WAS HILARIOUS.
HE JUST WOULDN'T BELIEVE HER.
THAT WAS SO GREAT.
PERFECT TIMING.
ASKING SOMEONE OUT'S MORE...
OH...
WATARU?

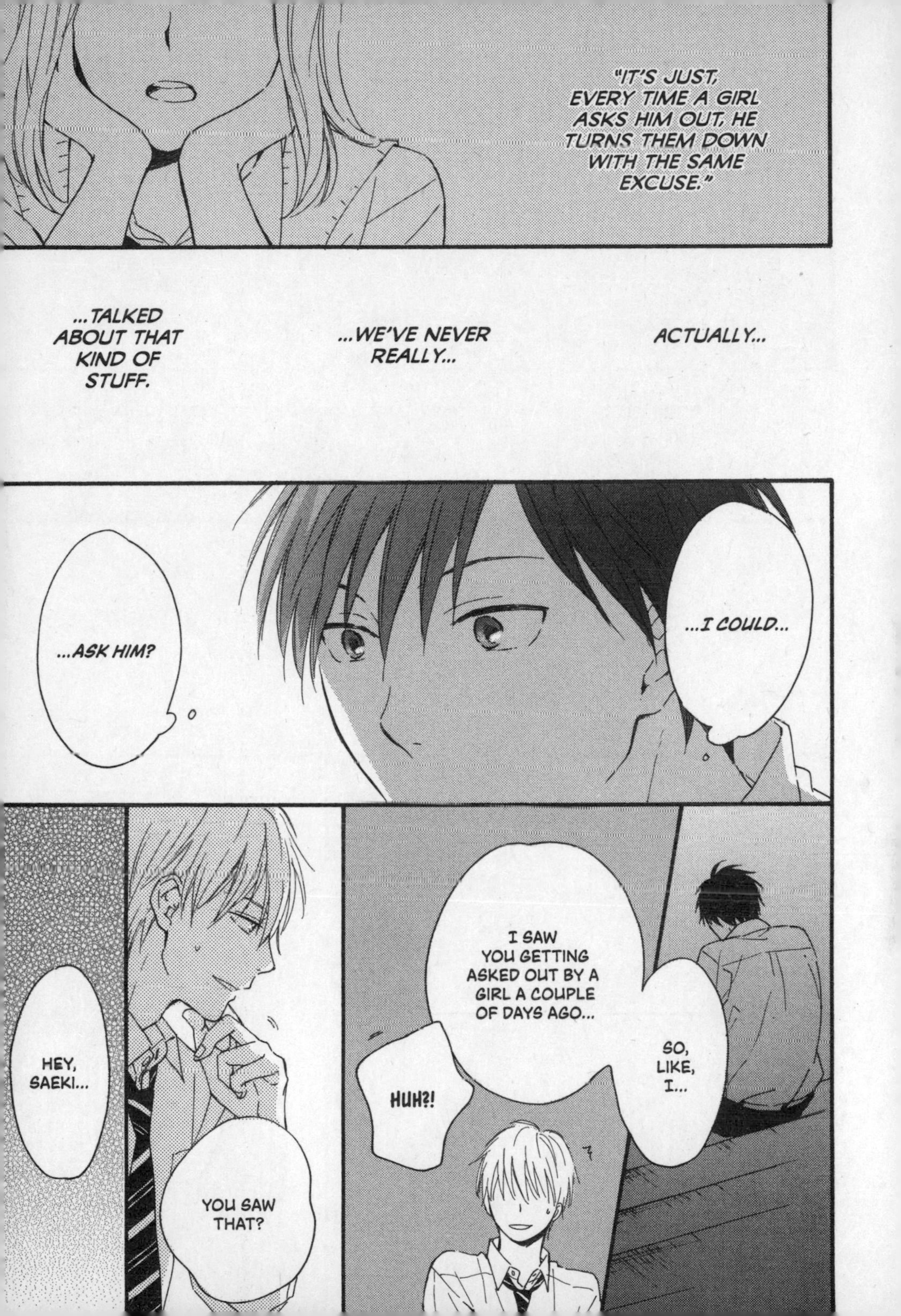
"IT'S JUST, EVERY TIME A GIRL ASKS HIM OUT, HE TURNS THEM DOWN WITH THE SAME EXCUSE."
ACTUALLY...
...WE'VE NEVER REALLY...
...TALKED ABOUT THAT KIND OF STUFF.
...I COULD...
...ASK HIM?
I SAW YOU GETTING ASKED OUT BY A GIRL A COUPLE OF DAYS AGO...
SO, LIKE, I...
HUH?!
HEY, SAEKI...
YOU SAW THAT?

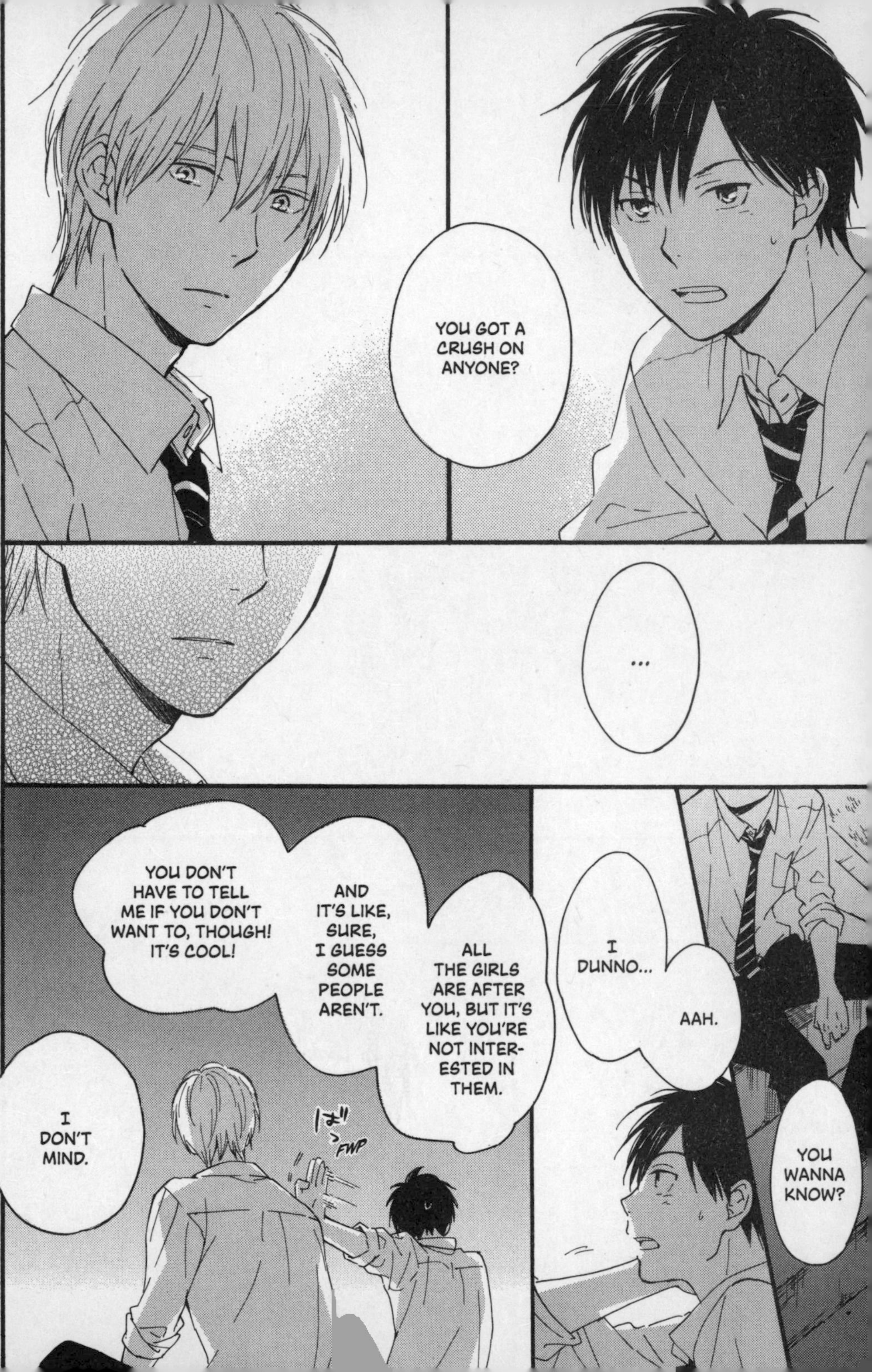
YOU GOT A CRUSH ON ANYONE?
...
I DUNNO...
AAH.
YOU WANNA KNOW?
ALL THE GIRLS ARE AFTER YOU, BUT IT'S LIKE YOU'RE NOT INTER-ESTED IN THEM.
AND IT'S LIKE, SURE, I GUESS SOME PEOPLE AREN'T.
YOU DON'T HAVE TO TELL ME IF YOU DON'T WANT TO, THOUGH! IT'S COOL!
FWP
I DON'T MIND.

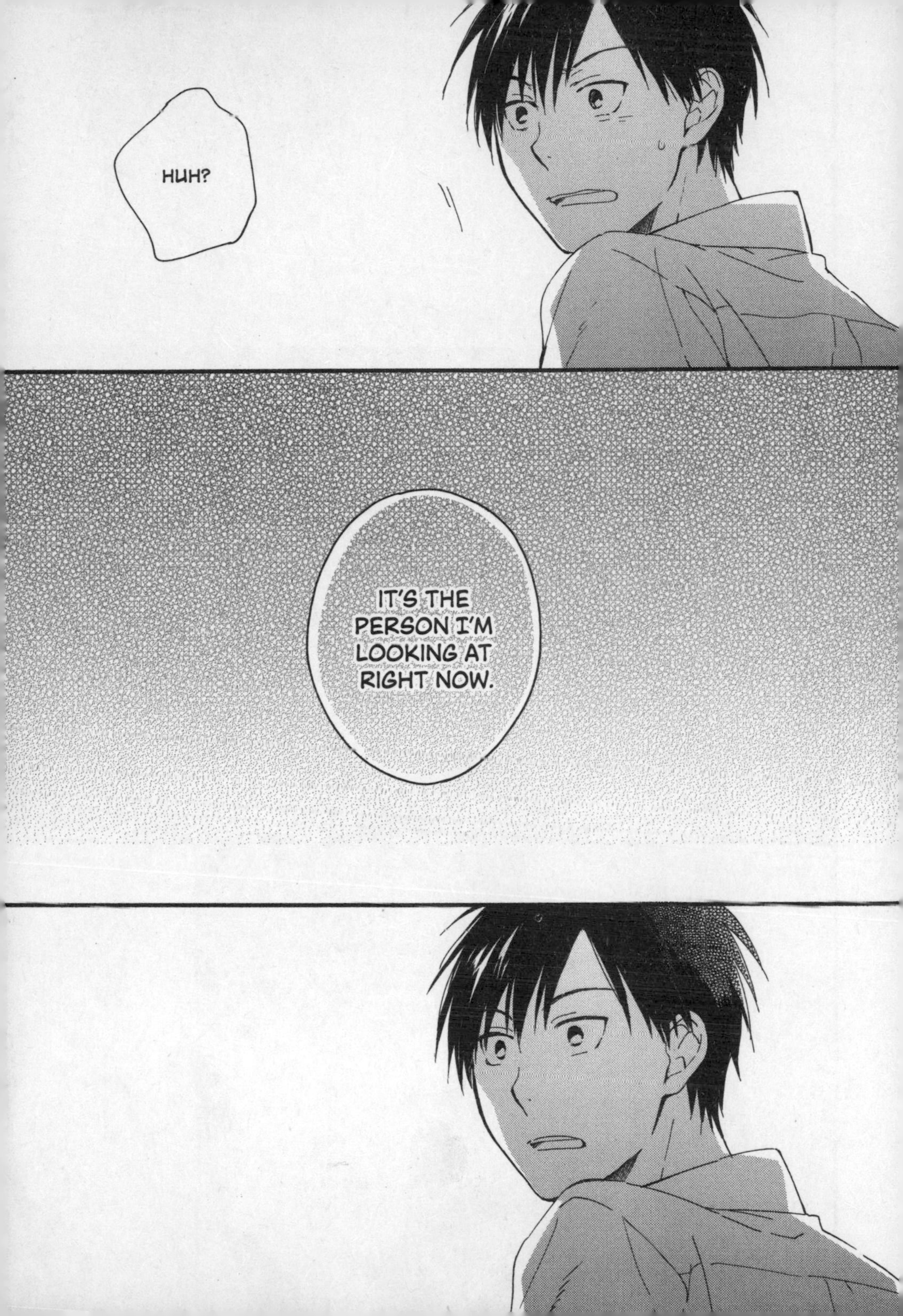
HUH?
IT'S THE PERSON I'M LOOKING AT RIGHT NOW.

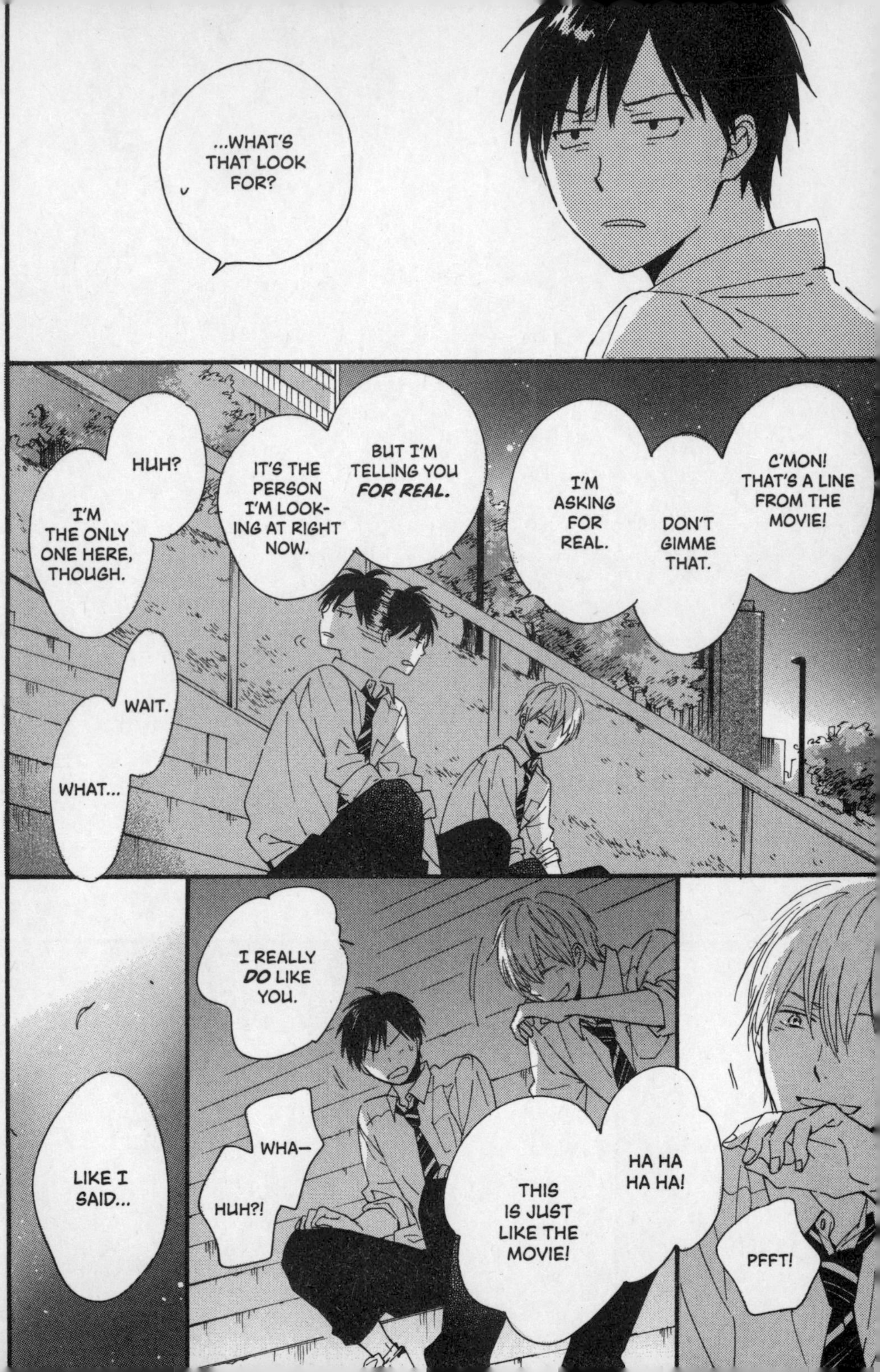
...WHAT'S THAT LOOK FOR?
C'MON! THAT'S A LINE FROM THE MOVIE!
DON'T GIMME THAT.
I'M ASKING FOR REAL.
BUT I'M TELLING YOU *FOR REAL.*
IT'S THE PERSON I'M LOOK-ING AT RIGHT NOW.
HUH?
I'M THE ONLY ONE HERE, THOUGH.
WAIT.
WHAT...
PFFT!
HA HA HA HA!
THIS IS JUST LIKE THE MOVIE!
WHA—
HUH?!
LIKE I SAID...
I REALLY *DO* LIKE YOU.

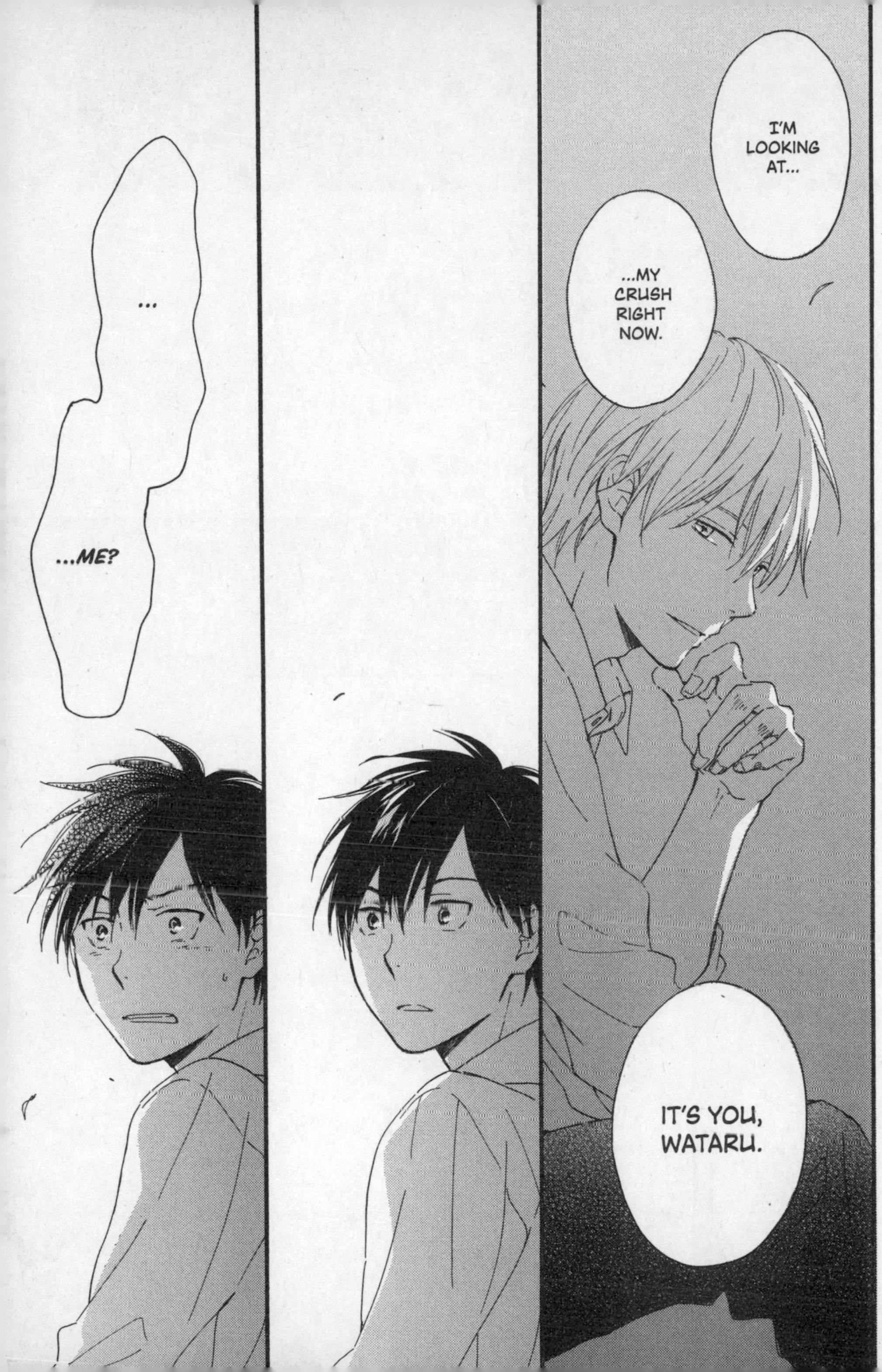
I'M LOOKING AT...
...MY CRUSH RIGHT NOW.
IT'S YOU, WATARU.
...
...ME?

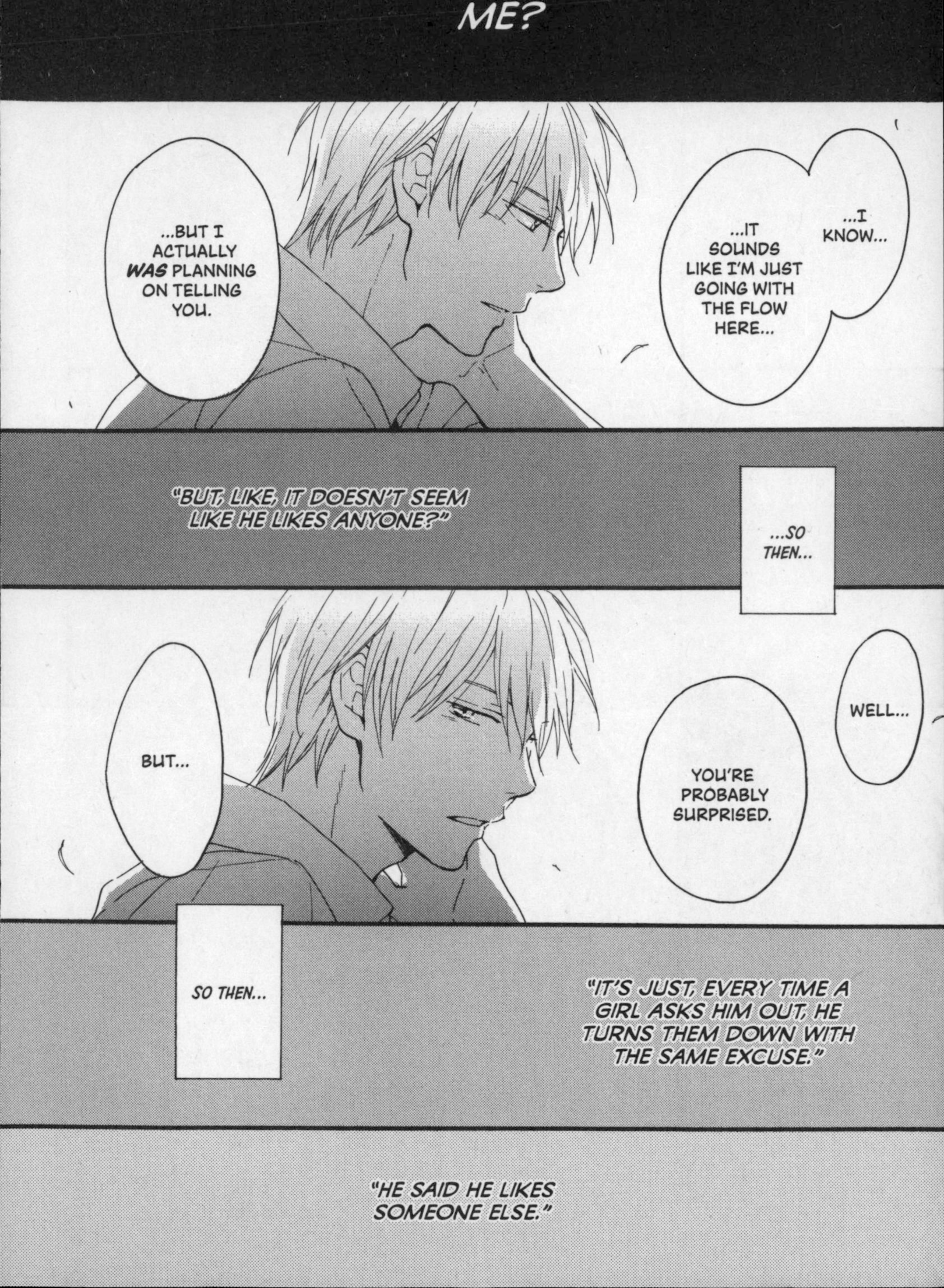
ME?
...I KNOW...
...IT SOUNDS LIKE I'M JUST GOING WITH THE FLOW HERE...
...BUT I ACTUALLY **WAS** PLANNING ON TELLING YOU.
...SO THEN...
"BUT, LIKE, IT DOESN'T SEEM LIKE HE LIKES ANYONE?"
WELL...
YOU'RE PROBABLY SURPRISED.
BUT...
"IT'S JUST, EVERY TIME A GIRL ASKS HIM OUT, HE TURNS THEM DOWN WITH THE SAME EXCUSE."
SO THEN...
"HE SAID HE LIKES SOMEONE ELSE."

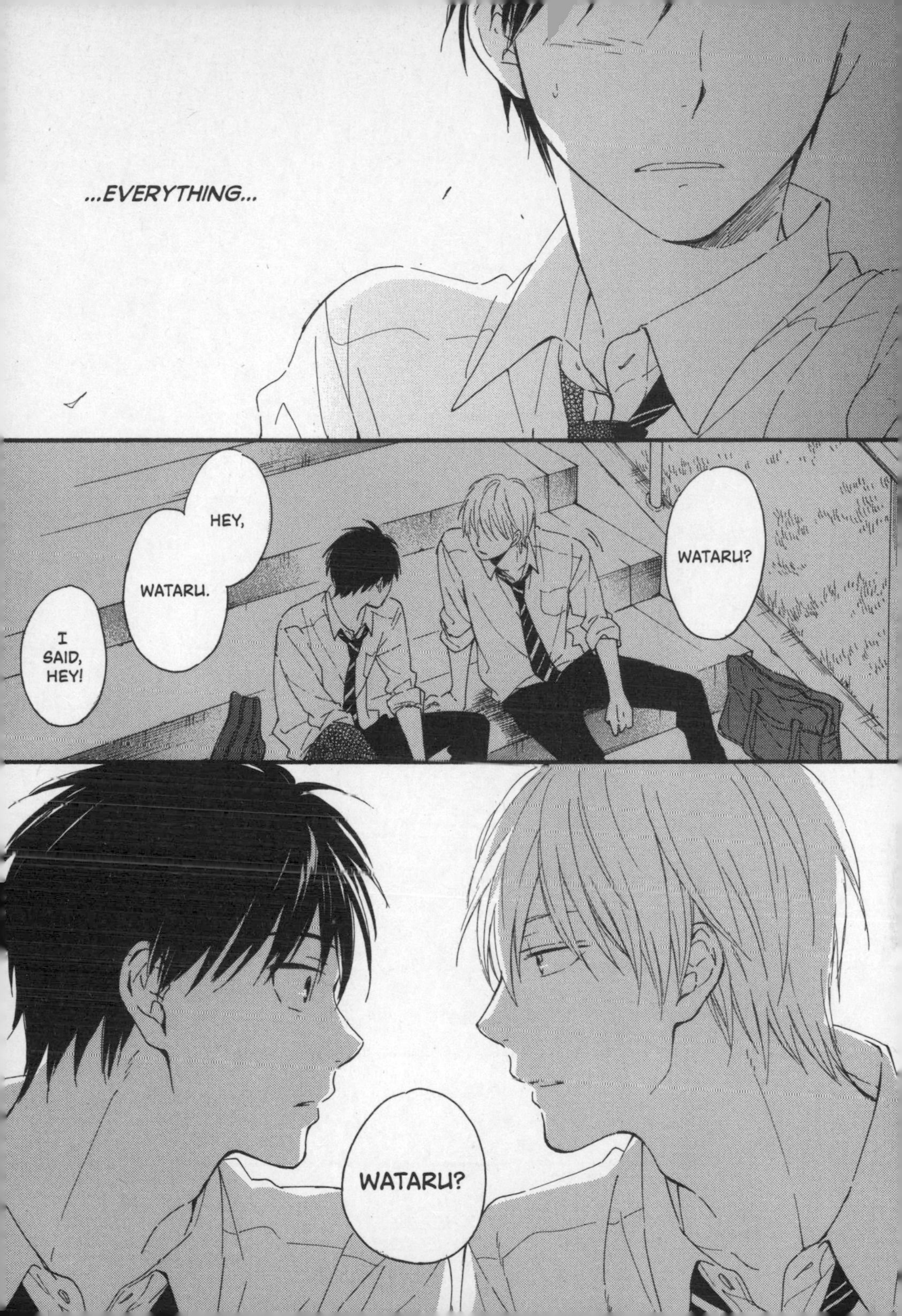
...EVERYTHING...
WATARU?
HEY,
WATARU.
I SAID, HEY!
WATARU?

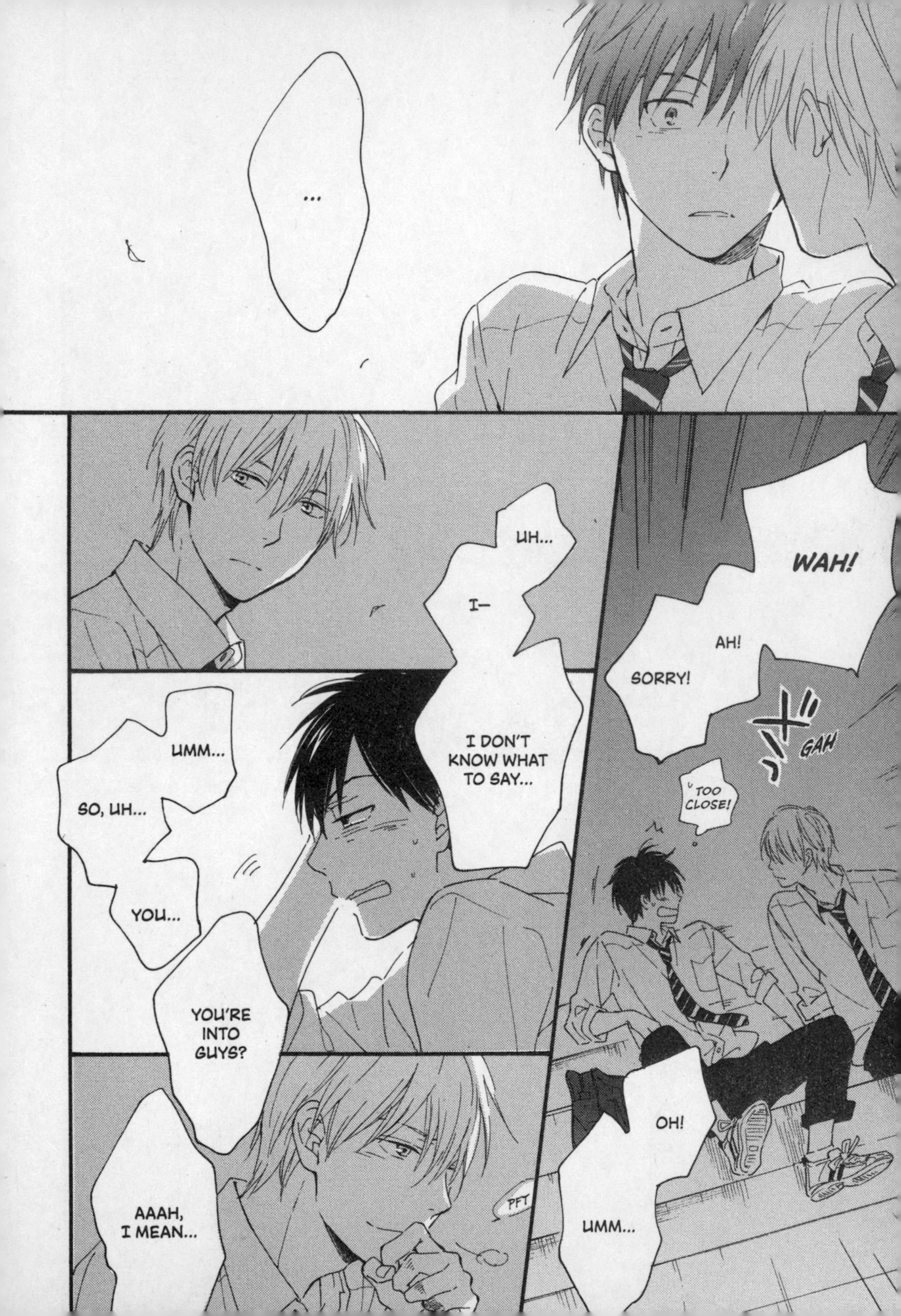
...
WAH!
AH!
SORRY!
GAH
TOO CLOSE!
OH!
UMM...
UH...
I—
I DON'T KNOW WHAT TO SAY...
UMM...
SO, UH...
YOU...
YOU'RE INTO GUYS?
PFT
AAAH, I MEAN...

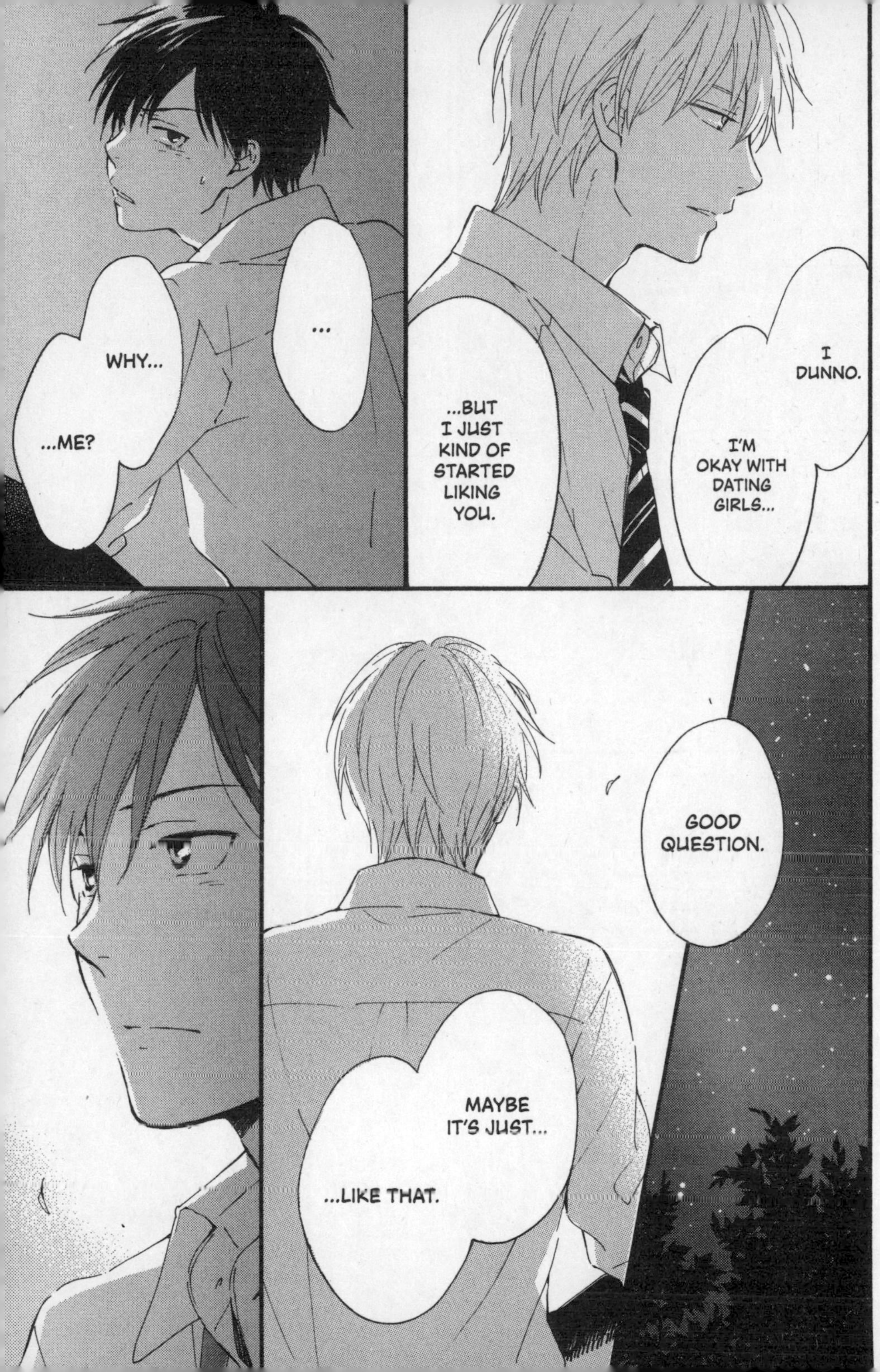
I DUNNO.
I'M OKAY WITH DATING GIRLS...
...BUT I JUST KIND OF STARTED LIKING YOU.
...
WHY...
...ME?
GOOD QUESTION.
MAYBE IT'S JUST...
...LIKE THAT.

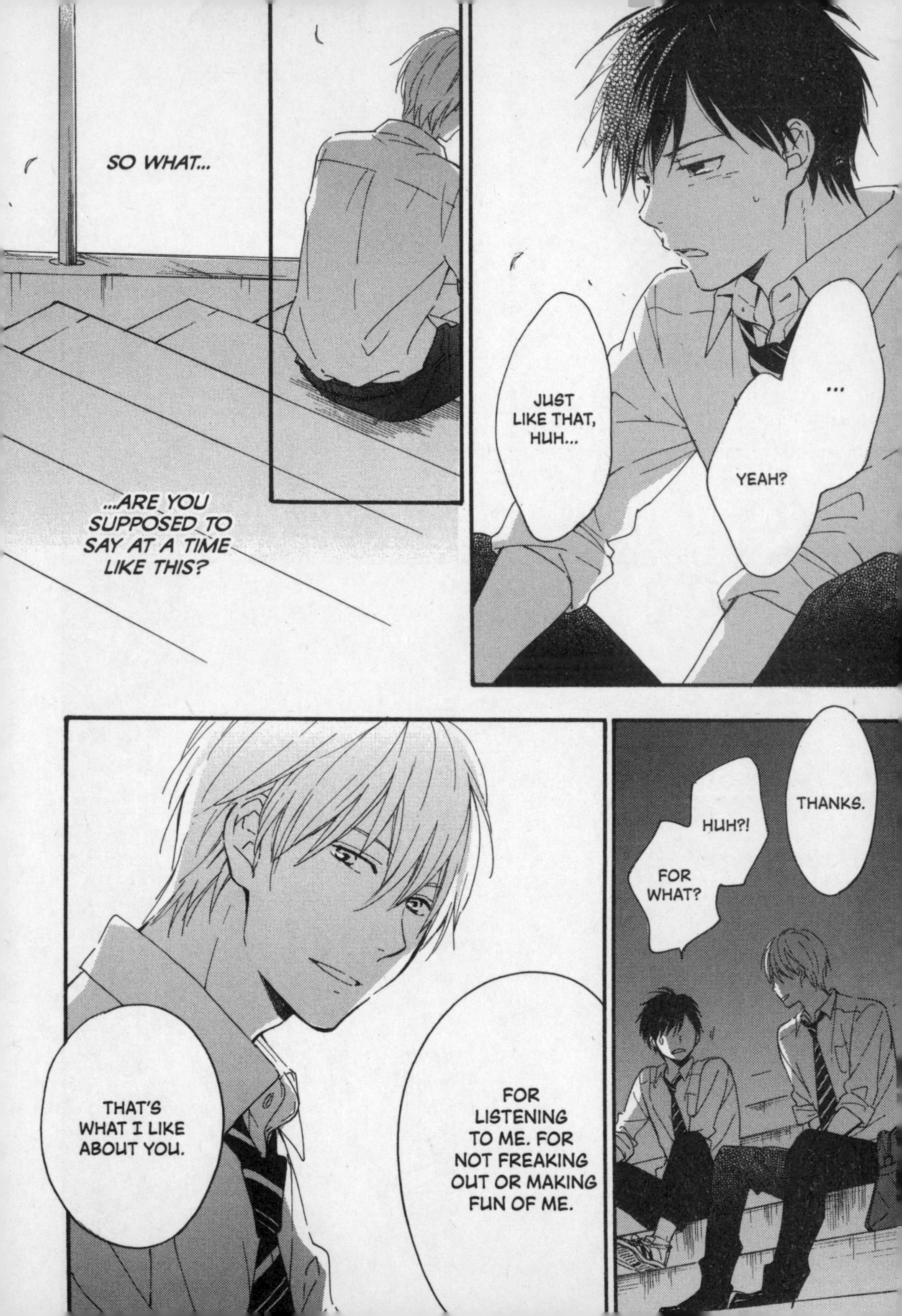
... YEAH?
JUST LIKE THAT, HUH...
SO WHAT...
...ARE YOU SUPPOSED TO SAY AT A TIME LIKE THIS?
THANKS.
HUH?! FOR WHAT?
FOR LISTENING TO ME. FOR NOT FREAKING OUT OR MAKING FUN OF ME.
THAT'S WHAT I LIKE ABOUT YOU.

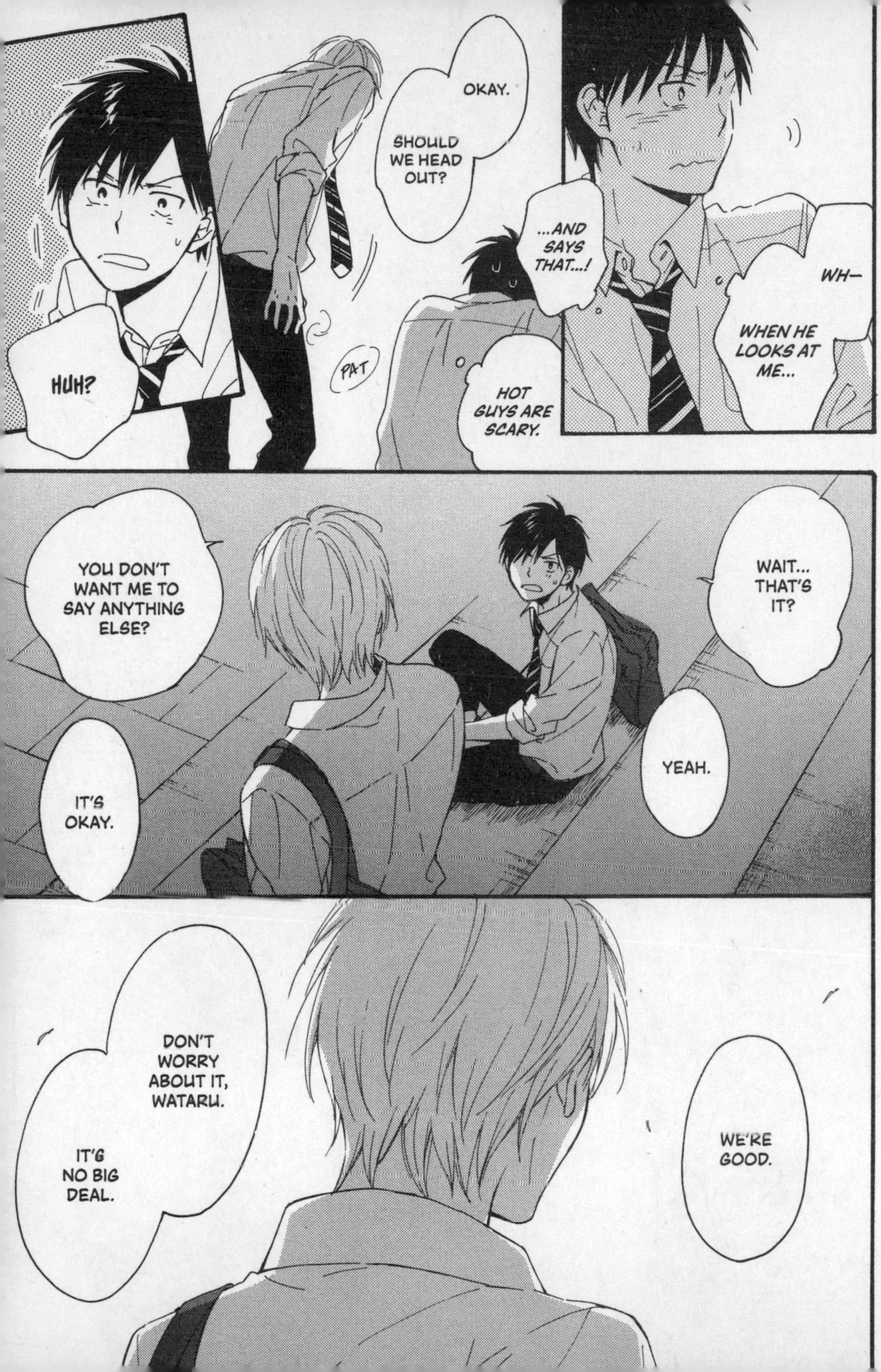
WH—
WHEN HE LOOKS AT ME...
...AND SAYS THAT...!
HOT GUYS ARE SCARY.
OKAY.
SHOULD WE HEAD OUT?
PAT
HUH?
WAIT... THAT'S IT?
YEAH.
YOU DON'T WANT ME TO SAY ANYTHING ELSE?
IT'S OKAY.
WE'RE GOOD.
DON'T WORRY ABOUT IT, WATARU.
IT'S NO BIG DEAL.

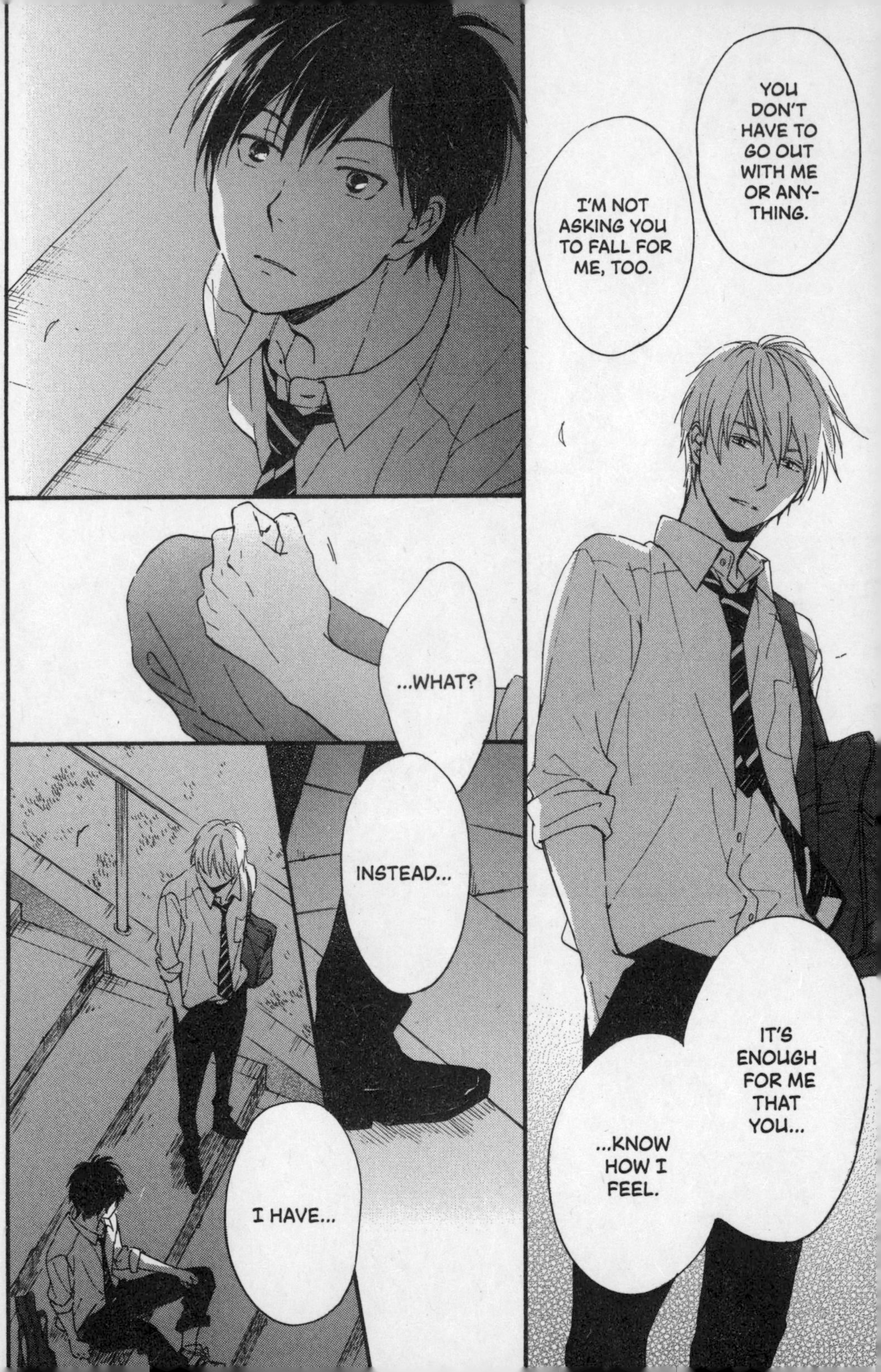
YOU DON'T HAVE TO GO OUT WITH ME OR ANY-THING.
I'M NOT ASKING YOU TO FALL FOR ME, TOO.
IT'S ENOUGH FOR ME THAT YOU...
...KNOW HOW I FEEL.
...WHAT?
INSTEAD...
I HAVE...

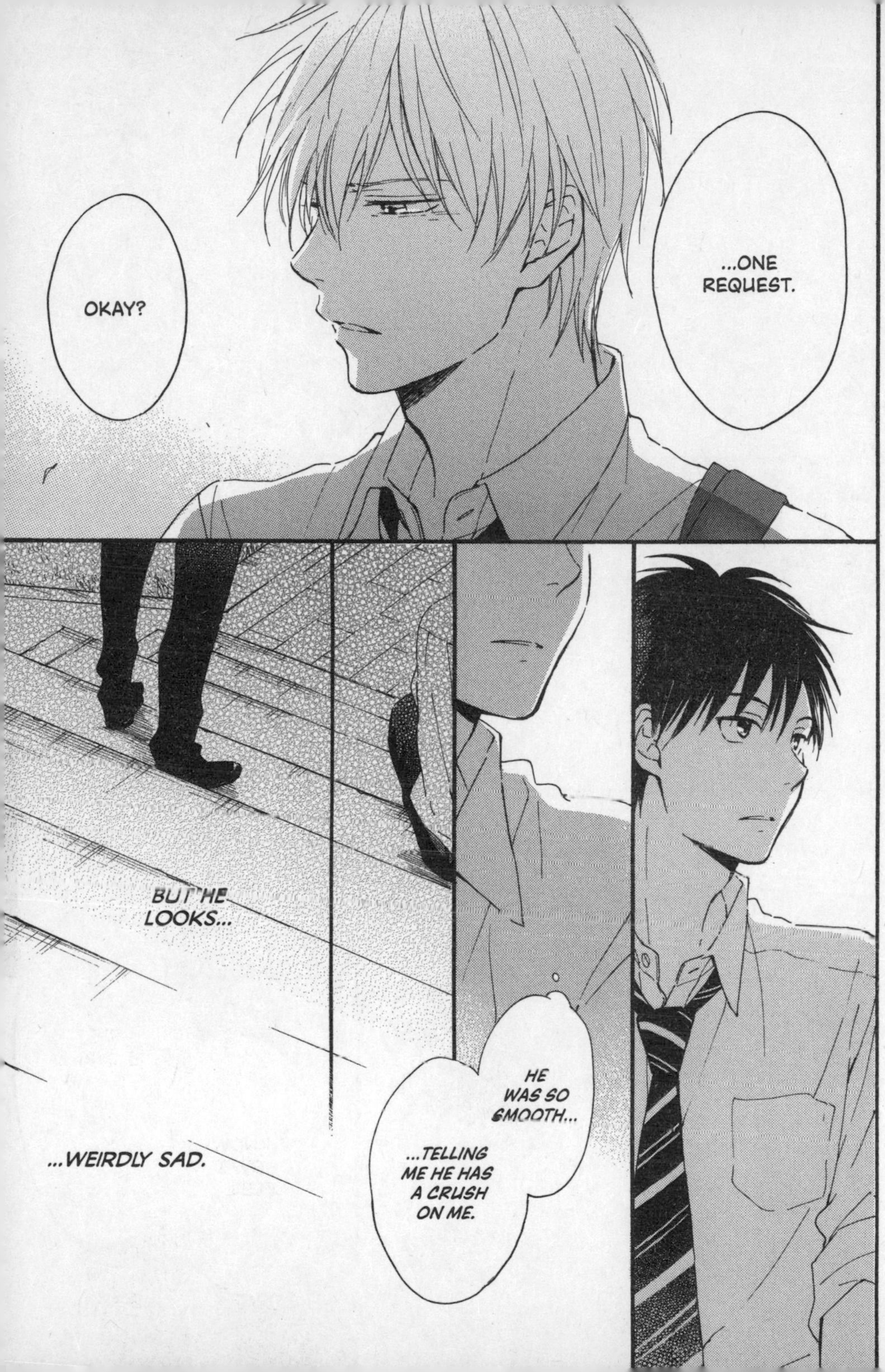
...ONE REQUEST.
OKAY?
HE WAS SO SMOOTH...
...TELLING ME HE HAS A CRUSH ON ME.
BUT HE LOOKS...
...WEIRDLY SAD.

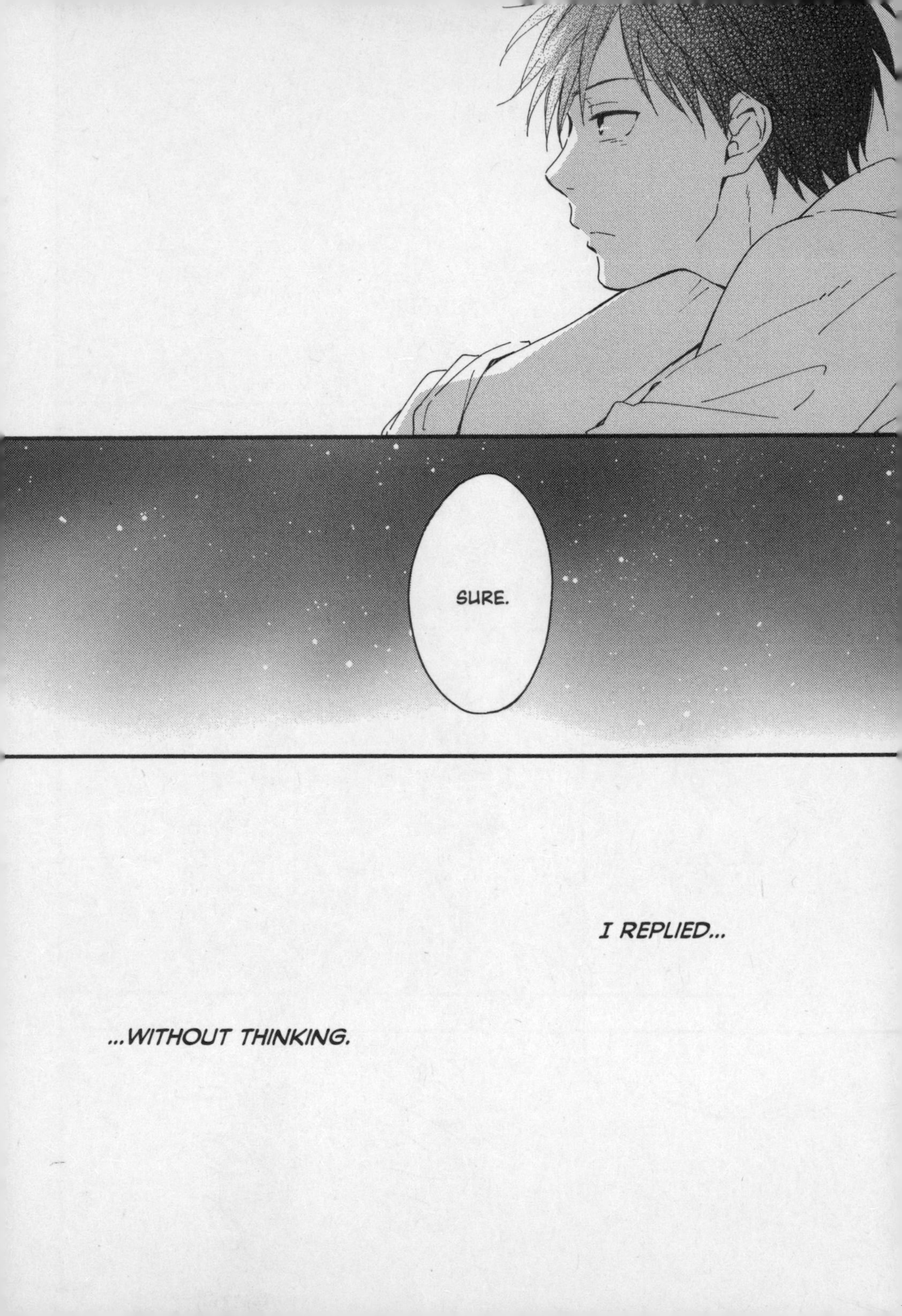
SURE.
I REPLIED...
...WITHOUT THINKING.

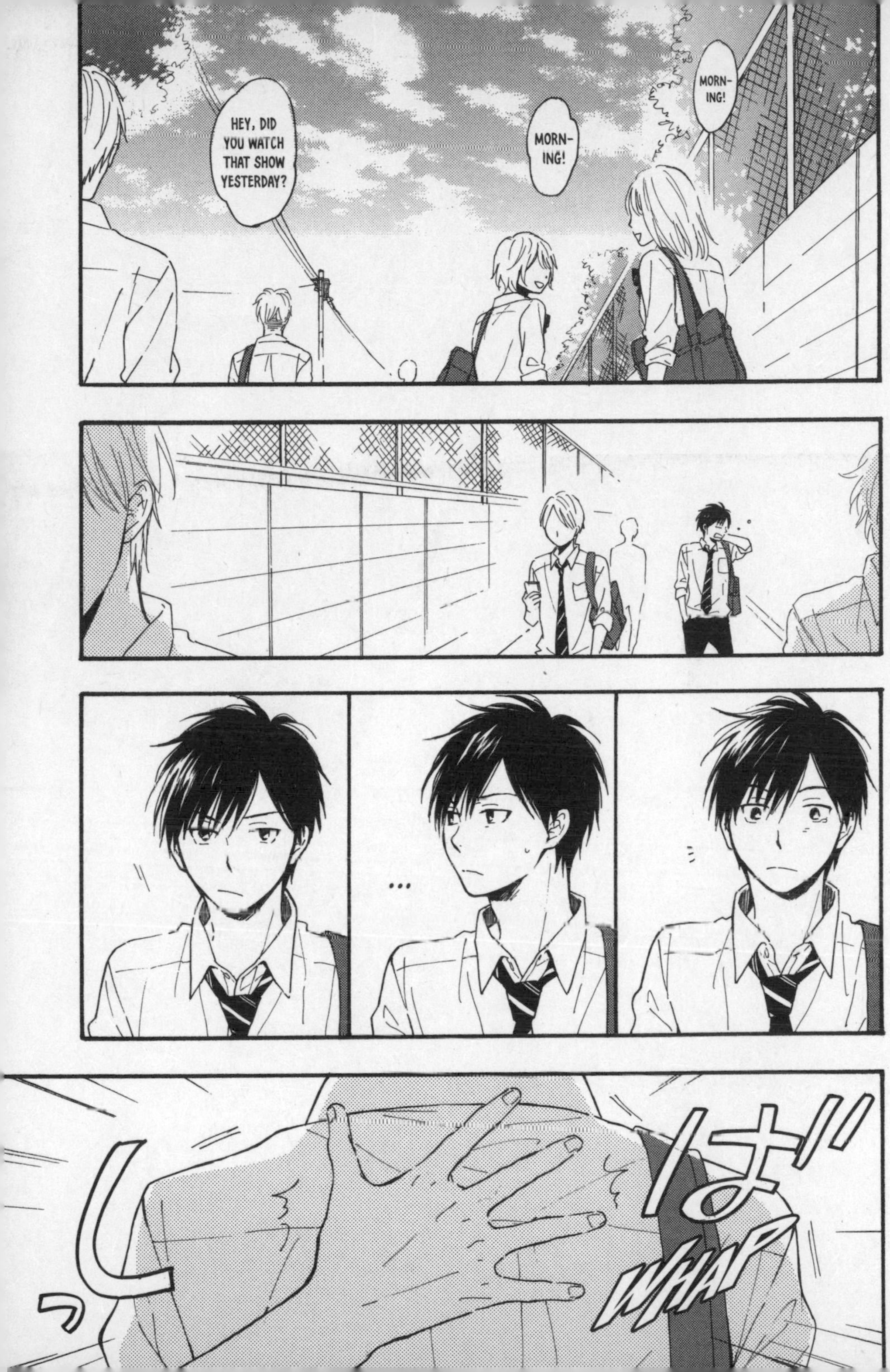
MORN-ING!
MORN-ING!
HEY, DID YOU WATCH THAT SHOW YESTERDAY?
...
ば
WHAP
しっ

Chapter 2

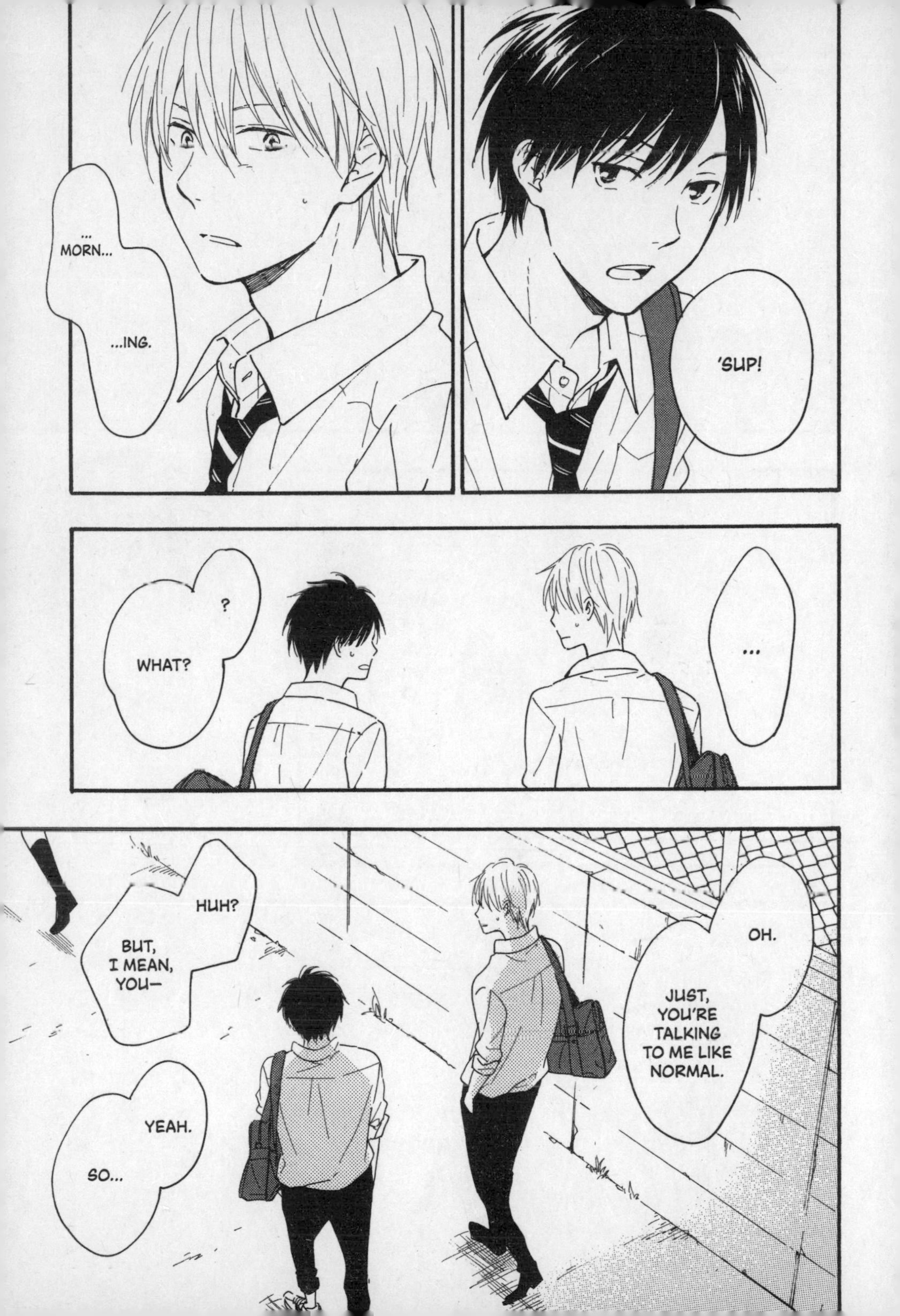
'SUP!
... MORN...
...ING.
...
? WHAT?
OH.
JUST, YOU'RE TALKING TO ME LIKE NORMAL.
HUH?
BUT, I MEAN, YOU—
YEAH.
SO...

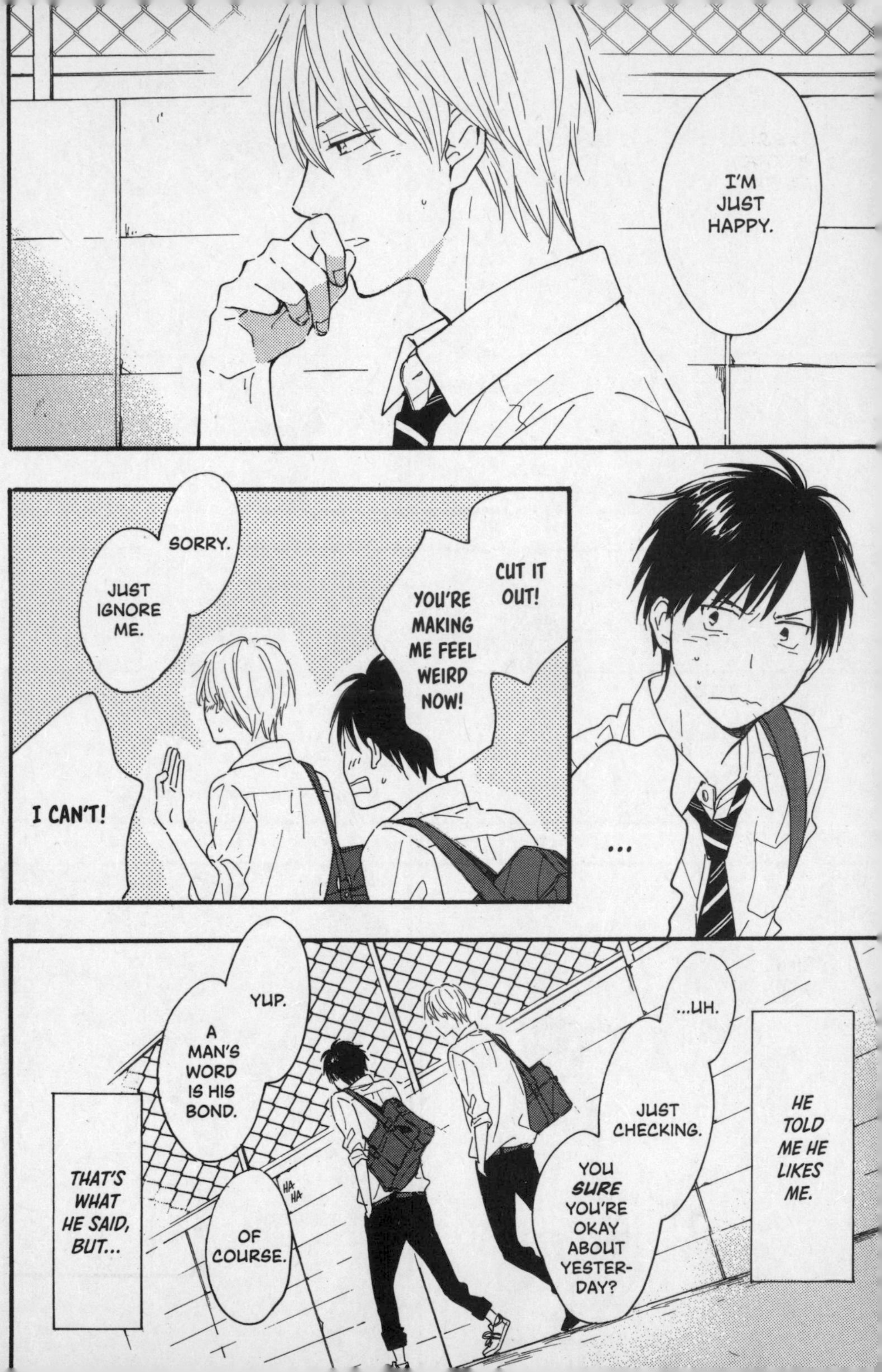
I'M JUST HAPPY.
...
CUT IT OUT!
YOU'RE MAKING ME FEEL WEIRD NOW!
SORRY.
JUST IGNORE ME.
I CAN'T!
HE TOLD ME HE LIKES ME.
...UH.
JUST CHECKING.
YOU *SURE* YOU'RE OKAY ABOUT YESTER-DAY?
YUP.
A MAN'S WORD IS HIS BOND.
HA HA
OF COURSE.
THAT'S WHAT HE SAID, BUT...

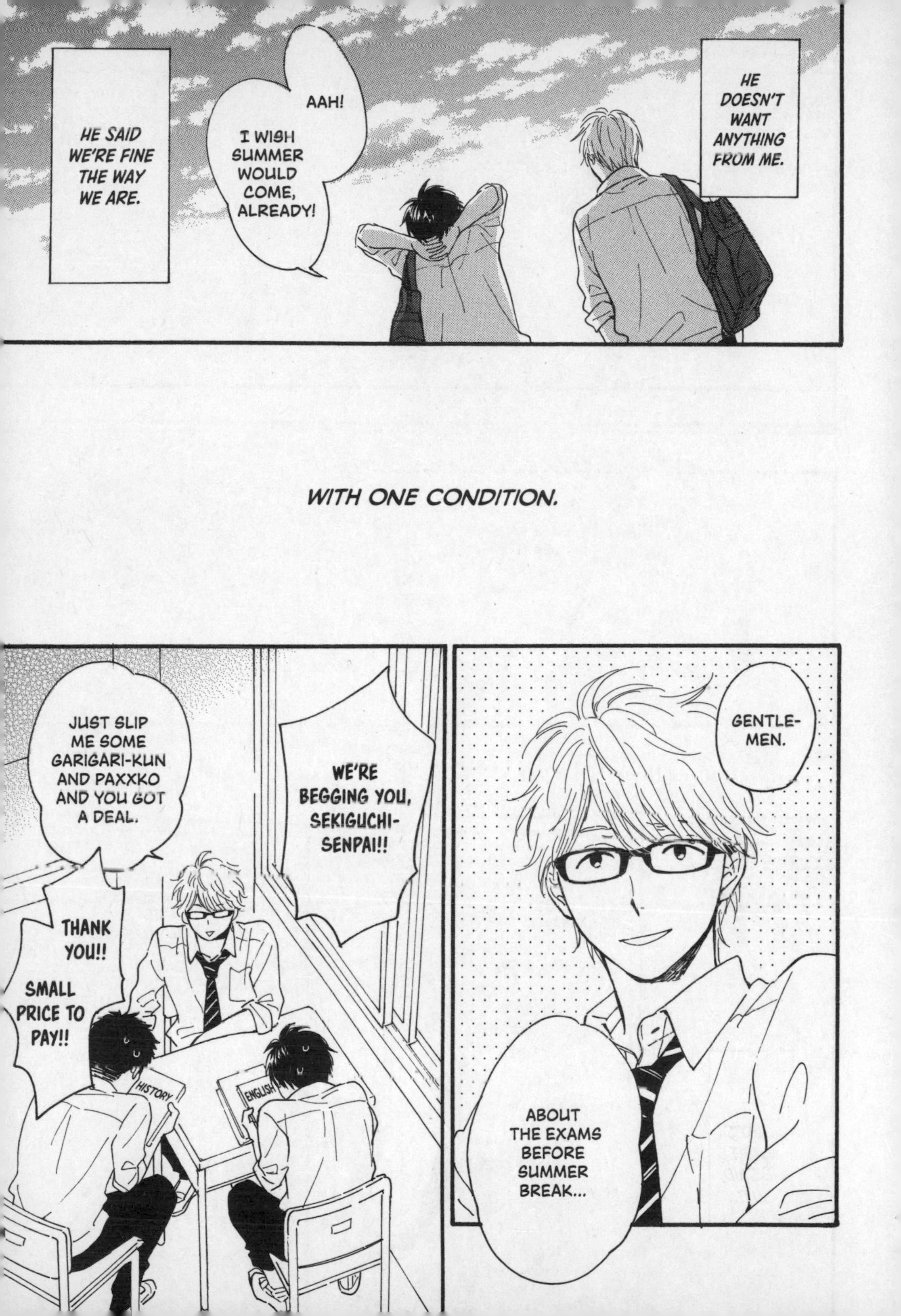
HE DOESN'T WANT ANYTHING FROM ME.
AAH! I WISH SUMMER WOULD COME, ALREADY!
HE SAID WE'RE FINE THE WAY WE ARE.
WITH ONE CONDITION.
GENTLEMEN.
ABOUT THE EXAMS BEFORE SUMMER BREAK...
WE'RE BEGGING YOU, SEKIGUCHI-SENPAI!!
JUST SLIP ME SOME GARIGARI-KUN AND PAXXKO AND YOU GOT A DEAL.
THANK YOU!!
SMALL PRICE TO PAY!!
HISTORY
ENGLISH

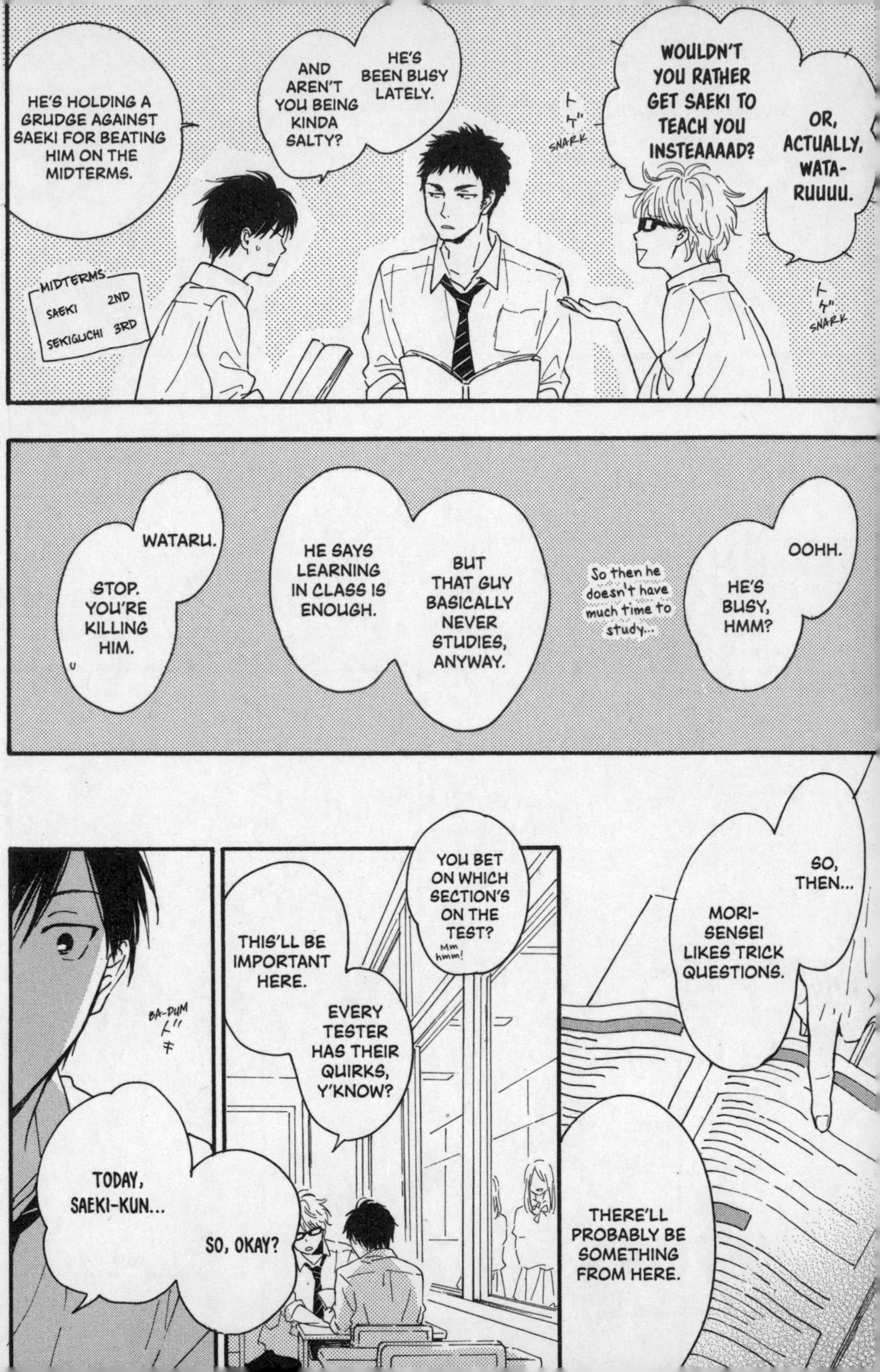
OR, ACTUALLY, WATA-RUUUU.
WOULDN'T YOU RATHER GET SAEKI TO TEACH YOU INSTEAAAAD?
SNARK
SNARK
HE'S BEEN BUSY LATELY.
AND AREN'T YOU BEING KINDA SALTY?
HE'S HOLDING A GRUDGE AGAINST SAEKI FOR BEATING HIM ON THE MIDTERMS.
MIDTERMS
SAEKI 2ND
SEKIGUCHI 3RD
OOHH.
HE'S BUSY, HMM?
So then he doesn't have much time to study...
BUT THAT GUY BASICALLY NEVER STUDIES, ANYWAY.
HE SAYS LEARNING IN CLASS IS ENOUGH.
WATARU.
STOP. YOU'RE KILLING HIM.
SO, THEN...
MORI-SENSEI LIKES TRICK QUESTIONS.
THERE'LL PROBABLY BE SOMETHING FROM HERE.
YOU BET ON WHICH SECTION'S ON THE TEST?
Mm hmm!
THIS'LL BE IMPORTANT HERE.
EVERY TESTER HAS THEIR QUIRKS, Y'KNOW?
BA-DUM
TODAY, SAEKI-KUN...
SO, OKAY?

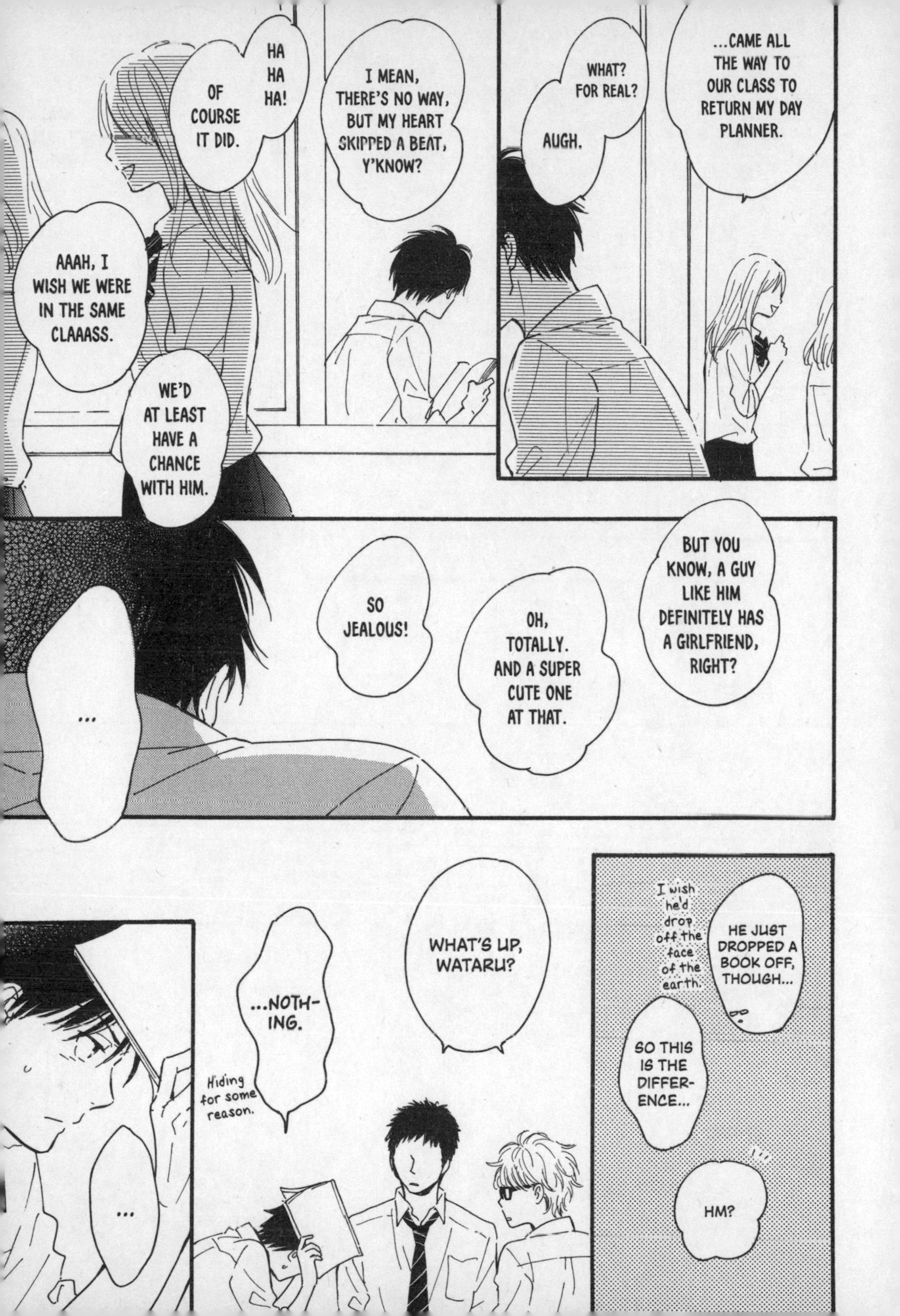

...CAME ALL THE WAY TO OUR CLASS TO RETURN MY DAY PLANNER.
WHAT? FOR REAL?
AUGH.
I MEAN, THERE'S NO WAY, BUT MY HEART SKIPPED A BEAT, Y'KNOW?
HA HA HA!
OF COURSE IT DID.
AAAH, I WISH WE WERE IN THE SAME CLAAASS.
WE'D AT LEAST HAVE A CHANCE WITH HIM.
BUT YOU KNOW, A GUY LIKE HIM DEFINITELY HAS A GIRLFRIEND, RIGHT?
OH, TOTALLY. AND A SUPER CUTE ONE AT THAT.
SO JEALOUS!
...
HE JUST DROPPED A BOOK OFF, THOUGH...
I wish he'd drop off the face of the earth.
SO THIS IS THE DIFFERENCE...
HM?
WHAT'S UP, WATARU?
...NOTH-ING.
Hiding for some reason.
...

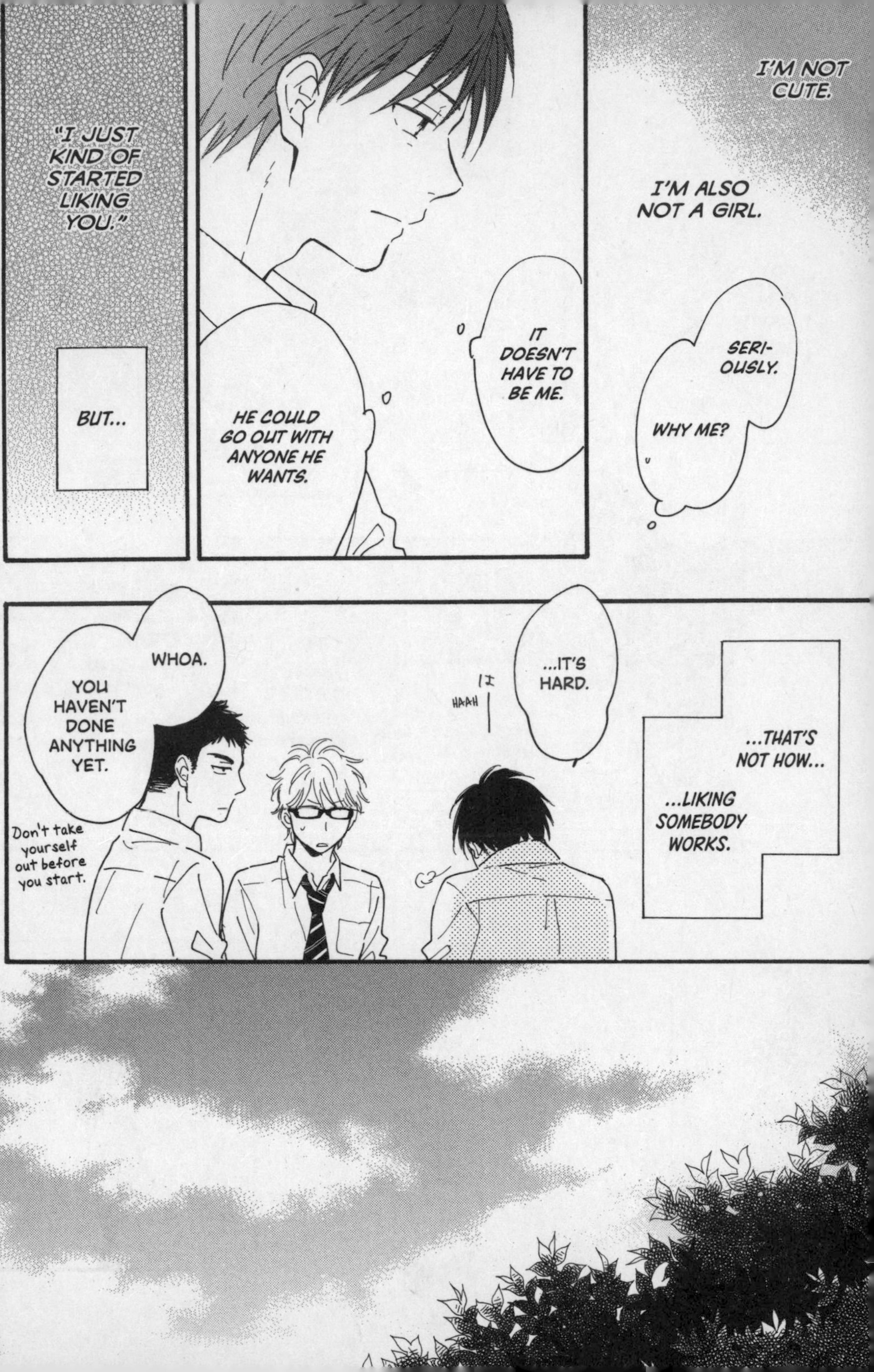
I'M NOT CUTE.
I'M ALSO NOT A GIRL.
SERI-OUSLY. WHY ME?
IT DOESN'T HAVE TO BE ME.
HE COULD GO OUT WITH ANYONE HE WANTS.
"I JUST KIND OF STARTED LIKING YOU."
BUT...
...THAT'S NOT HOW...
...LIKING SOMEBODY WORKS.
...IT'S HARD.
HAAH
WHOA. YOU HAVEN'T DONE ANYTHING YET.
Don't take yourself out before you start.

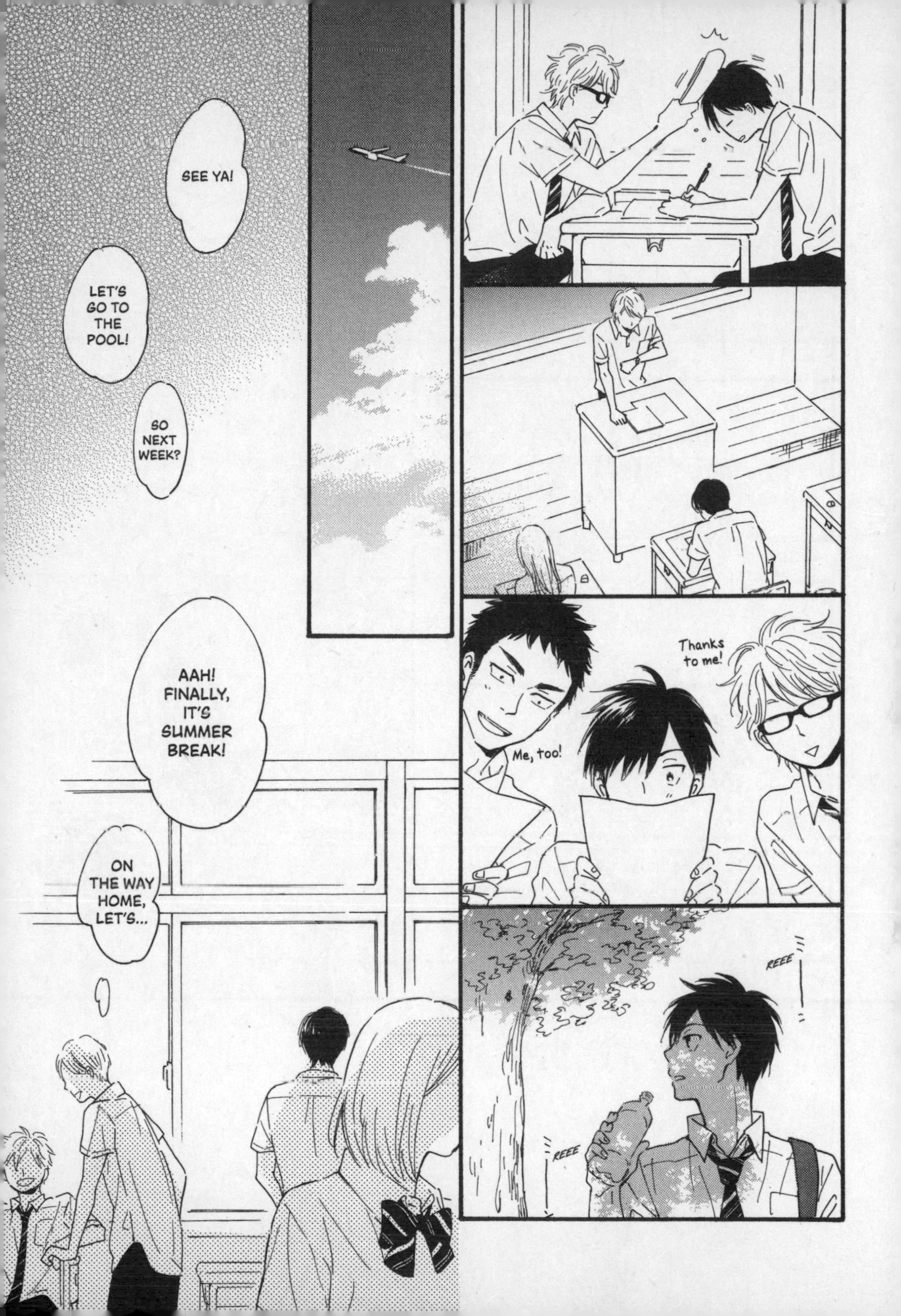
Thanks to me!
Me, too!
REEE
REEE
SEE YA!
LET'S GO TO THE POOL!
SO NEXT WEEK?
AAH! FINALLY, IT'S SUMMER BREAK!
ON THE WAY HOME, LET'S...

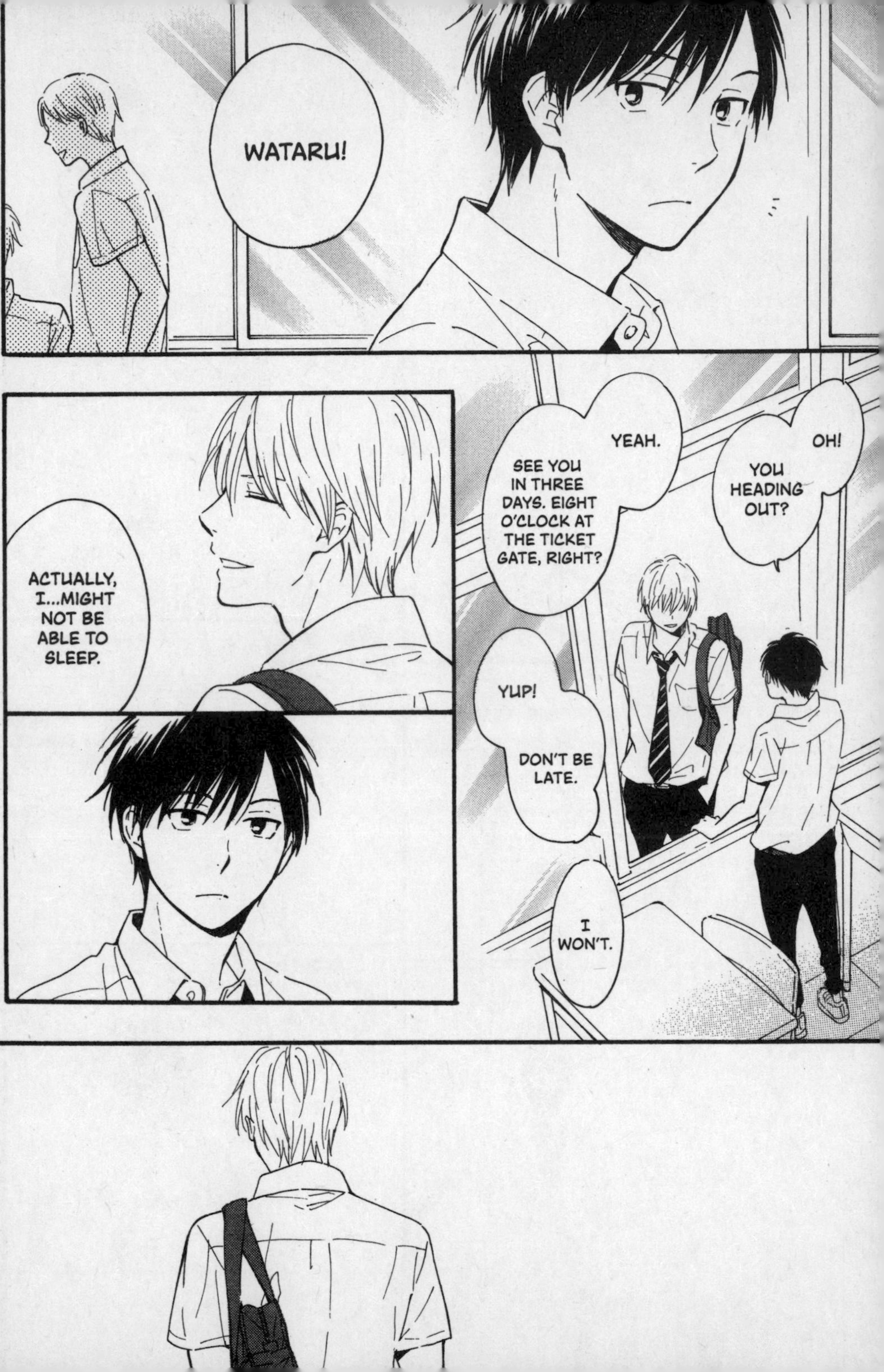
WATARU!
OH! YOU HEADING OUT?
YEAH. SEE YOU IN THREE DAYS. EIGHT O'CLOCK AT THE TICKET GATE, RIGHT?
YUP! DON'T BE LATE.
I WON'T.
ACTUALLY, I...MIGHT NOT BE ABLE TO SLEEP.

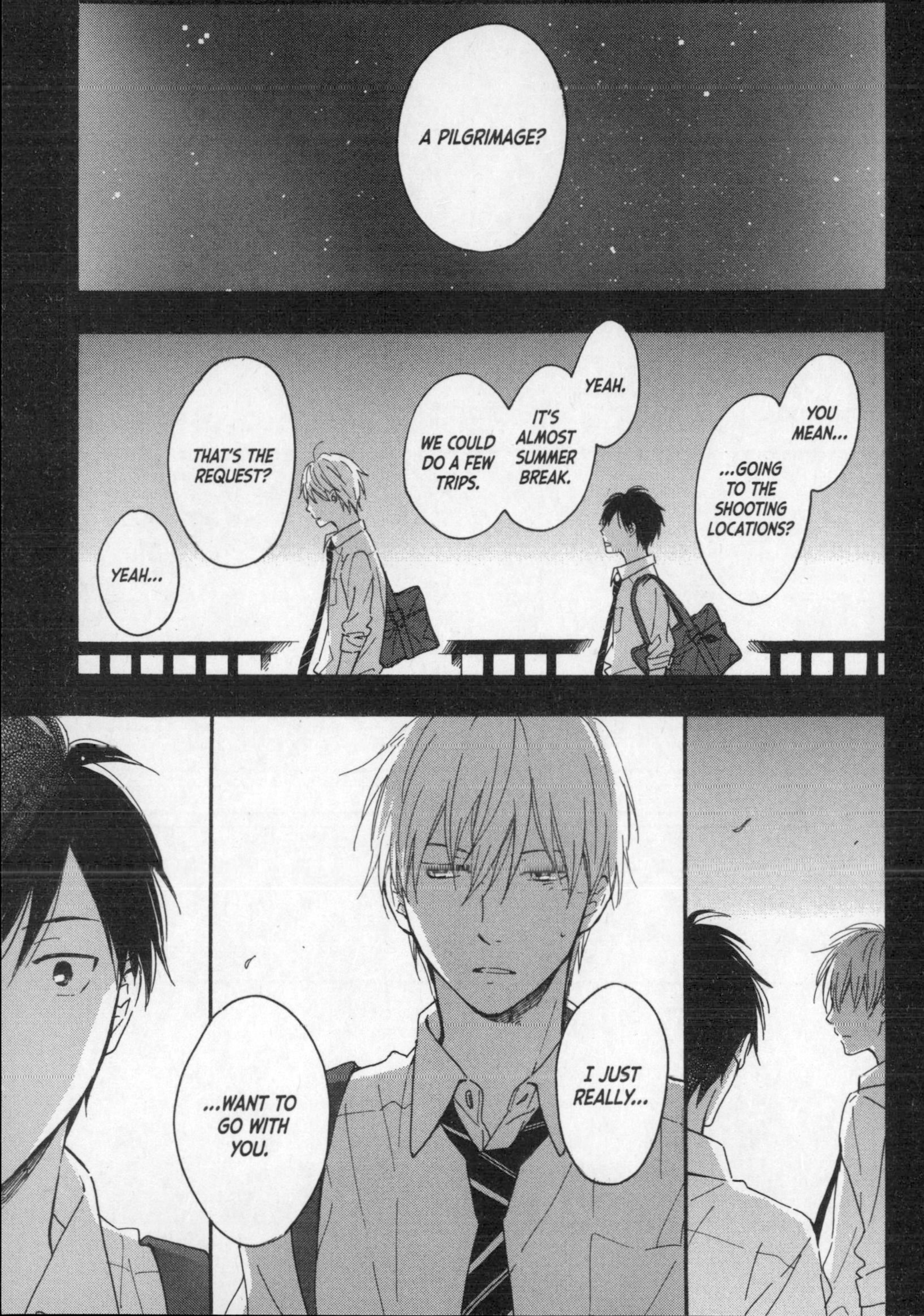
A PILGRIMAGE?
YOU MEAN...
...GOING TO THE SHOOTING LOCATIONS?
YEAH.
IT'S ALMOST SUMMER BREAK.
WE COULD DO A FEW TRIPS.
THAT'S THE REQUEST?
YEAH...
I JUST REALLY...
...WANT TO GO WITH YOU.

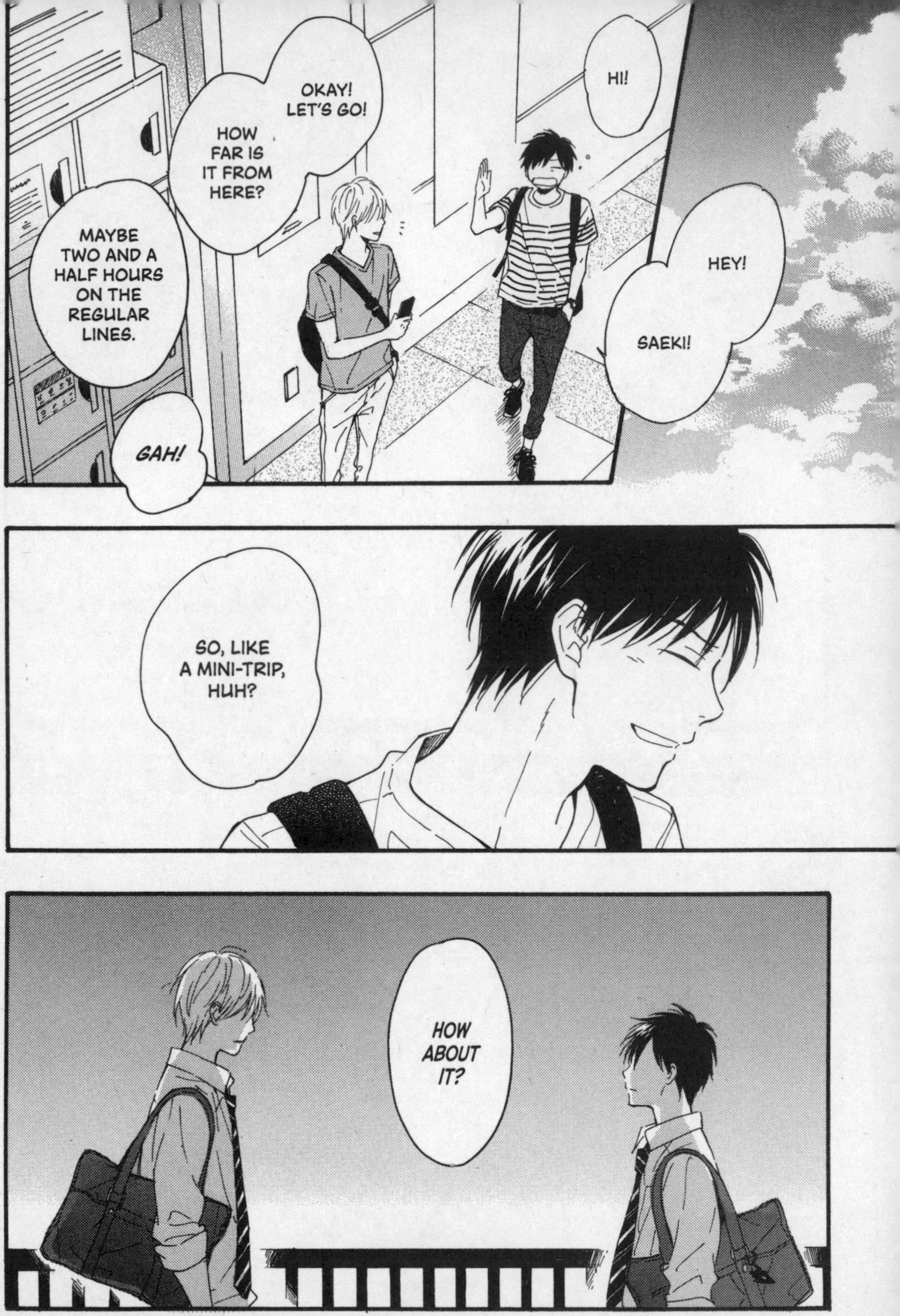
HI!
HEY!
SAEKI!
OKAY! LET'S GO!
HOW FAR IS IT FROM HERE?
MAYBE TWO AND A HALF HOURS ON THE REGULAR LINES.
GAH!
SO, LIKE A MINI-TRIP, HUH?
HOW ABOUT IT?

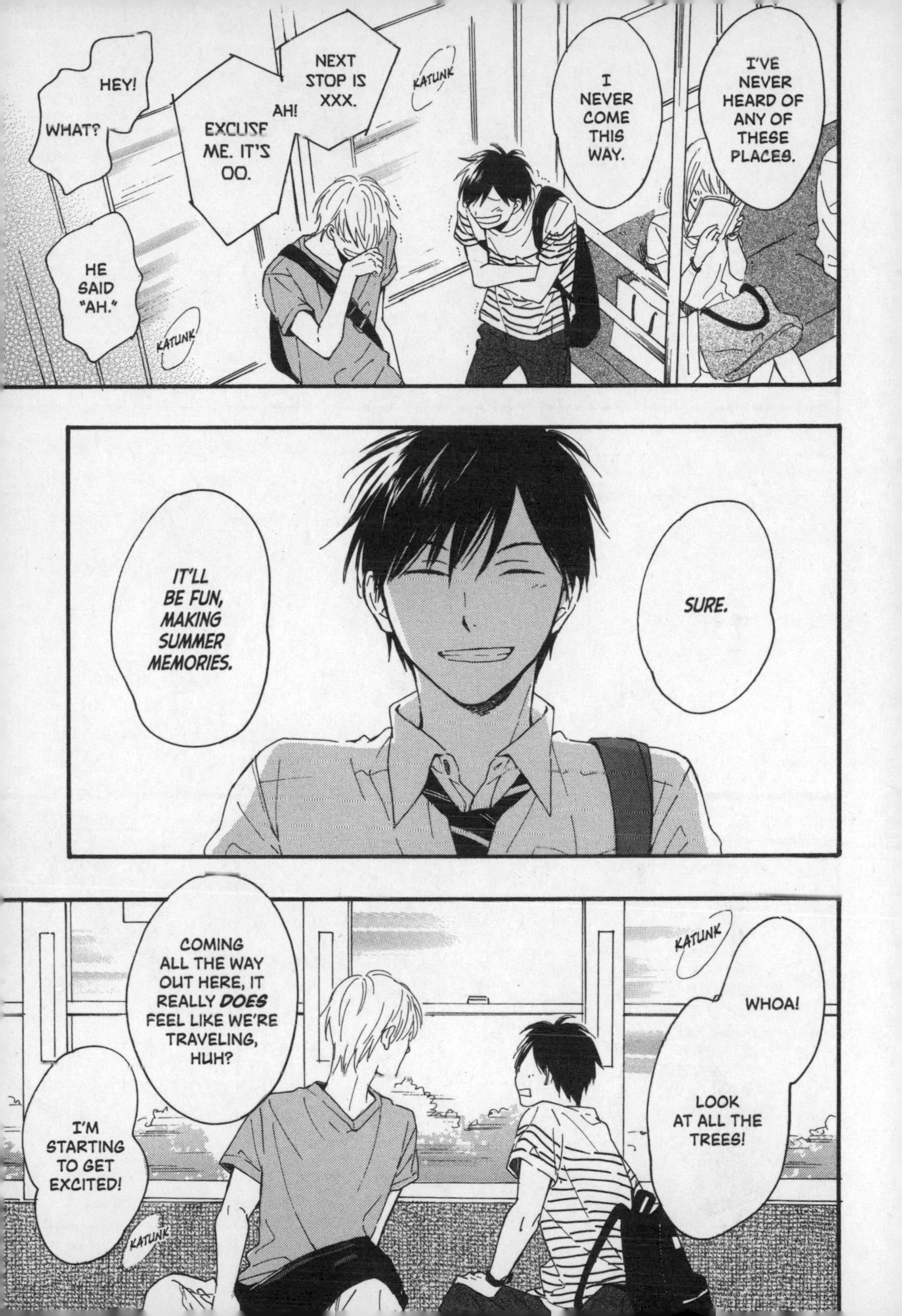
I'VE NEVER HEARD OF ANY OF THESE PLACES.
I NEVER COME THIS WAY.
KATUNK
NEXT STOP IS XXX.
AH!
EXCUSE ME. IT'S OO.
HEY!
WHAT?
HE SAID "AH."
KATUNK
SURE.
IT'LL BE FUN, MAKING SUMMER MEMORIES.
KATUNK
WHOA!
LOOK AT ALL THE TREES!
COMING ALL THE WAY OUT HERE, IT REALLY *DOES* FEEL LIKE WE'RE TRAVELING, HUH?
I'M STARTING TO GET EXCITED!
KATUNK

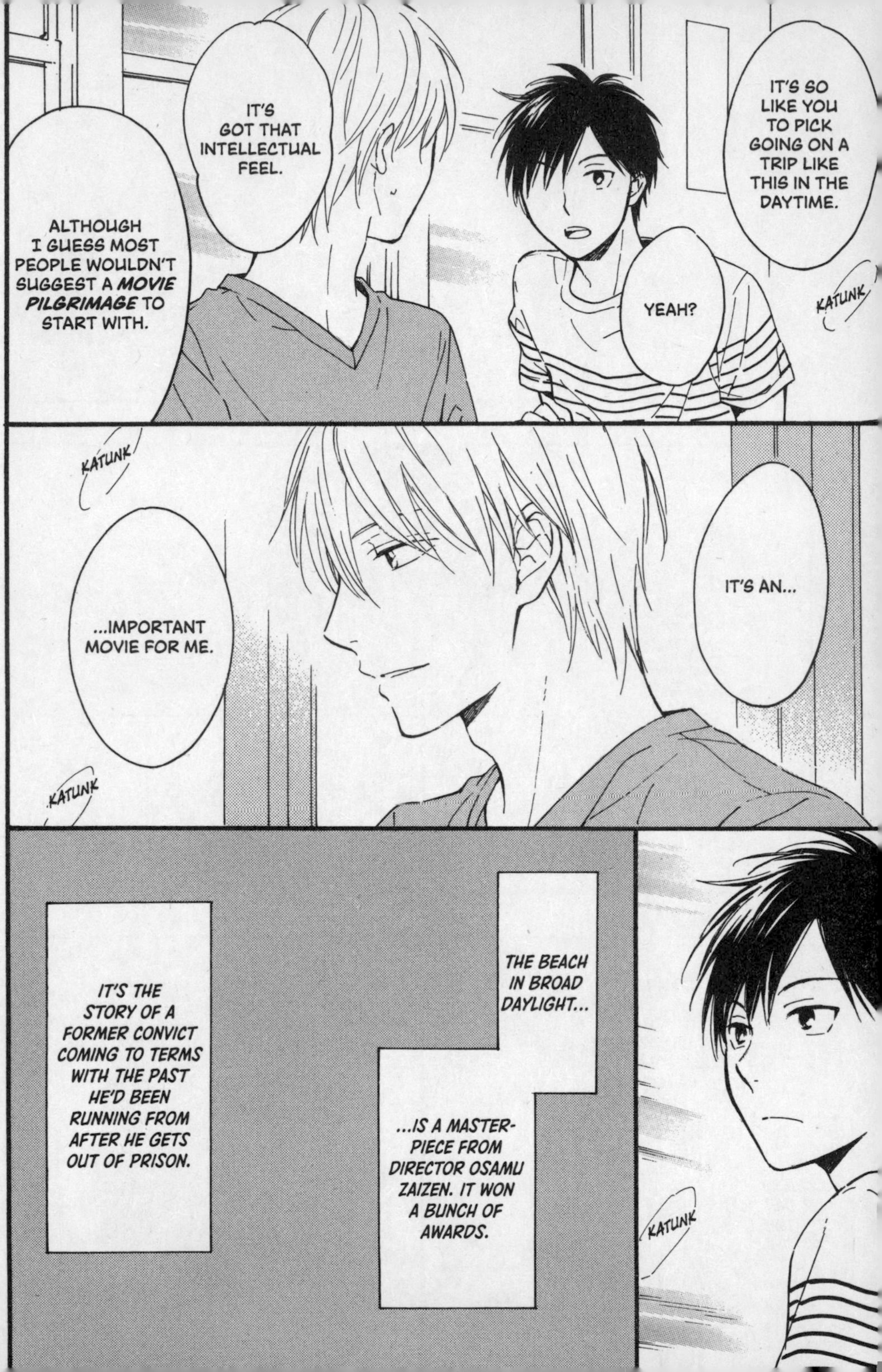
IT'S SO LIKE YOU TO PICK GOING ON A TRIP LIKE THIS IN THE DAYTIME.
KATUNK
YEAH?
IT'S GOT THAT INTELLECTUAL FEEL.
ALTHOUGH I GUESS MOST PEOPLE WOULDN'T SUGGEST A *MOVIE PILGRIMAGE* TO START WITH.
IT'S AN...
KATUNK
...IMPORTANT MOVIE FOR ME.
KATUNK
KATUNK
THE BEACH IN BROAD DAYLIGHT...
...IS A MASTER-PIECE FROM DIRECTOR OSAMU ZAIZEN. IT WON A BUNCH OF AWARDS.
IT'S THE STORY OF A FORMER CONVICT COMING TO TERMS WITH THE PAST HE'D BEEN RUNNING FROM AFTER HE GETS OUT OF PRISON.

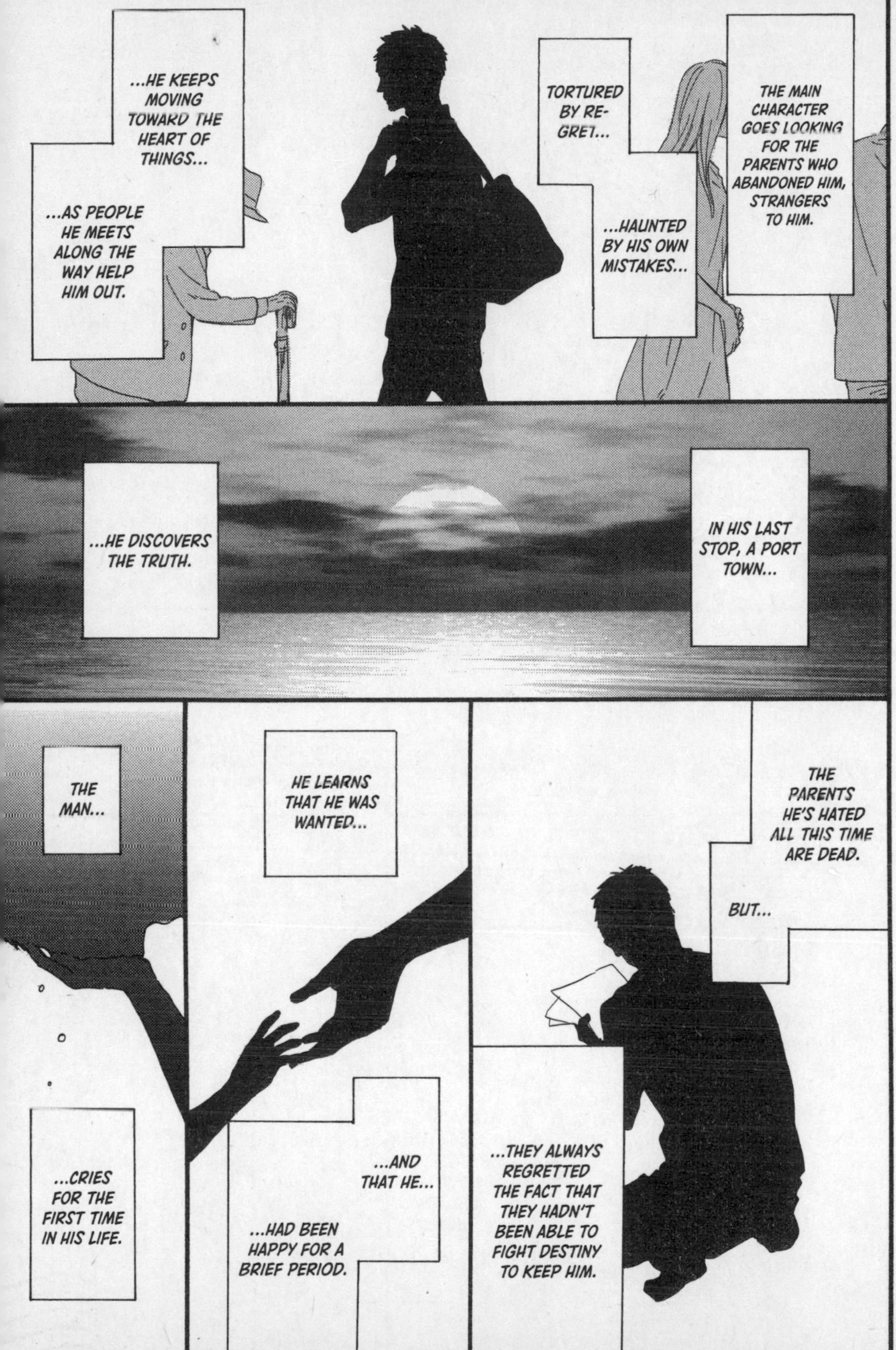
THE MAIN CHARACTER GOES LOOKING FOR THE PARENTS WHO ABANDONED HIM, STRANGERS TO HIM.
TORTURED BY RE-GRET...
...HAUNTED BY HIS OWN MISTAKES...
...HE KEEPS MOVING TOWARD THE HEART OF THINGS...
...AS PEOPLE HE MEETS ALONG THE WAY HELP HIM OUT.
IN HIS LAST STOP, A PORT TOWN...
...HE DISCOVERS THE TRUTH.
THE PARENTS HE'S HATED ALL THIS TIME ARE DEAD.
BUT...
...THEY ALWAYS REGRETTED THE FACT THAT THEY HADN'T BEEN ABLE TO FIGHT DESTINY TO KEEP HIM.
HE LEARNS THAT HE WAS WANTED...
...AND THAT HE...
...HAD BEEN HAPPY FOR A BRIEF PERIOD.
THE MAN...
...CRIES FOR THE FIRST TIME IN HIS LIFE.

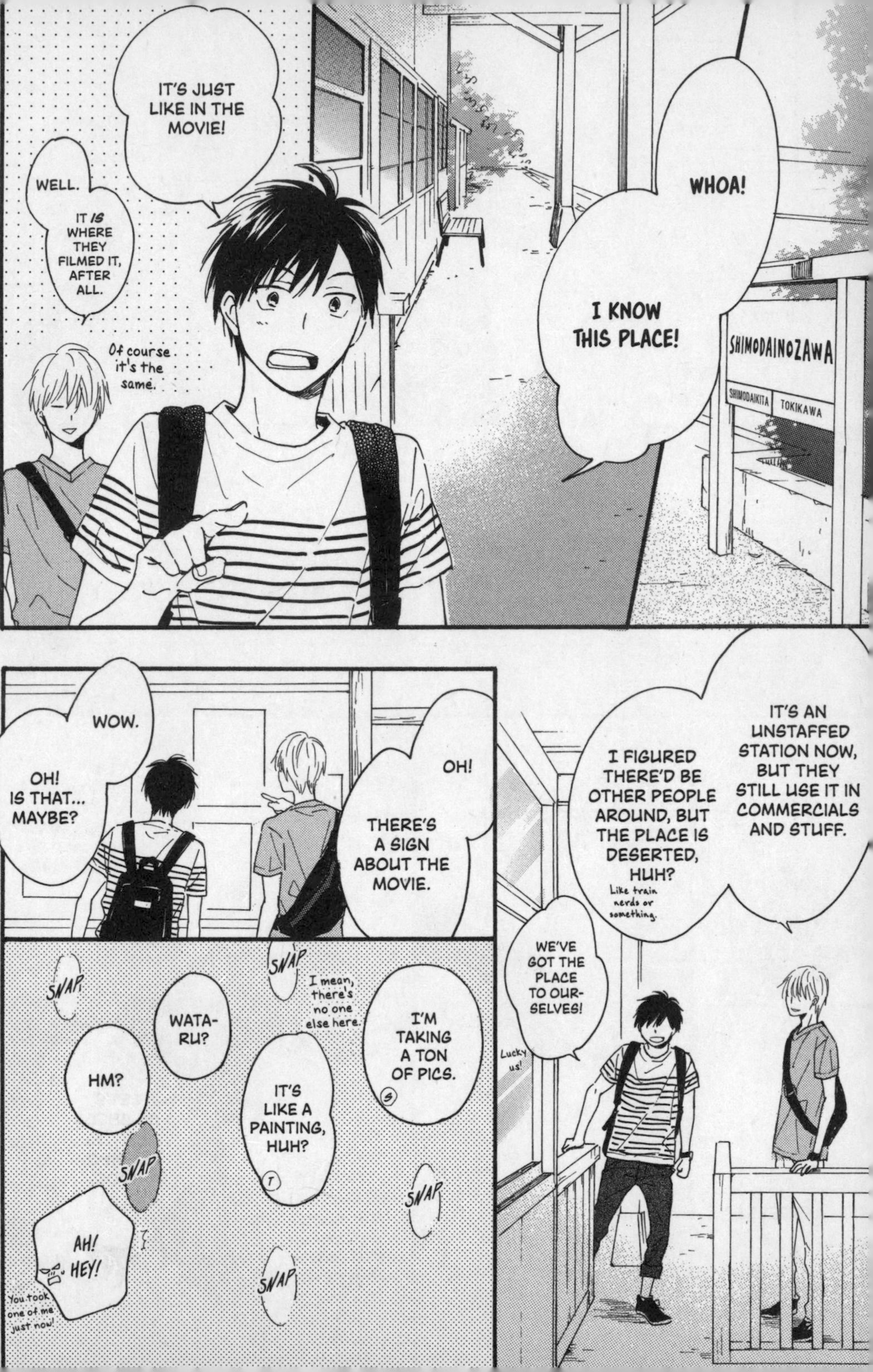
WHOA!
I KNOW THIS PLACE!
SHIMODAINOZAWA
SHIMODAIKITA
TOKIKAWA
IT'S JUST LIKE IN THE MOVIE!
WELL.
IT *IS* WHERE THEY FILMED IT, AFTER ALL.
Of course it's the same.
IT'S AN UNSTAFFED STATION NOW, BUT THEY STILL USE IT IN COMMERCIALS AND STUFF.
I FIGURED THERE'D BE OTHER PEOPLE AROUND, BUT THE PLACE IS DESERTED, HUH?
Like train nerds or something.
WE'VE GOT THE PLACE TO OURSELVES!
Lucky us!
OH!
THERE'S A SIGN ABOUT THE MOVIE.
WOW.
OH! IS THAT... MAYBE?
SNAP
I'M TAKING A TON OF PICS.
I mean, there's no one else here.
WATA-RU?
SNAP
HM?
IT'S LIKE A PAINTING, HUH?
SNAP
SNAP
SNAP
AH! HEY!
You took one of me just now!

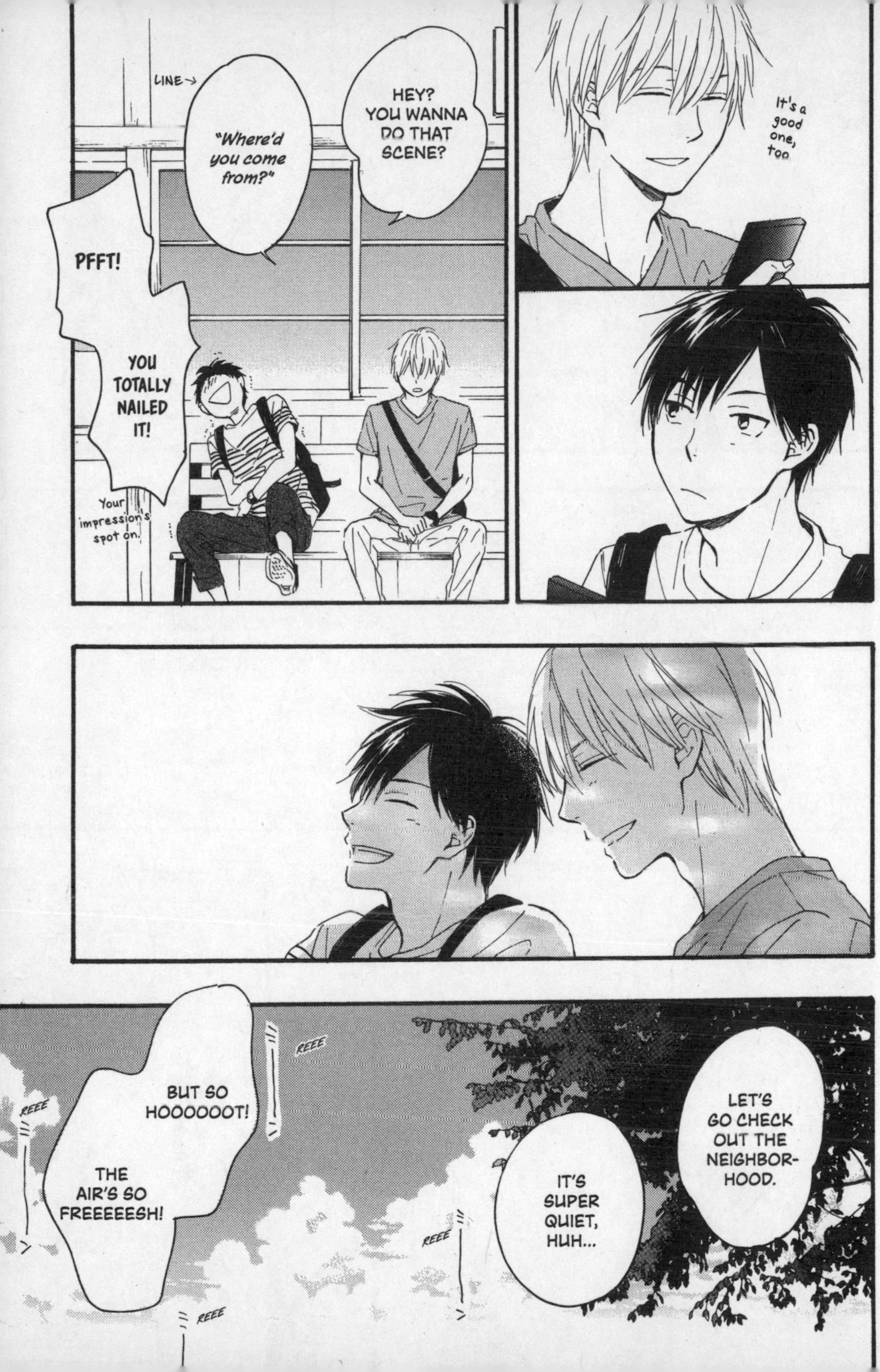
It's a good one, too.
HEY? YOU WANNA DO THAT SCENE?
LINE→
"Where'd you come from?"
PFFT!
YOU TOTALLY NAILED IT!
Your impression's spot on.
LET'S GO CHECK OUT THE NEIGHBOR-HOOD.
IT'S SUPER QUIET, HUH...
REEE
REEE
BUT SO HOOOOOOT!
THE AIR'S SO FREEEEESH!
REEE
REEE

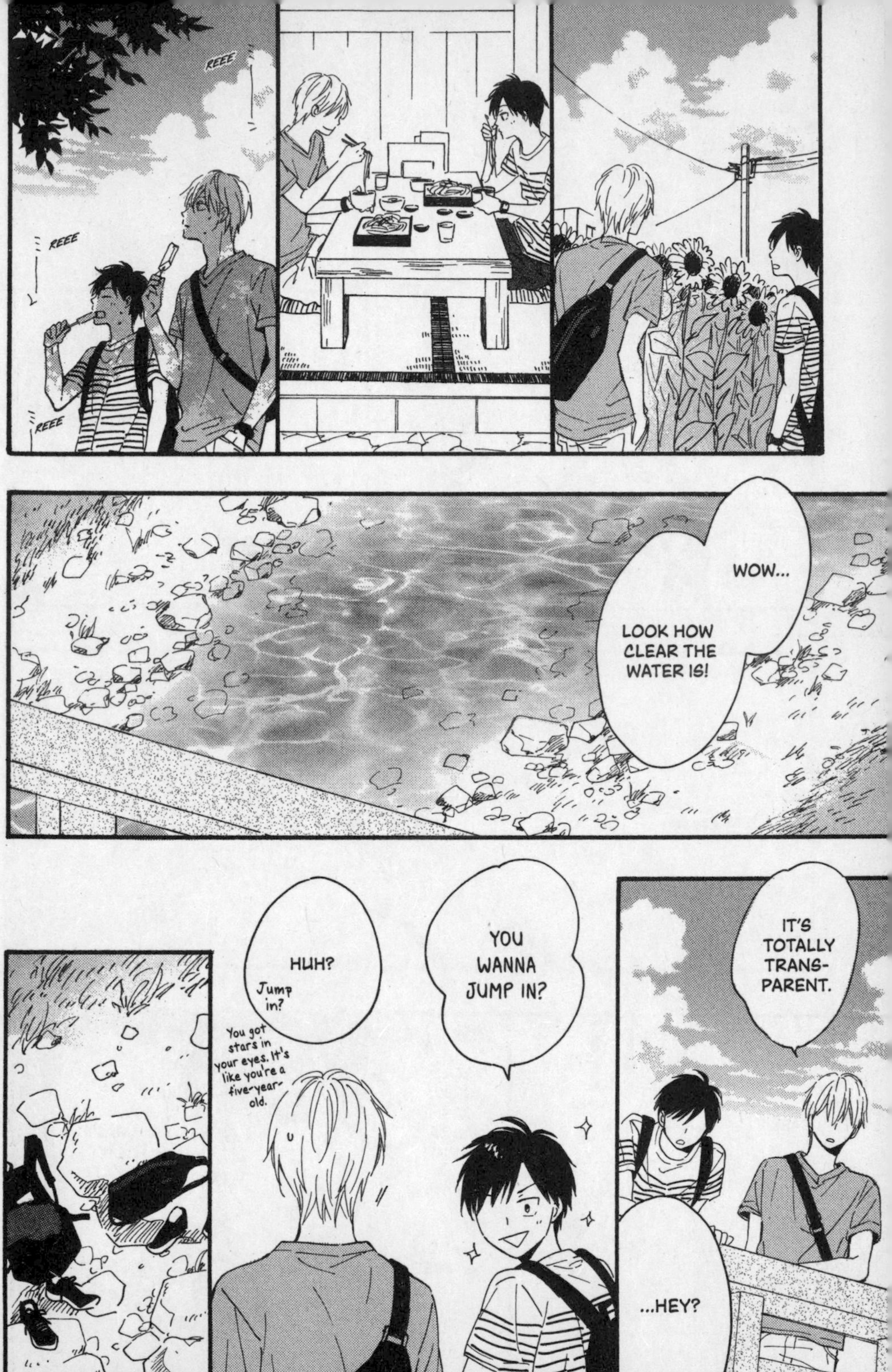
REEE
REEE
REEE
WOW...
LOOK HOW CLEAR THE WATER IS!
IT'S TOTALLY TRANS-PARENT.
...HEY?
YOU WANNA JUMP IN?
HUH?
Jump in?
You got stars in your eyes. It's like you're a five-year-old.

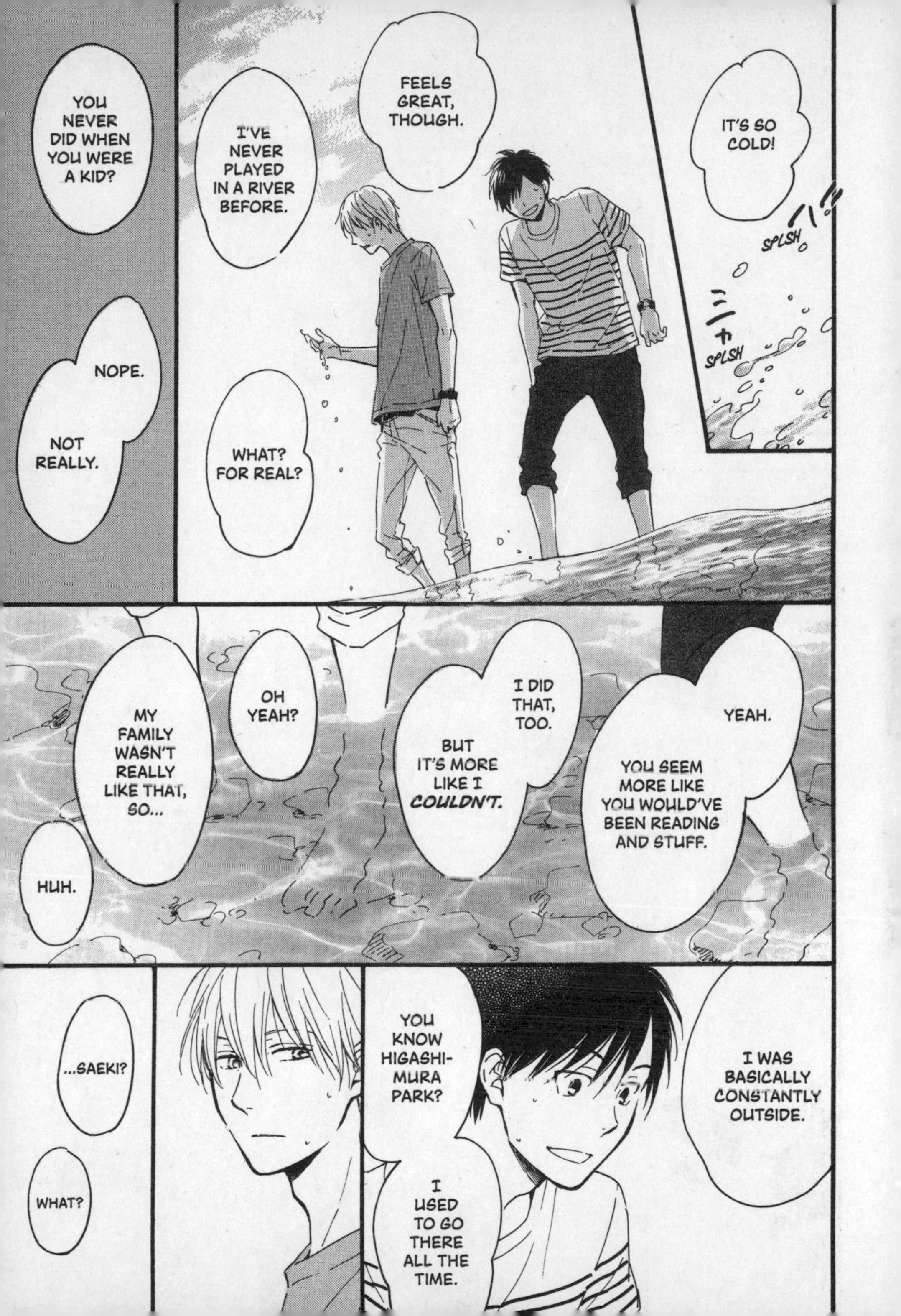
IT'S SO COLD!
SPLSH
SPLSH
FEELS GREAT, THOUGH.
I'VE NEVER PLAYED IN A RIVER BEFORE.
WHAT? FOR REAL?
YOU NEVER DID WHEN YOU WERE A KID?
NOPE.
NOT REALLY.
YEAH.
YOU SEEM MORE LIKE YOU WOULD'VE BEEN READING AND STUFF.
I DID THAT, TOO.
BUT IT'S MORE LIKE I *COULDN'T.*
OH YEAH?
MY FAMILY WASN'T REALLY LIKE THAT, SO...
HUH.
I WAS BASICALLY CONSTANTLY OUTSIDE.
YOU KNOW HIGASHI-MURA PARK?
I USED TO GO THERE ALL THE TIME.
...SAEKI?
WHAT?

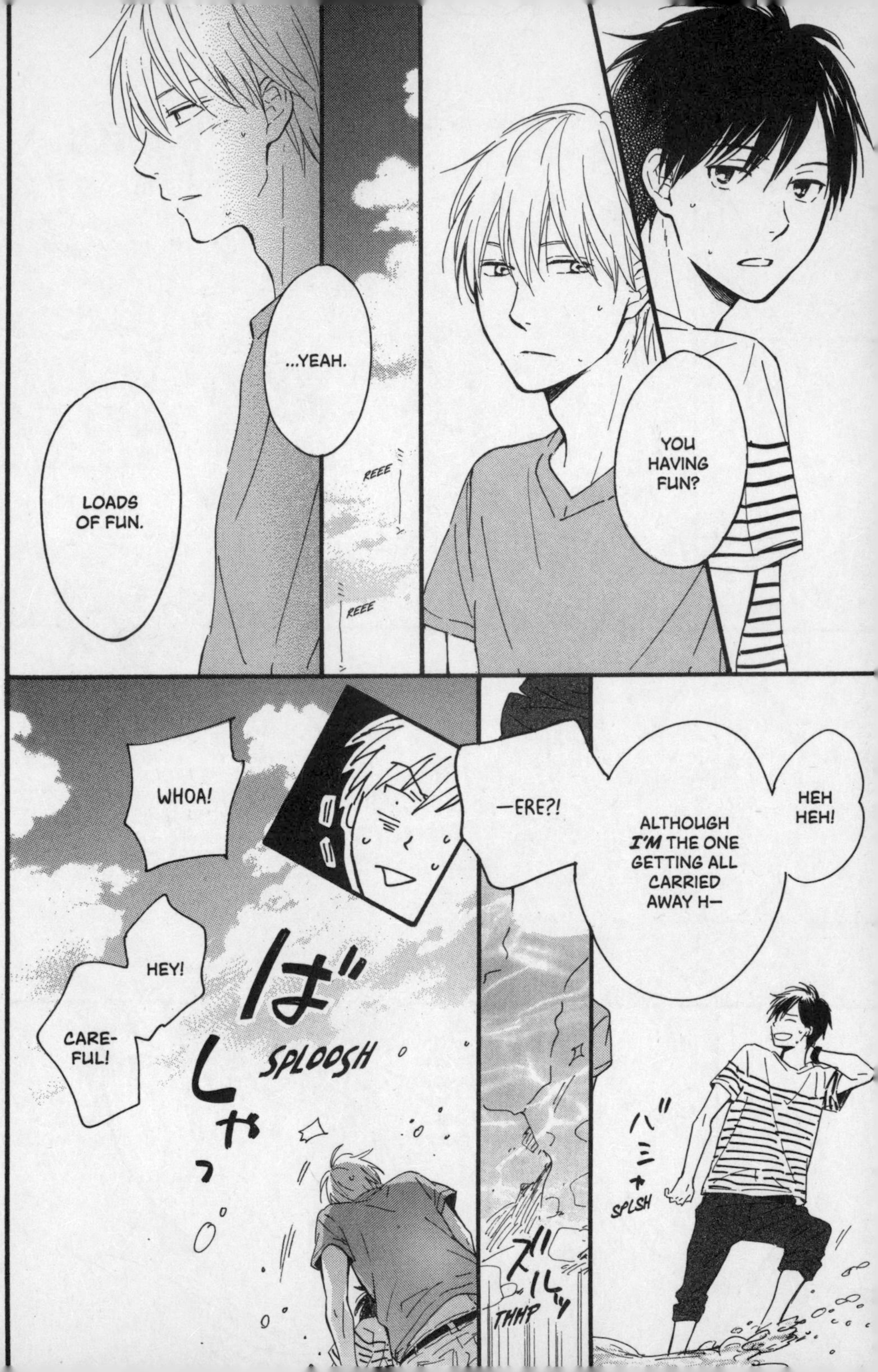
YOU HAVING FUN?
REEE
REEE
...YEAH.
LOADS OF FUN.
HEH HEH!
ALTHOUGH *I'M* THE ONE GETTING ALL CARRIED AWAY H—
バシャ
SPLSH
—ERE?!
ズルッ
THHP
WHOA!
ばしゃっ
SPLOOSH
HEY!
CARE-FUL!

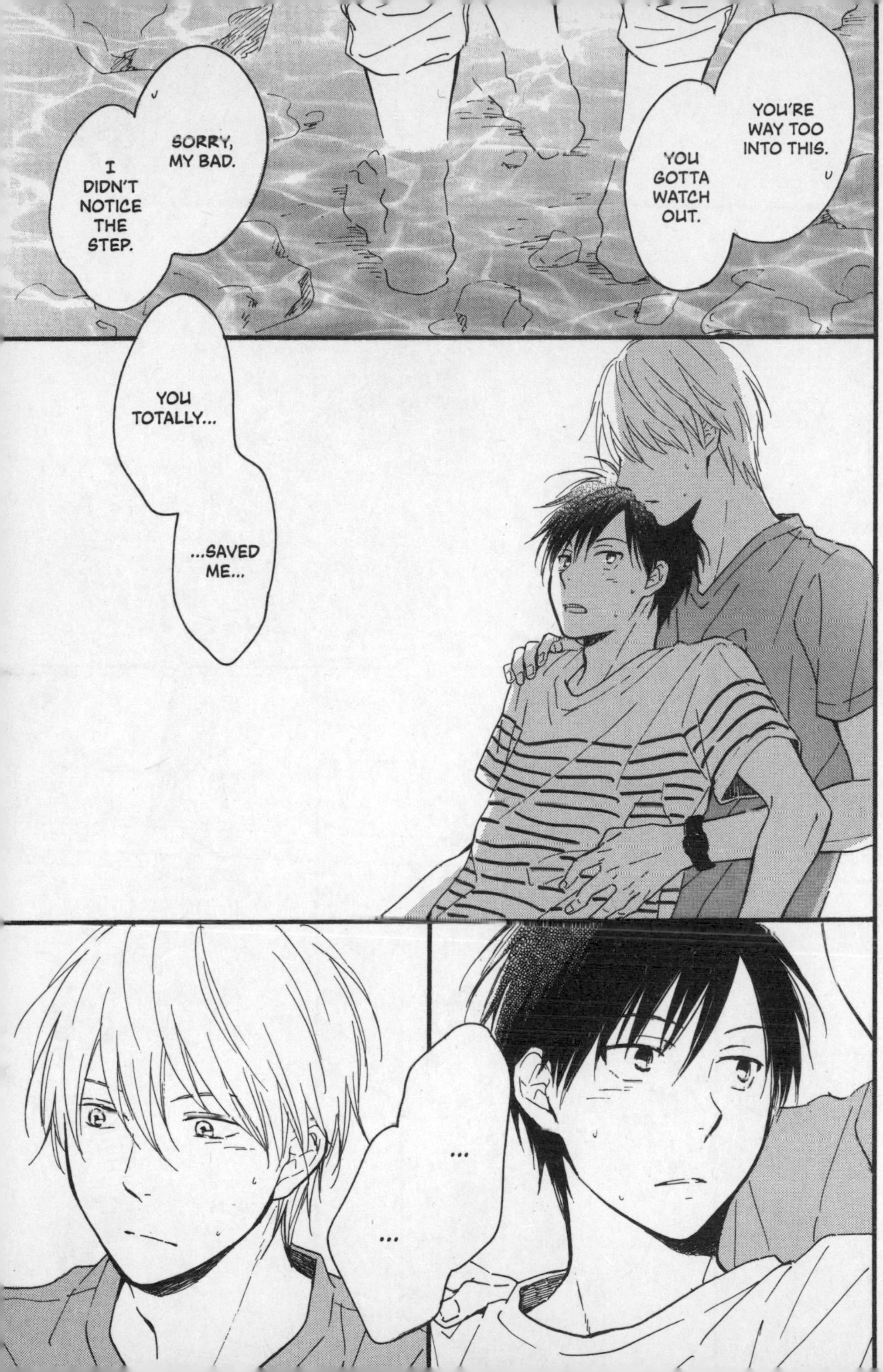

YOU'RE WAY TOO INTO THIS.
YOU GOTTA WATCH OUT.
SORRY, MY BAD.
I DIDN'T NOTICE THE STEP.
YOU TOTALLY...
...SAVED ME...
...
...

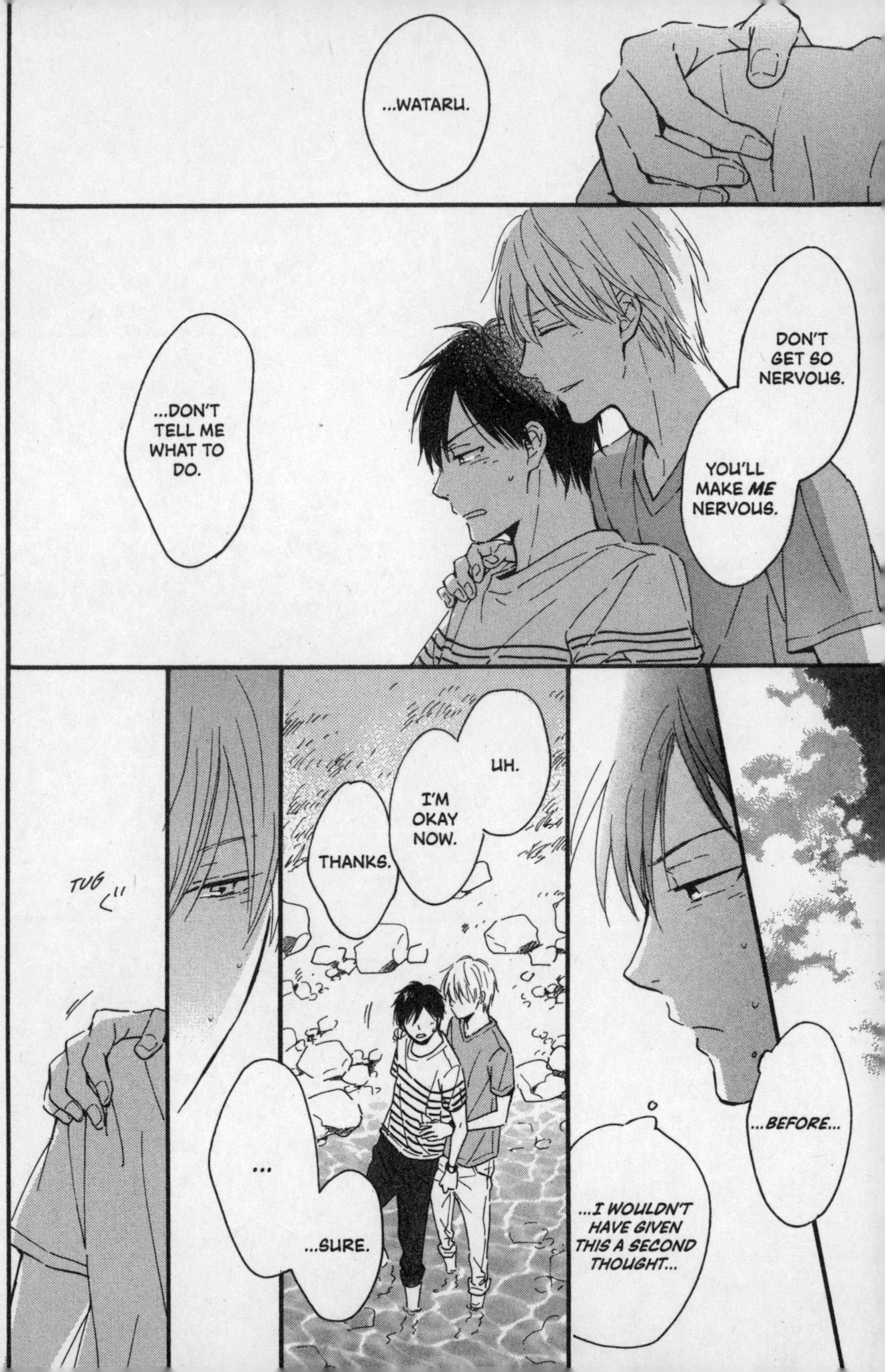
...WATARU.
DON'T GET SO NERVOUS.
YOU'LL MAKE *ME* NERVOUS.
...DON'T TELL ME WHAT TO DO.
...BEFORE...
...I WOULDN'T HAVE GIVEN THIS A SECOND THOUGHT...
UH.
I'M OKAY NOW.
THANKS.
...
...SURE.
TUG

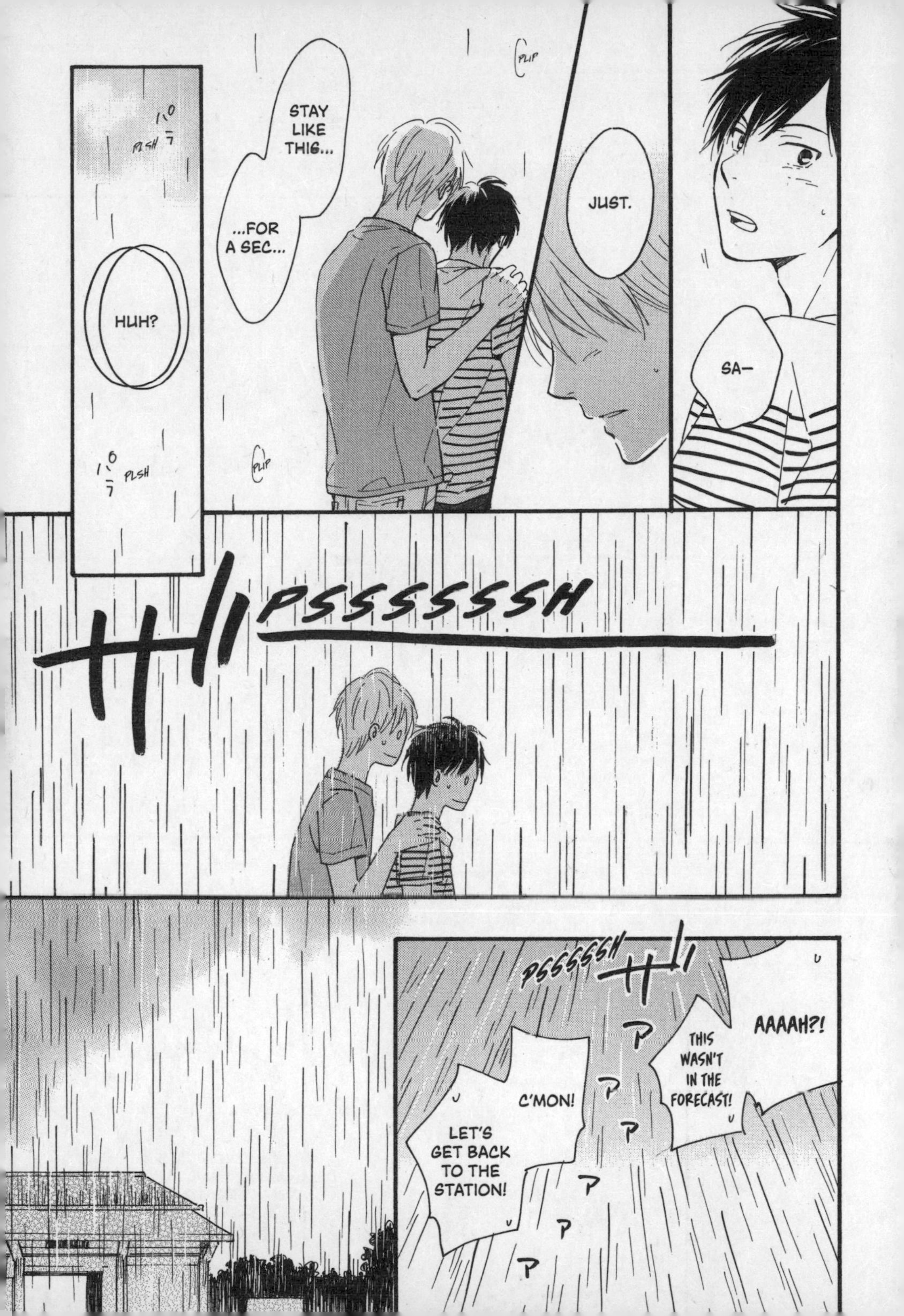
SA—
JUST.
PLIP
STAY LIKE THIS...
...FOR A SEC...
PLIP
PLSH
HUH?
PLSH
PSSSSSSH
AAAAH?!
THIS WASN'T IN THE FORECAST!
C'MON!
LET'S GET BACK TO THE STATION!
PSSSSSH

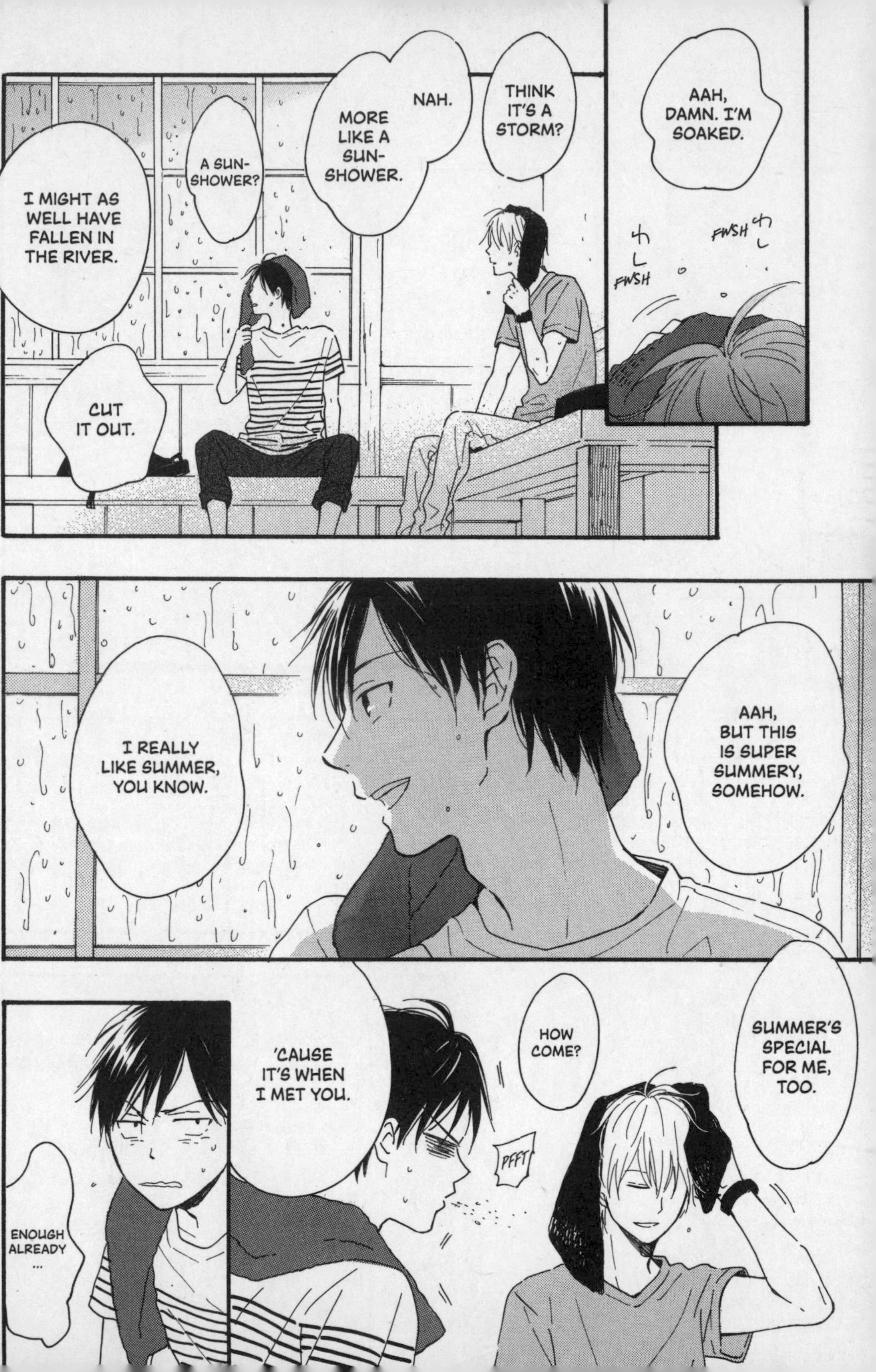
AAH, DAMN. I'M SOAKED.
FWSH
FWSH
THINK IT'S A STORM?
NAH.
MORE LIKE A SUN-SHOWER.
A SUN-SHOWER?
I MIGHT AS WELL HAVE FALLEN IN THE RIVER.
CUT IT OUT.
AAH, BUT THIS IS SUPER SUMMERY, SOMEHOW.
I REALLY LIKE SUMMER, YOU KNOW.
SUMMER'S SPECIAL FOR ME, TOO.
HOW COME?
'CAUSE IT'S WHEN I MET YOU.
PFFT
ENOUGH ALREADY ...

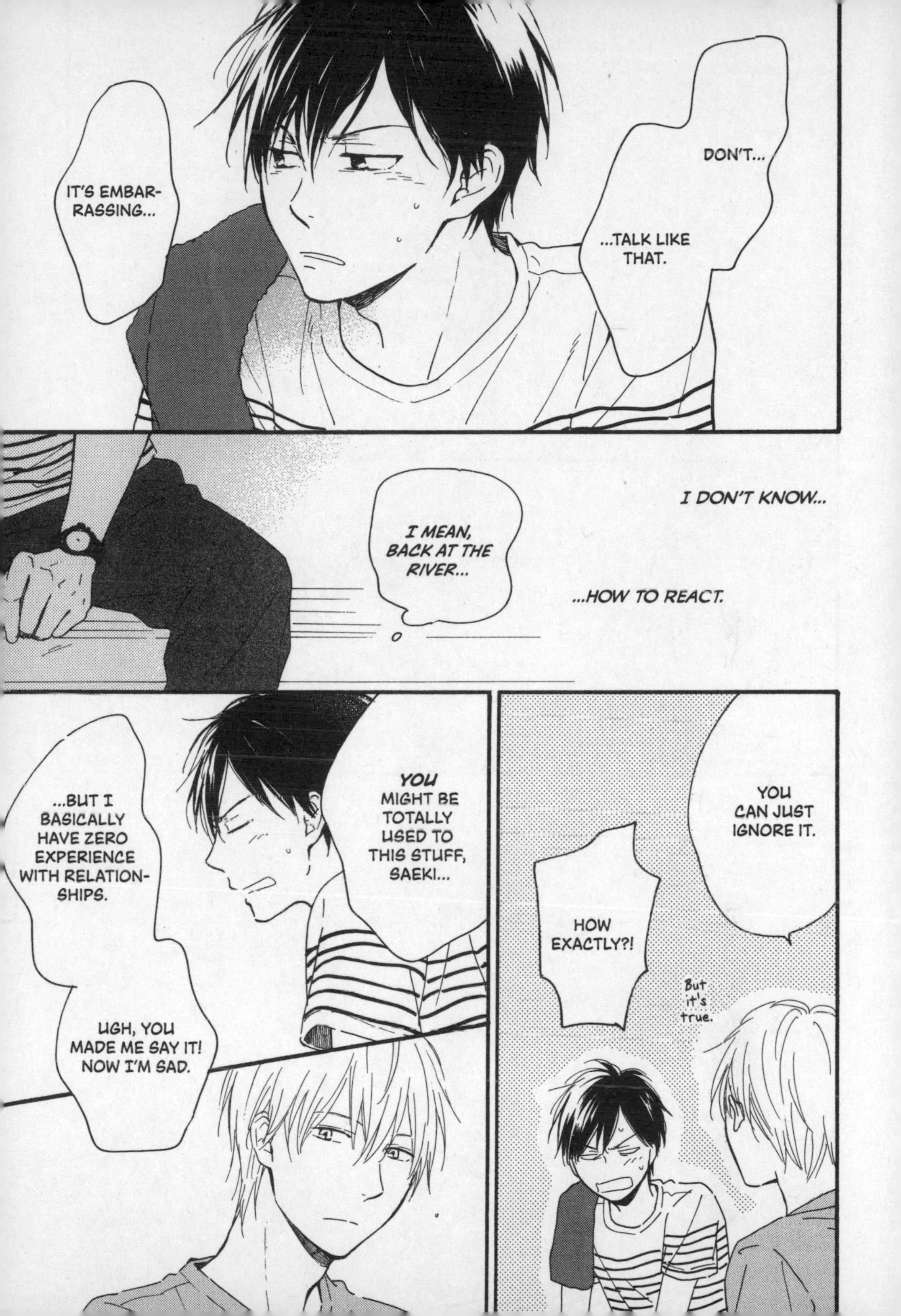
DON'T...
...TALK LIKE THAT.
IT'S EMBARRASSING...
I DON'T KNOW...
...HOW TO REACT.
I MEAN, BACK AT THE RIVER...
YOU CAN JUST IGNORE IT.
HOW EXACTLY?!
But it's true.
YOU MIGHT BE TOTALLY USED TO THIS STUFF, SAEKI...
...BUT I BASICALLY HAVE ZERO EXPERIENCE WITH RELATIONSHIPS.
UGH, YOU MADE ME SAY IT! NOW I'M SAD.

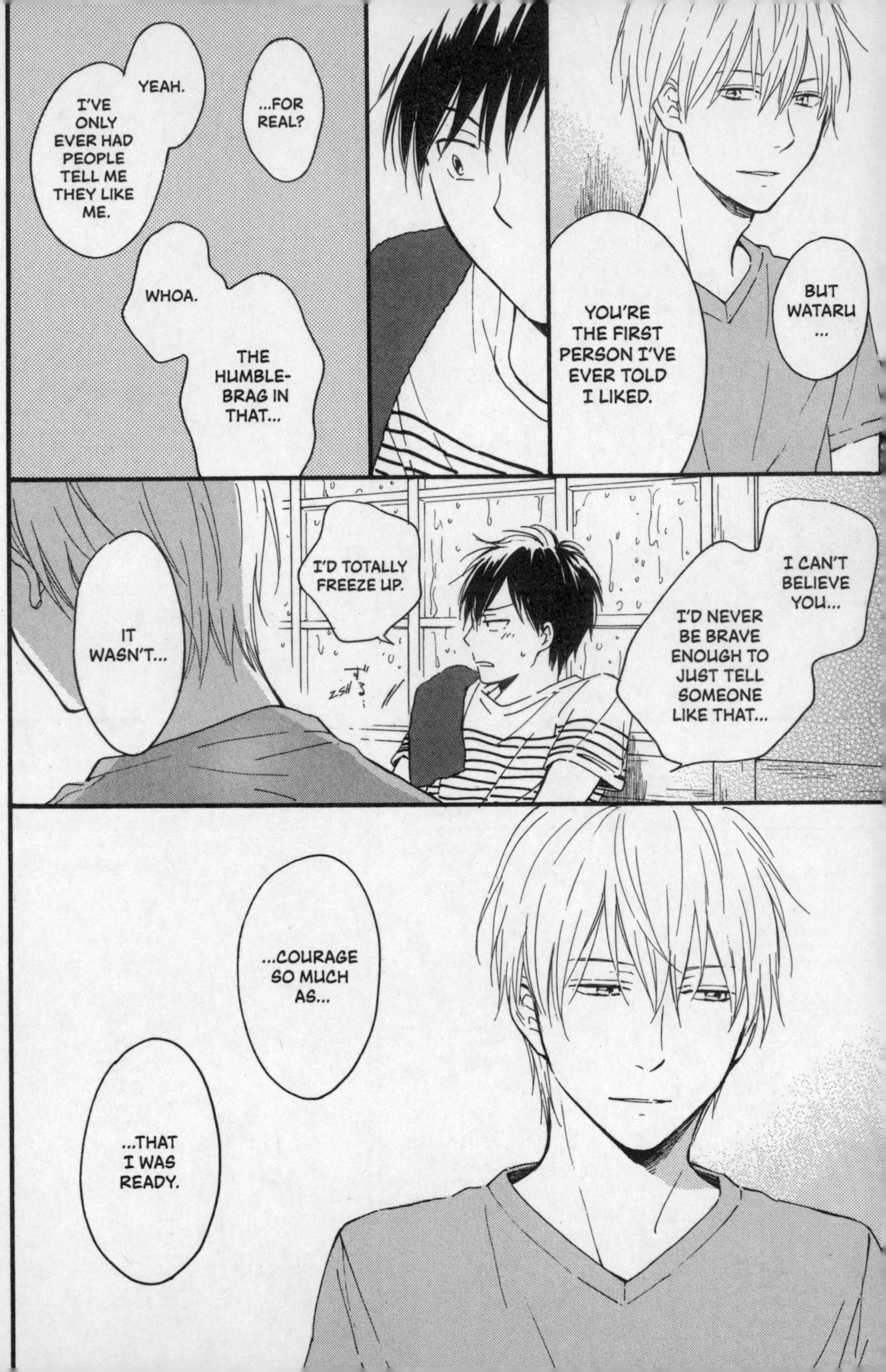
BUT WATARU...
YOU'RE THE FIRST PERSON I'VE EVER TOLD I LIKED.
...FOR REAL?
YEAH. I'VE ONLY EVER HAD PEOPLE TELL ME THEY LIKE ME.
WHOA.
THE HUMBLE-BRAG IN THAT...
I CAN'T BELIEVE YOU...
I'D NEVER BE BRAVE ENOUGH TO JUST TELL SOMEONE LIKE THAT...
I'D TOTALLY FREEZE UP.
ZSH
IT WASN'T...
...COURAGE SO MUCH AS...
...THAT I WAS READY.

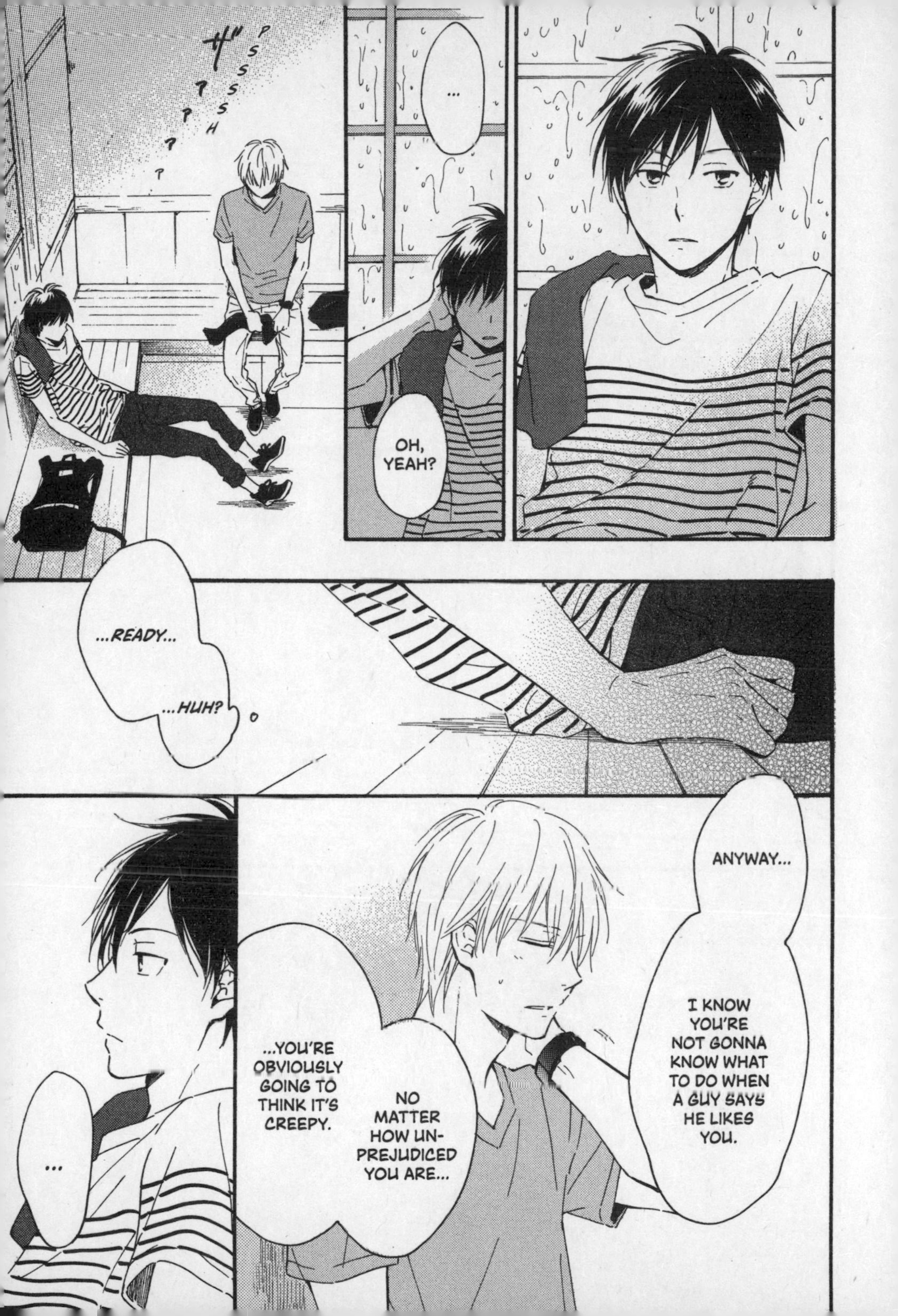
...
OH, YEAH?
PSSSSH
...READY...
...HUH?
ANYWAY...
I KNOW YOU'RE NOT GONNA KNOW WHAT TO DO WHEN A GUY SAYS HE LIKES YOU.
NO MATTER HOW UN-PREJUDICED YOU ARE...
...YOU'RE OBVIOUSLY GOING TO THINK IT'S CREEPY.
...

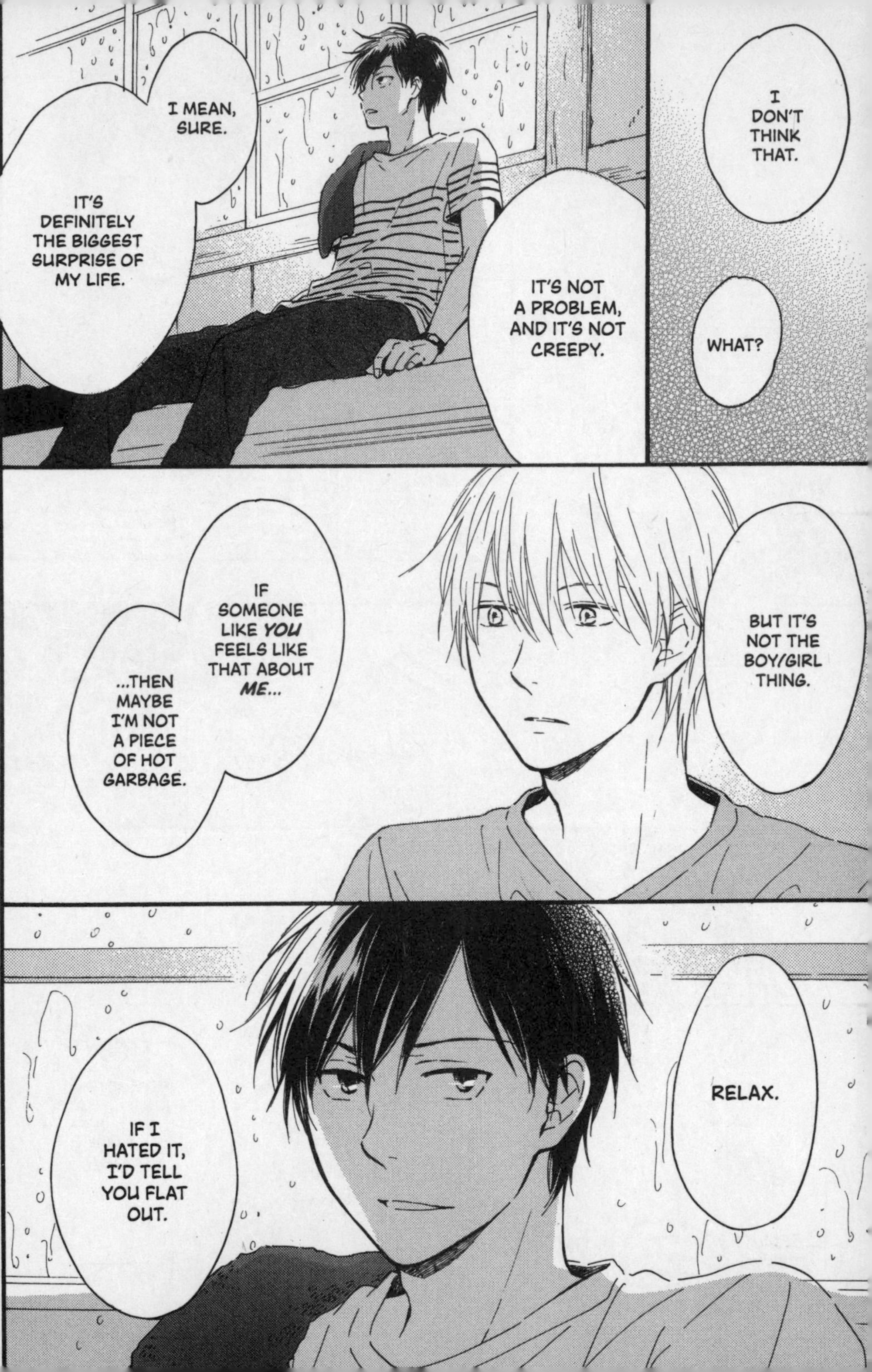
I DON'T THINK THAT.
WHAT?
IT'S NOT A PROBLEM, AND IT'S NOT CREEPY.
I MEAN, SURE.
IT'S DEFINITELY THE BIGGEST SURPRISE OF MY LIFE.
BUT IT'S NOT THE BOY/GIRL THING.
IF SOMEONE LIKE *YOU* FEELS LIKE THAT ABOUT *ME*...
...THEN MAYBE I'M NOT A PIECE OF HOT GARBAGE.
RELAX.
IF I HATED IT, I'D TELL YOU FLAT OUT.

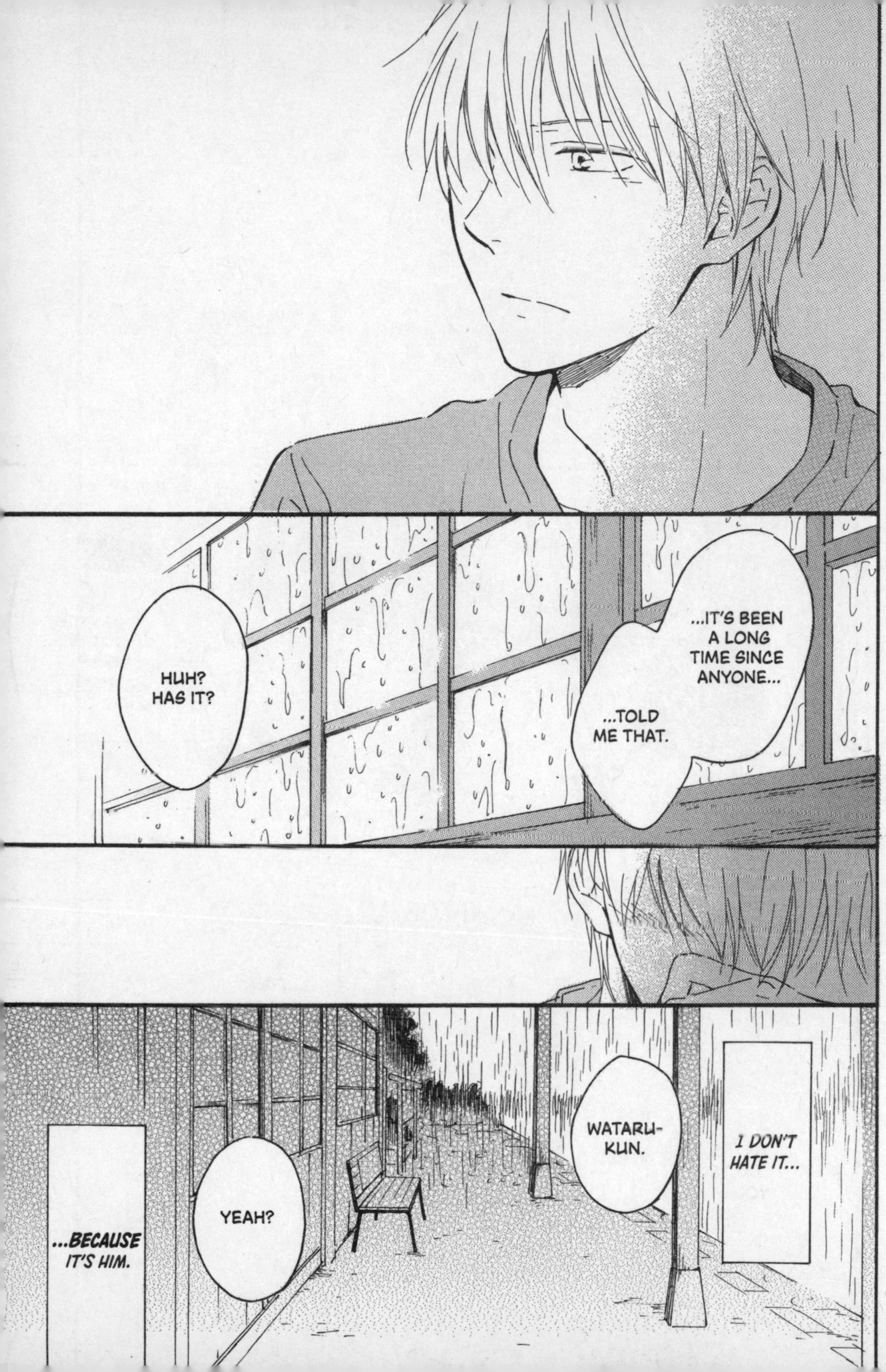
...IT'S BEEN A LONG TIME SINCE ANYONE...
...TOLD ME THAT.
HUH? HAS IT?
I DON'T HATE IT...
WATARU-KUN.
YEAH?
...BECAUSE IT'S HIM.

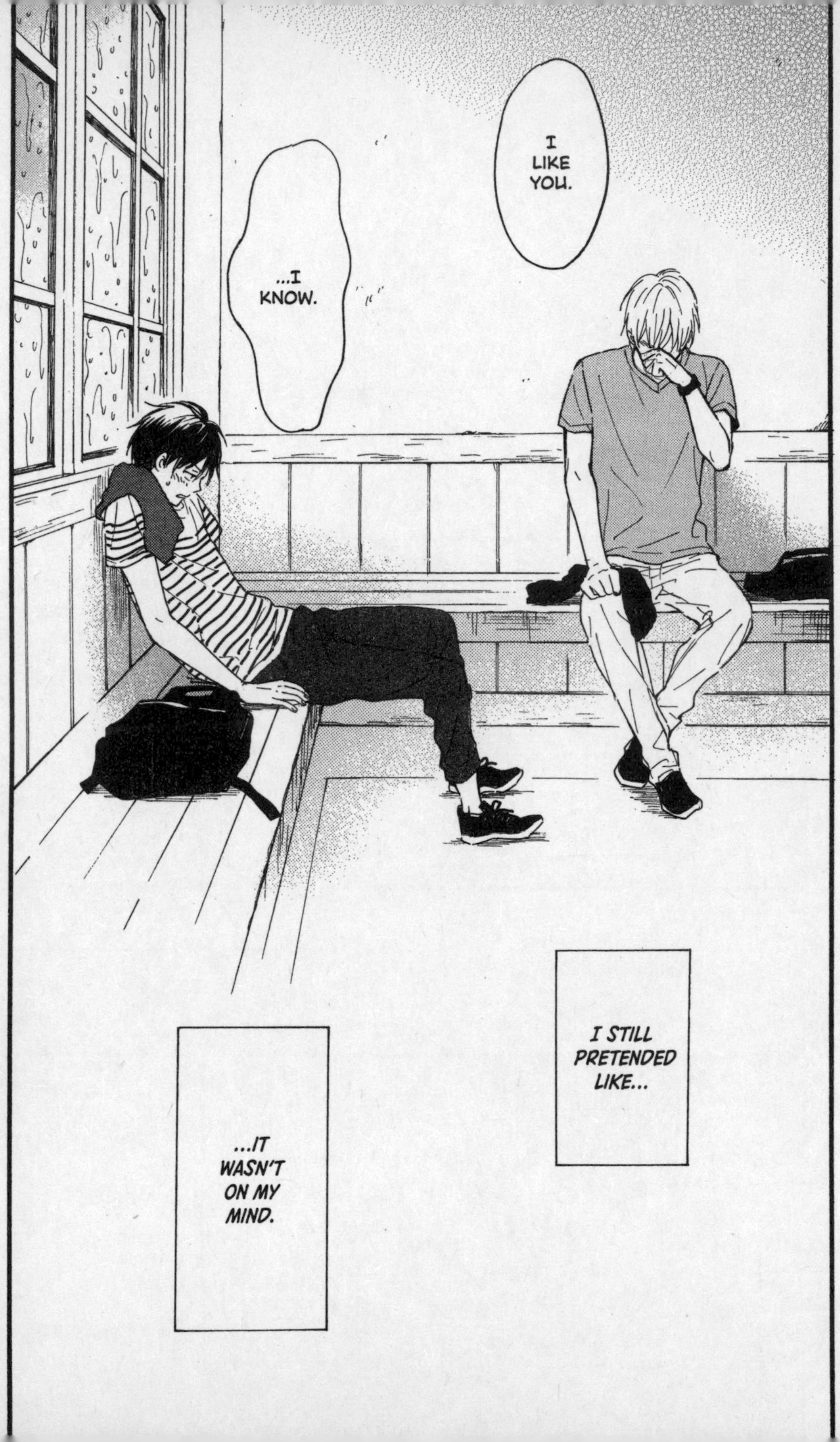
I LIKE YOU.
...I KNOW.
I STILL PRETENDED LIKE...
...IT WASN'T ON MY MIND.

Chapter 3

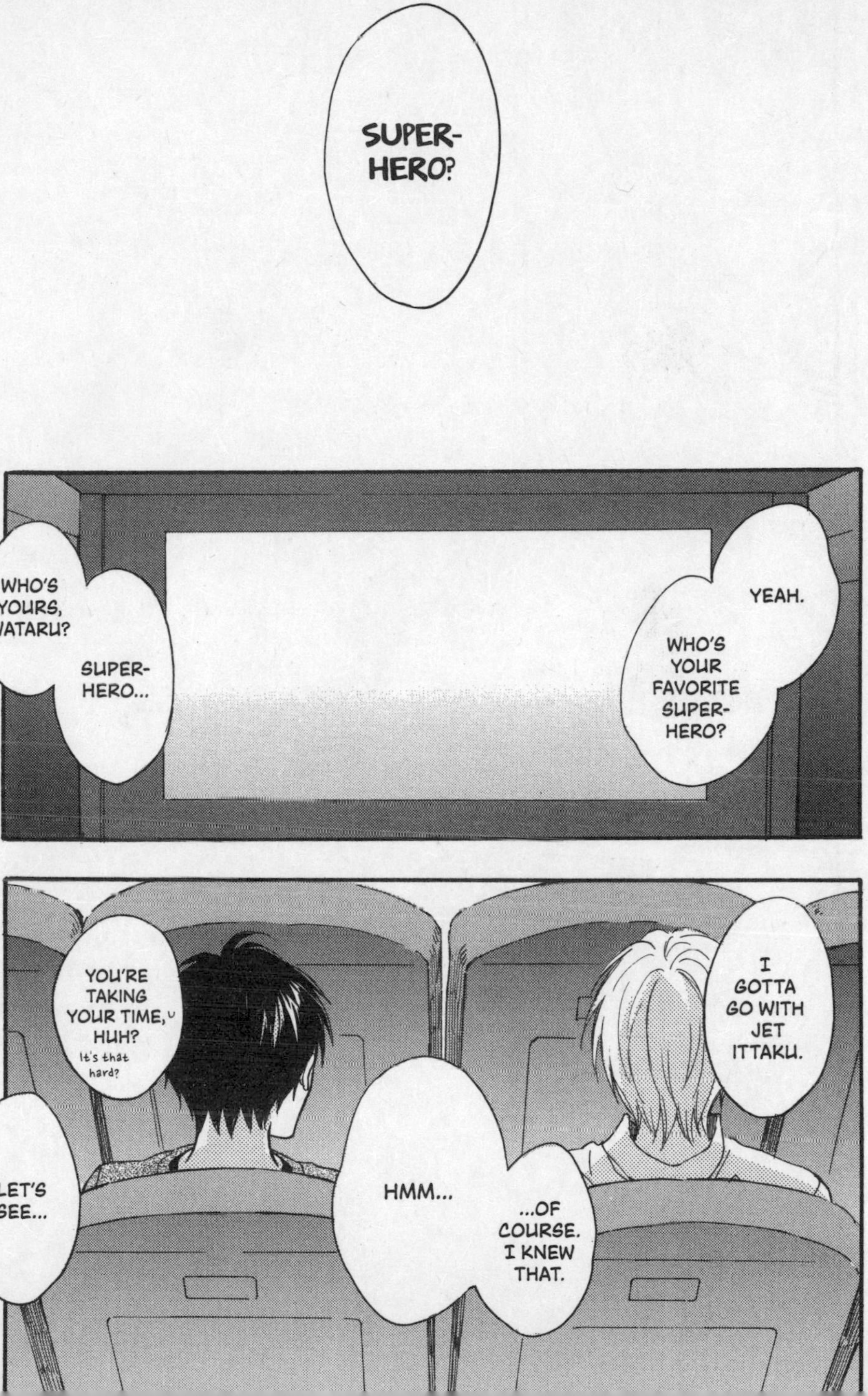
SUPER-HERO?
YEAH.
WHO'S YOUR FAVORITE SUPER-HERO?
SUPER-HERO...
WHO'S YOURS, WATARU?
I GOTTA GO WITH JET ITTAKU.
YOU'RE TAKING YOUR TIME, HUH?
It's that hard?
...OF COURSE. I KNEW THAT.
HMM...
LET'S SEE...

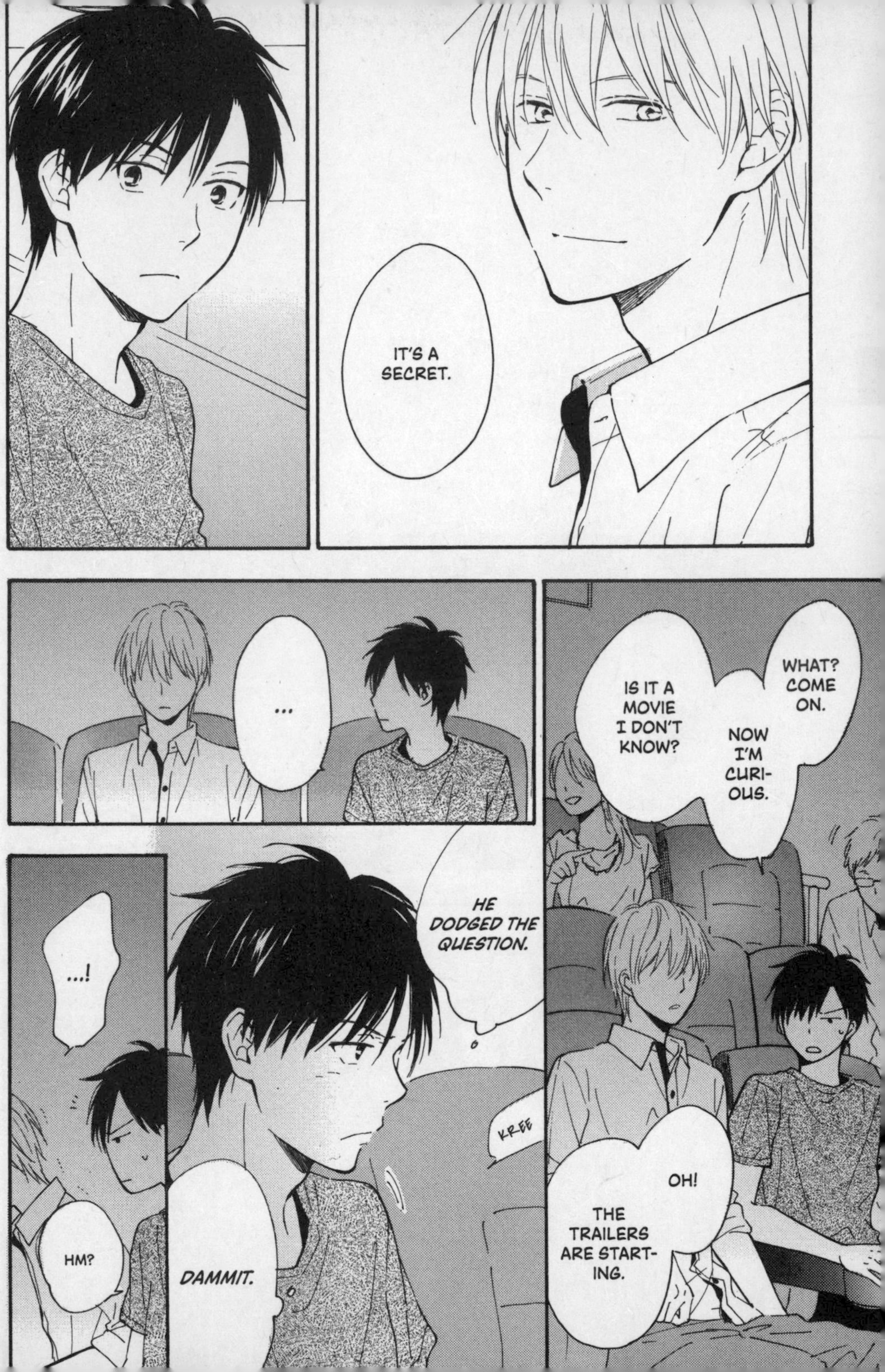
IT'S A SECRET.
WHAT? COME ON. NOW I'M CURIOUS.
IS IT A MOVIE I DON'T KNOW?
OH! THE TRAILERS ARE STARTING.
...
HE DODGED THE QUESTION.
KREE
DAMMIT.
...!
HM?

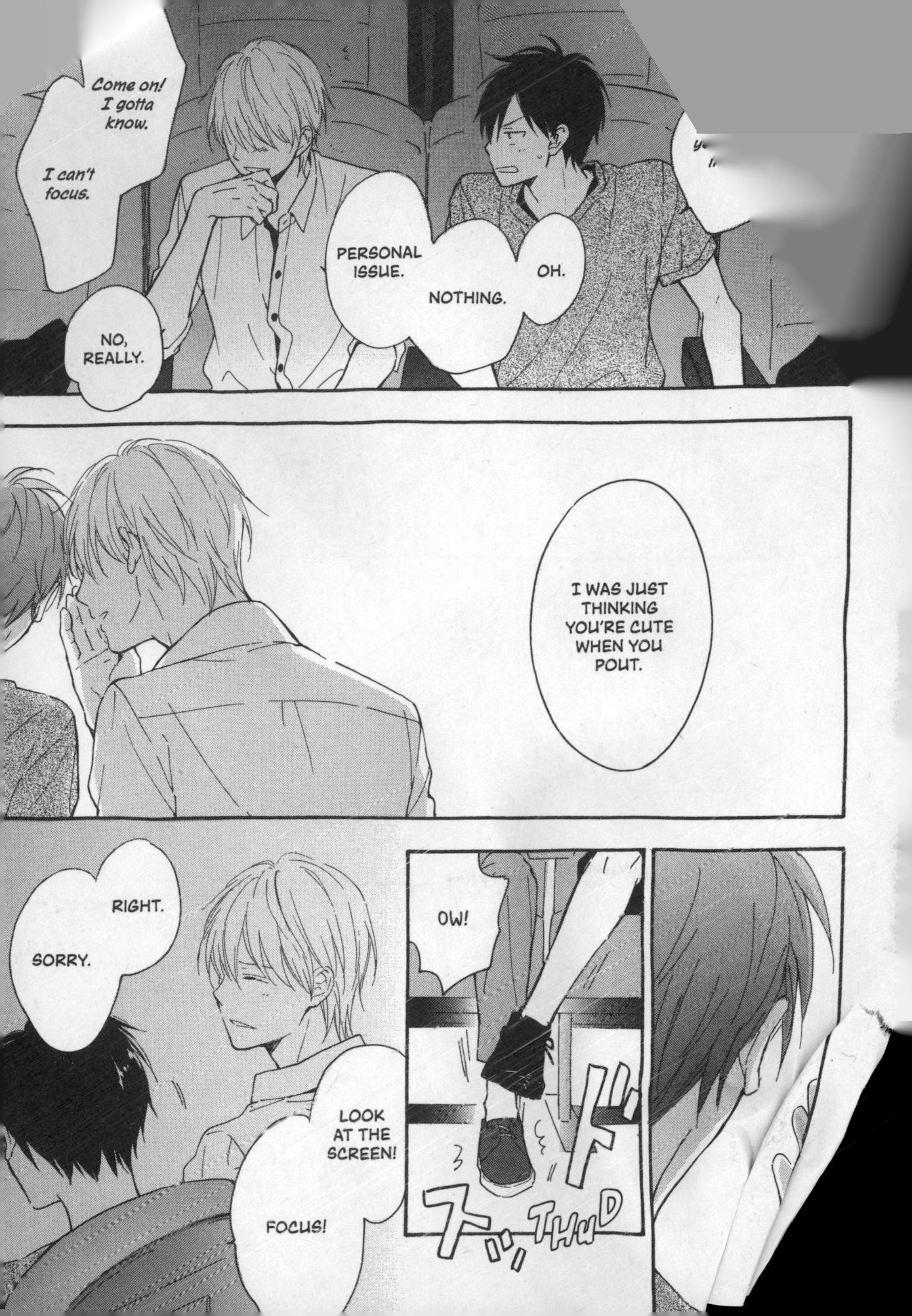

Come on! I gotta know.
I can't focus.
PERSONAL ISSUE.
NOTHING.
OH.
NO, REALLY.
I WAS JUST THINKING YOU'RE CUTE WHEN YOU POUT.
OW!
THUD
LOOK AT THE SCREEN!
FOCUS!
RIGHT.
SORRY.

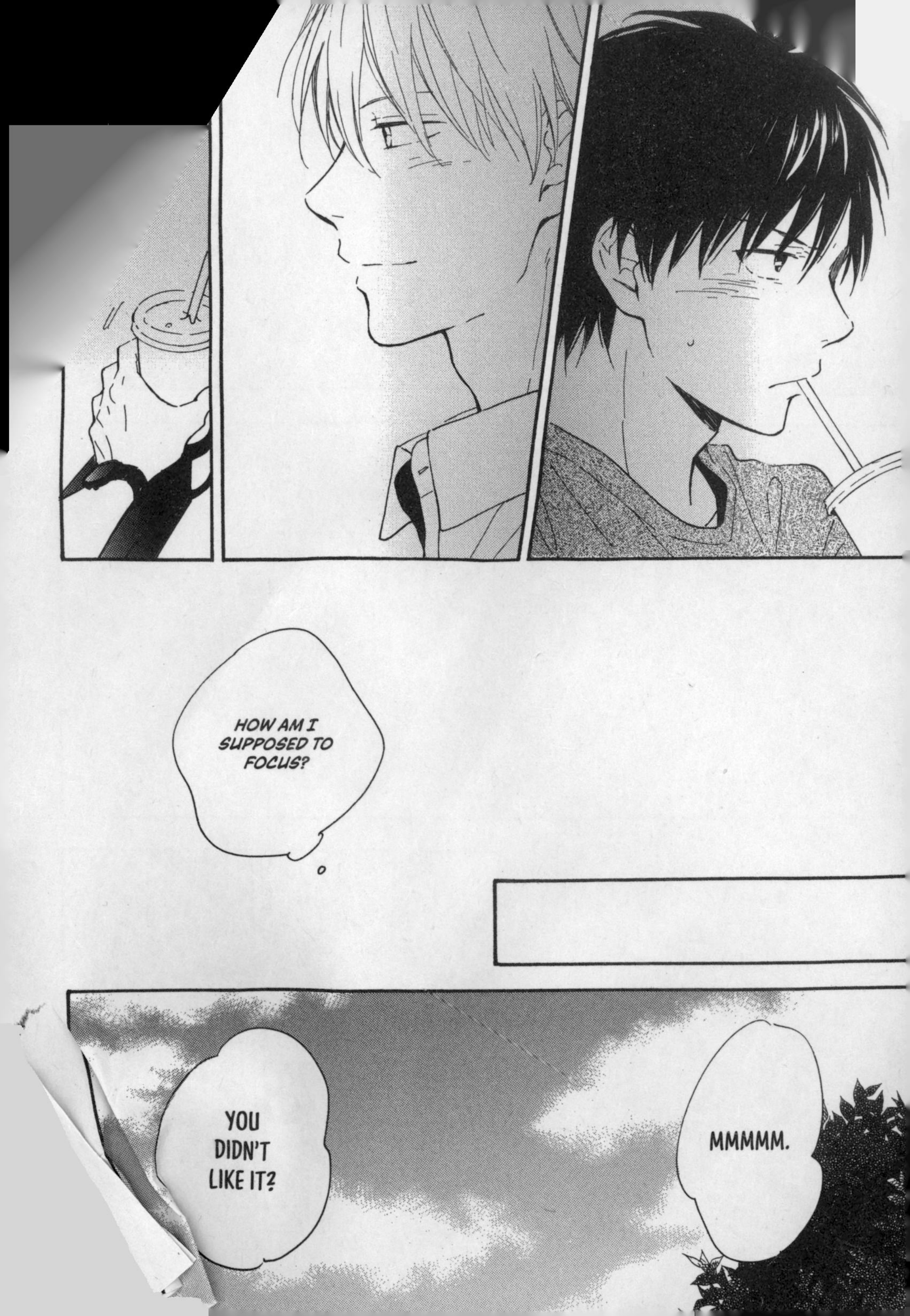
HOW AM I SUPPOSED TO FOCUS?
MMMMM.
YOU DIDN'T LIKE IT?

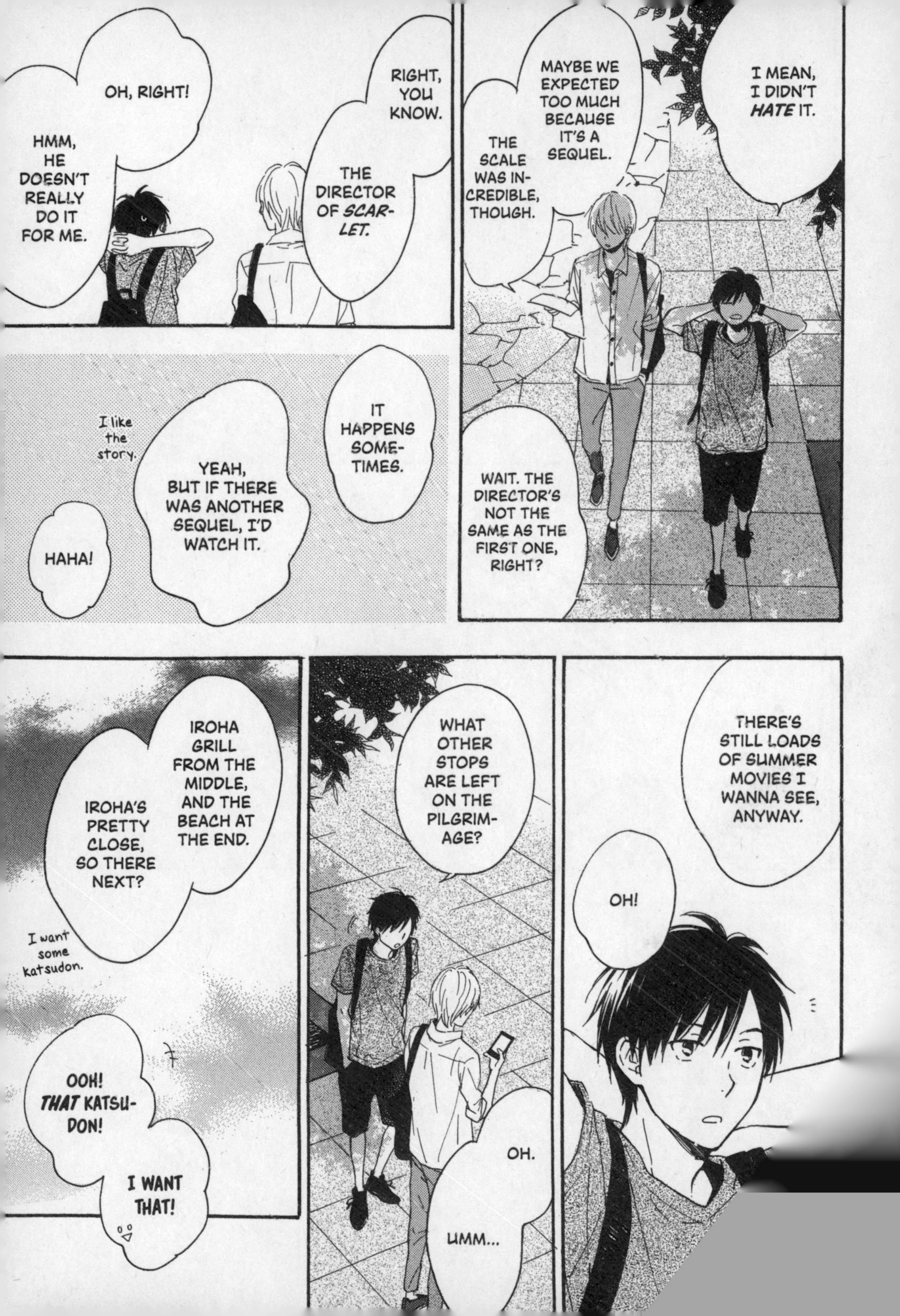
I MEAN, I DIDN'T *HATE* IT.
MAYBE WE EXPECTED TOO MUCH BECAUSE IT'S A SEQUEL.
THE SCALE WAS IN-CREDIBLE, THOUGH.
WAIT. THE DIRECTOR'S NOT THE SAME AS THE FIRST ONE, RIGHT?
RIGHT, YOU KNOW.
THE DIRECTOR OF *SCAR-LET.*
OH, RIGHT!
HMM, HE DOESN'T REALLY DO IT FOR ME.
IT HAPPENS SOME-TIMES.
YEAH, BUT IF THERE WAS ANOTHER SEQUEL, I'D WATCH IT.
I like the story.
HAHA!
THERE'S STILL LOADS OF SUMMER MOVIES I WANNA SEE, ANYWAY.
OH!
WHAT OTHER STOPS ARE LEFT ON THE PILGRIM-AGE?
OH.
UMM...
IROHA GRILL FROM THE MIDDLE, AND THE BEACH AT THE END.
IROHA'S PRETTY CLOSE, SO THERE NEXT?
I want some katsudon.
OOH! *THAT* KATSU-DON!
I WANT THAT!

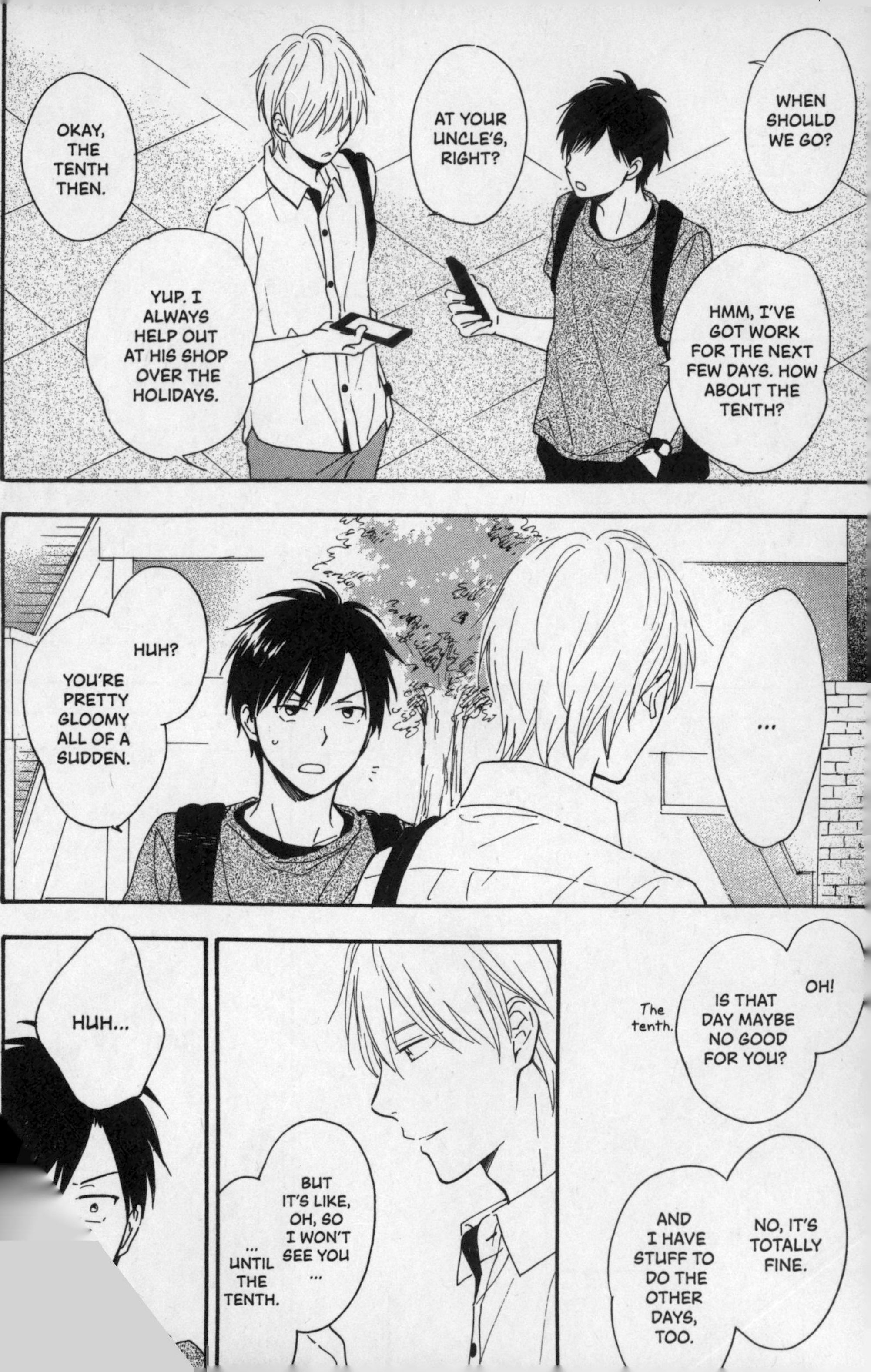
WHEN SHOULD WE GO?
HMM, I'VE GOT WORK FOR THE NEXT FEW DAYS. HOW ABOUT THE TENTH?
OKAY, THE TENTH THEN.
AT YOUR UNCLE'S, RIGHT?
YUP. I ALWAYS HELP OUT AT HIS SHOP OVER THE HOLIDAYS.
...
HUH?
YOU'RE PRETTY GLOOMY ALL OF A SUDDEN.
The tenth.
OH!
IS THAT DAY MAYBE NO GOOD FOR YOU?
NO, IT'S TOTALLY FINE.
AND I HAVE STUFF TO DO THE OTHER DAYS, TOO.
BUT IT'S LIKE, OH, SO I WON'T SEE YOU ...
... UNTIL THE TENTH.
HUH...

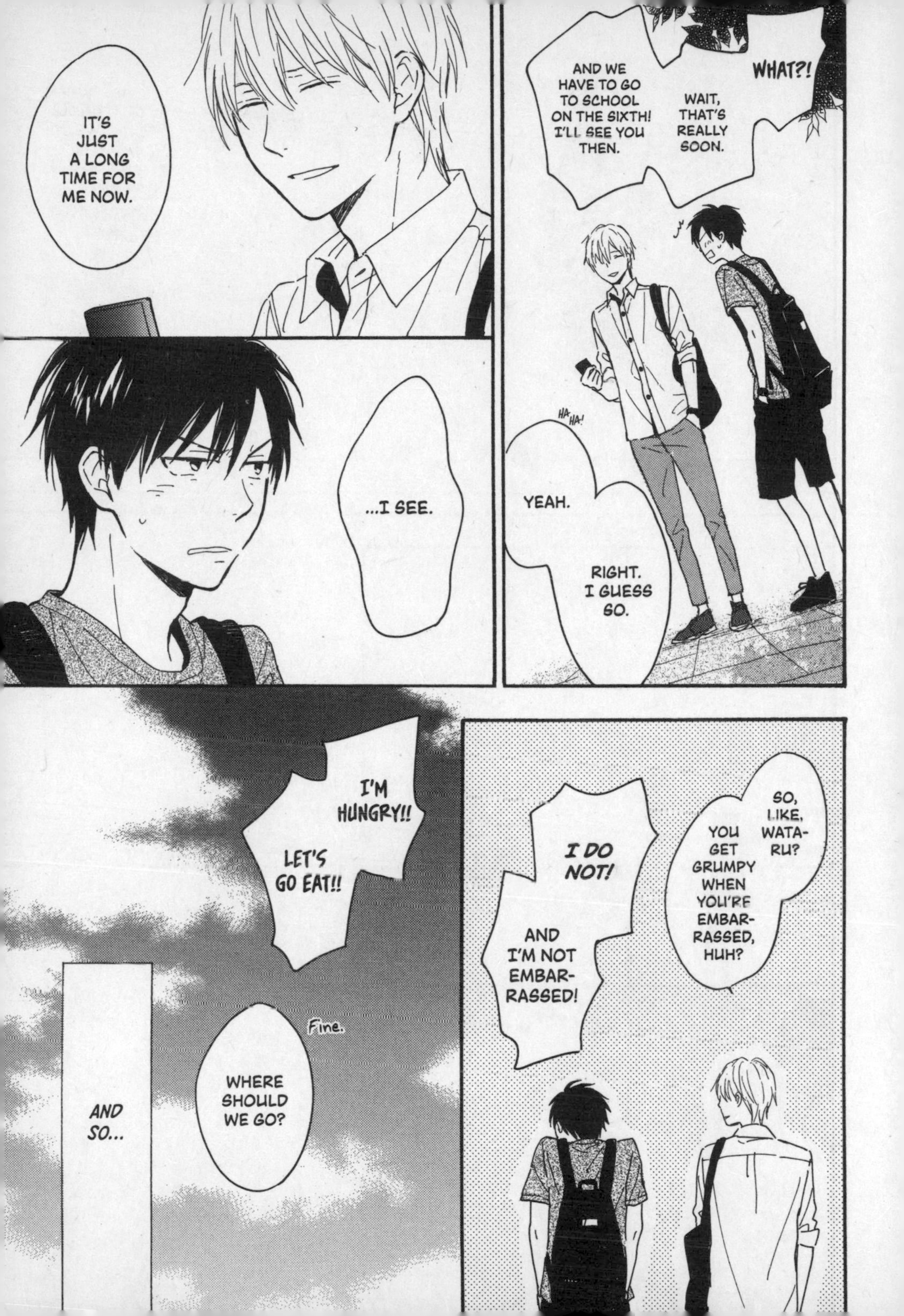
WHAT?!
WAIT, THAT'S REALLY SOON.
AND WE HAVE TO GO TO SCHOOL ON THE SIXTH! I'LL SEE YOU THEN.
HA HA!
YEAH.
RIGHT. I GUESS SO.
IT'S JUST A LONG TIME FOR ME NOW.
...I SEE.
SO, LIKE, WATARU?
YOU GET GRUMPY WHEN YOU'RE EMBARRASSED, HUH?
I DO NOT!
AND I'M NOT EMBARRASSED!
I'M HUNGRY!!
LET'S GO EAT!!
Fine.
WHERE SHOULD WE GO?
AND SO...

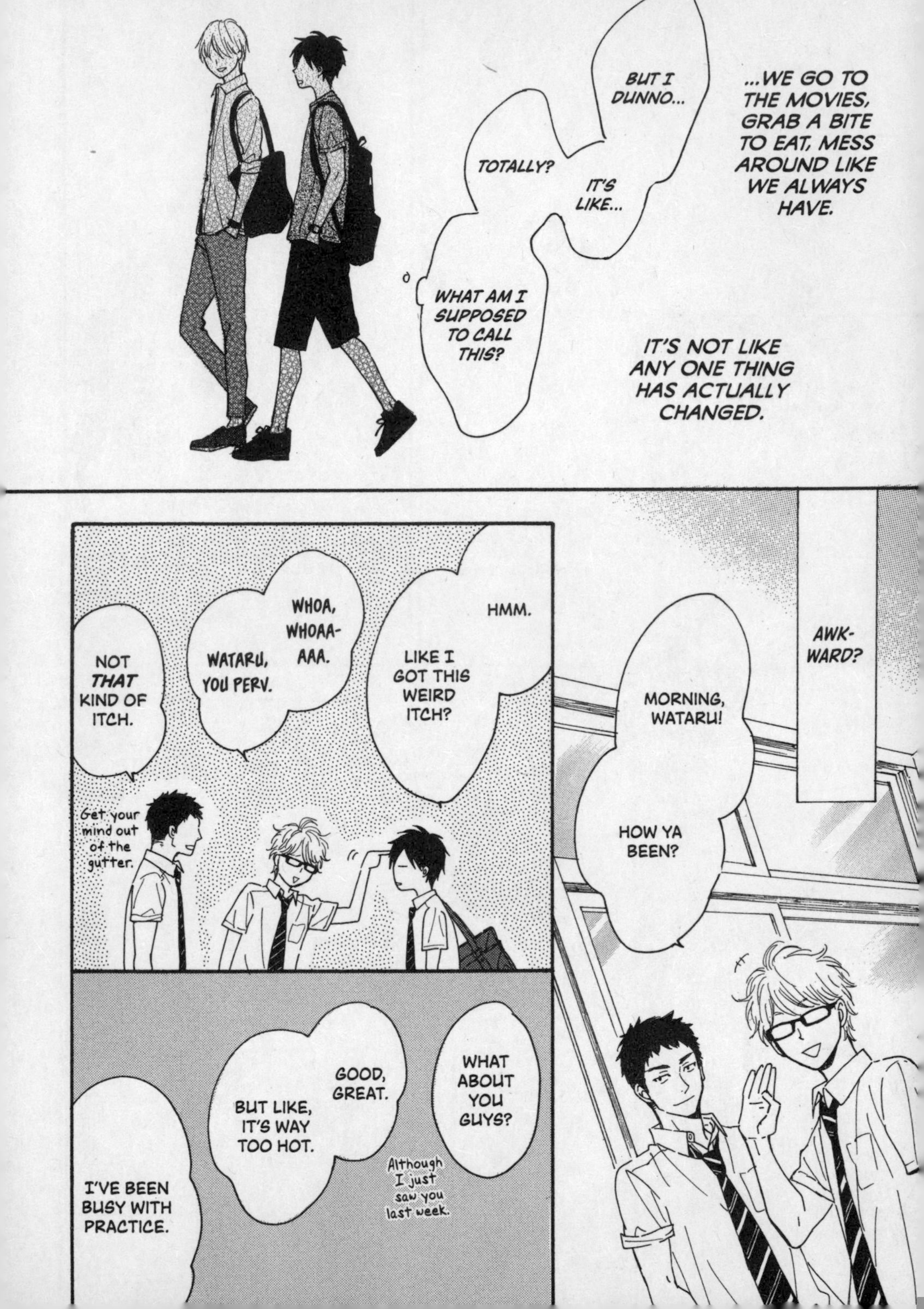
...WE GO TO THE MOVIES, GRAB A BITE TO EAT, MESS AROUND LIKE WE ALWAYS HAVE.
IT'S NOT LIKE ANY ONE THING HAS ACTUALLY CHANGED.
BUT I DUNNO...
IT'S LIKE...
TOTALLY?
WHAT AM I SUPPOSED TO CALL THIS?
AWK-WARD?
MORNING, WATARU!
HOW YA BEEN?
HMM.
LIKE I GOT THIS WEIRD ITCH?
WHOA, WHOAA-AAA.
WATARU, YOU PERV.
NOT *THAT* KIND OF ITCH.
Get your mind out of the gutter.
WHAT ABOUT YOU GUYS?
GOOD, GREAT.
BUT LIKE, IT'S WAY TOO HOT.
Although I just saw you last week.
I'VE BEEN BUSY WITH PRACTICE.

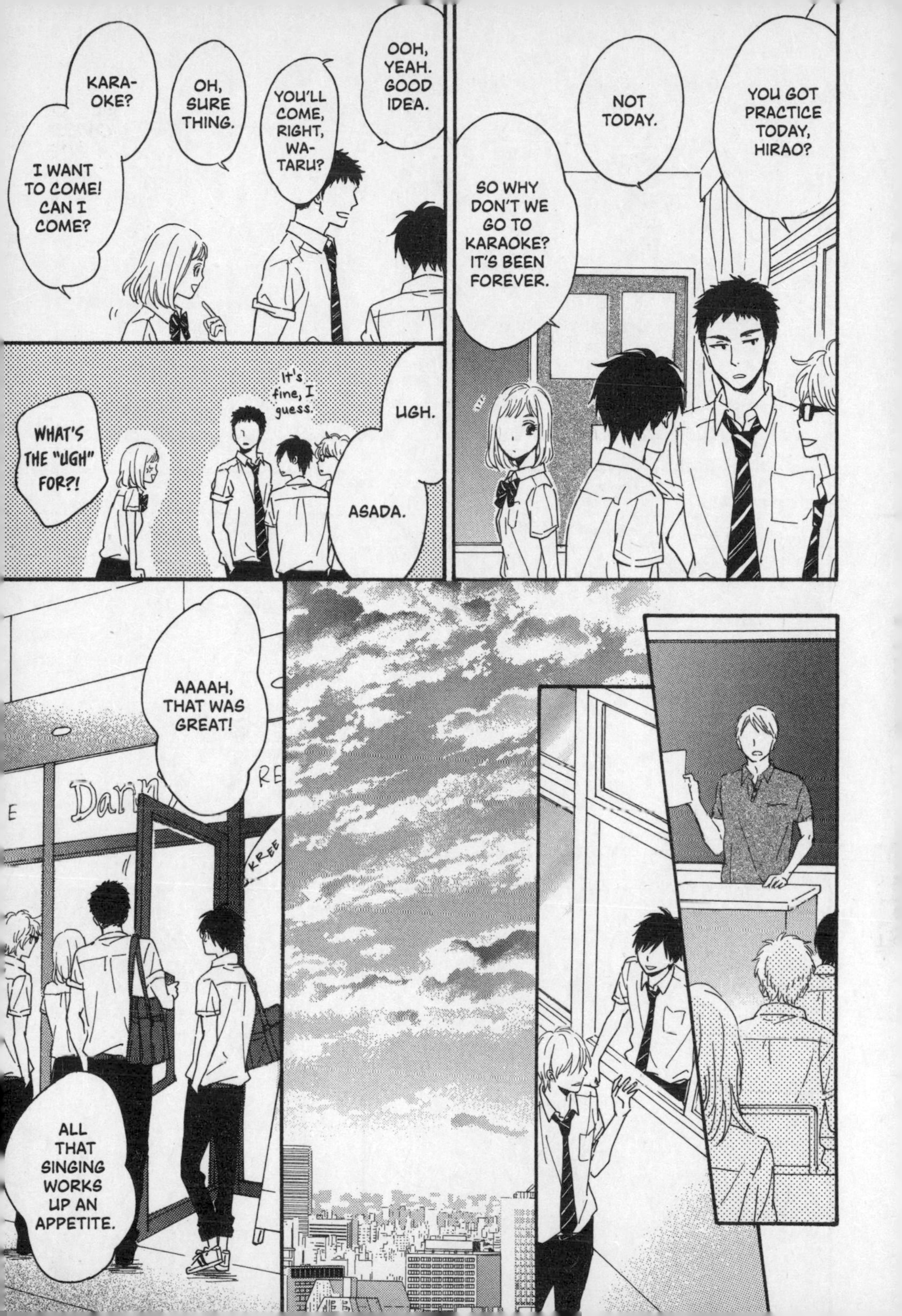

YOU GOT PRACTICE TODAY, HIRAO?
NOT TODAY.
SO WHY DON'T WE GO TO KARAOKE? IT'S BEEN FOREVER.
OOH, YEAH. GOOD IDEA.
YOU'LL COME, RIGHT, WA-TARU?
OH, SURE THING.
KARA-OKE?
I WANT TO COME! CAN I COME?
UGH.
ASADA.
It's fine, I guess.
WHAT'S THE "UGH" FOR?!
AAAAH, THAT WAS GREAT!
KREE
ALL THAT SINGING WORKS UP AN APPETITE.

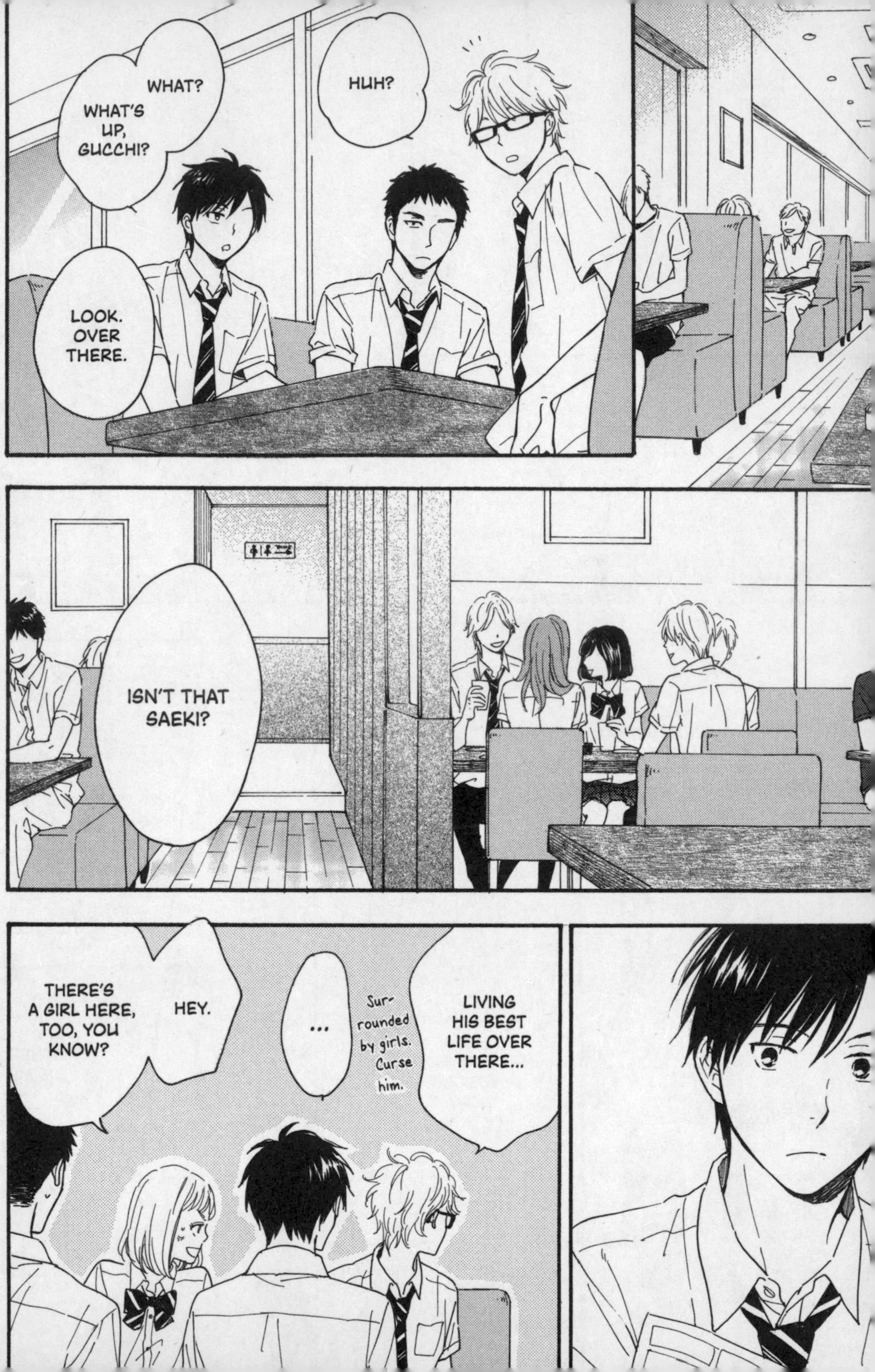
HUH?
WHAT? WHAT'S UP, GUCCHI?
LOOK. OVER THERE.
ISN'T THAT SAEKI?
LIVING HIS BEST LIFE OVER THERE...
Sur-rounded by girls. Curse him.
...
HEY.
THERE'S A GIRL HERE, TOO, YOU KNOW?

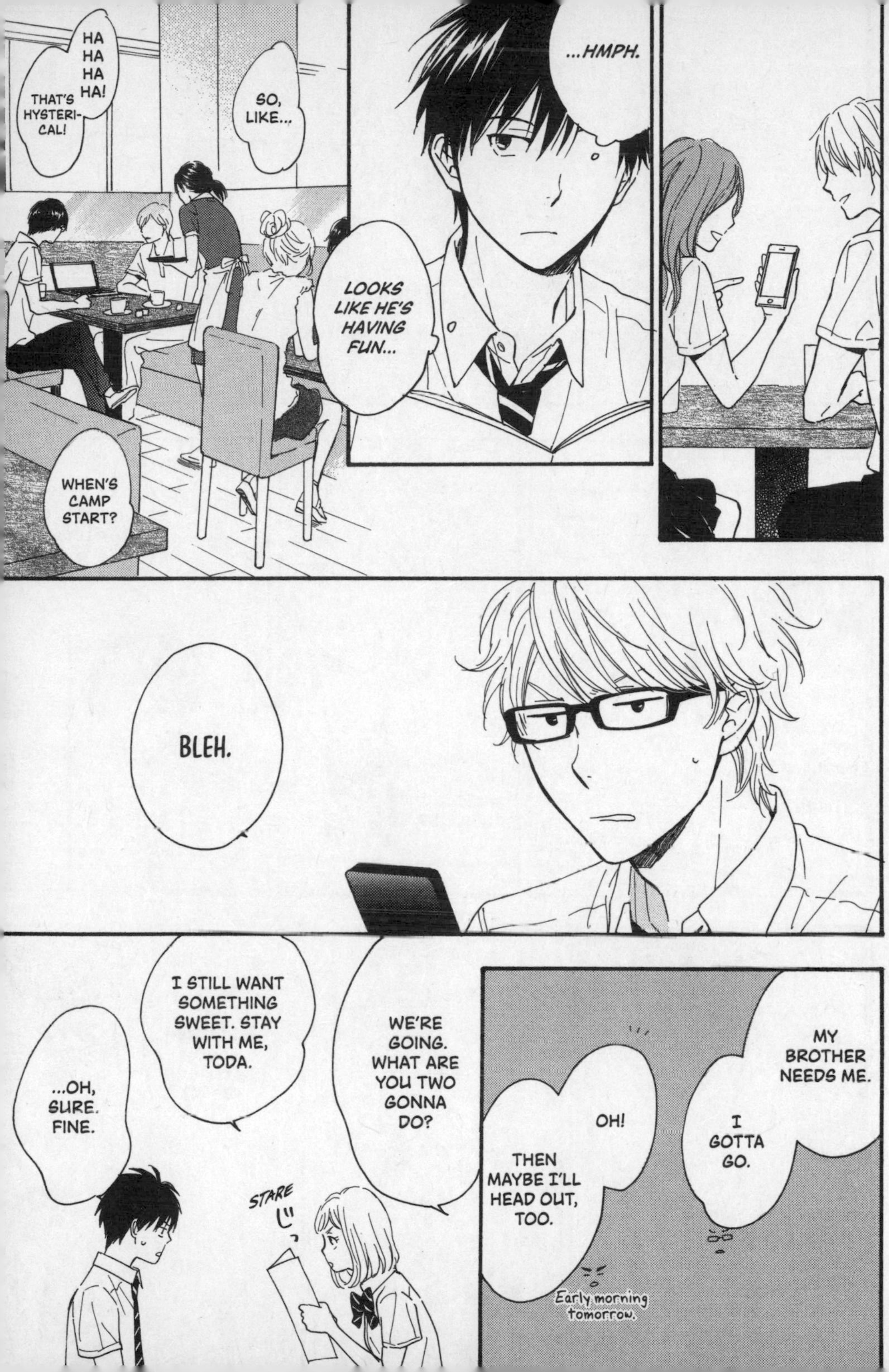
...HMPH.
LOOKS LIKE HE'S HAVING FUN...
SO, LIKE...
HA HA HA HA! THAT'S HYSTERICAL!
WHEN'S CAMP START?
BLEH.
MY BROTHER NEEDS ME.
I GOTTA GO.
OH!
THEN MAYBE I'LL HEAD OUT, TOO.
Early morning tomorrow.
WE'RE GOING. WHAT ARE YOU TWO GONNA DO?
I STILL WANT SOMETHING SWEET. STAY WITH ME, TODA.
STARE
...OH, SURE. FINE.

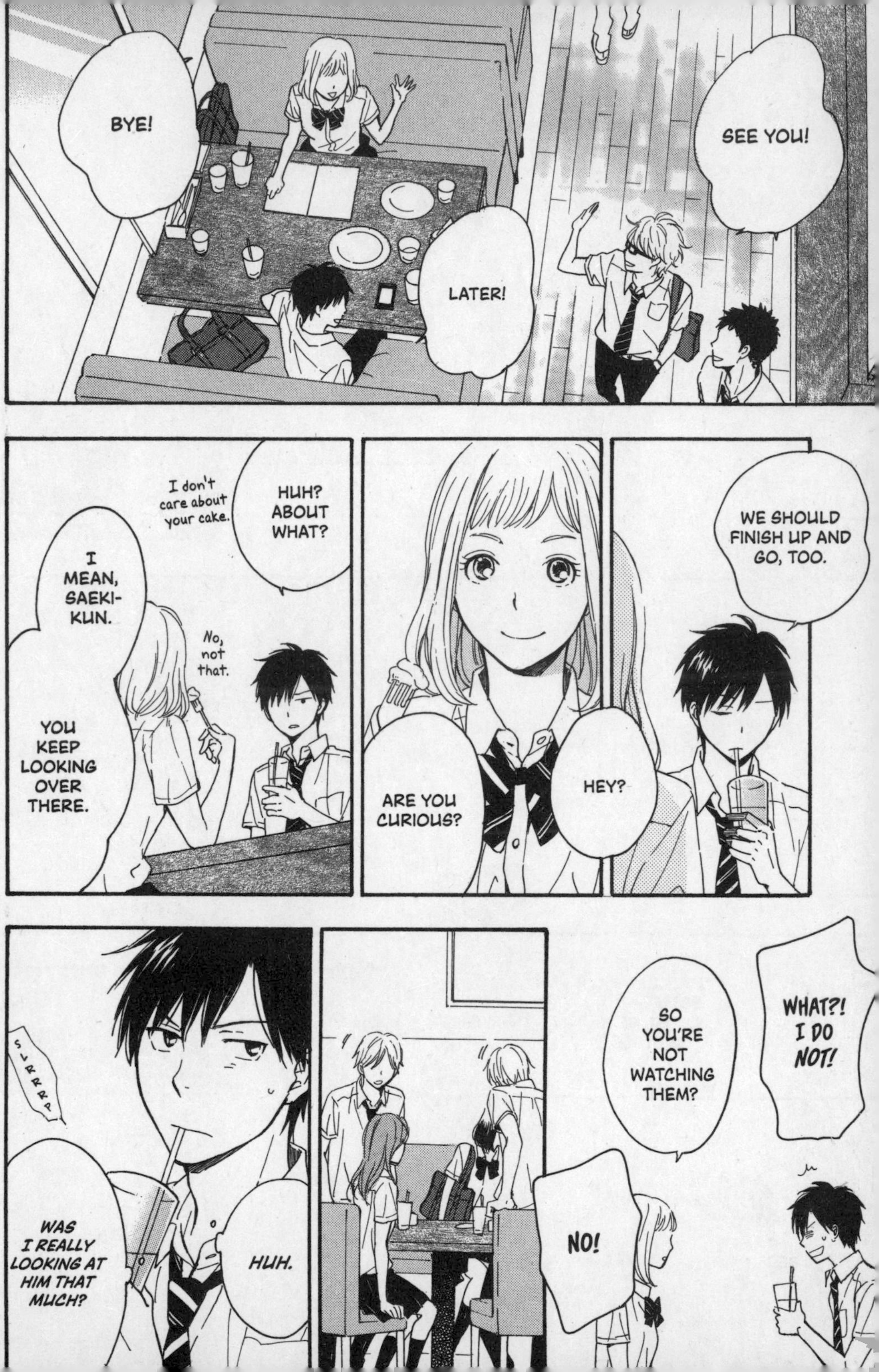
SEE YOU!
BYE!
LATER!
WE SHOULD FINISH UP AND GO, TOO.
HEY?
ARE YOU CURIOUS?
HUH? ABOUT WHAT?
I don't care about your cake.
I MEAN, SAEKI-KUN.
No, not that.
YOU KEEP LOOKING OVER THERE.
WHAT?! I DO NOT!
SO YOU'RE NOT WATCHING THEM?
NO!
SLRRRP
HUH.
WAS I REALLY LOOKING AT HIM THAT MUCH?

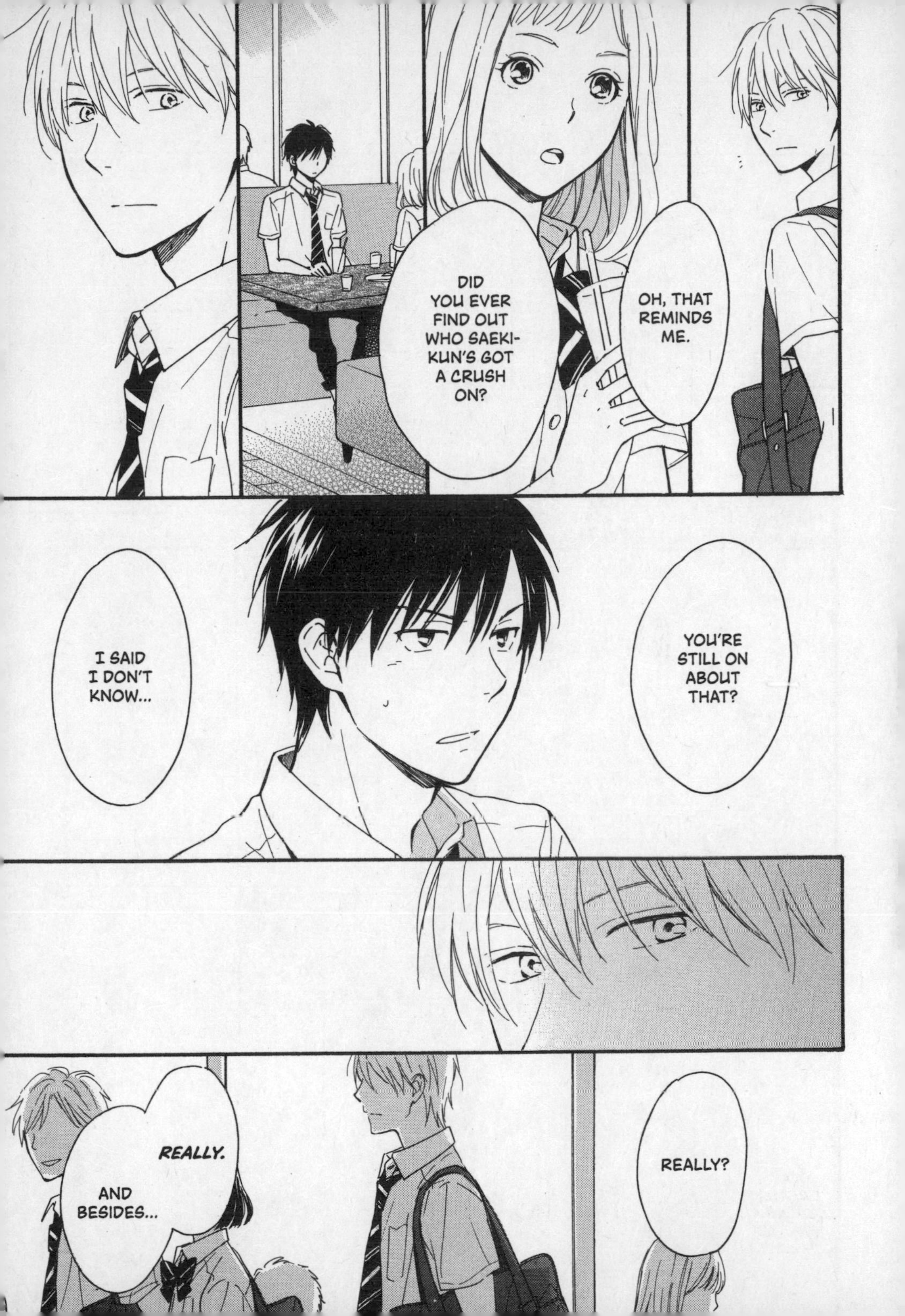
OH, THAT REMINDS ME.
DID YOU EVER FIND OUT WHO SAEKI-KUN'S GOT A CRUSH ON?
YOU'RE STILL ON ABOUT THAT?
I SAID I DON'T KNOW...
REALLY?
REALLY.
AND BESIDES...

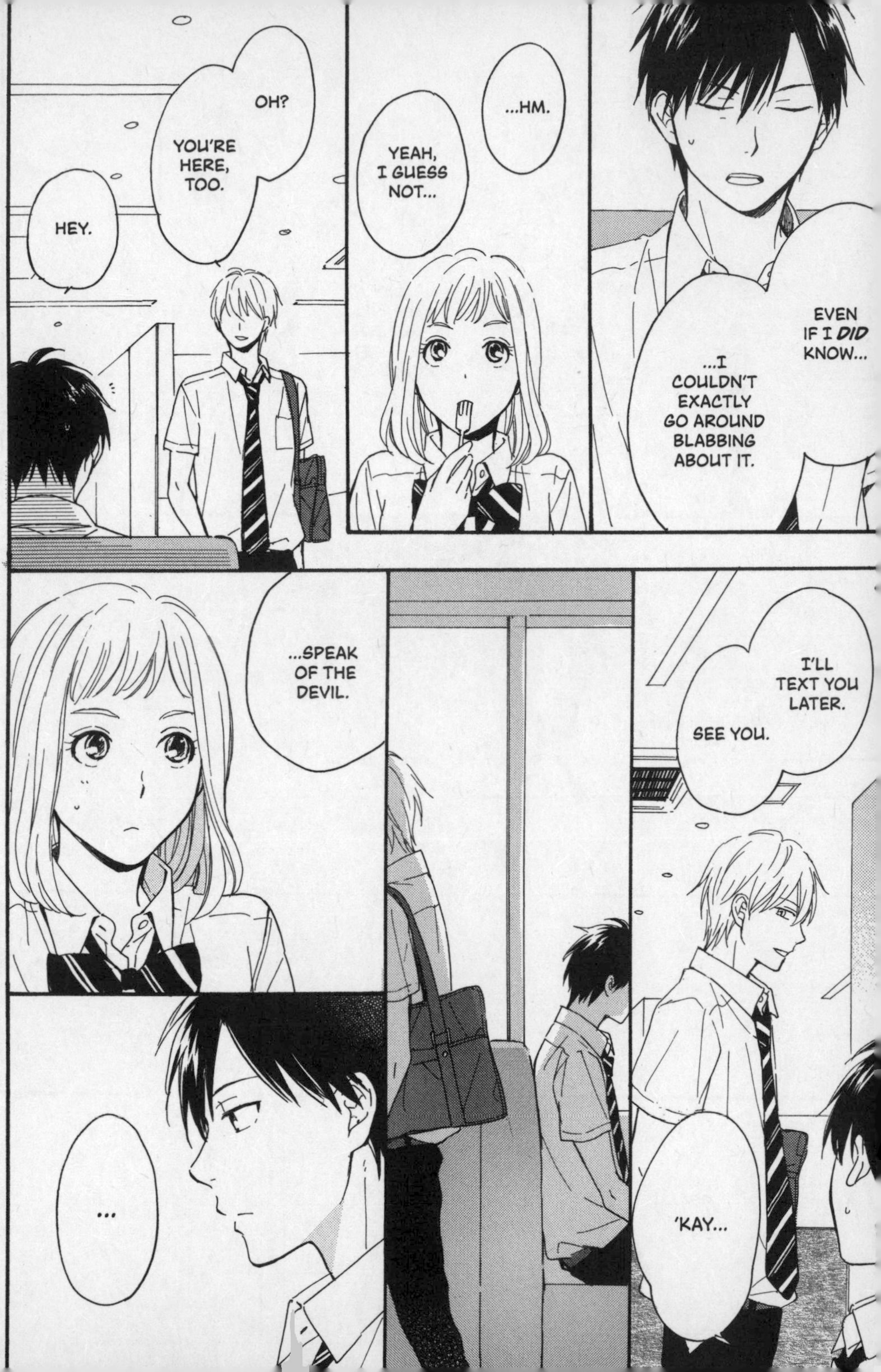
EVEN IF I *DID* KNOW...
...I COULDN'T EXACTLY GO AROUND BLABBING ABOUT IT.
...HM.
YEAH, I GUESS NOT...
OH? YOU'RE HERE, TOO.
HEY.
I'LL TEXT YOU LATER. SEE YOU.
'KAY...
...SPEAK OF THE DEVIL.
...

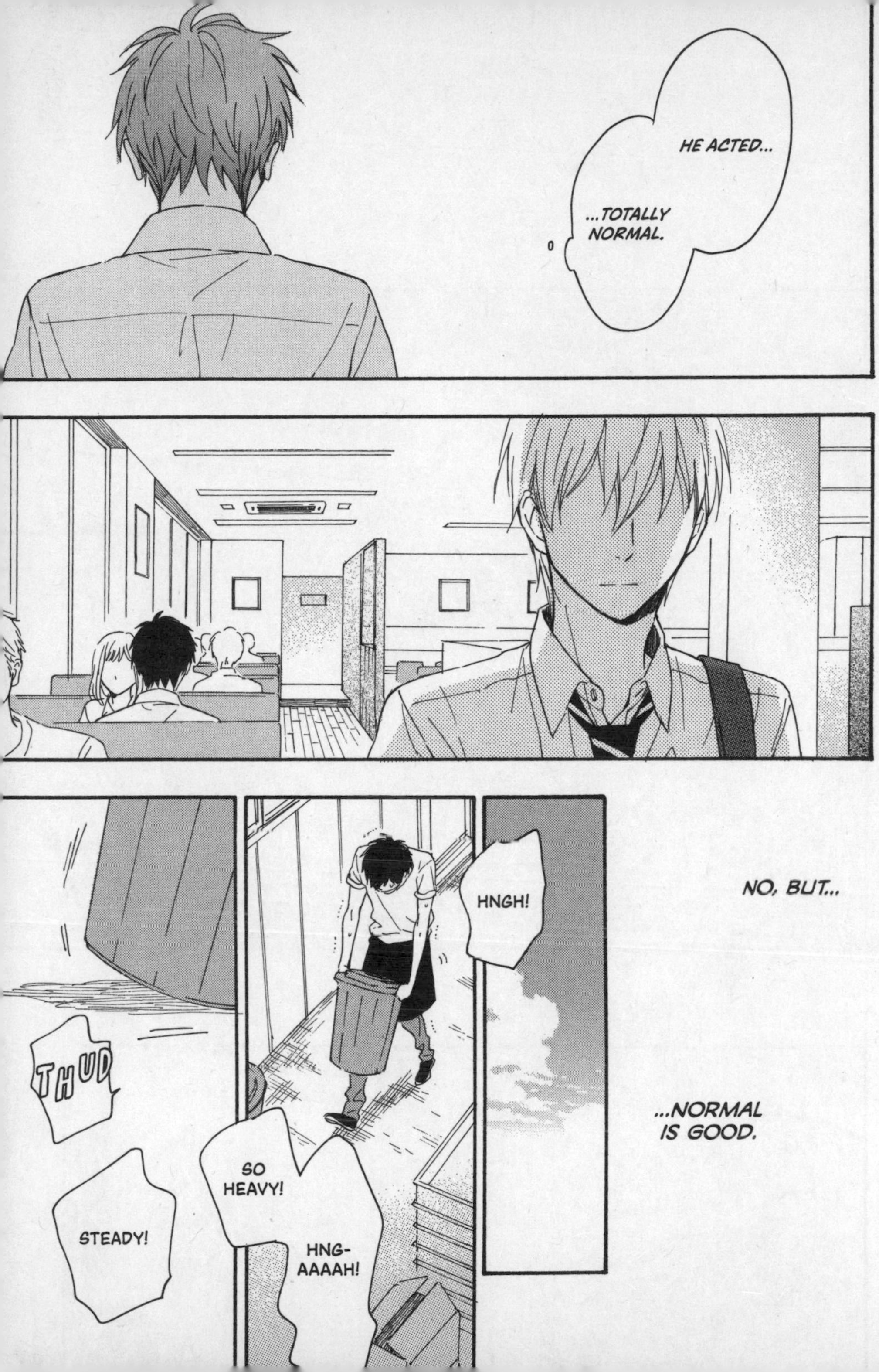
HE ACTED...
...TOTALLY NORMAL.
NO, BUT...
...NORMAL IS GOOD.
HNGH!
SO HEAVY!
HNG-AAAAH!
THUD
STEADY!

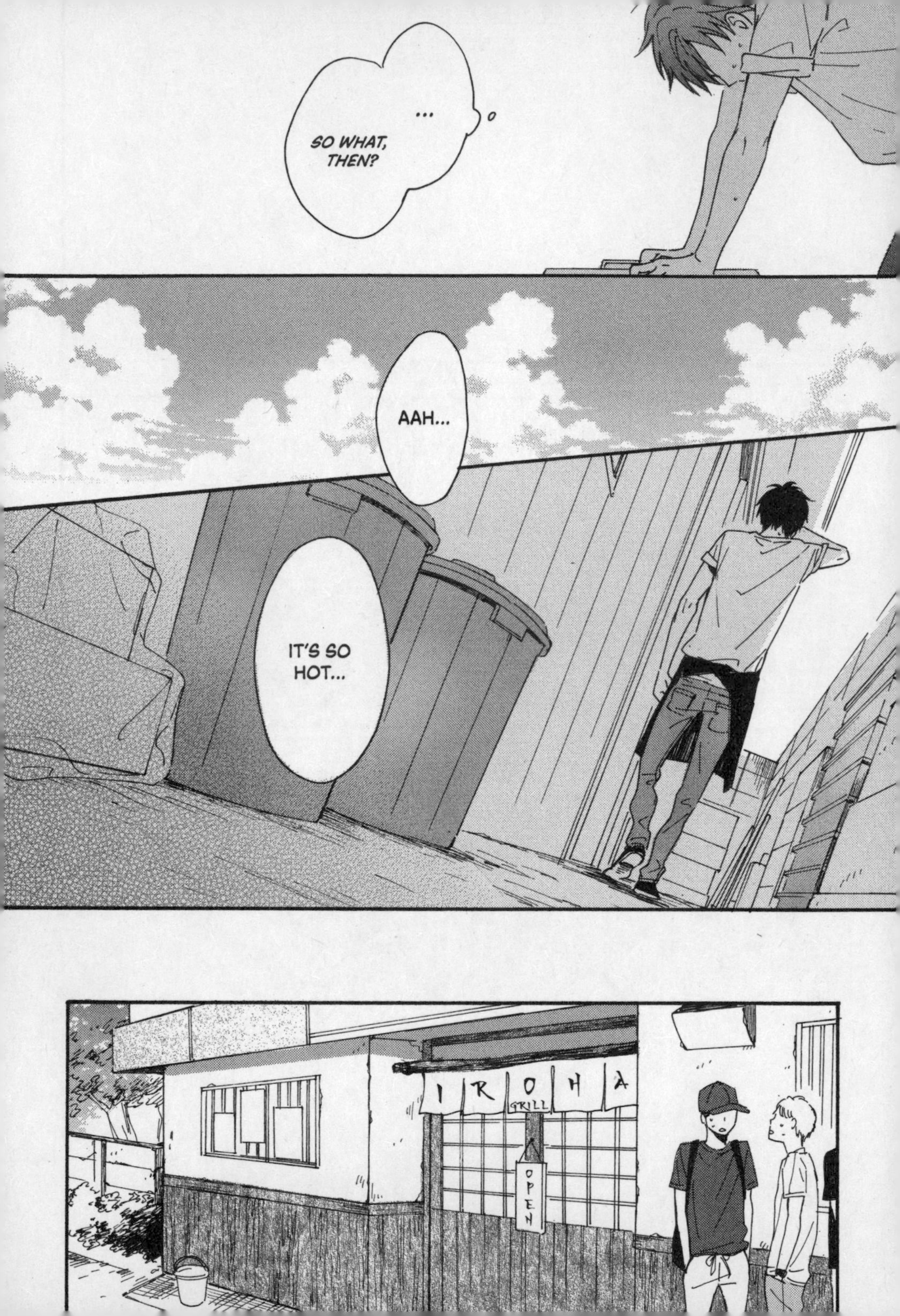
...
SO WHAT, THEN?
AAH...
IT'S SO HOT...
I R O H A
GRILL
OPEN

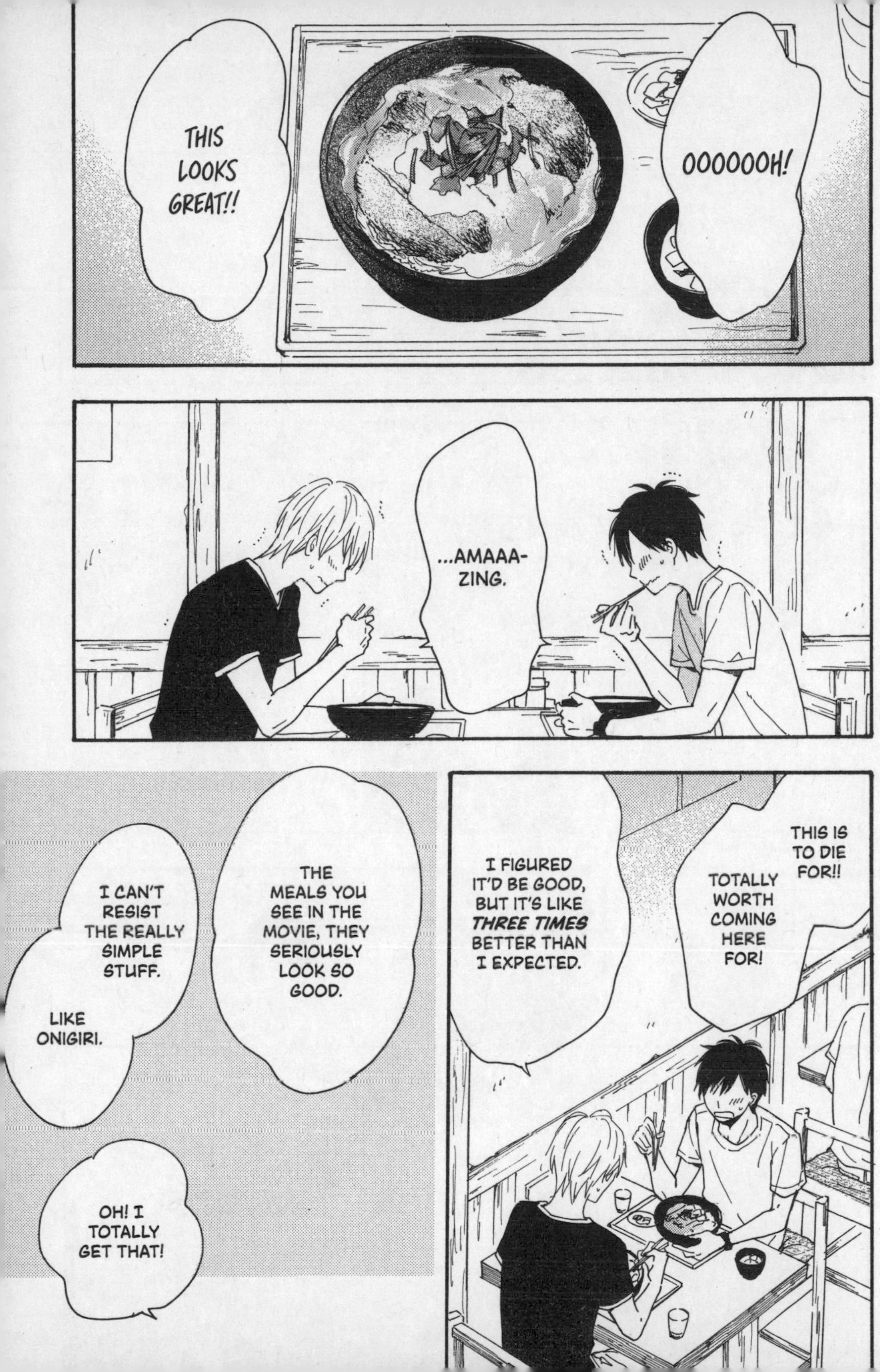
OOOOOOH!
THIS LOOKS GREAT!!
...AMAAA-ZING.
THIS IS TO DIE FOR!!
TOTALLY WORTH COMING HERE FOR!
I FIGURED IT'D BE GOOD, BUT IT'S LIKE *THREE TIMES* BETTER THAN I EXPECTED.
THE MEALS YOU SEE IN THE MOVIE, THEY SERIOUSLY LOOK SO GOOD.
I CAN'T RESIST THE REALLY SIMPLE STUFF.
LIKE ONIGIRI.
OH! I TOTALLY GET THAT!

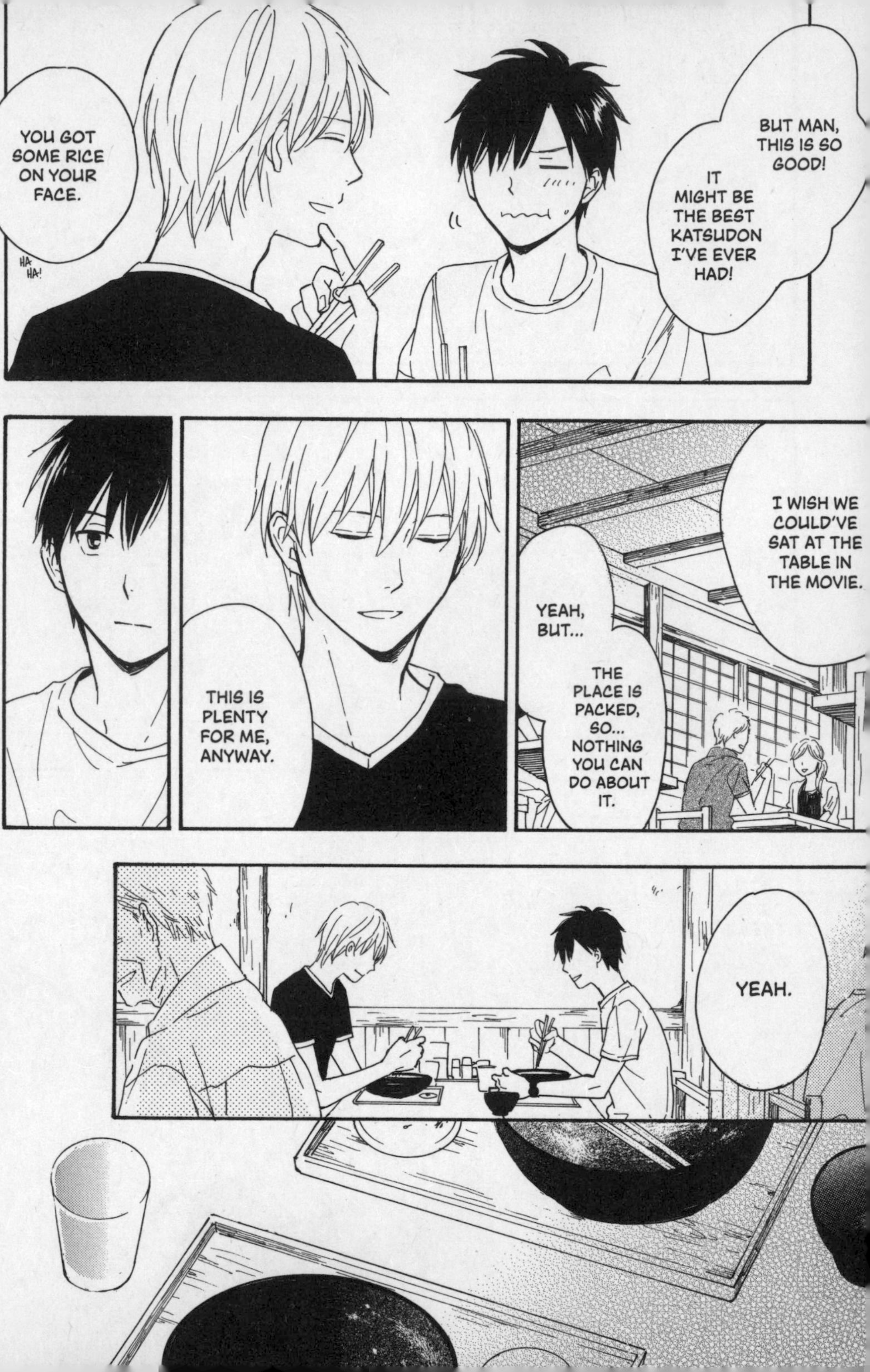
BUT MAN, THIS IS SO GOOD!
IT MIGHT BE THE BEST KATSUDON I'VE EVER HAD!
YOU GOT SOME RICE ON YOUR FACE.
HA HA!
I WISH WE COULD'VE SAT AT THE TABLE IN THE MOVIE.
YEAH, BUT...
THE PLACE IS PACKED, SO... NOTHING YOU CAN DO ABOUT IT.
THIS IS PLENTY FOR ME, ANYWAY.
YEAH.

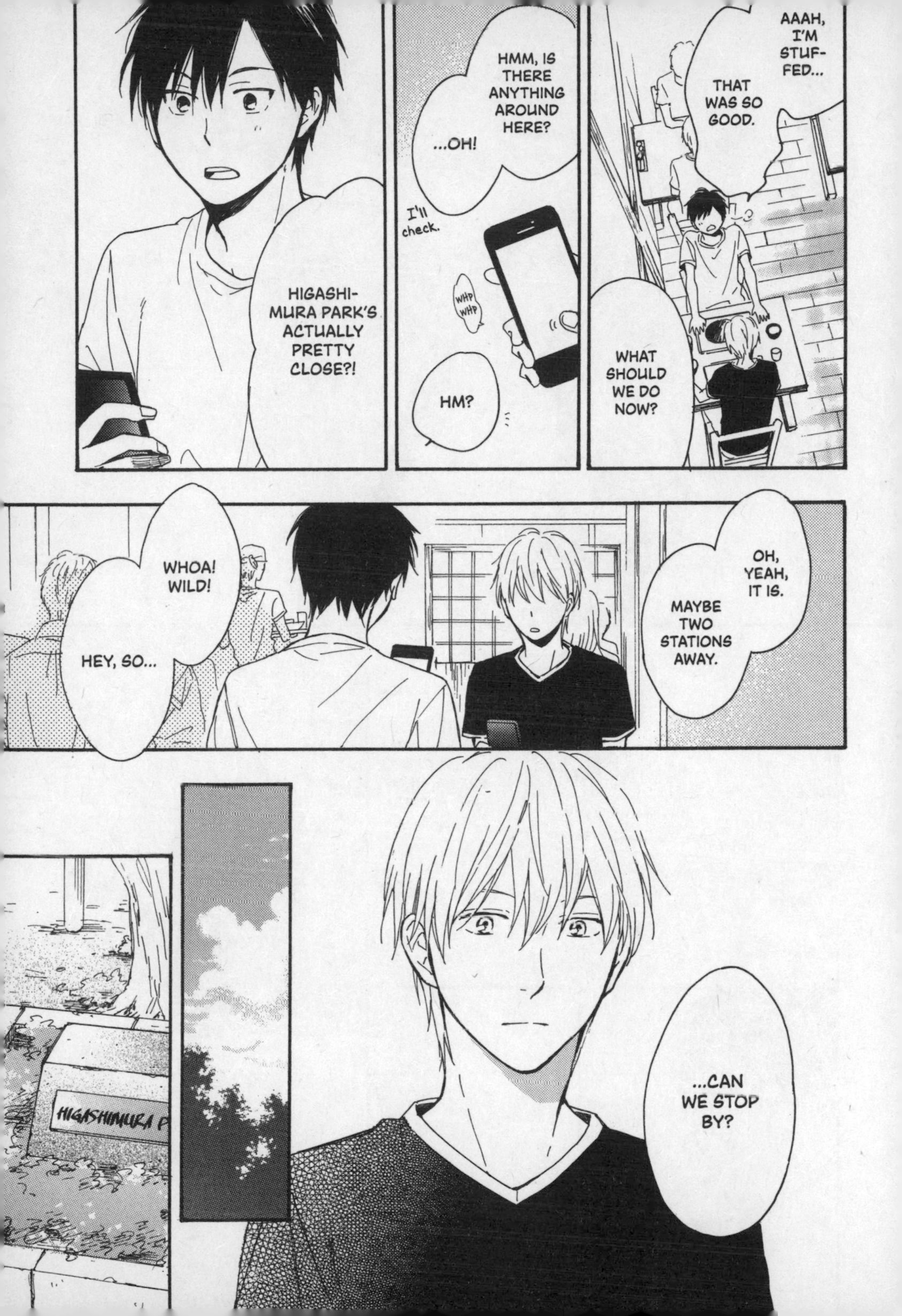
AAAH, I'M STUFFED...
THAT WAS SO GOOD.
WHAT SHOULD WE DO NOW?
HMM, IS THERE ANYTHING AROUND HERE?
...OH!
I'll check.
WHP WHP
HM?
HIGASHIMURA PARK'S ACTUALLY PRETTY CLOSE?!
OH, YEAH, IT IS.
MAYBE TWO STATIONS AWAY.
WHOA! WILD!
HEY, SO...
...CAN WE STOP BY?
HIGASHIMURA P

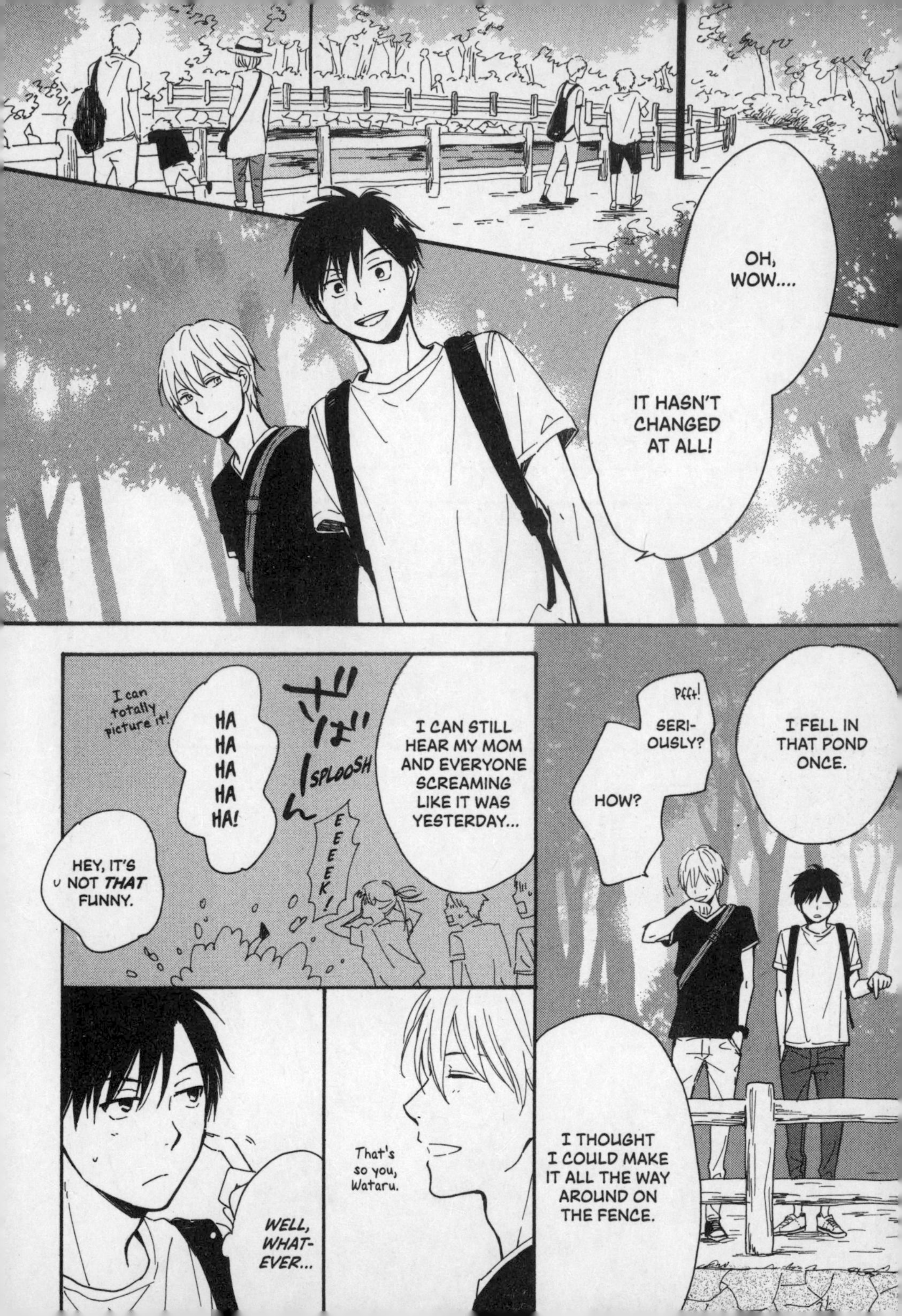
OH, WOW....
IT HASN'T CHANGED AT ALL!
I FELL IN THAT POND ONCE.
Pfft!
SERI-OUSLY?
HOW?
I THOUGHT I COULD MAKE IT ALL THE WAY AROUND ON THE FENCE.
I CAN STILL HEAR MY MOM AND EVERYONE SCREAMING LIKE IT WAS YESTERDAY...
ざばーん SPLOOSH
EEEEEK!
HA HA HA HA HA!
I can totally picture it!
HEY, IT'S NOT *THAT* FUNNY.
That's so you, Wataru.
WELL, WHAT-EVER...

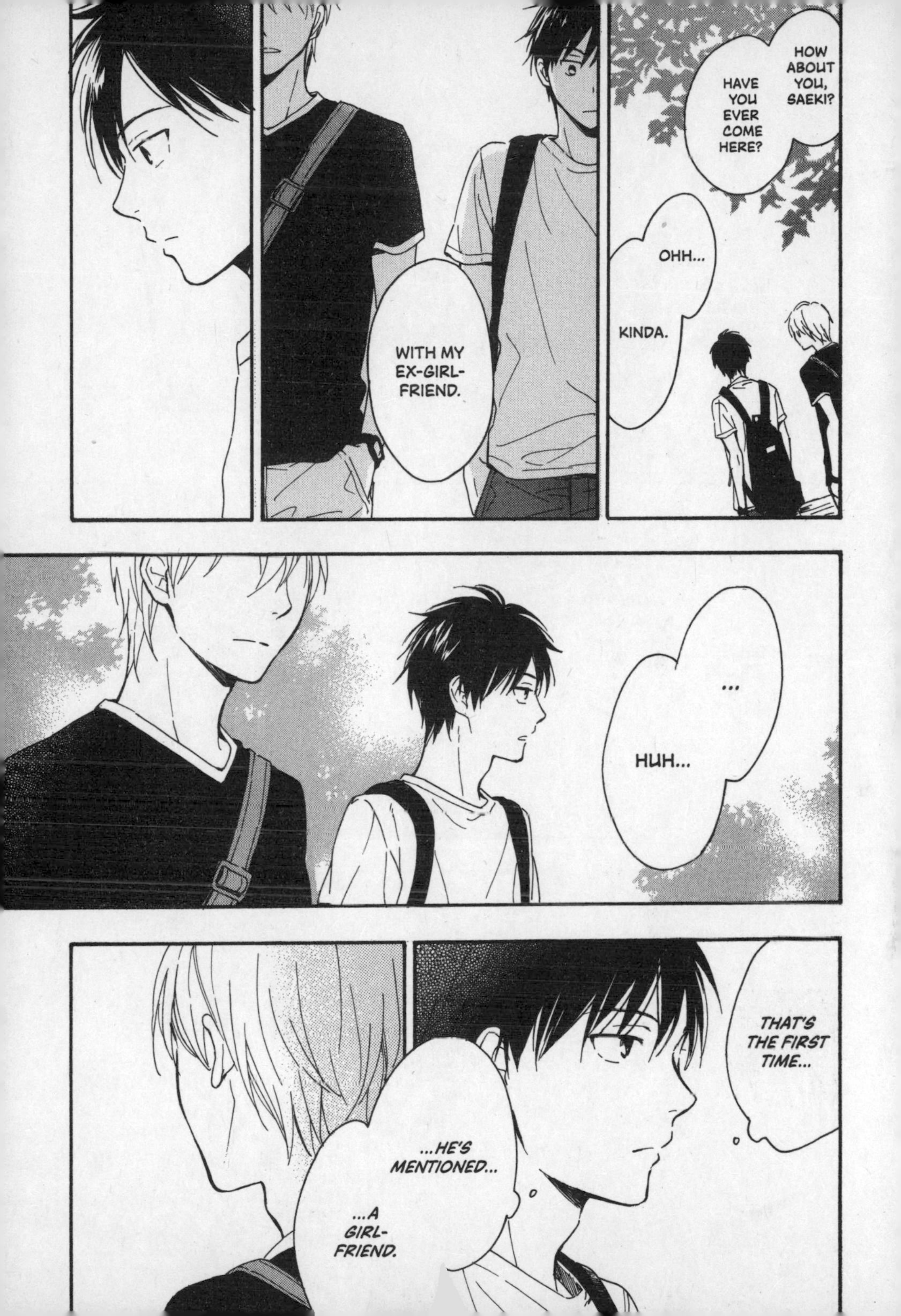
HOW ABOUT YOU, SAEKI?
HAVE YOU EVER COME HERE?
OHH...
KINDA.
WITH MY EX-GIRL-FRIEND.
...
HUH...
THAT'S THE FIRST TIME...
...HE'S MENTIONED...
...A GIRL-FRIEND.

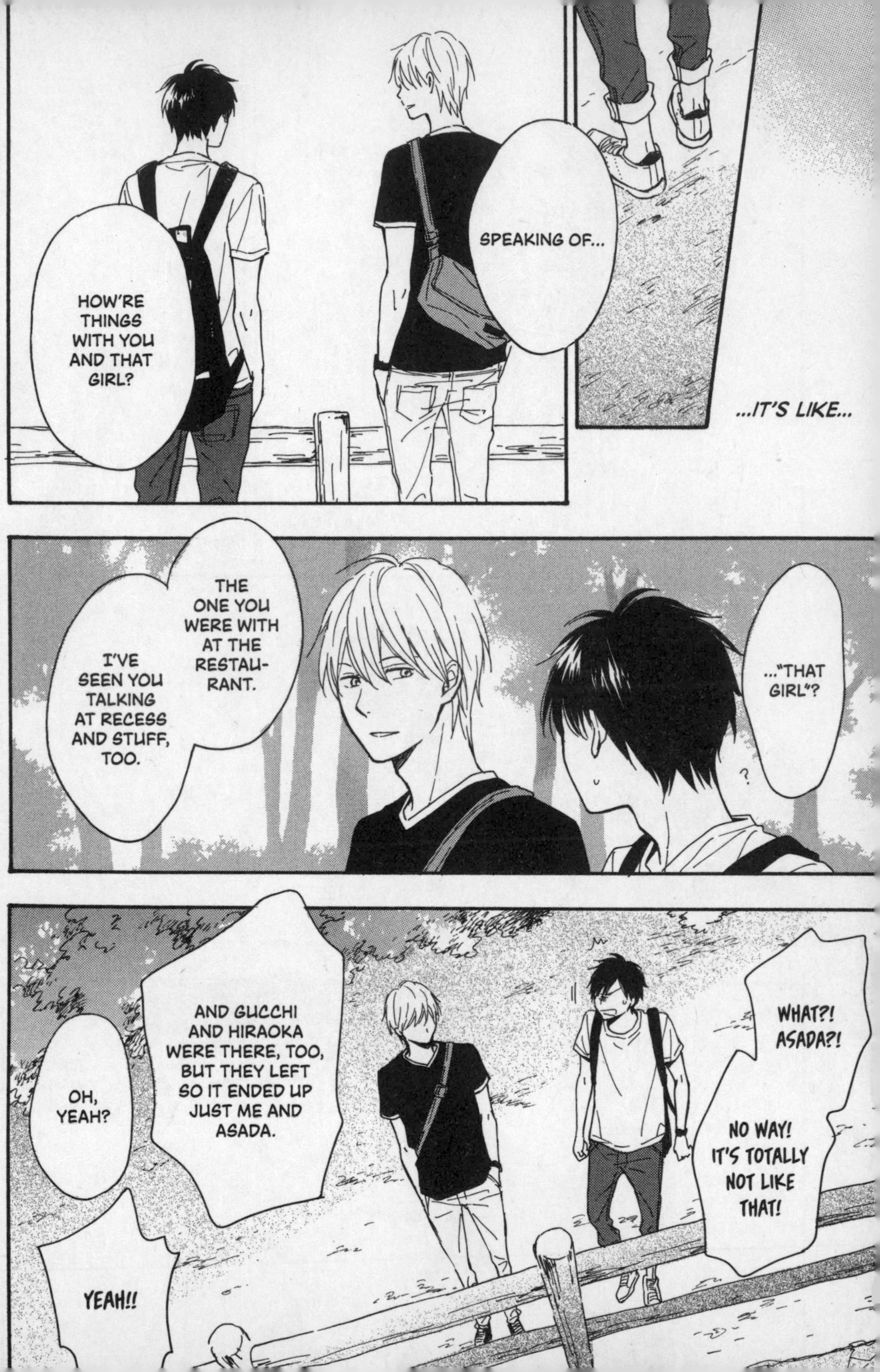
...IT'S LIKE...
SPEAKING OF...
HOW'RE THINGS WITH YOU AND THAT GIRL?
..."THAT GIRL"?
THE ONE YOU WERE WITH AT THE RESTAU-RANT.
I'VE SEEN YOU TALKING AT RECESS AND STUFF, TOO.
WHAT?! ASADA?!
NO WAY! IT'S TOTALLY NOT LIKE THAT!
AND GUCCHI AND HIRAOKA WERE THERE, TOO, BUT THEY LEFT SO IT ENDED UP JUST ME AND ASADA.
OH, YEAH?
YEAH!!

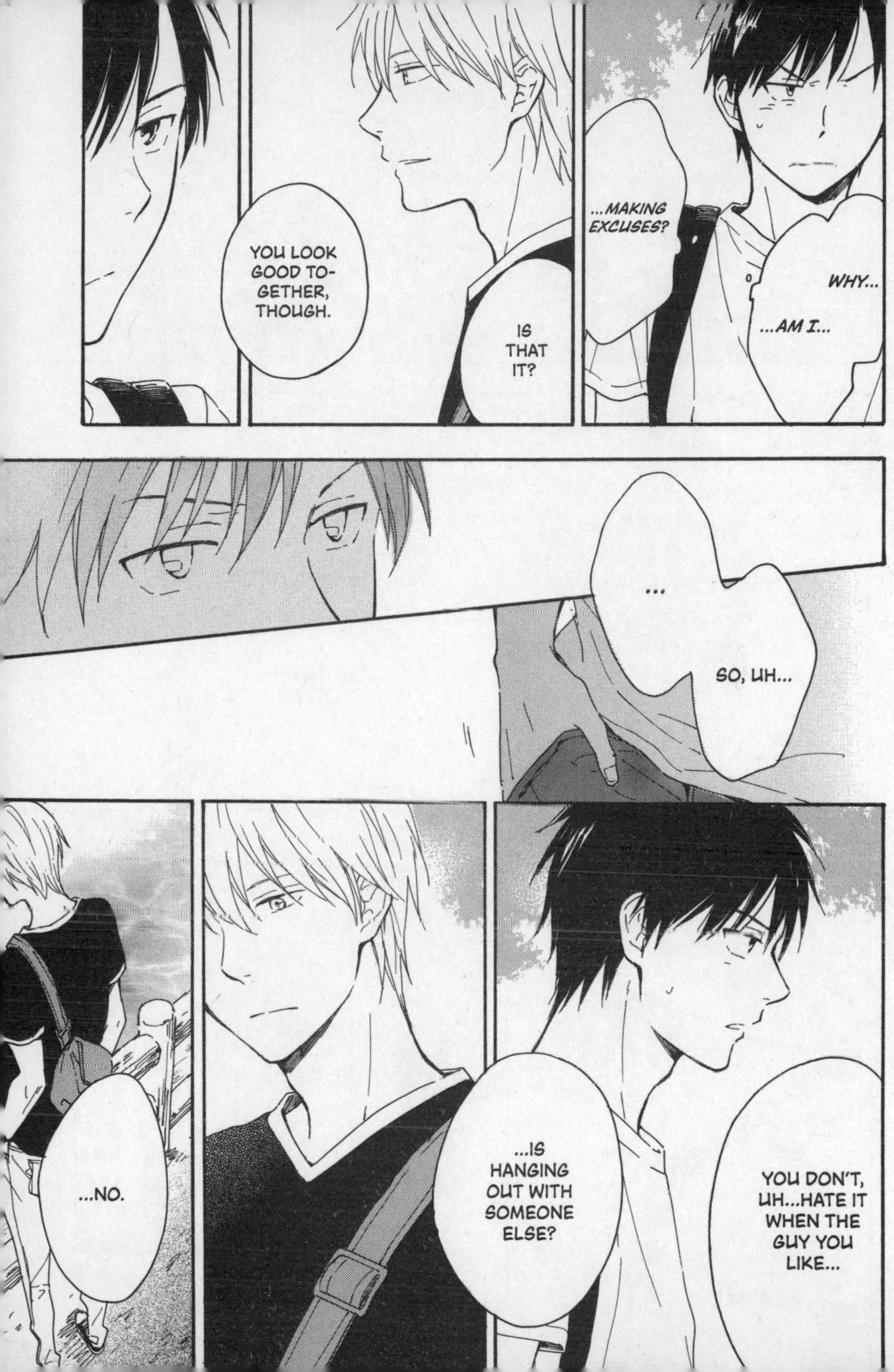
WHY...
...AM I...
...MAKING EXCUSES?
IS THAT IT?
YOU LOOK GOOD TO-GETHER, THOUGH.
...
SO, UH...
YOU DON'T, UH...HATE IT WHEN THE GUY YOU LIKE...
...IS HANGING OUT WITH SOMEONE ELSE?
...NO.

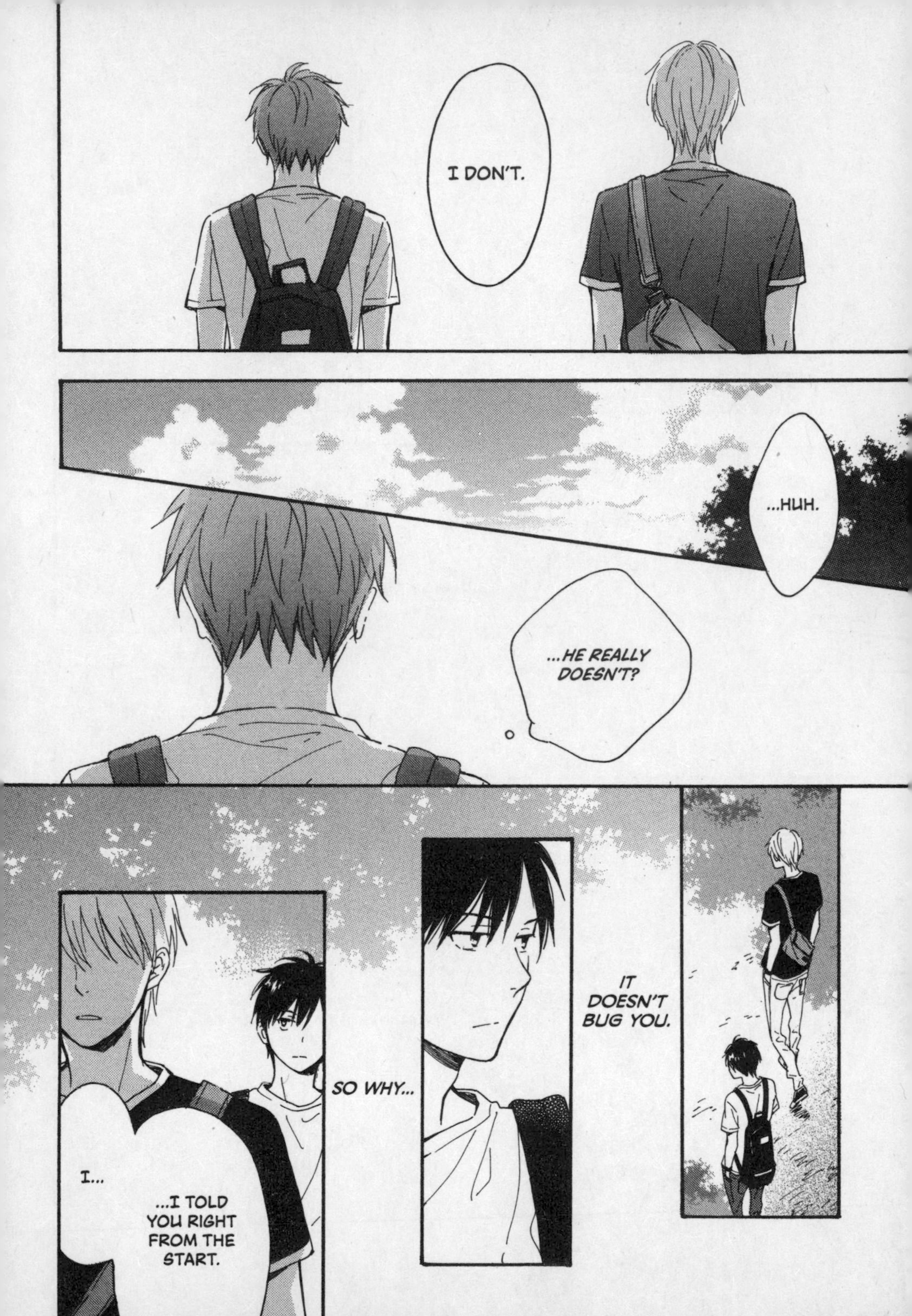
I DON'T.
...HUH.
...HE REALLY DOESN'T?
IT DOESN'T BUG YOU.
SO WHY...
I...
...I TOLD YOU RIGHT FROM THE START.

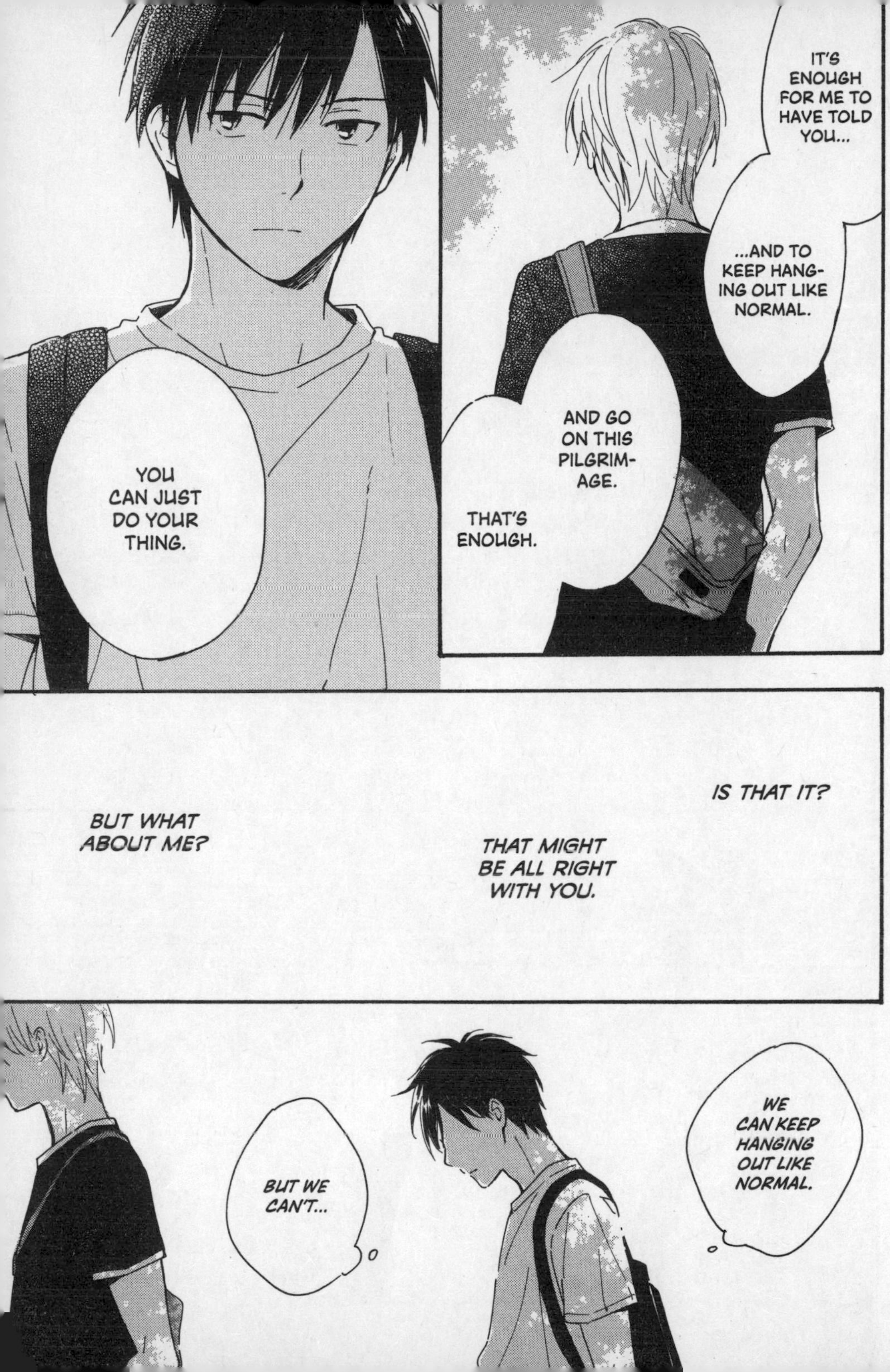
IT'S ENOUGH FOR ME TO HAVE TOLD YOU...
...AND TO KEEP HANGING OUT LIKE NORMAL.
AND GO ON THIS PILGRIMAGE.
THAT'S ENOUGH.
YOU CAN JUST DO YOUR THING.
IS THAT IT?
THAT MIGHT BE ALL RIGHT WITH YOU.
BUT WHAT ABOUT ME?
WE CAN KEEP HANGING OUT LIKE NORMAL.
BUT WE CAN'T...

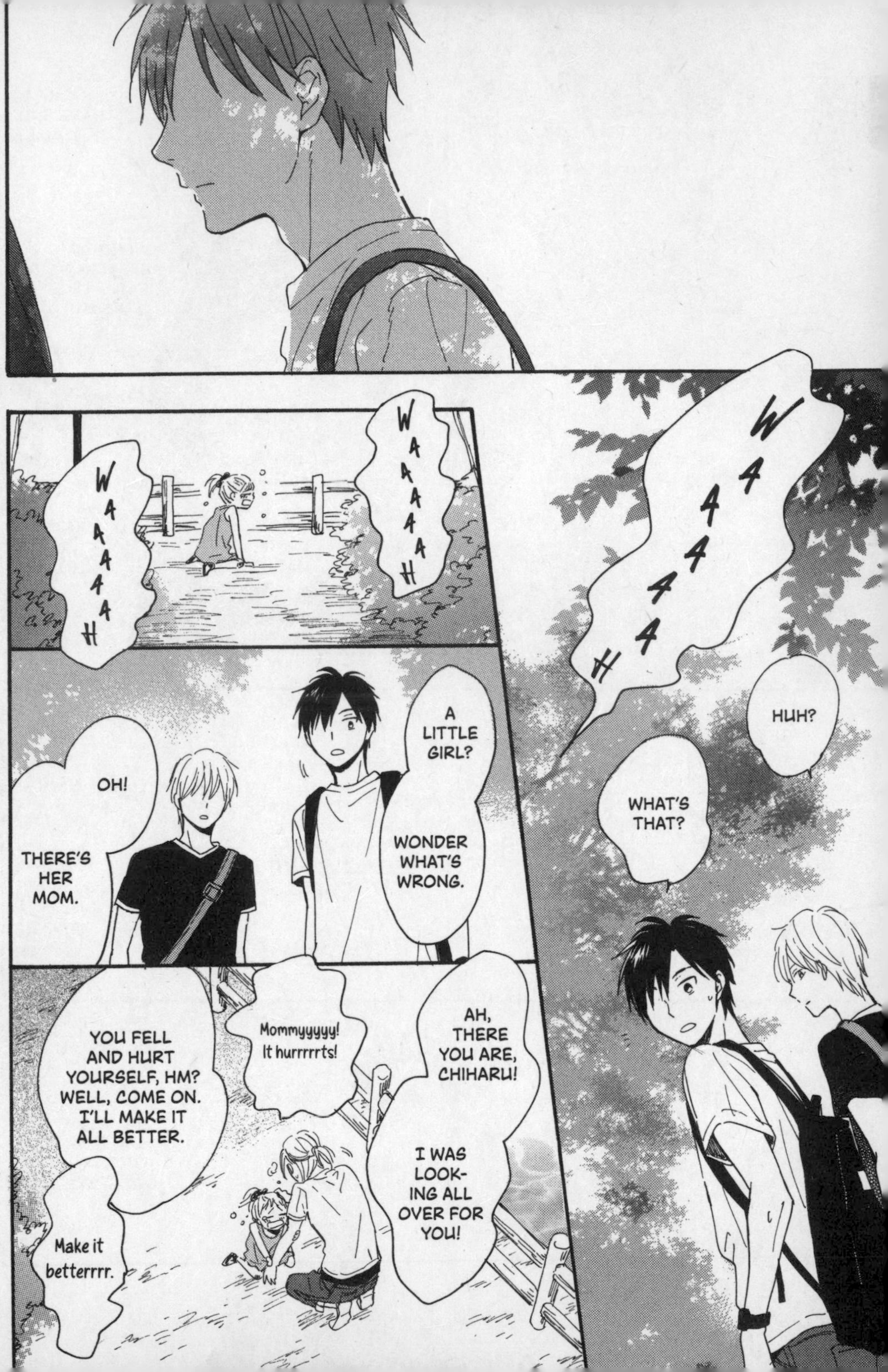
WAAAAAAH
HUH?
WHAT'S THAT?
WAAAAAH
WAAAAAH
A LITTLE GIRL?
WONDER WHAT'S WRONG.
OH!
THERE'S HER MOM.
AH, THERE YOU ARE, CHIHARU!
I WAS LOOKING ALL OVER FOR YOU!
Mommyyyyy! It hurrrrrts!
YOU FELL AND HURT YOURSELF, HM? WELL, COME ON. I'LL MAKE IT ALL BETTER.
Make it betterrrr.

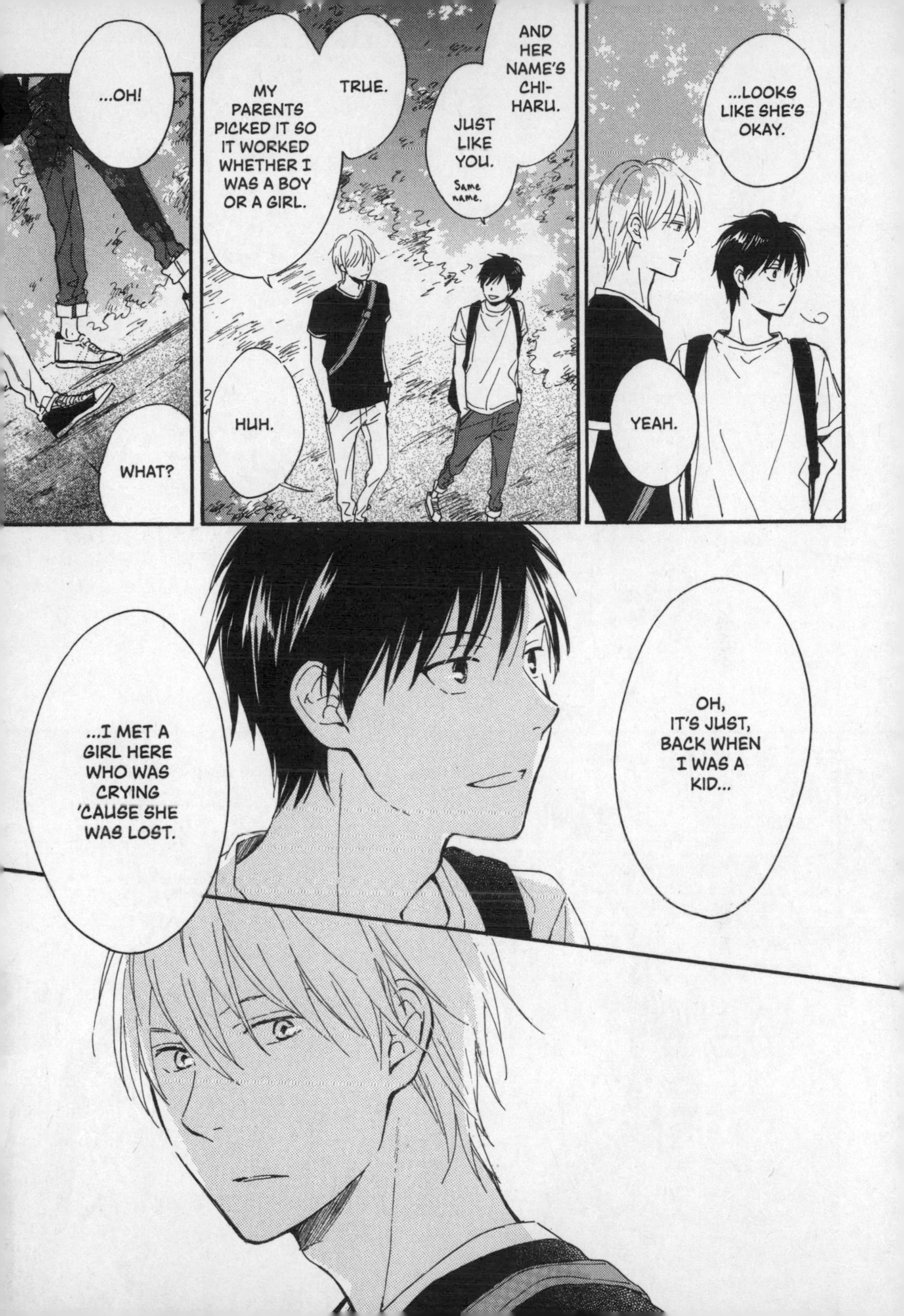
...LOOKS LIKE SHE'S OKAY.
YEAH.
AND HER NAME'S CHI-HARU.
JUST LIKE YOU.
Same name.
TRUE.
MY PARENTS PICKED IT SO IT WORKED WHETHER I WAS A BOY OR A GIRL.
HUH.
...OH!
WHAT?
OH, IT'S JUST, BACK WHEN I WAS A KID...
...I MET A GIRL HERE WHO WAS CRYING 'CAUSE SHE WAS LOST.

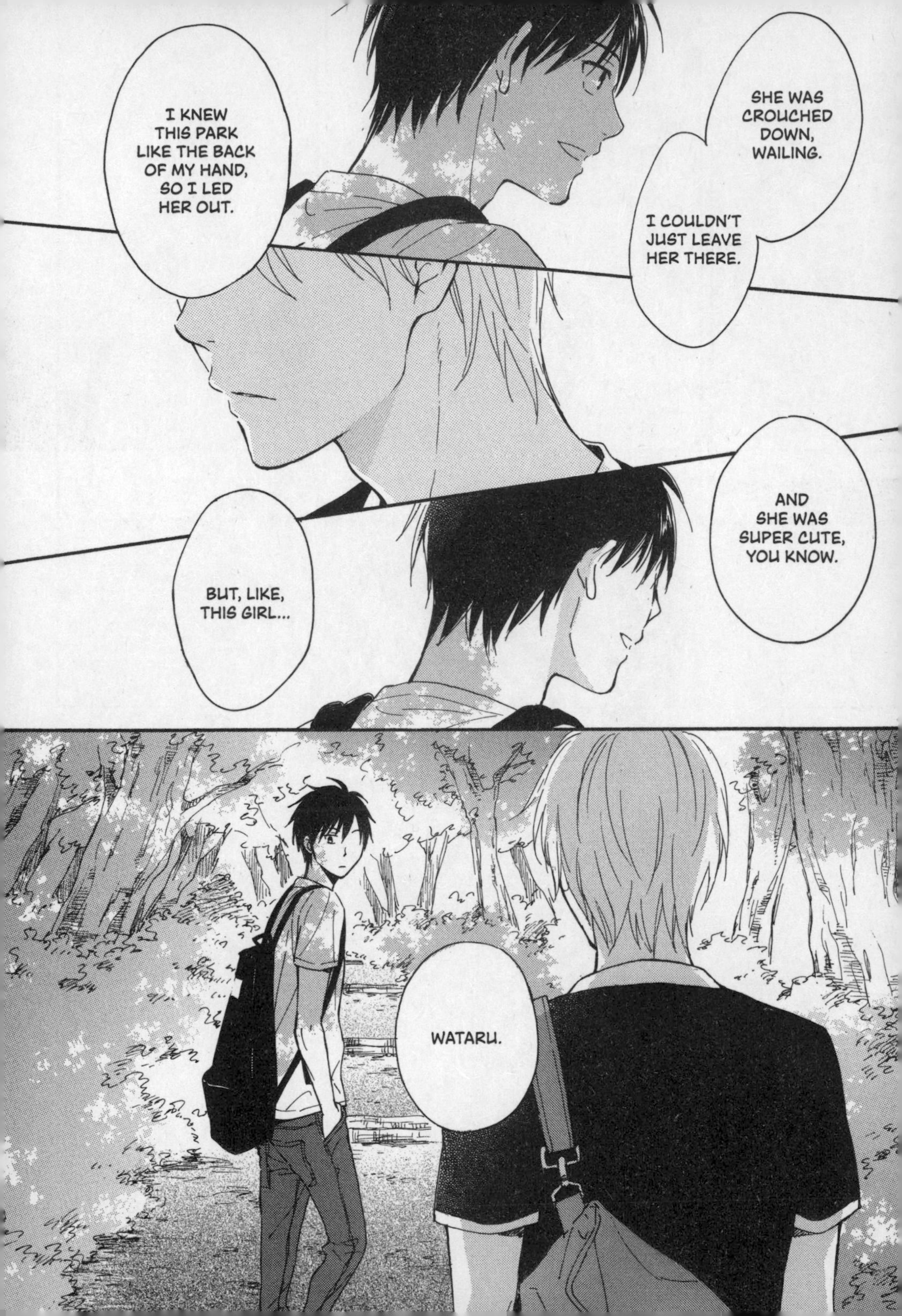
SHE WAS CROUCHED DOWN, WAILING.
I COULDN'T JUST LEAVE HER THERE.
I KNEW THIS PARK LIKE THE BACK OF MY HAND, SO I LED HER OUT.
AND SHE WAS SUPER CUTE, YOU KNOW.
BUT, LIKE, THIS GIRL...
WATARU.

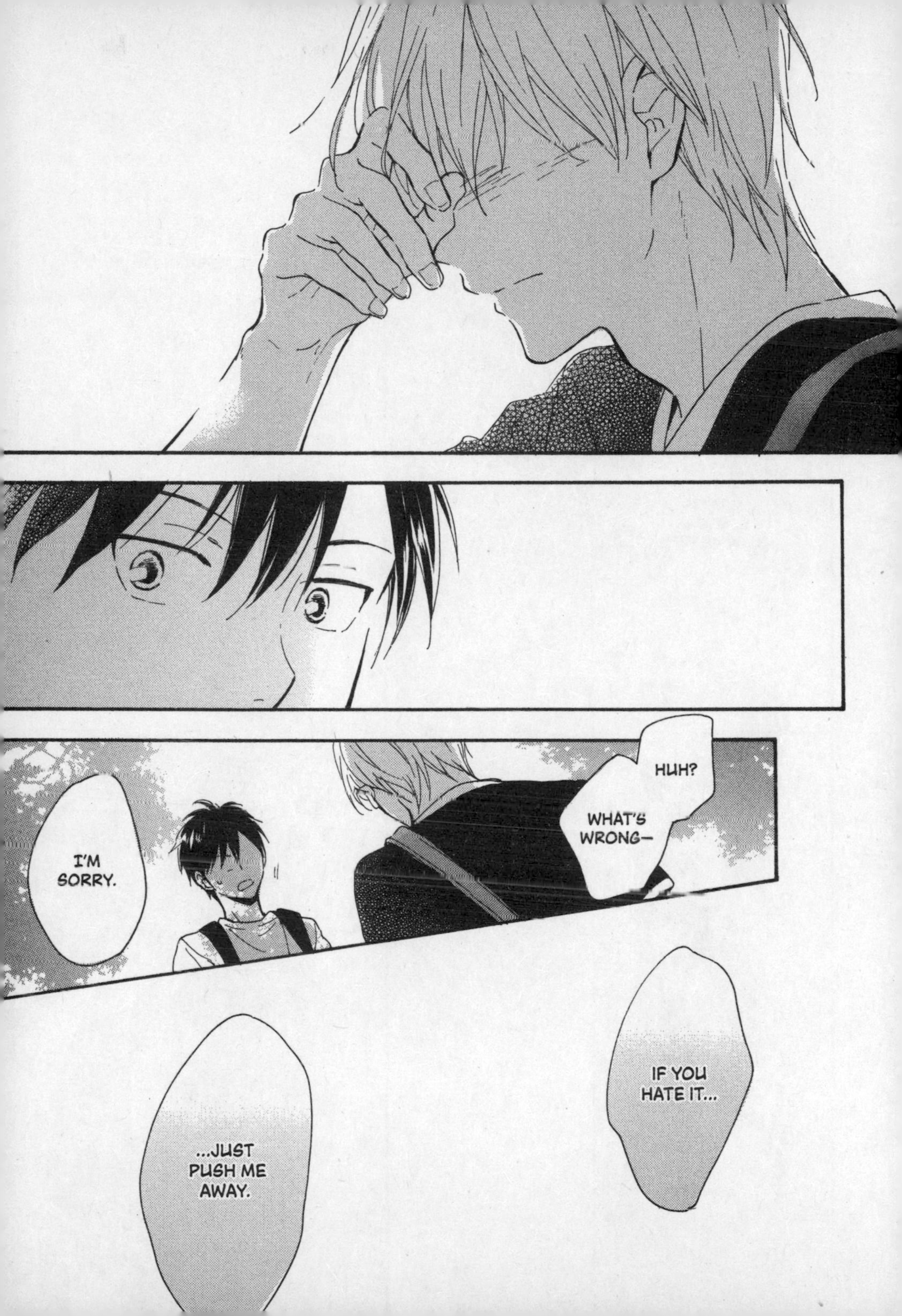
HUH?
WHAT'S WRONG—
I'M SORRY.
IF YOU HATE IT...
...JUST PUSH ME AWAY.

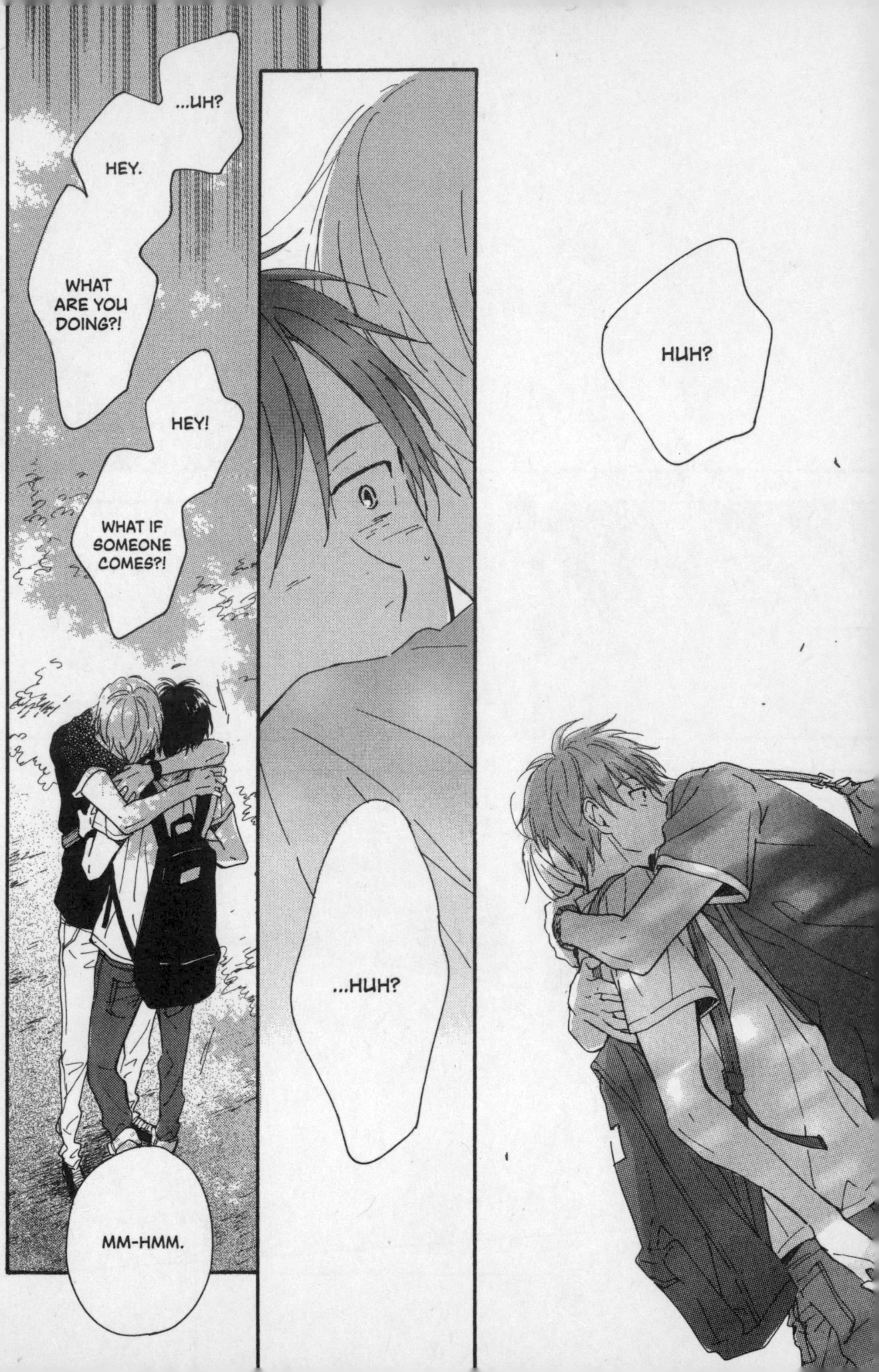
HUH?
...HUH?
...UH?
HEY.
WHAT ARE YOU DOING?!
HEY!
WHAT IF SOMEONE COMES?!
MM-HMM.

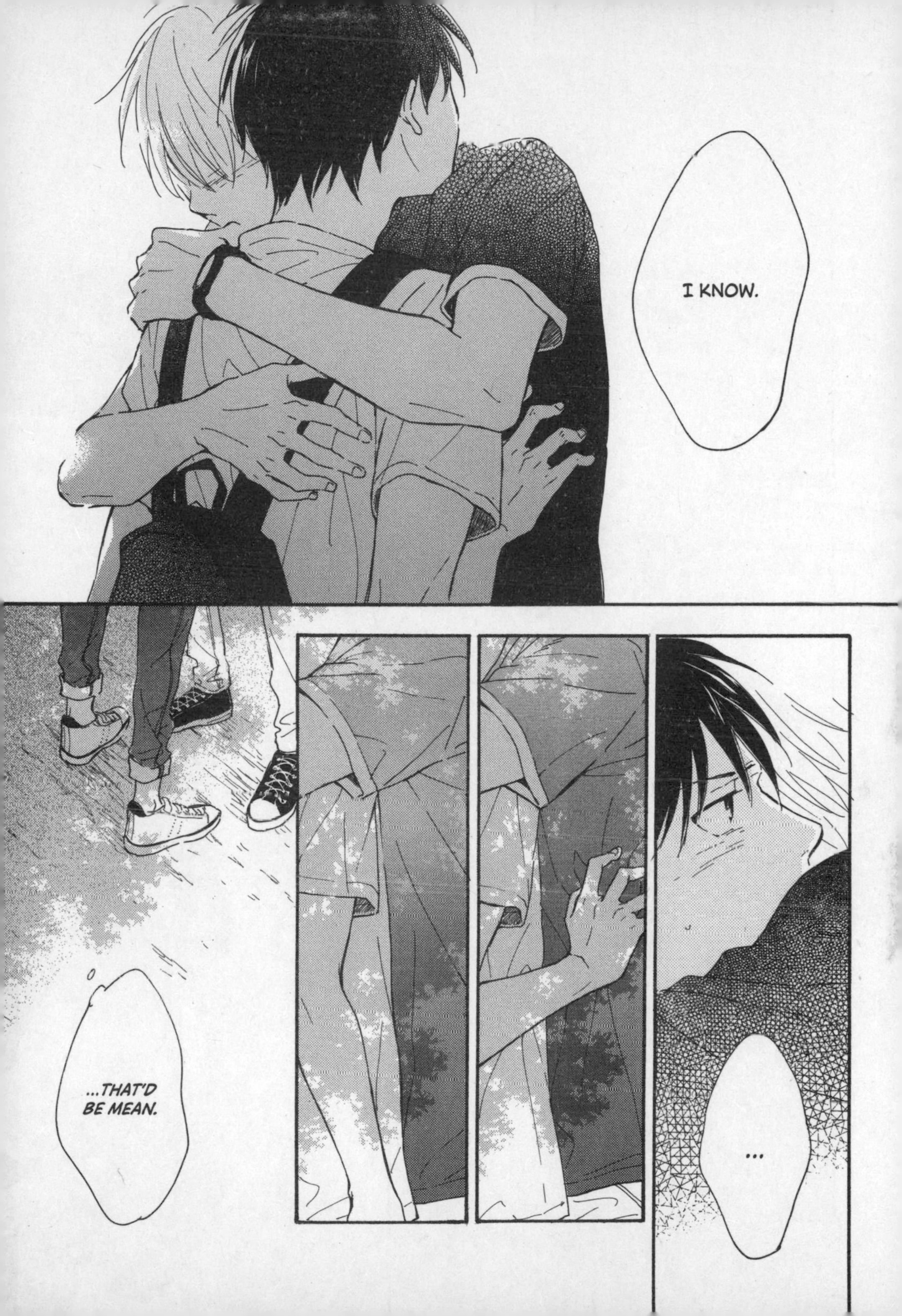
I KNOW.
...
...THAT'D BE MEAN.

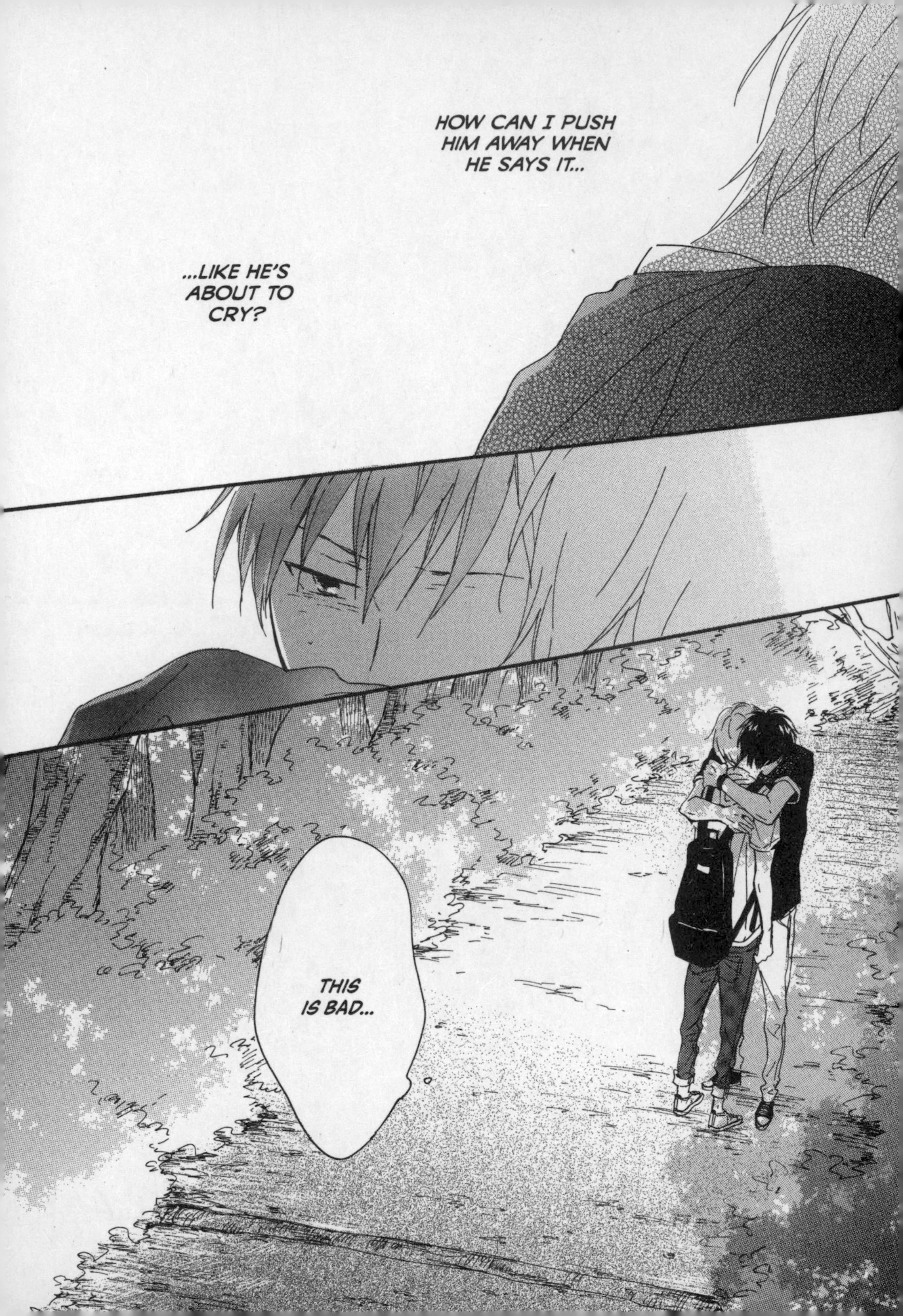
HOW CAN I PUSH HIM AWAY WHEN HE SAYS IT...
...LIKE HE'S ABOUT TO CRY?
THIS IS BAD...

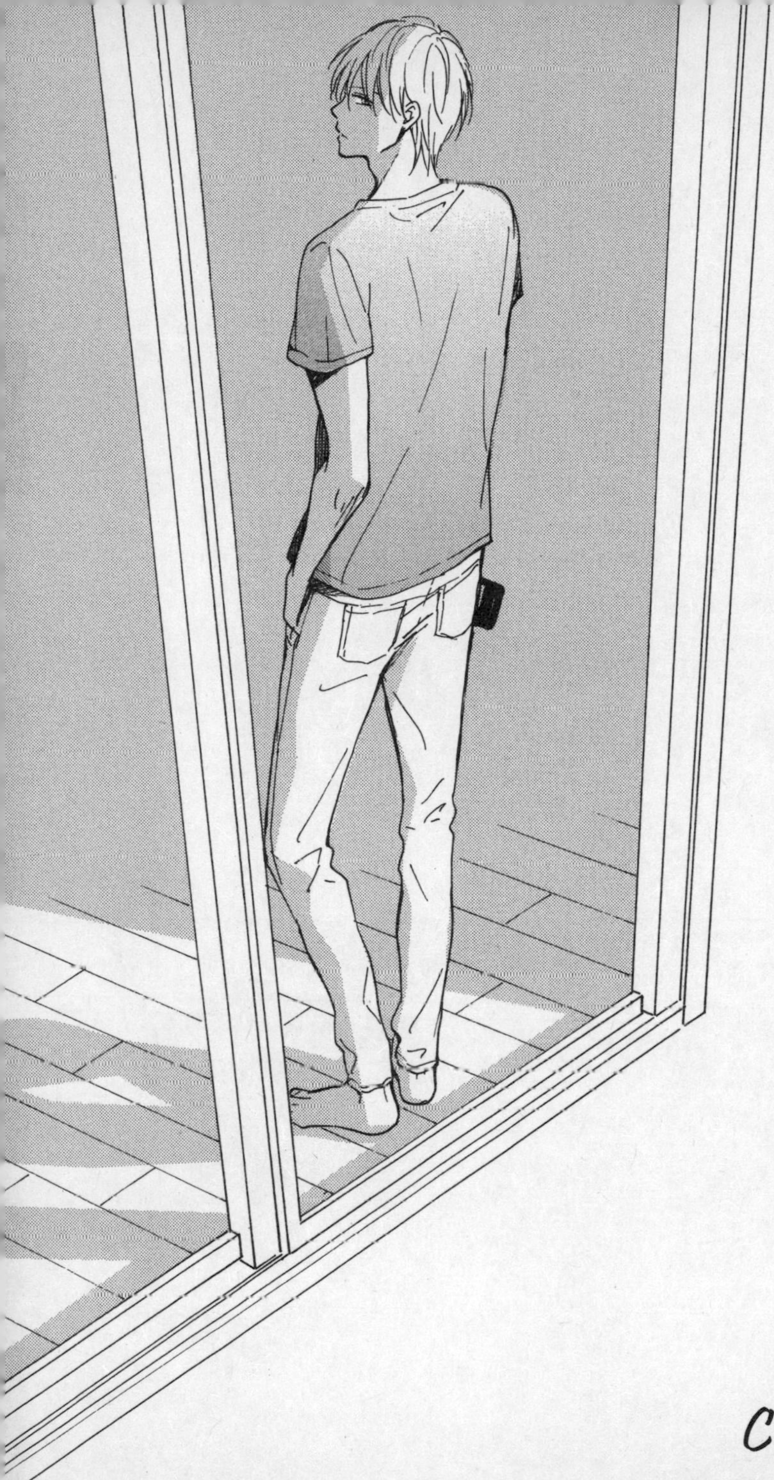

Chapter 4

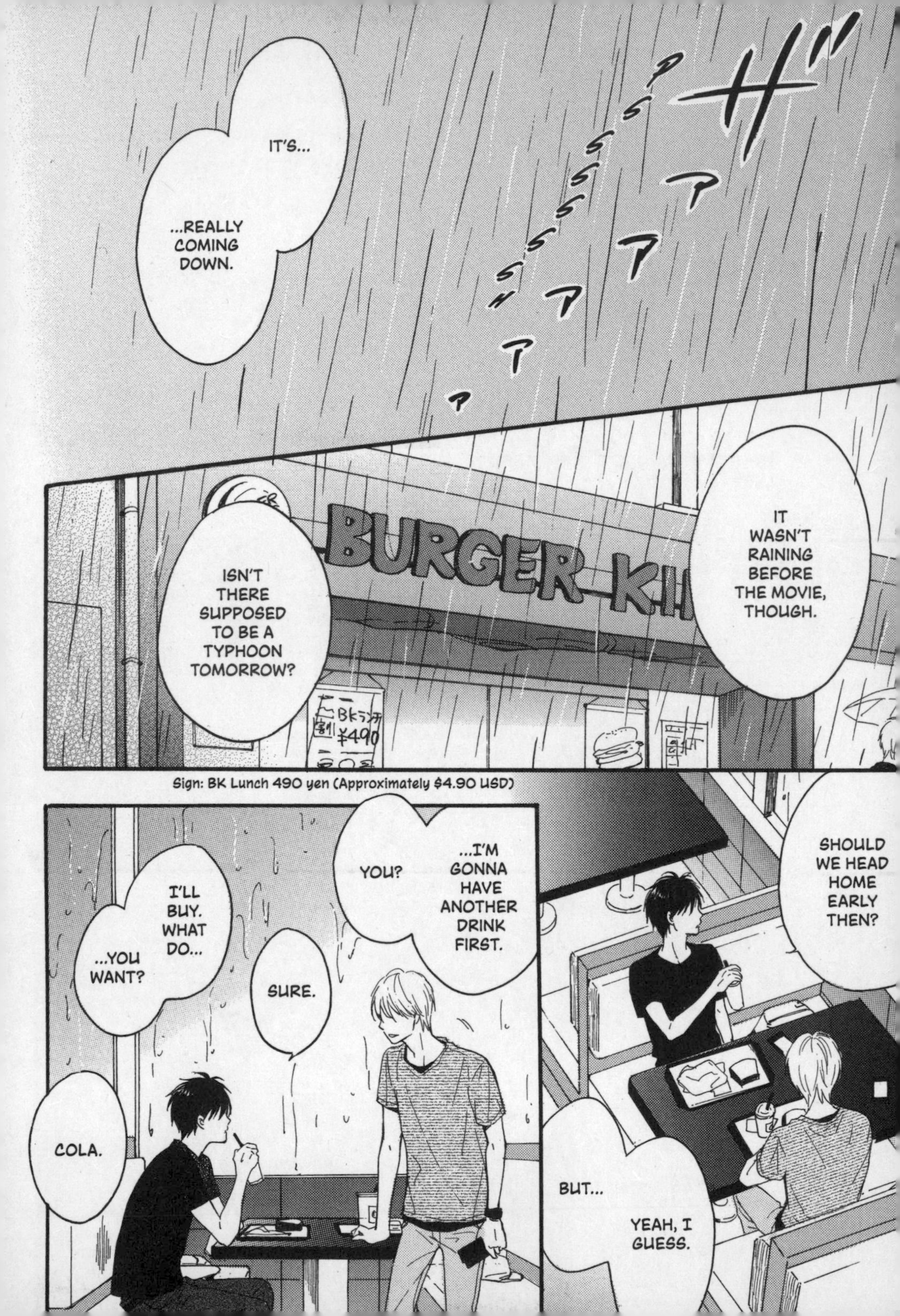
ザアアアアア
PSSSSSSH
IT'S...
...REALLY COMING DOWN.
IT WASN'T RAINING BEFORE THE MOVIE, THOUGH.
BURGER KI
ISN'T THERE SUPPOSED TO BE A TYPHOON TOMORROW?
BKランチ
割 ¥490
SHOULD WE HEAD HOME EARLY THEN?
BUT...
YEAH, I GUESS.
...I'M GONNA HAVE ANOTHER DRINK FIRST.
SURE.
I'LL BUY. WHAT DO...
YOU?
...YOU WANT?
COLA.

Sign: BK Lunch 490 yen (Approximately $4.90 USD)

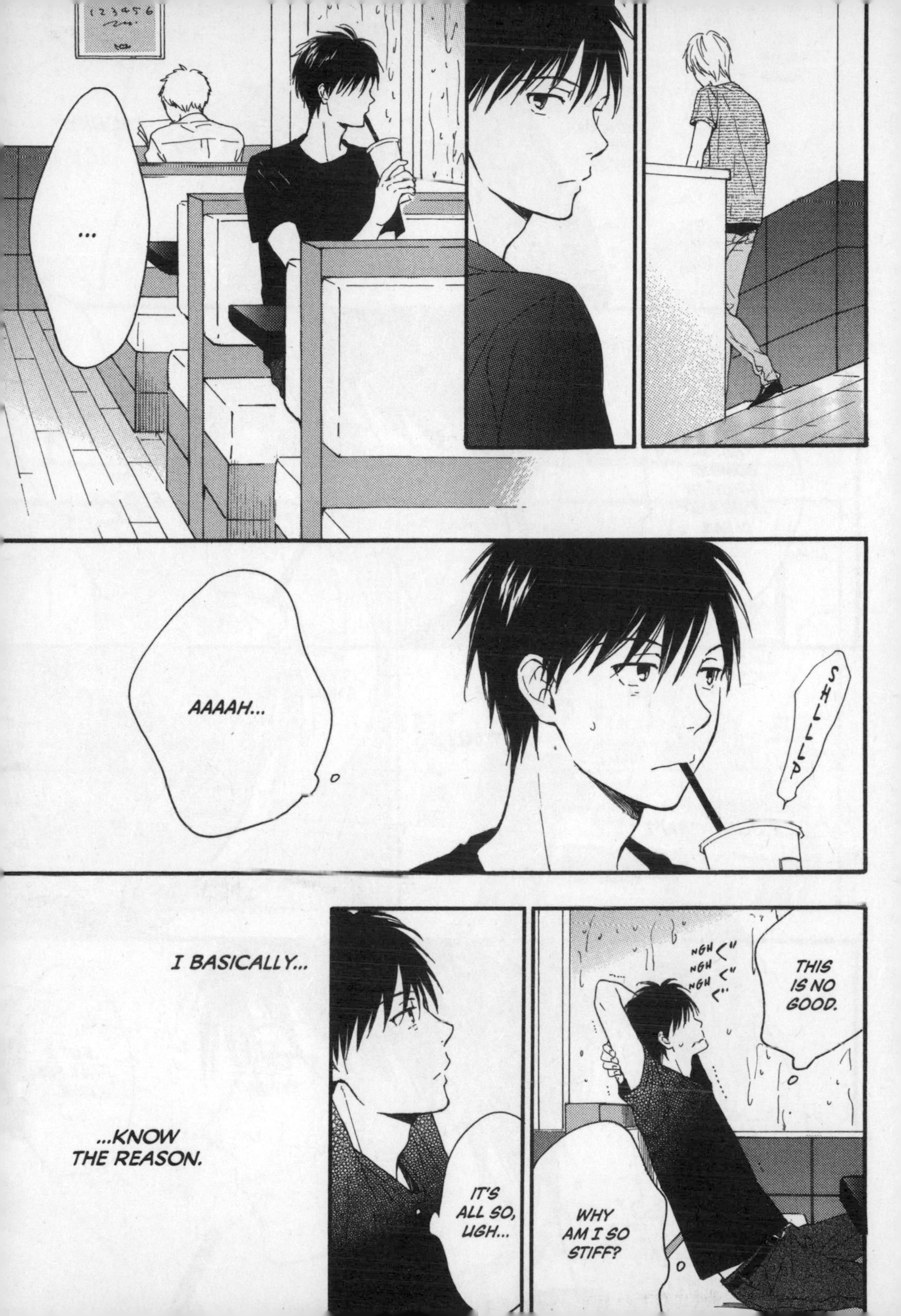
...
AAAAH...
SHLLLP
THIS IS NO GOOD.
NGH NGH NGH
WHY AM I SO STIFF?
IT'S ALL SO, UGH...
I BASICALLY...
...KNOW THE REASON.

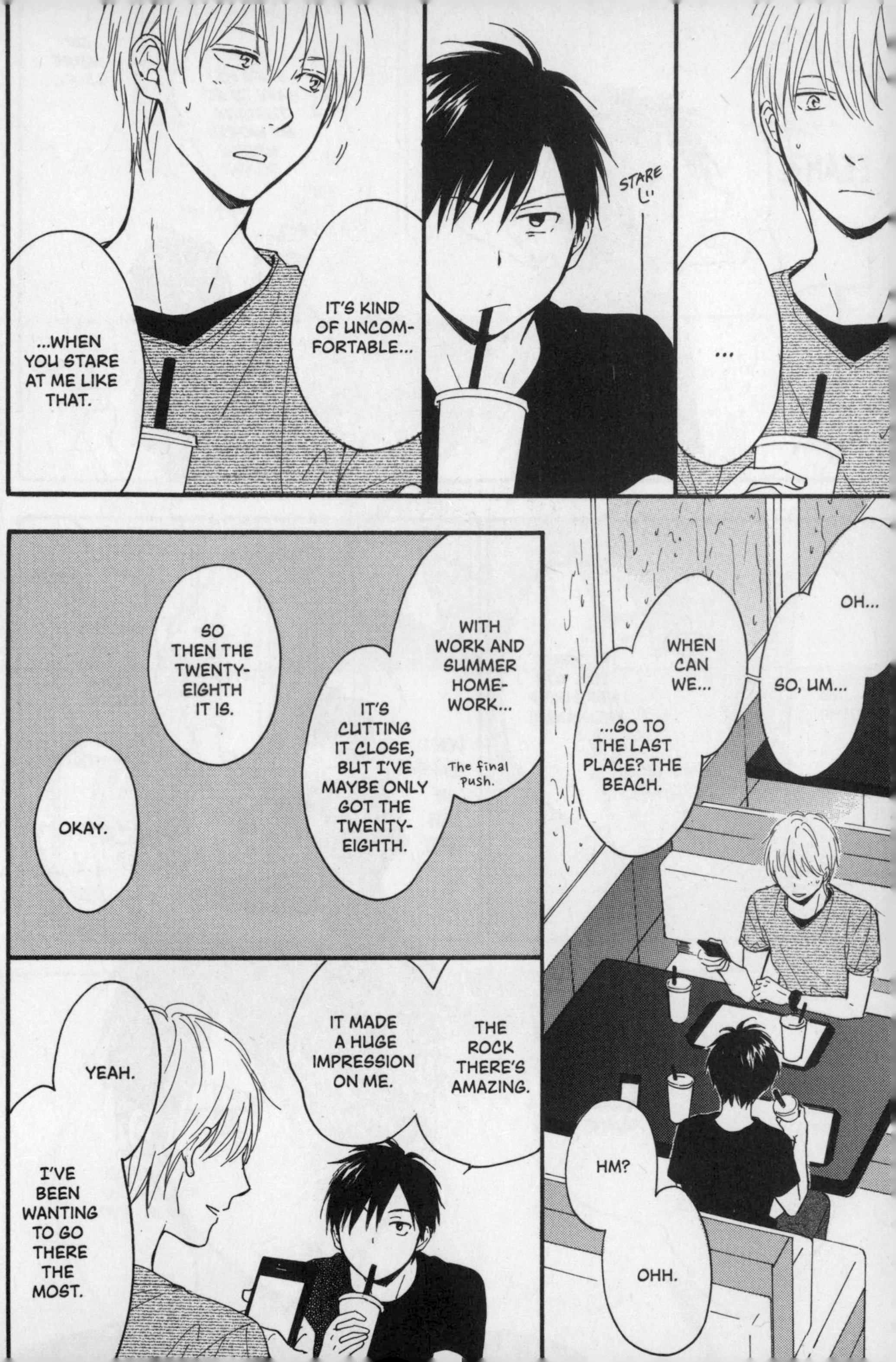
...
STARE
IT'S KIND OF UNCOMFORTABLE...
...WHEN YOU STARE AT ME LIKE THAT.
OH...
SO, UM...
WHEN CAN WE...
...GO TO THE LAST PLACE? THE BEACH.
HM?
OHH.
WITH WORK AND SUMMER HOMEWORK...
The final push.
IT'S CUTTING IT CLOSE, BUT I'VE MAYBE ONLY GOT THE TWENTY-EIGHTH.
SO THEN THE TWENTY-EIGHTH IT IS.
OKAY.
THE ROCK THERE'S AMAZING.
IT MADE A HUGE IMPRESSION ON ME.
YEAH.
I'VE BEEN WANTING TO GO THERE THE MOST.

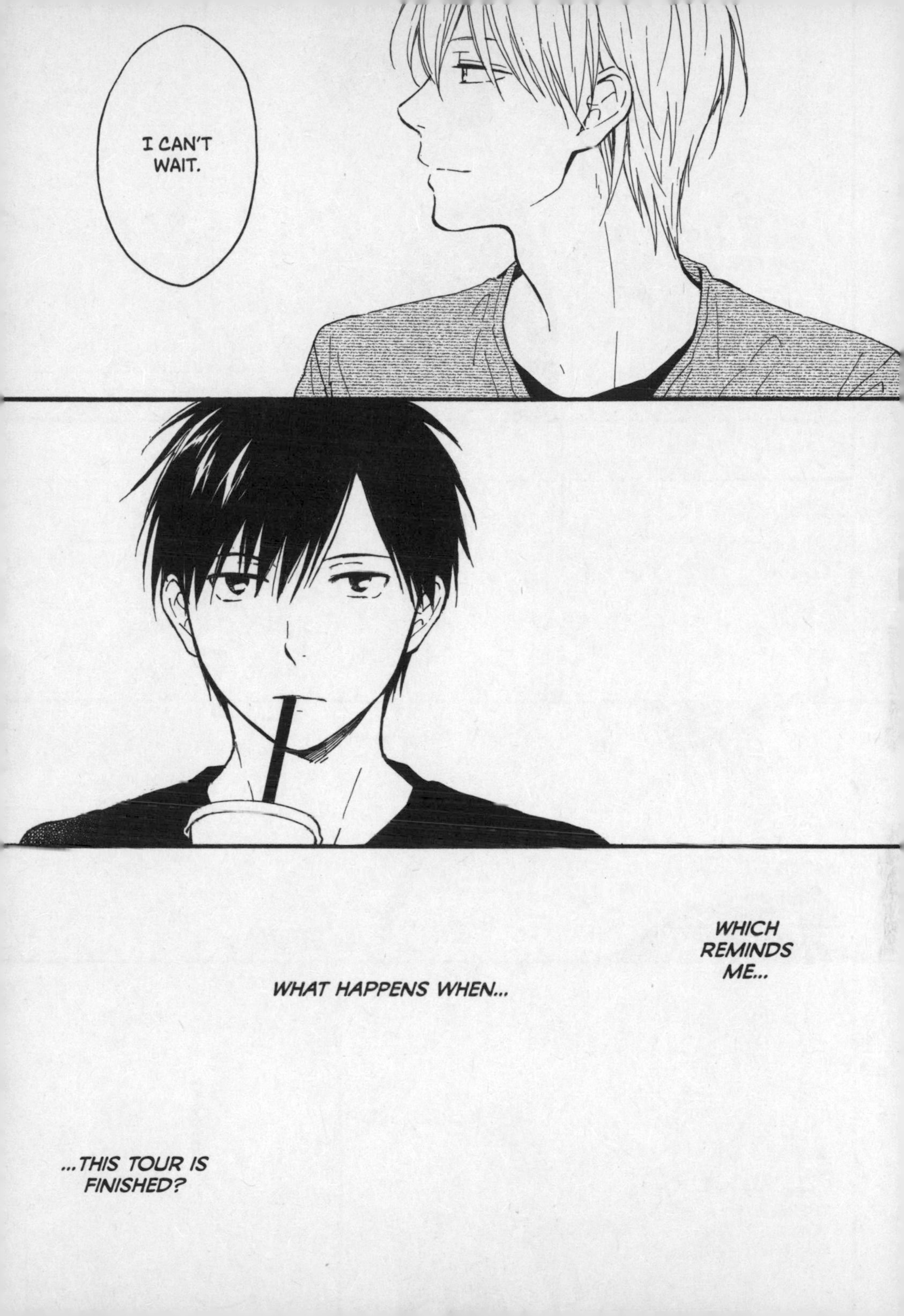
I CAN'T WAIT.
WHICH REMINDS ME...
WHAT HAPPENS WHEN...
...THIS TOUR IS FINISHED?

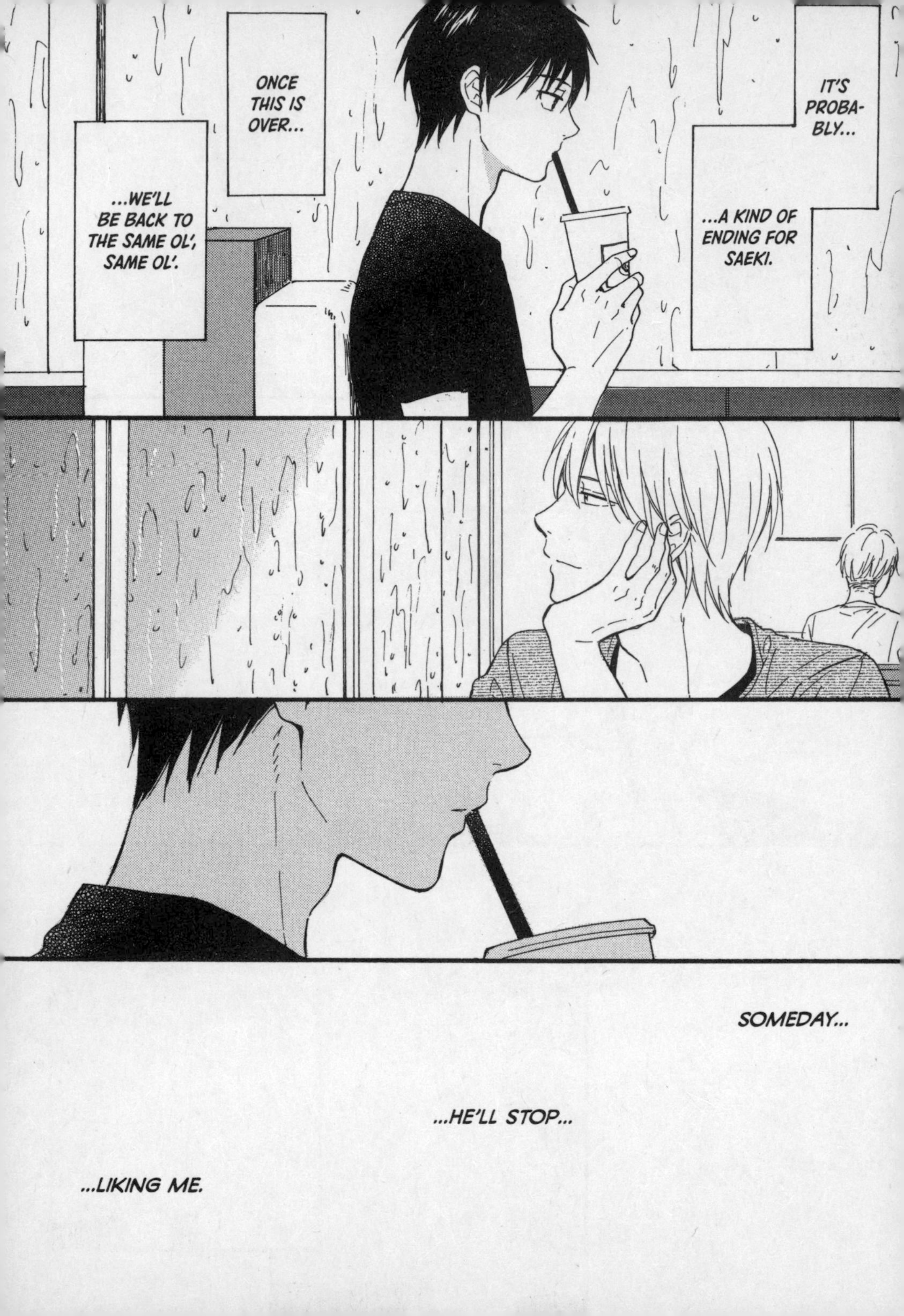
IT'S PROBA-BLY...
...A KIND OF ENDING FOR SAEKI.
ONCE THIS IS OVER...
...WE'LL BE BACK TO THE SAME OL', SAME OL'.
SOMEDAY...
...HE'LL STOP...
...LIKING ME.

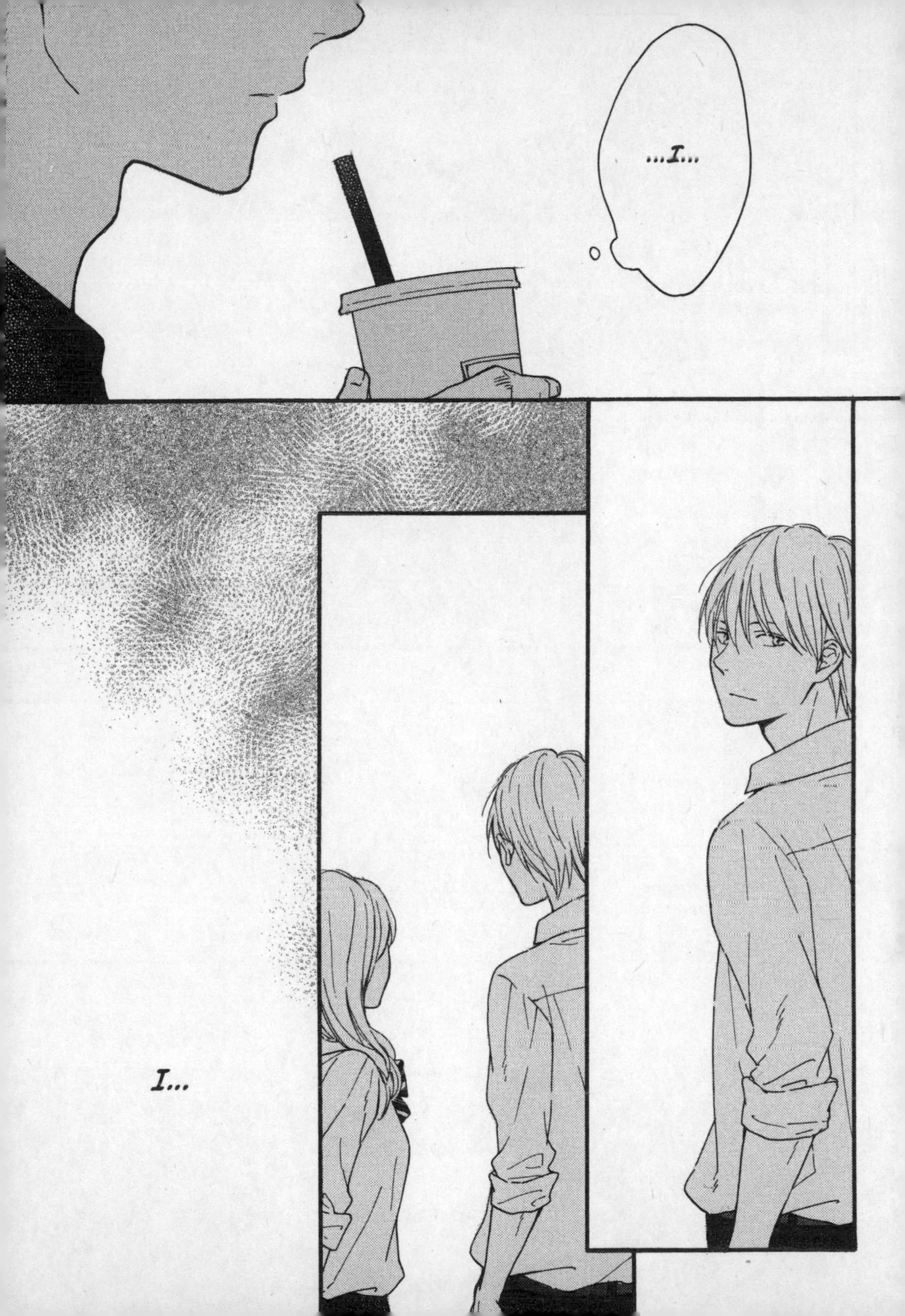
...I...
I...

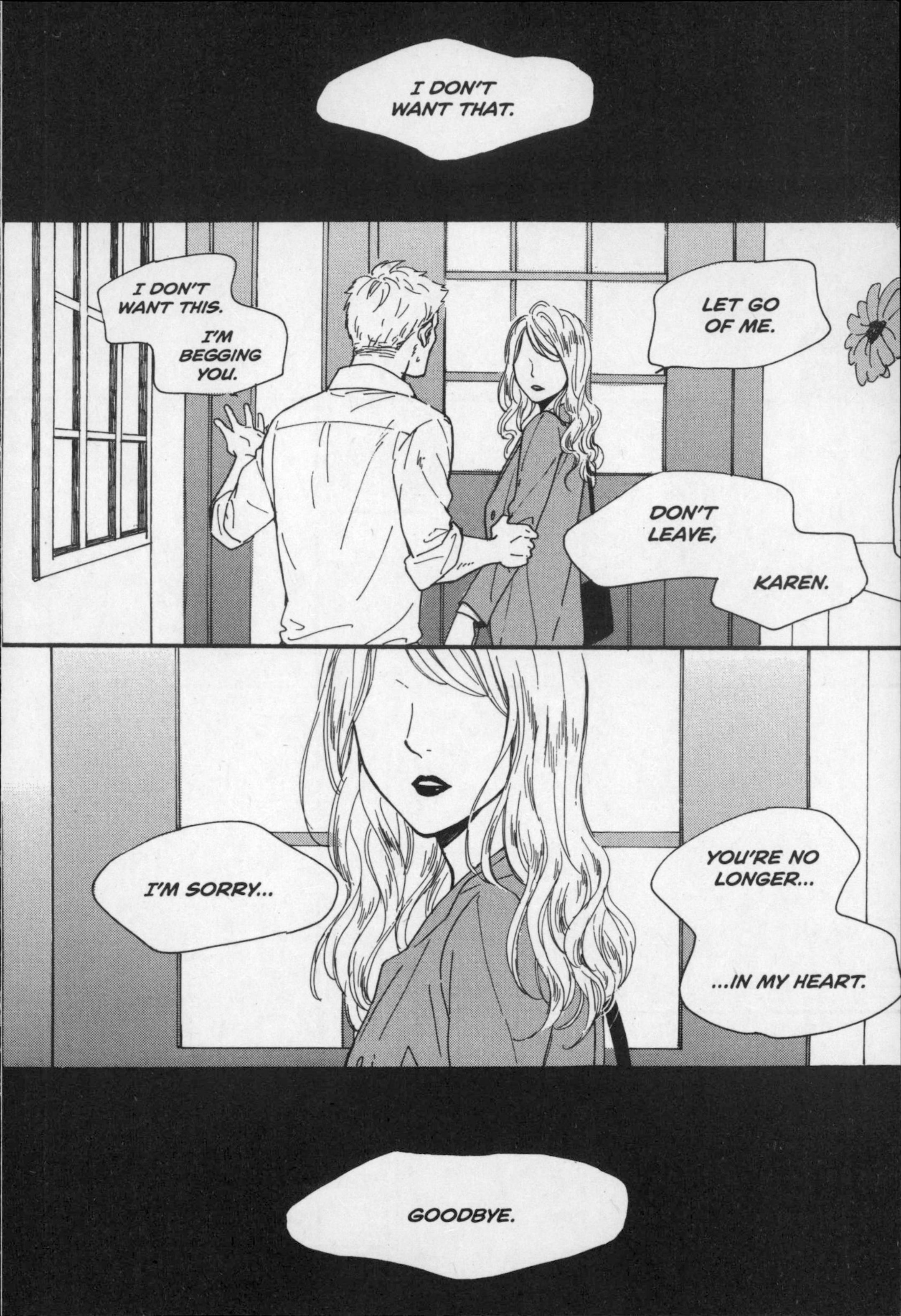
I DON'T WANT THAT.
LET GO OF ME.
I DON'T WANT THIS.
I'M BEGGING YOU.
DON'T LEAVE,
KAREN.
YOU'RE NO LONGER...
...IN MY HEART.
I'M SORRY...
GOODBYE.

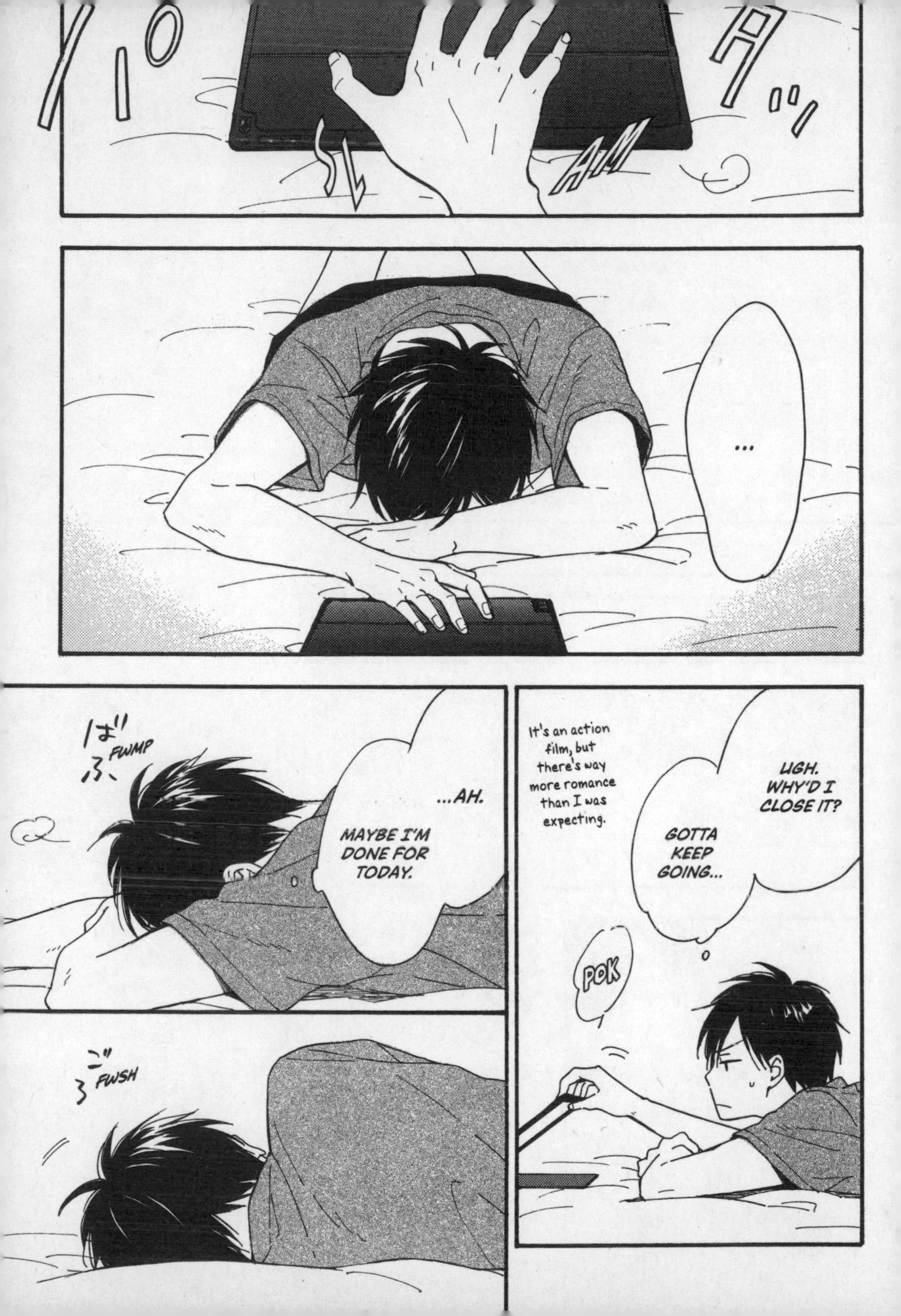
SLAM
...
UGH. WHY'D I CLOSE IT?
GOTTA KEEP GOING...
It's an action film, but there's way more romance than I was expecting.
POK
...AH.
MAYBE I'M DONE FOR TODAY.
ばふ
FWUMP
ごろ
FWSH

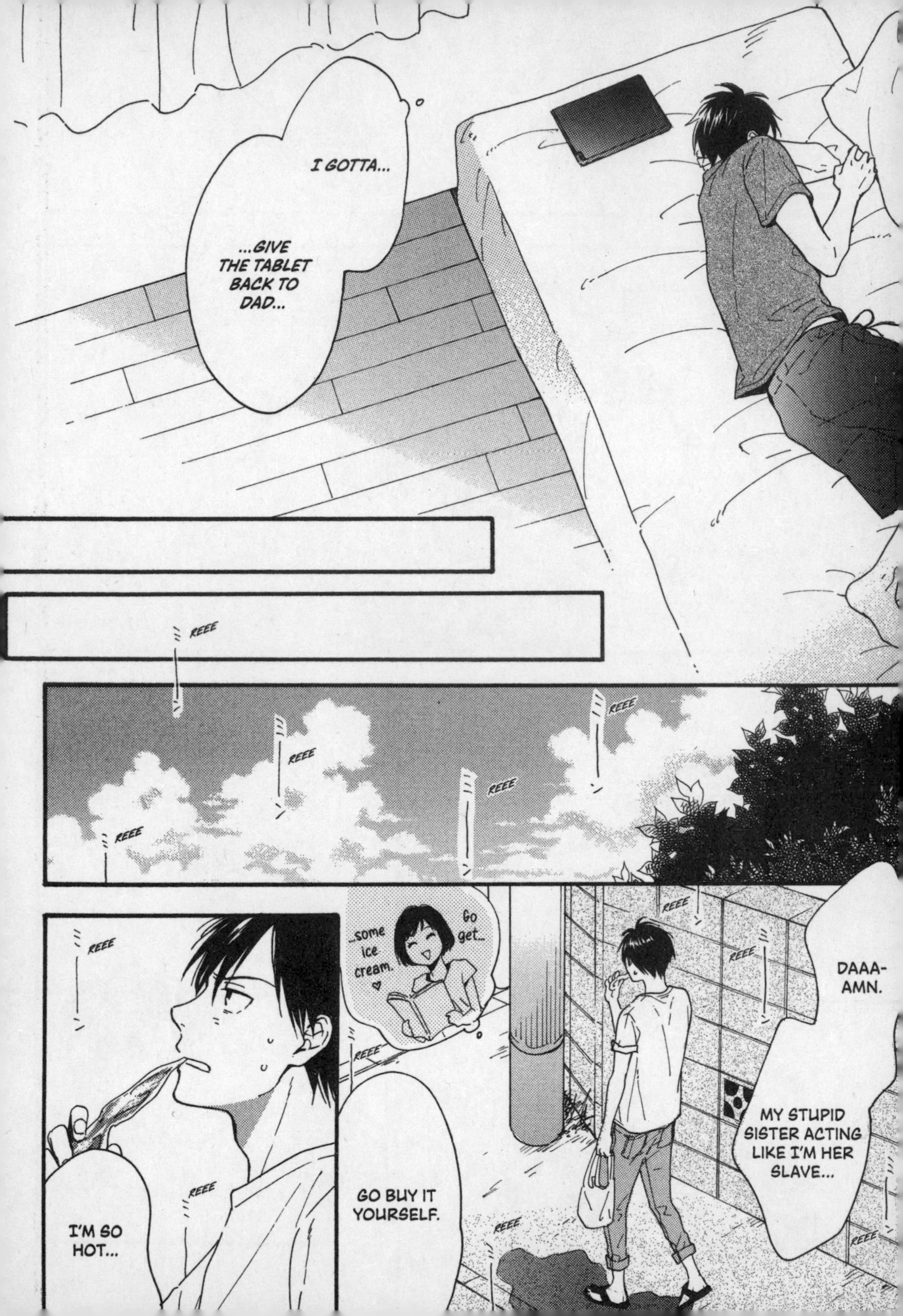
I GOTTA...
...GIVE THE TABLET BACK TO DAD...
REEE
REEE
REEE
REEE
REEE
REEE
DAAA-AMN.
MY STUPID SISTER ACTING LIKE I'M HER SLAVE...
REEE
REEE
REEE
Go get...
...some ice cream. ♥
REEE
GO BUY IT YOURSELF.
REEE
REEE
REEE
I'M SO HOT...

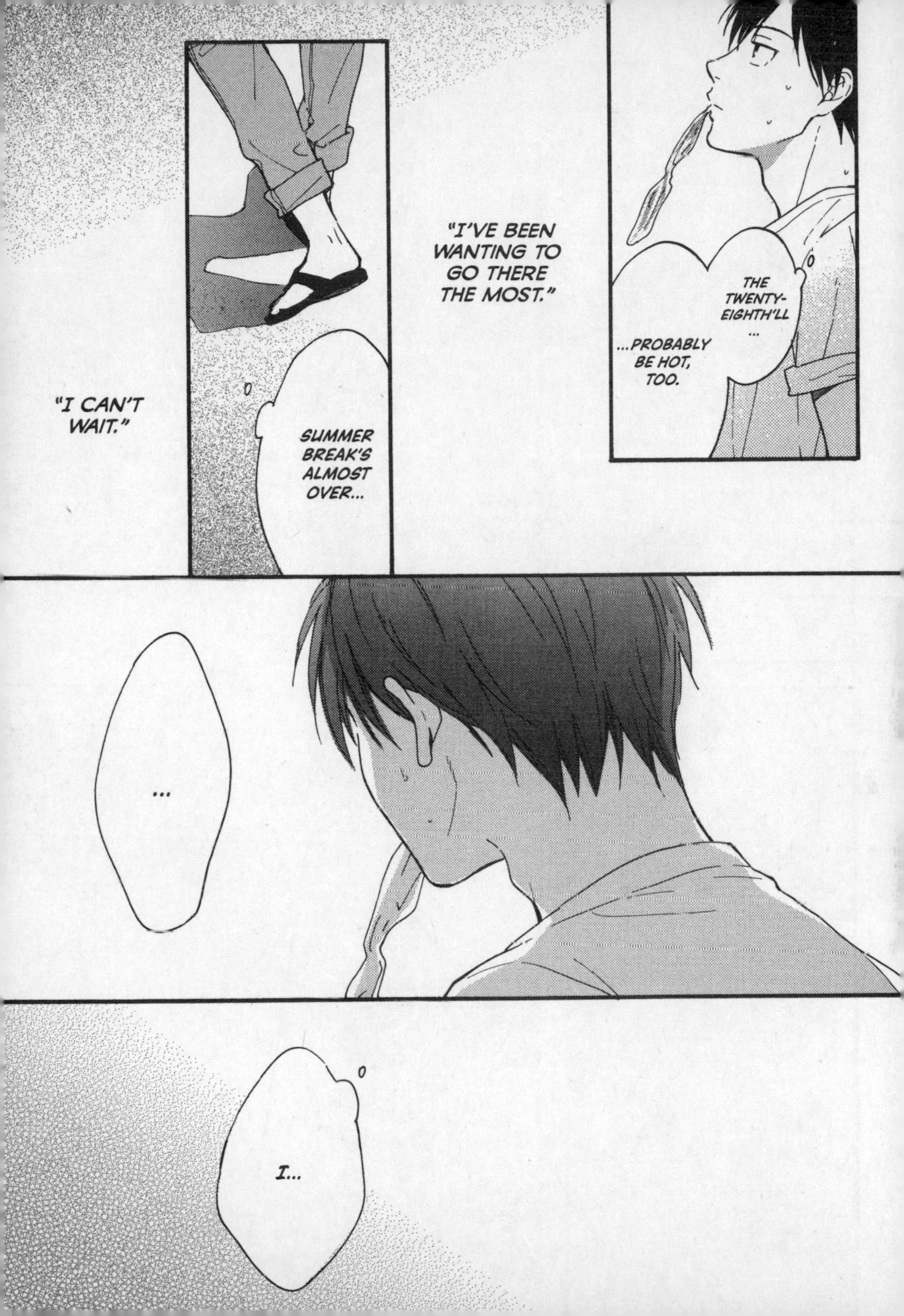
THE TWENTY-EIGHTH'LL ...
...PROBABLY BE HOT, TOO.
"I'VE BEEN WANTING TO GO THERE THE MOST."
SUMMER BREAK'S ALMOST OVER...
"I CAN'T WAIT."
...
I...

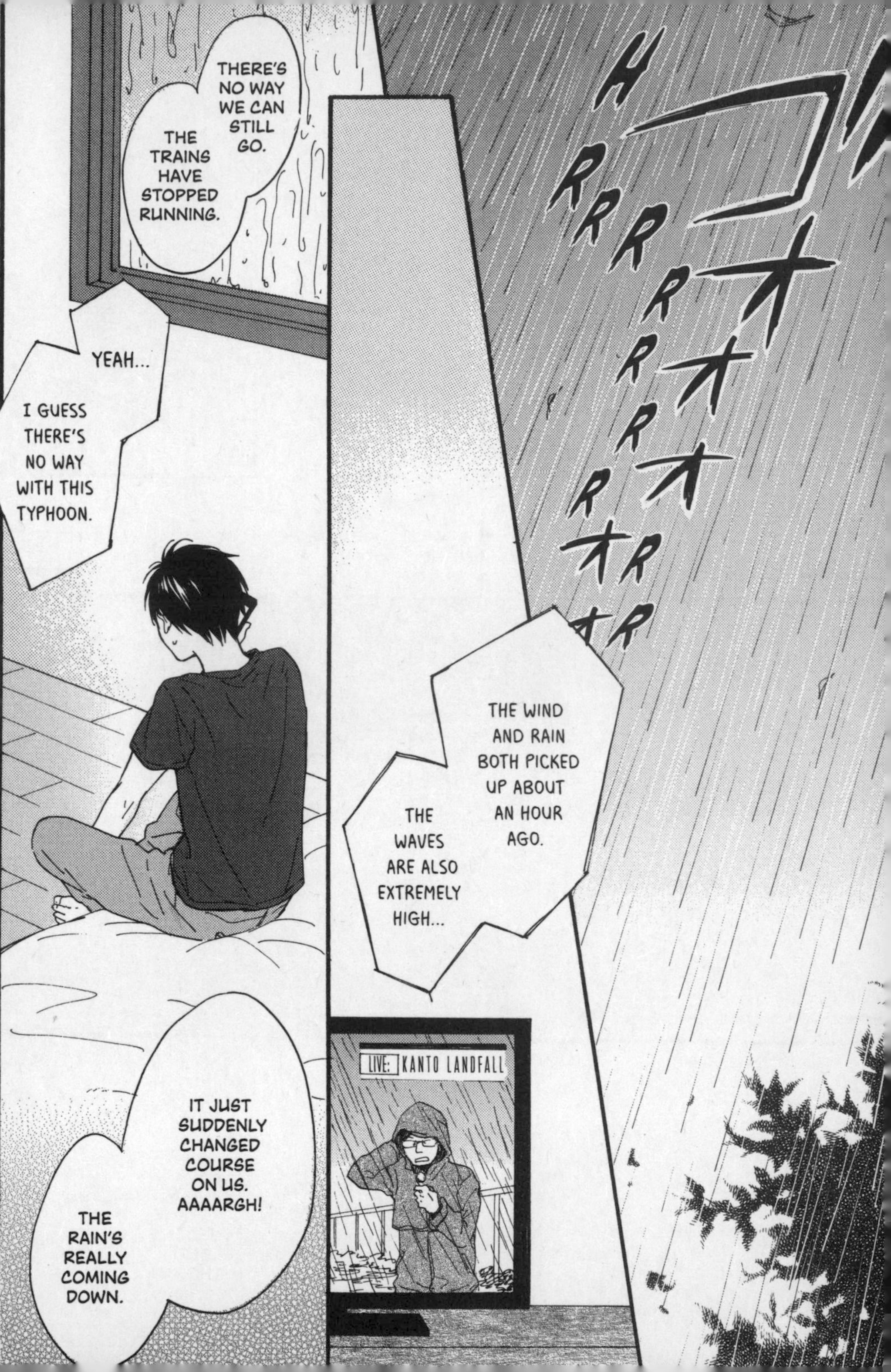
HRRRRRRRRRRR
LIVE: KANTO LANDFALL
THE WIND AND RAIN BOTH PICKED UP ABOUT AN HOUR AGO.
THE WAVES ARE ALSO EXTREMELY HIGH...
THERE'S NO WAY WE CAN STILL GO.
THE TRAINS HAVE STOPPED RUNNING.
YEAH...
I GUESS THERE'S NO WAY WITH THIS TYPHOON.
IT JUST SUDDENLY CHANGED COURSE ON US. AAAARGH!
THE RAIN'S REALLY COMING DOWN.

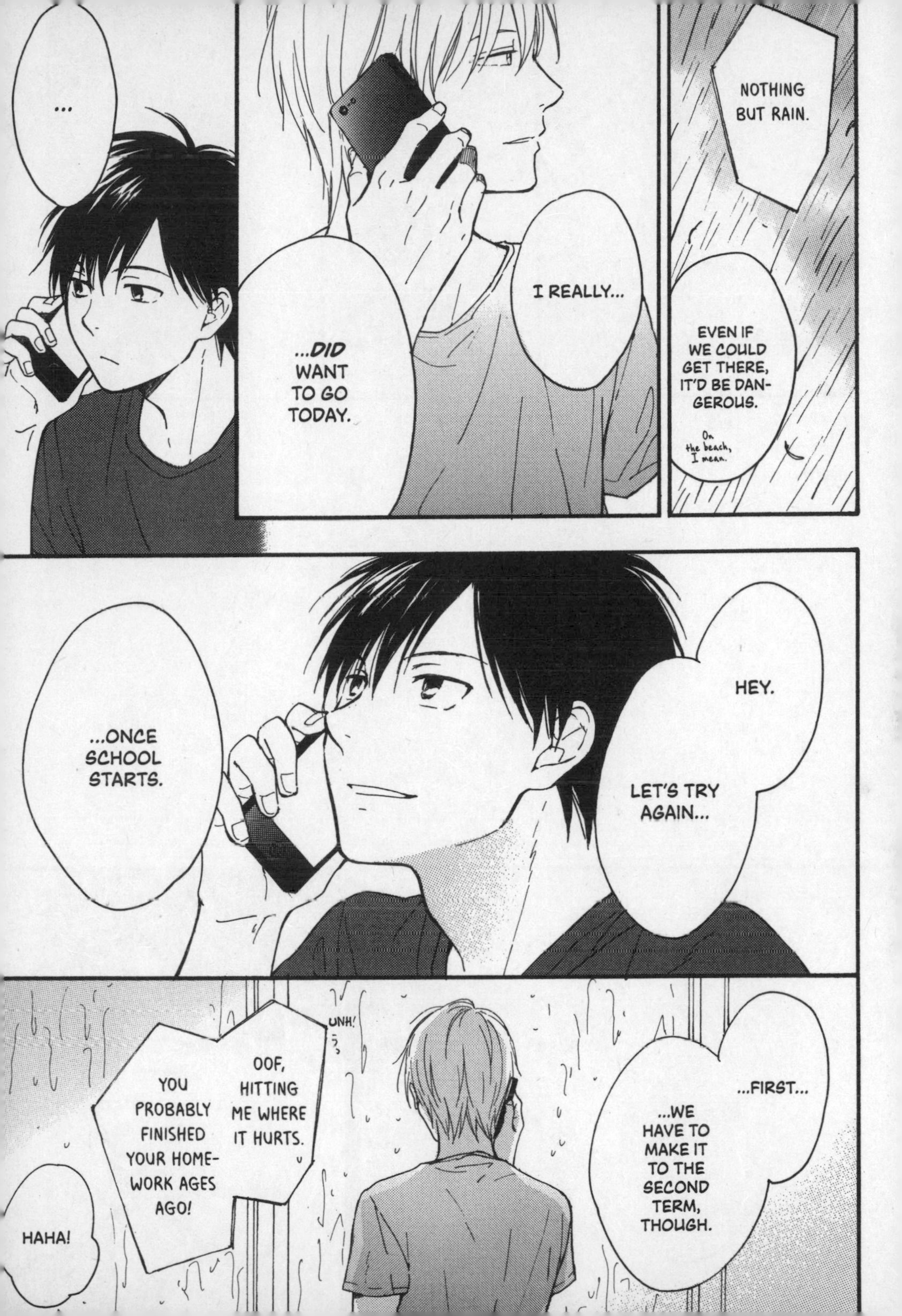
NOTHING BUT RAIN.
EVEN IF WE COULD GET THERE, IT'D BE DANGEROUS.
On the beach, I mean.
I REALLY...
...DID WANT TO GO TODAY.
...
HEY.
LET'S TRY AGAIN...
...ONCE SCHOOL STARTS.
...FIRST...
...WE HAVE TO MAKE IT TO THE SECOND TERM, THOUGH.
UNH!
OOF, HITTING ME WHERE IT HURTS.
YOU PROBABLY FINISHED YOUR HOME-WORK AGES AGO!
HAHA!

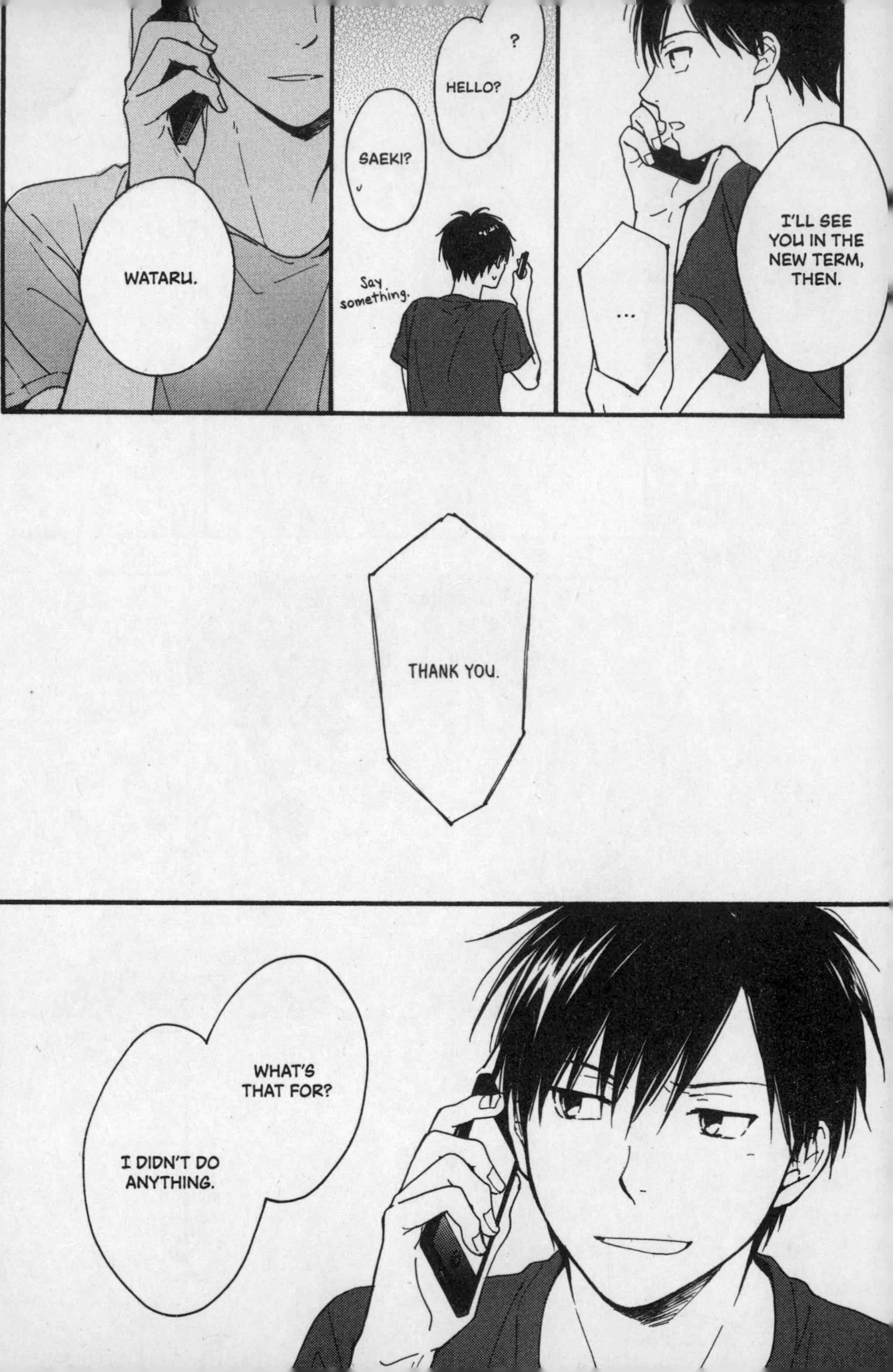
I'LL SEE YOU IN THE NEW TERM, THEN.
...
?
HELLO?
SAEKI?
Say something.
WATARU.
THANK YOU.
WHAT'S THAT FOR?
I DIDN'T DO ANYTHING.

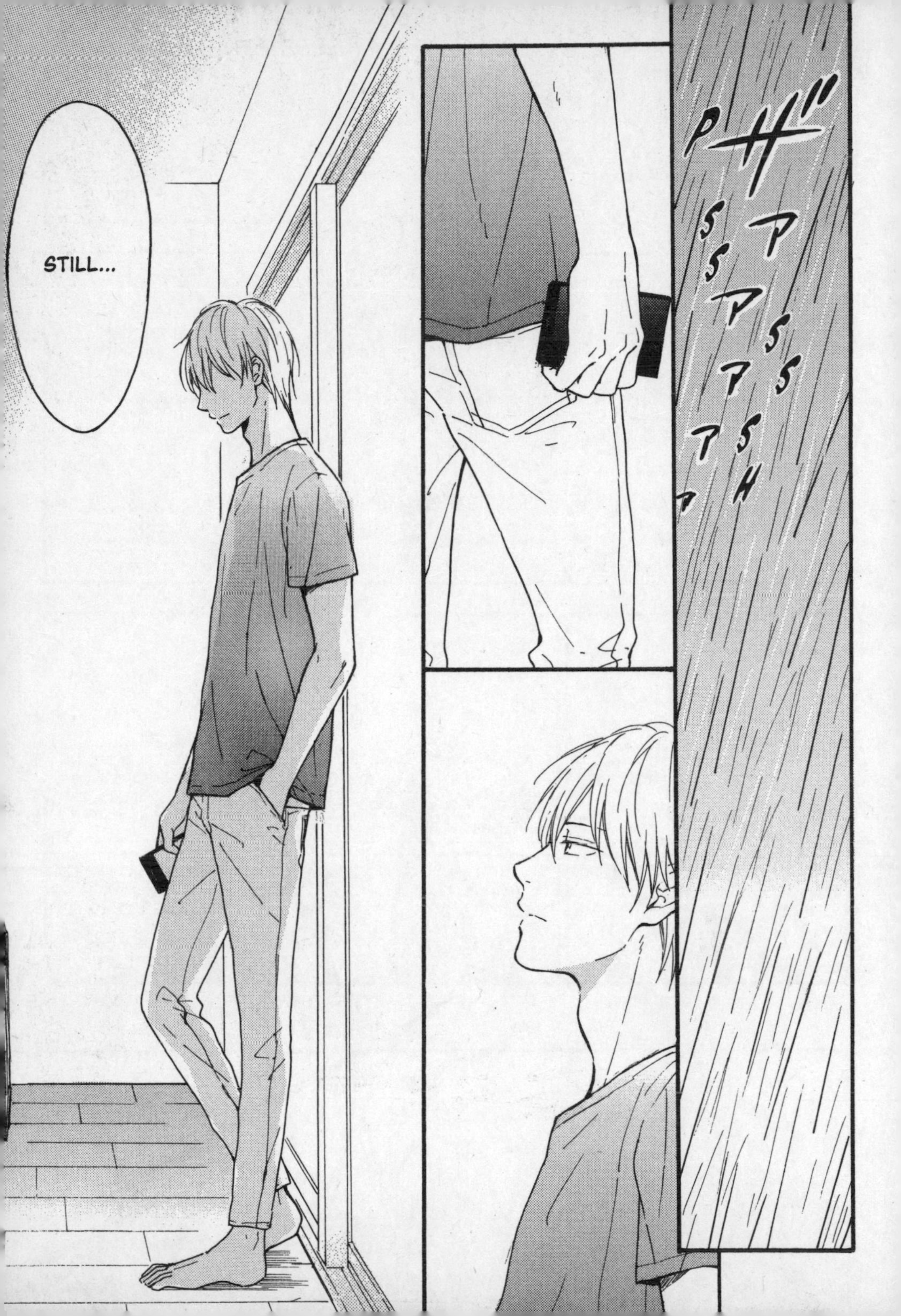
ザアアアアア
PSSSSSH
STILL...

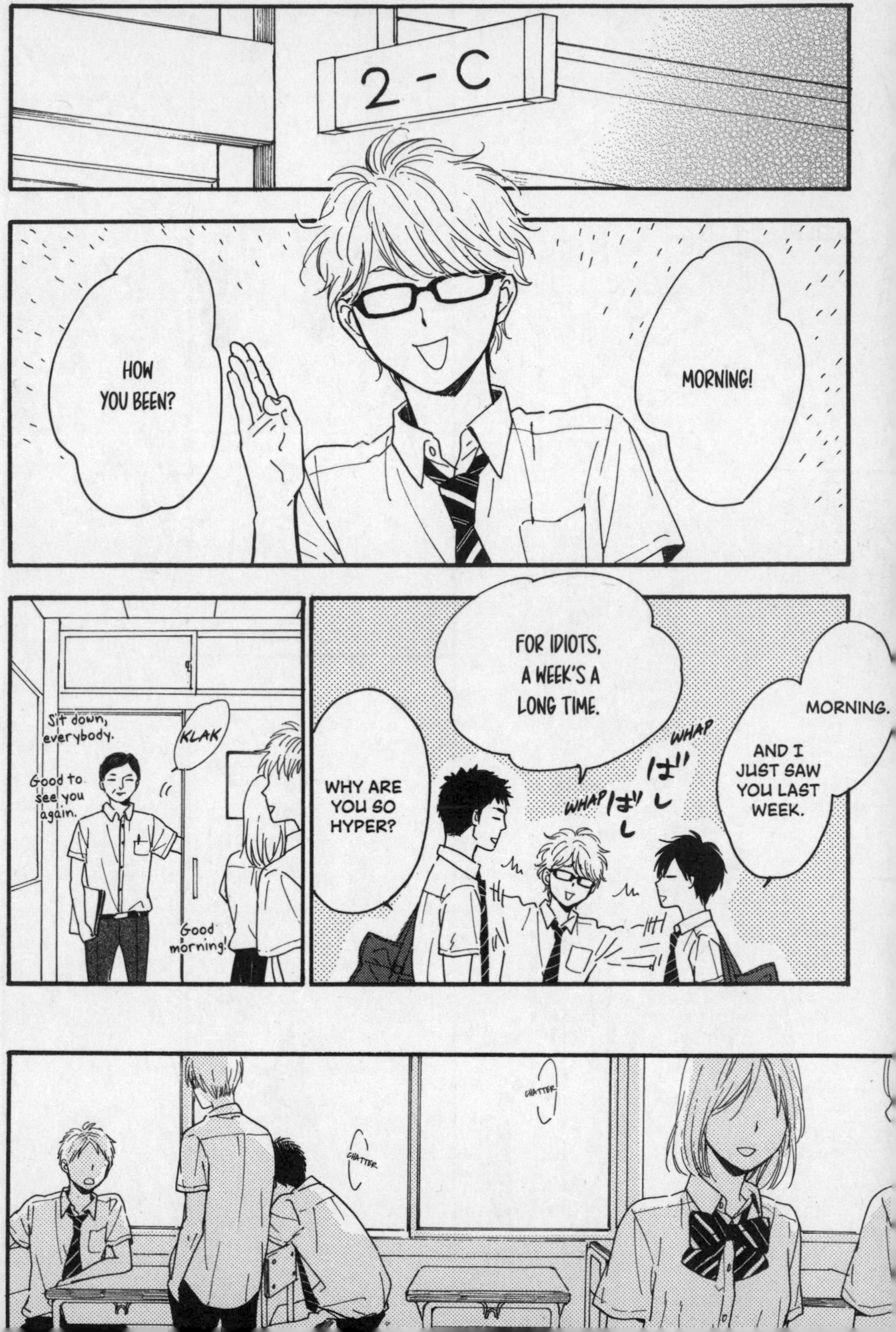
2-C
MORNING!
HOW YOU BEEN?
MORNING.
AND I JUST SAW YOU LAST WEEK.
WHAP ばし
WHAP ばし
FOR IDIOTS, A WEEK'S A LONG TIME.
WHY ARE YOU SO HYPER?
KLAK
Sit down, everybody.
Good to see you again.
Good morning!
CHATTER
CHATTER

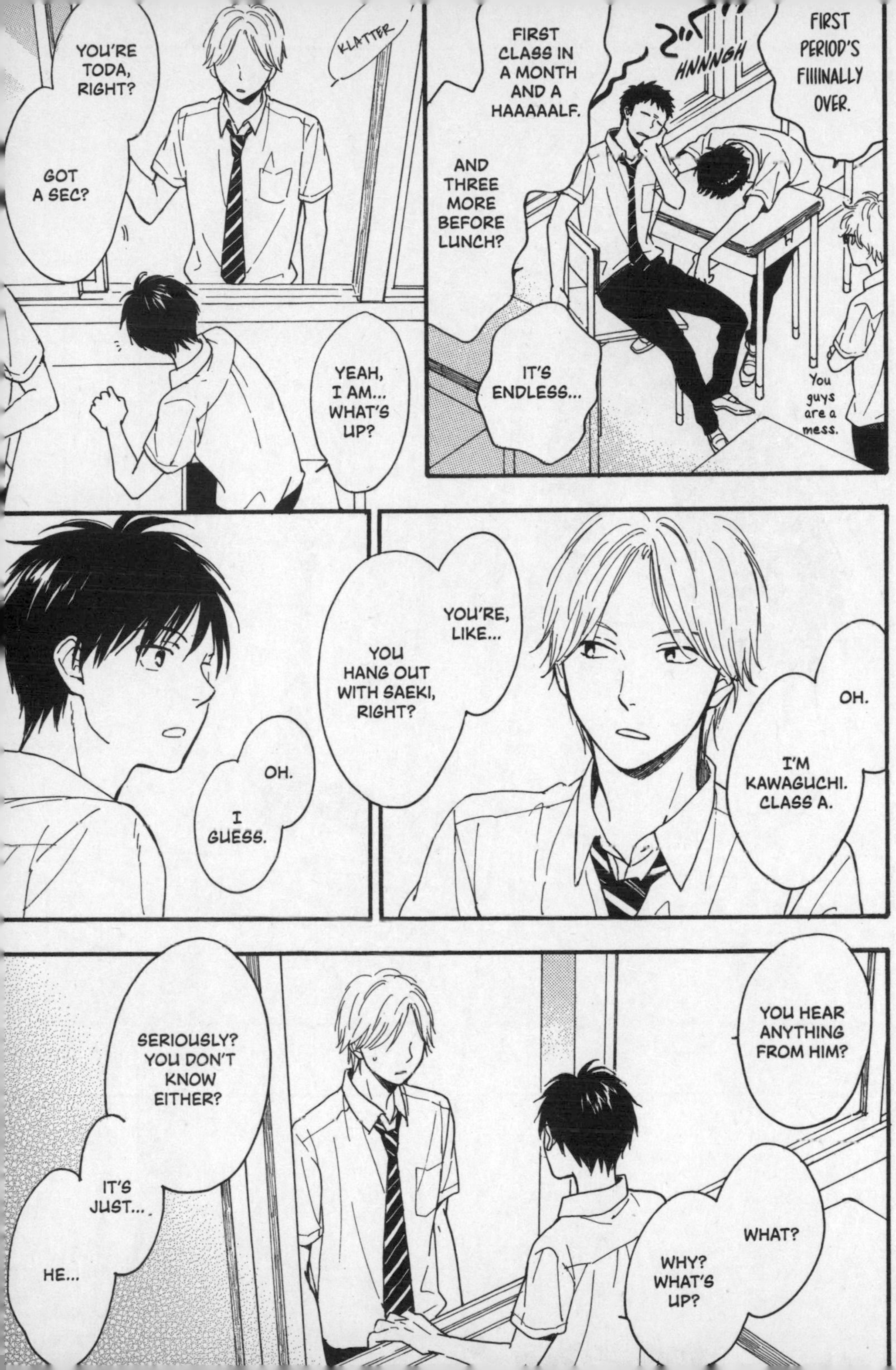
FIRST PERIOD'S FIIIINALLY OVER.
HNNNGH
FIRST CLASS IN A MONTH AND A HAAAAALF.
AND THREE MORE BEFORE LUNCH?
IT'S ENDLESS...
You guys are a mess.
KLATTER
YOU'RE TODA, RIGHT?
GOT A SEC?
YEAH, I AM... WHAT'S UP?
OH.
I'M KAWAGUCHI. CLASS A.
YOU'RE, LIKE...
YOU HANG OUT WITH SAEKI, RIGHT?
OH.
I GUESS.
YOU HEAR ANYTHING FROM HIM?
WHAT?
WHY? WHAT'S UP?
SERIOUSLY? YOU DON'T KNOW EITHER?
IT'S JUST...
HE...

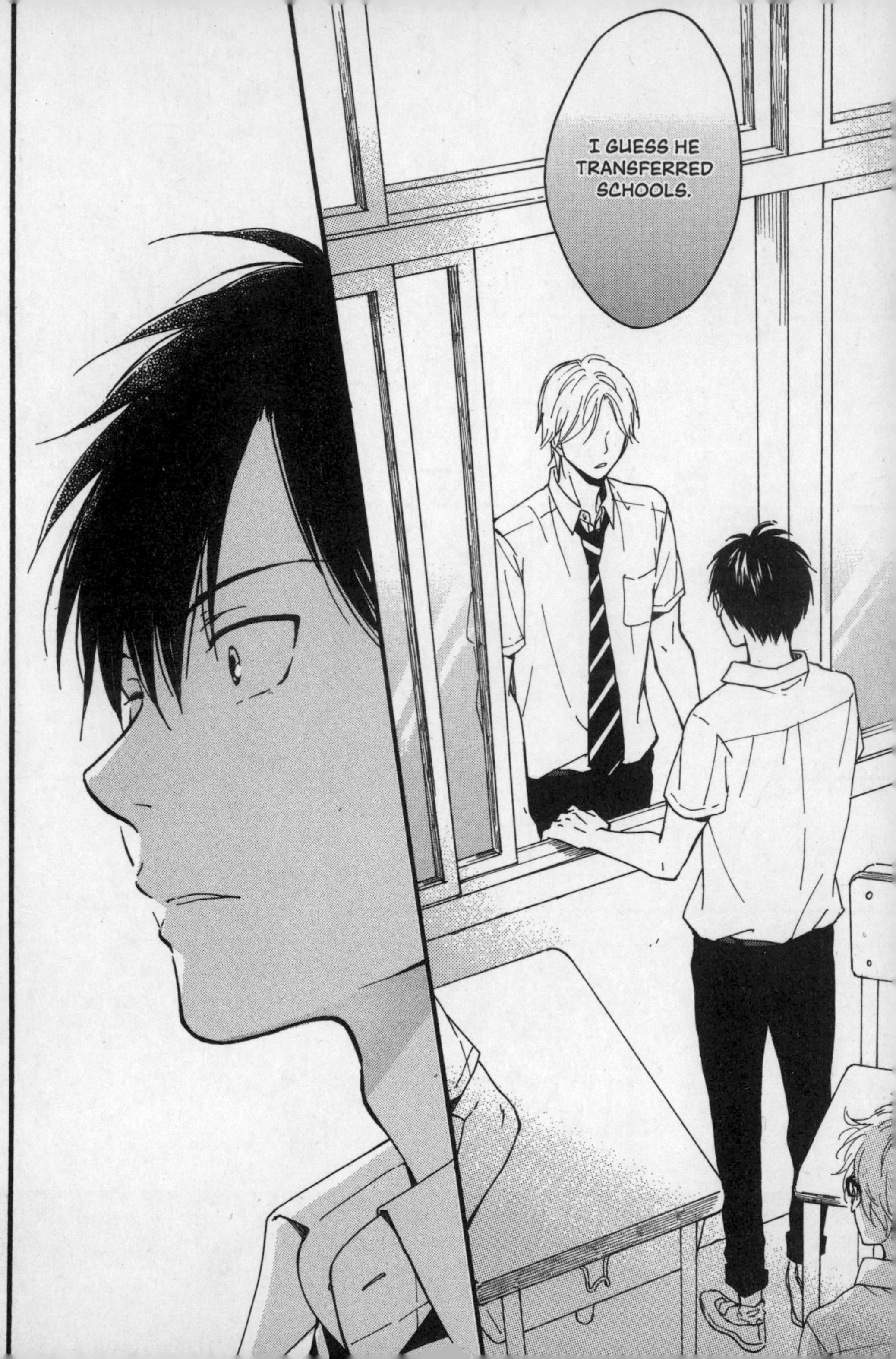
I GUESS HE TRANSFERRED SCHOOLS.

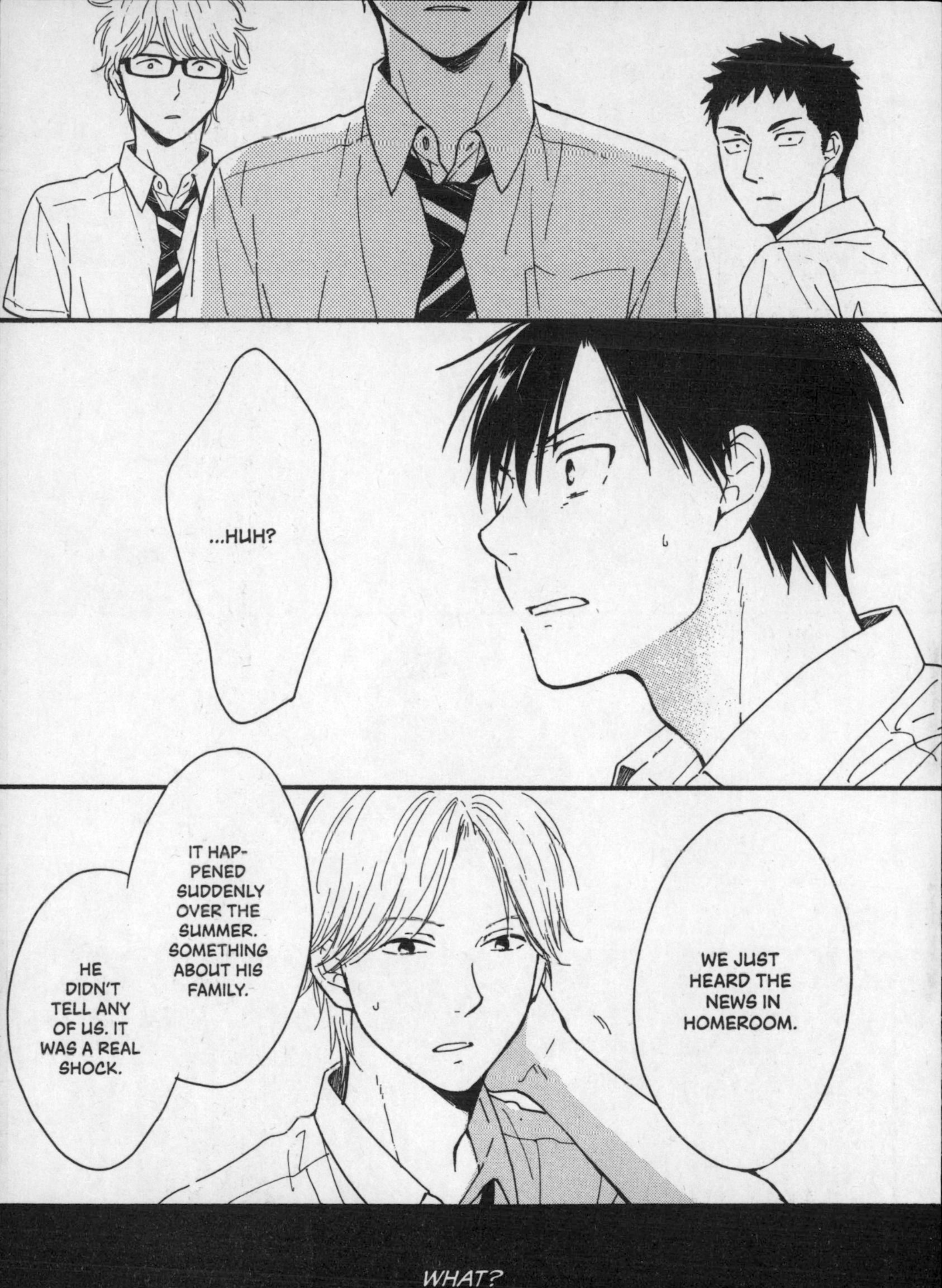
...HUH?
WE JUST HEARD THE NEWS IN HOMEROOM.
IT HAP-PENED SUDDENLY OVER THE SUMMER. SOMETHING ABOUT HIS FAMILY.
HE DIDN'T TELL ANY OF US. IT WAS A REAL SHOCK.
WHAT?

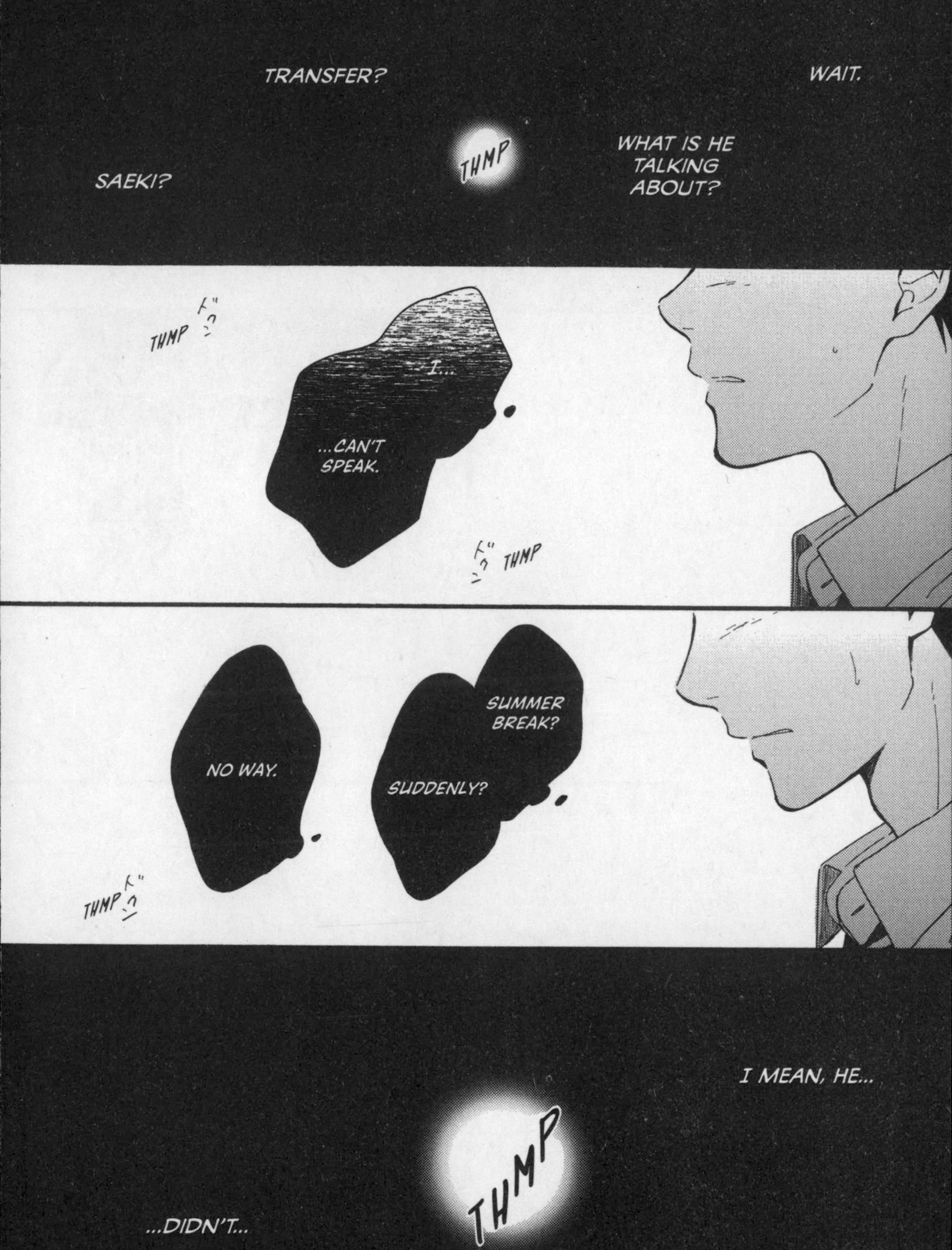
WAIT.
WHAT IS HE TALKING ABOUT?
TRANSFER?
THMP
SAEKI?
THMP ドッ
I...
...CAN'T SPEAK.
ドッ THMP
SUMMER BREAK?
SUDDENLY?
NO WAY.
THMP ドッ
I MEAN, HE...
THMP
...DIDN'T...

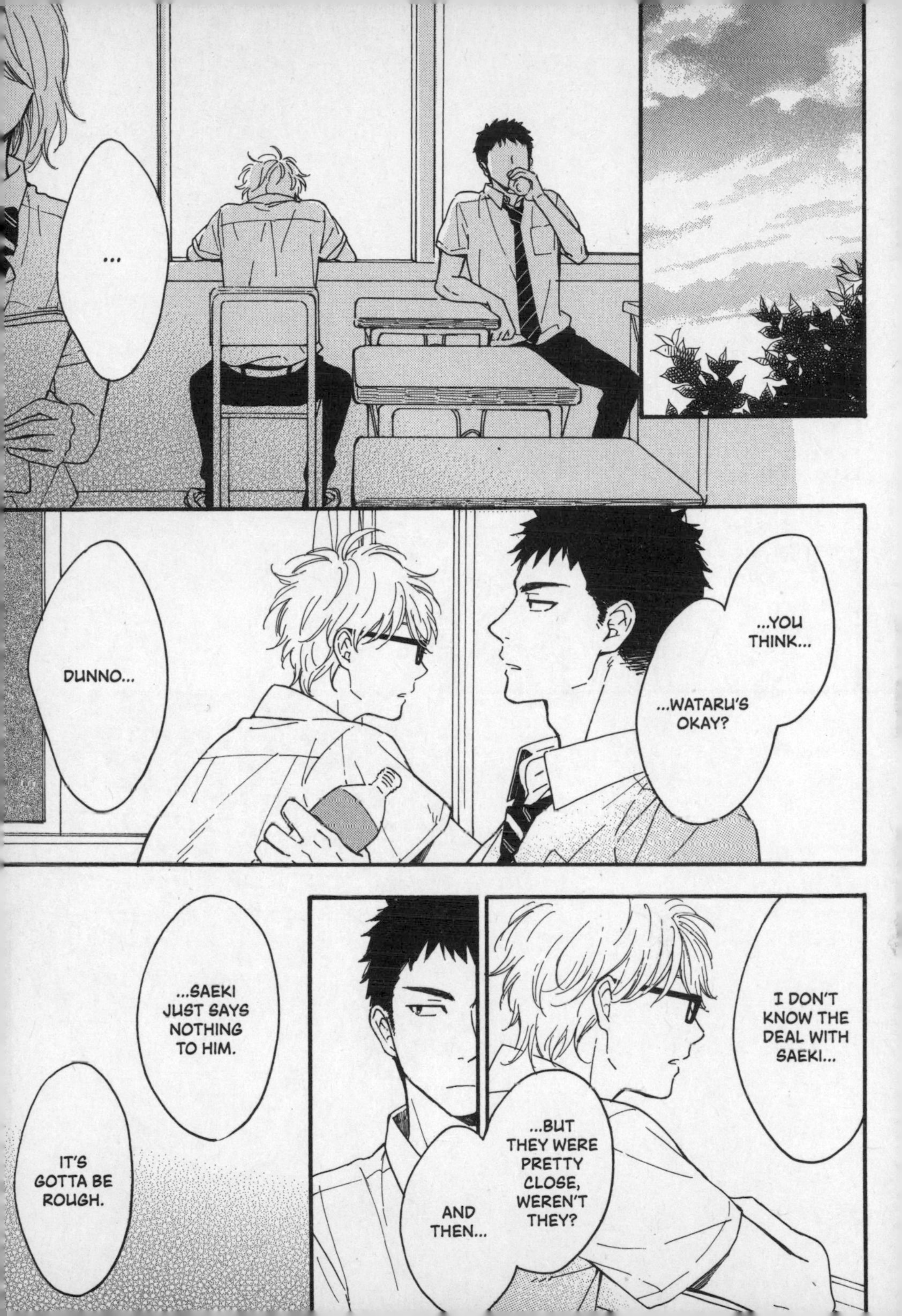
...
...YOU THINK... ...WATARU'S OKAY?
DUNNO...
I DON'T KNOW THE DEAL WITH SAEKI...
...BUT THEY WERE PRETTY CLOSE, WEREN'T THEY?
AND THEN...
...SAEKI JUST SAYS NOTHING TO HIM.
IT'S GOTTA BE ROUGH.

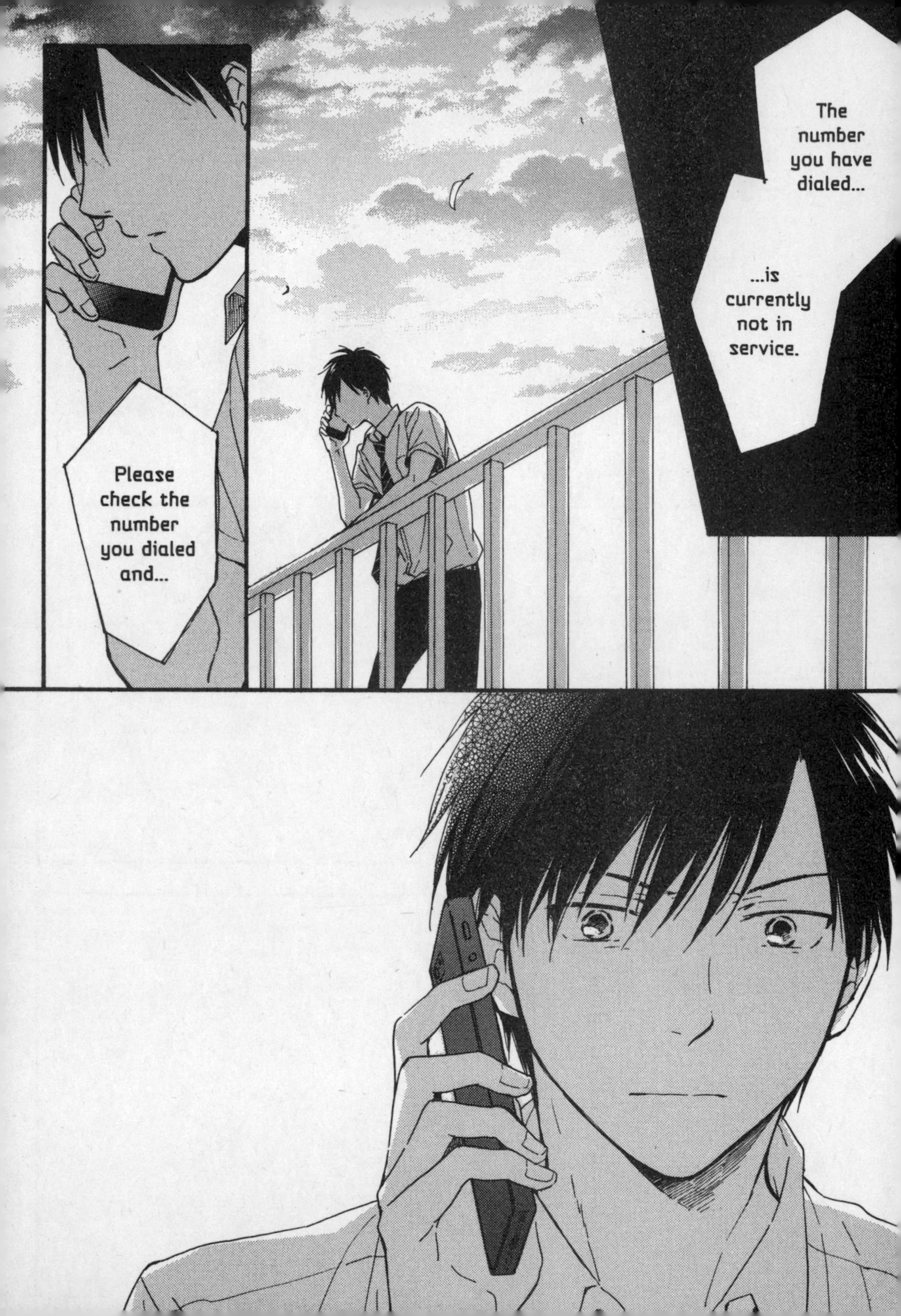
The number you have dialed...
...is currently not in service.
Please check the number you dialed and...

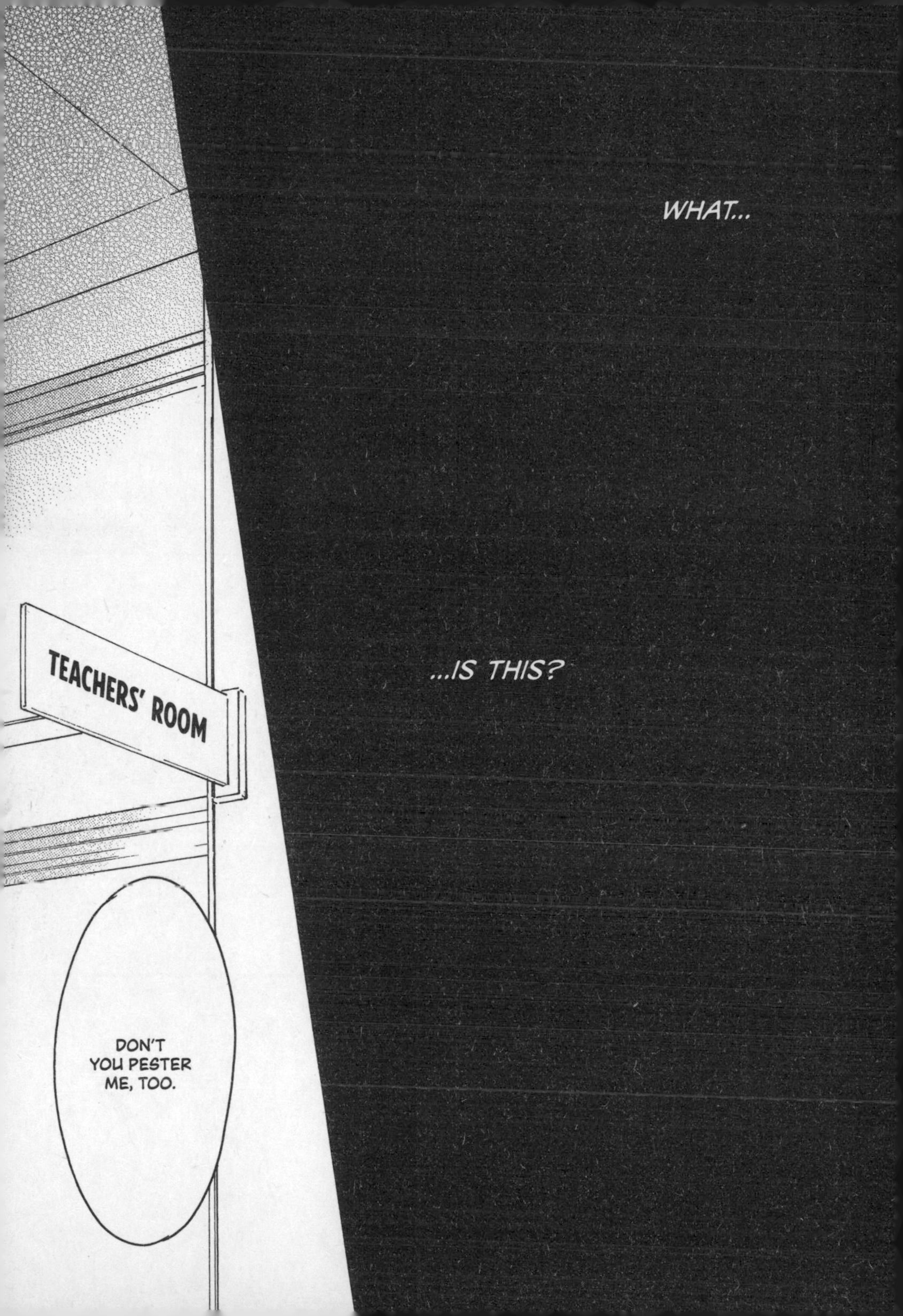
WHAT...
...IS THIS?
TEACHERS' ROOM
DON'T YOU PESTER ME, TOO.

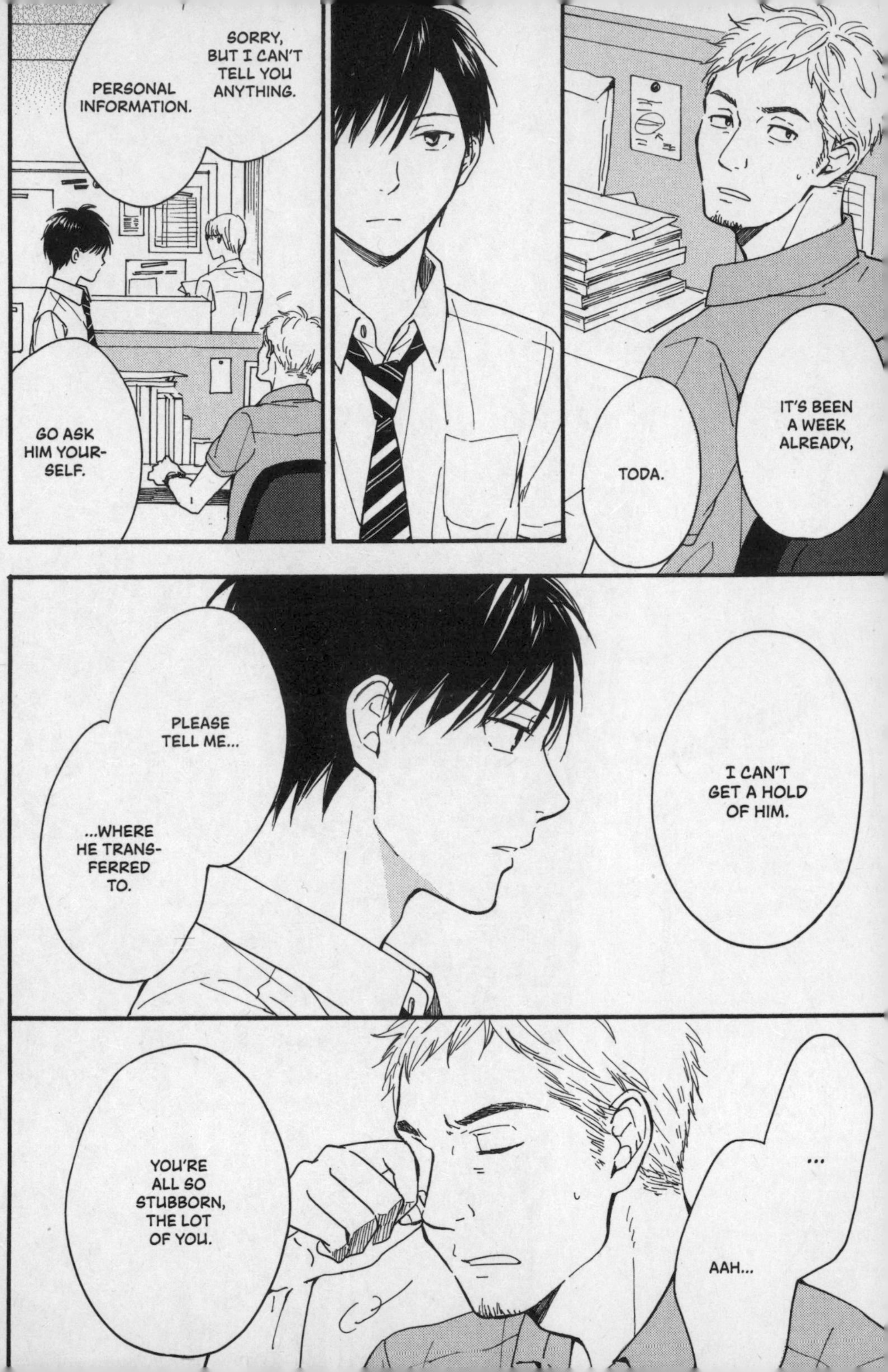
IT'S BEEN A WEEK ALREADY,
TODA.
SORRY, BUT I CAN'T TELL YOU ANYTHING.
PERSONAL INFORMATION.
GO ASK HIM YOUR-SELF.
I CAN'T GET A HOLD OF HIM.
PLEASE TELL ME...
...WHERE HE TRANS-FERRED TO.
...
AAH...
YOU'RE ALL SO STUBBORN, THE LOT OF YOU.

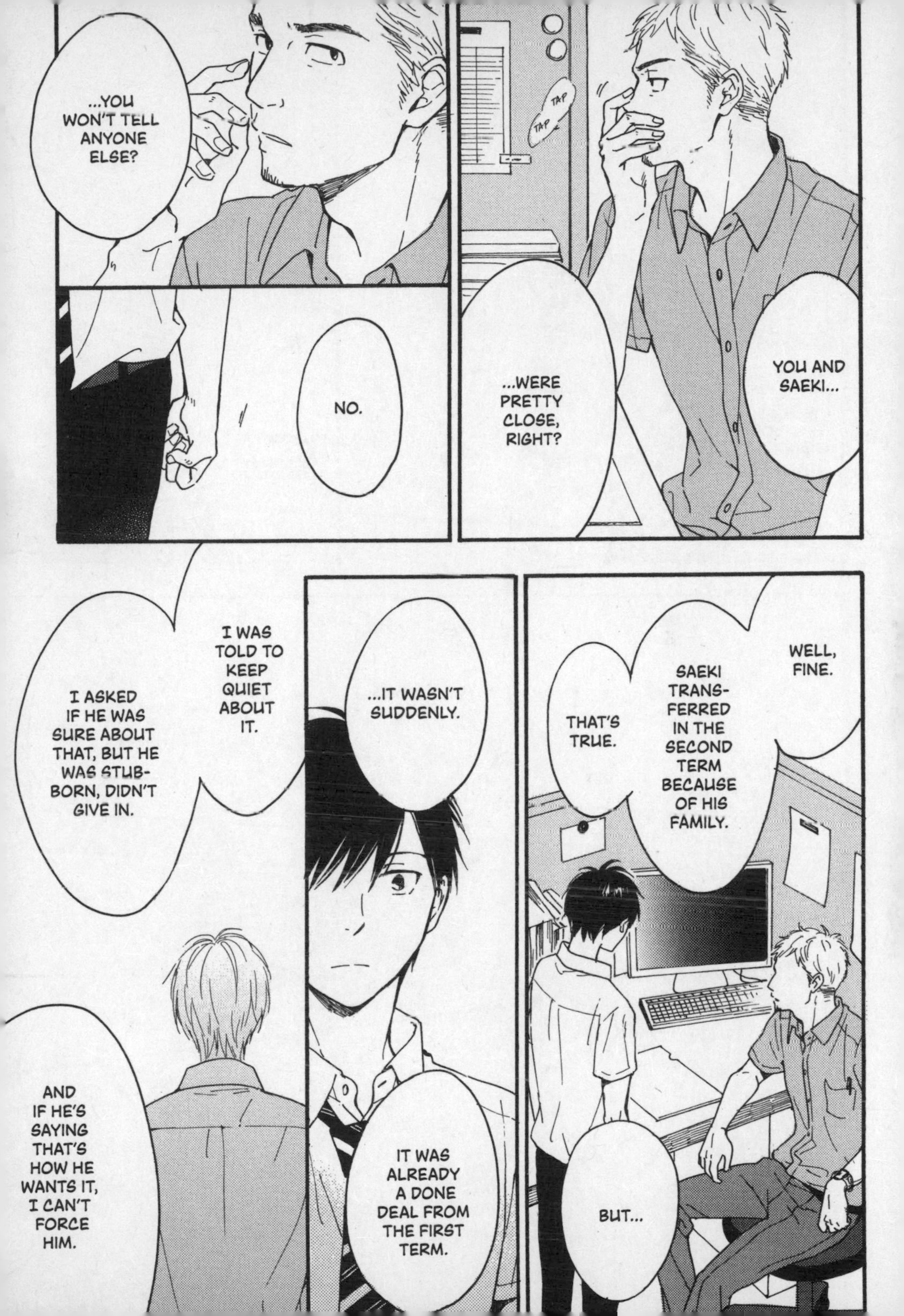
TAP
TAP
YOU AND SAEKI...
...WERE PRETTY CLOSE, RIGHT?
...YOU WON'T TELL ANYONE ELSE?
NO.
WELL, FINE.
SAEKI TRANSFERRED IN THE SECOND TERM BECAUSE OF HIS FAMILY.
THAT'S TRUE.
BUT...
...IT WASN'T SUDDENLY.
IT WAS ALREADY A DONE DEAL FROM THE FIRST TERM.
I WAS TOLD TO KEEP QUIET ABOUT IT.
I ASKED IF HE WAS SURE ABOUT THAT, BUT HE WAS STUBBORN, DIDN'T GIVE IN.
AND IF HE'S SAYING THAT'S HOW HE WANTS IT, I CAN'T FORCE HIM.

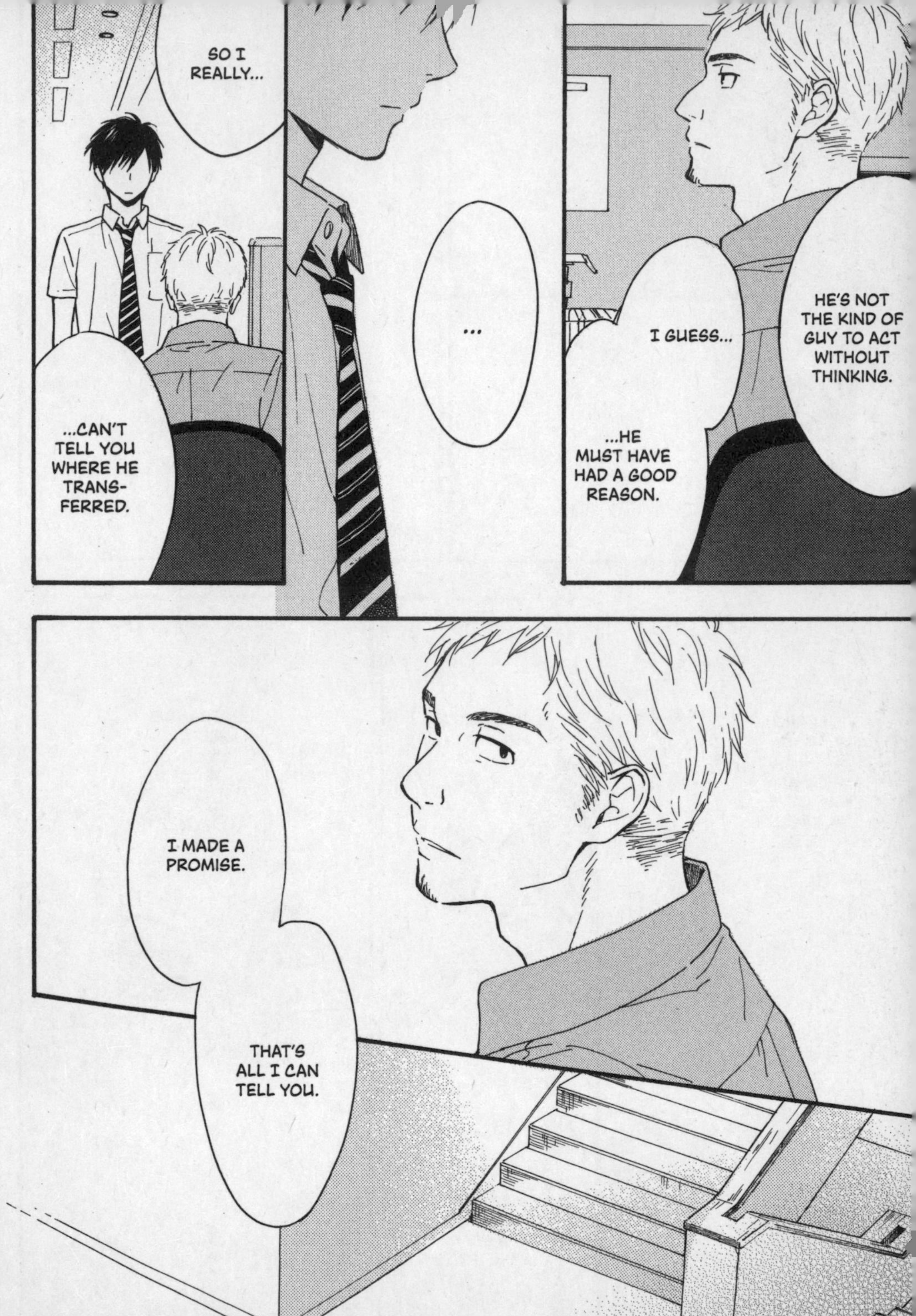
HE'S NOT THE KIND OF GUY TO ACT WITHOUT THINKING.
I GUESS...
...HE MUST HAVE HAD A GOOD REASON.
...
SO I REALLY...
...CAN'T TELL YOU WHERE HE TRANS-FERRED.
I MADE A PROMISE.
THAT'S ALL I CAN TELL YOU.

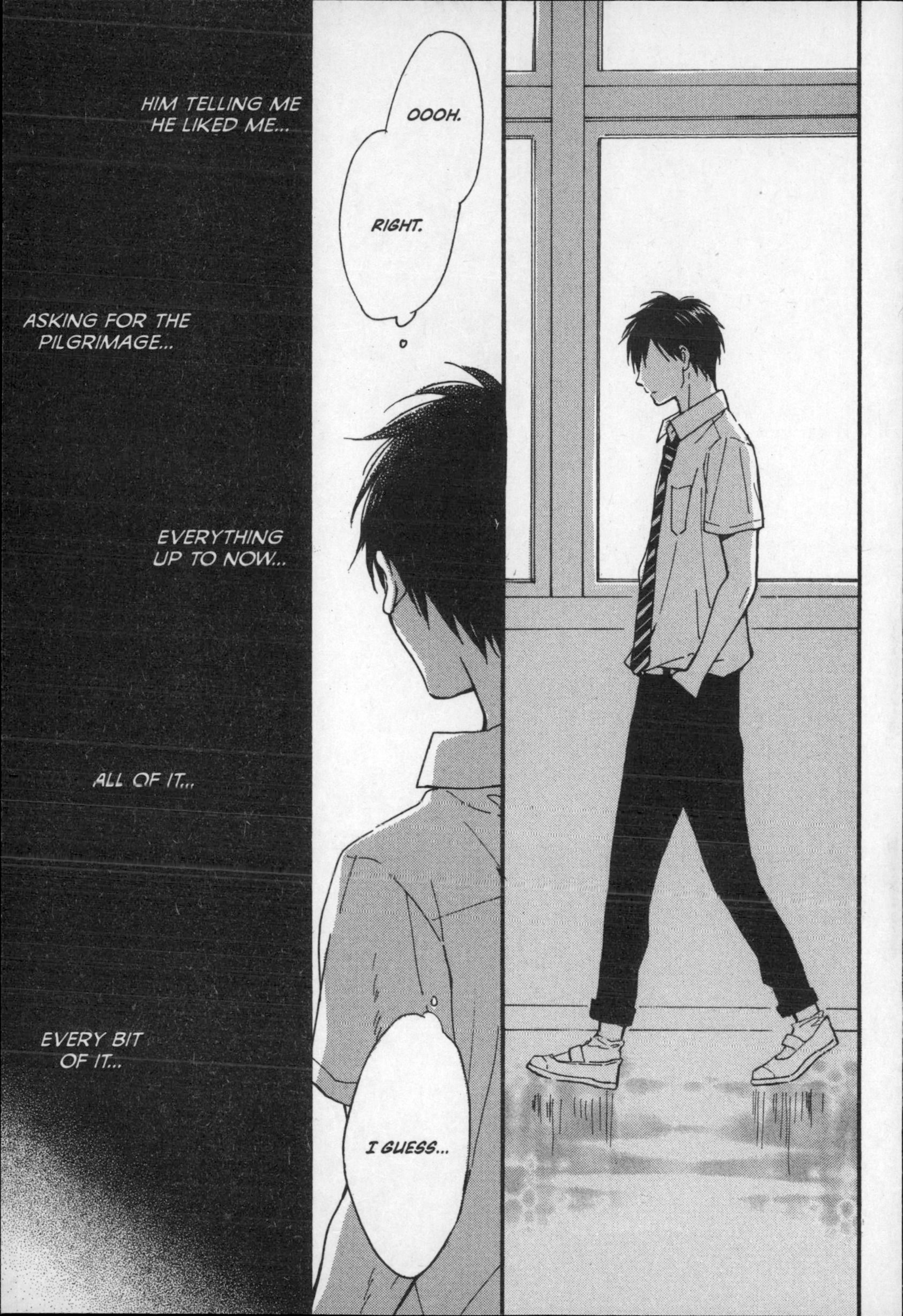
OOOH.
RIGHT.
I GUESS...
HIM TELLING ME HE LIKED ME...
ASKING FOR THE PILGRIMAGE...
EVERYTHING UP TO NOW...
ALL OF IT...
EVERY BIT OF IT...

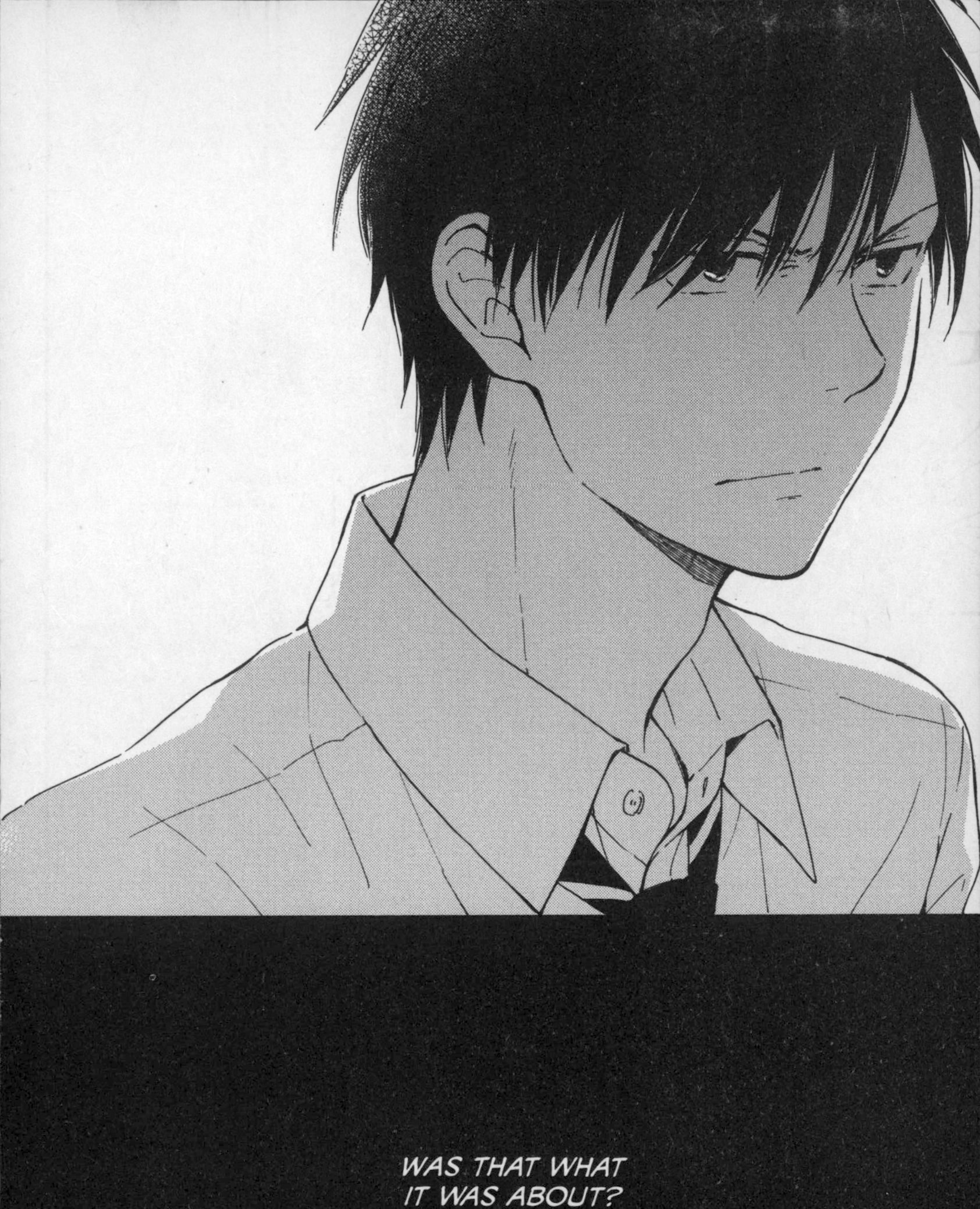
WAS THAT WHAT
IT WAS ABOUT?

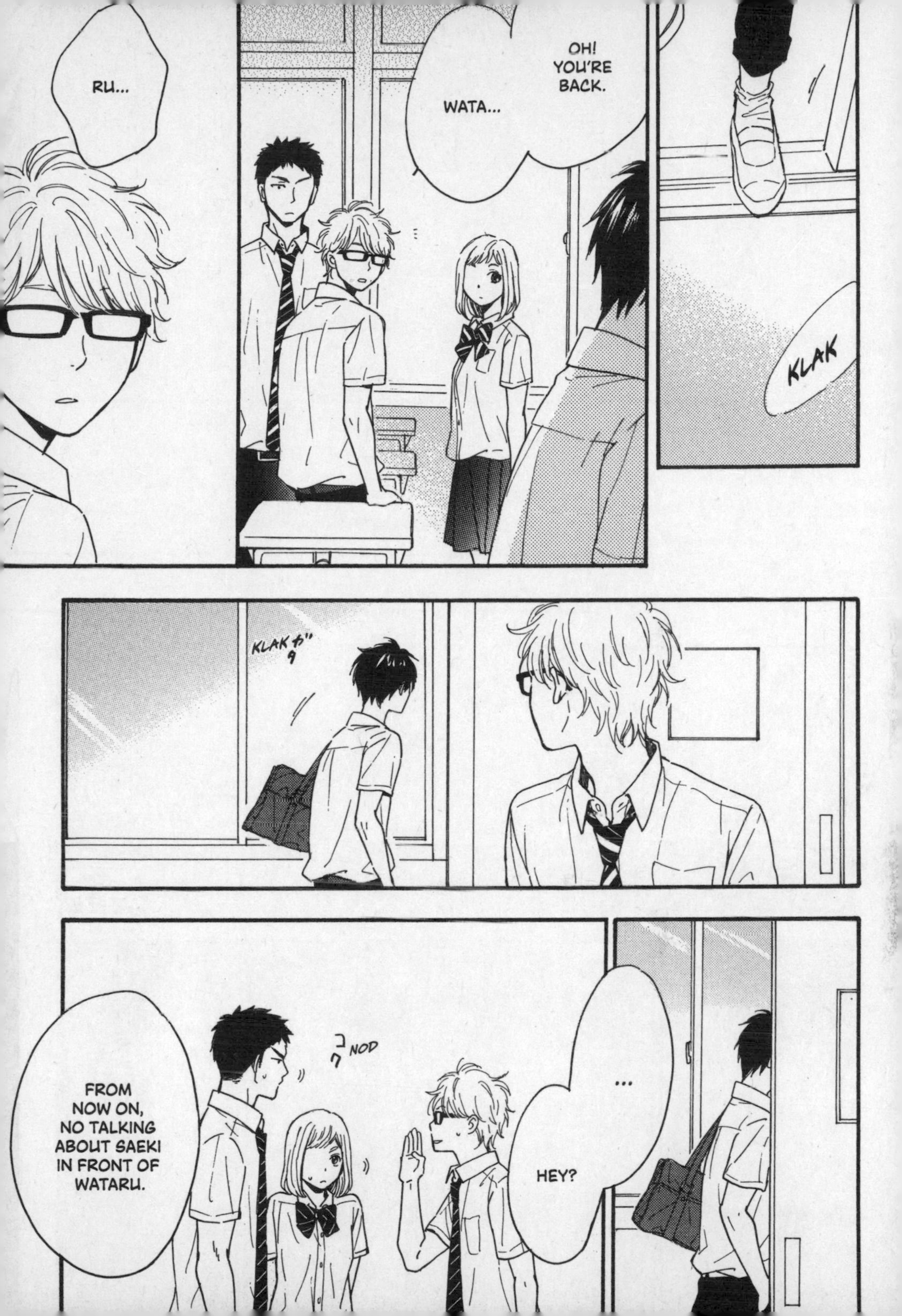
KLAK
OH! YOU'RE BACK.
WATA...
RU...
KLAK
...
HEY?
NOD
FROM NOW ON, NO TALKING ABOUT SAEKI IN FRONT OF WATARU.

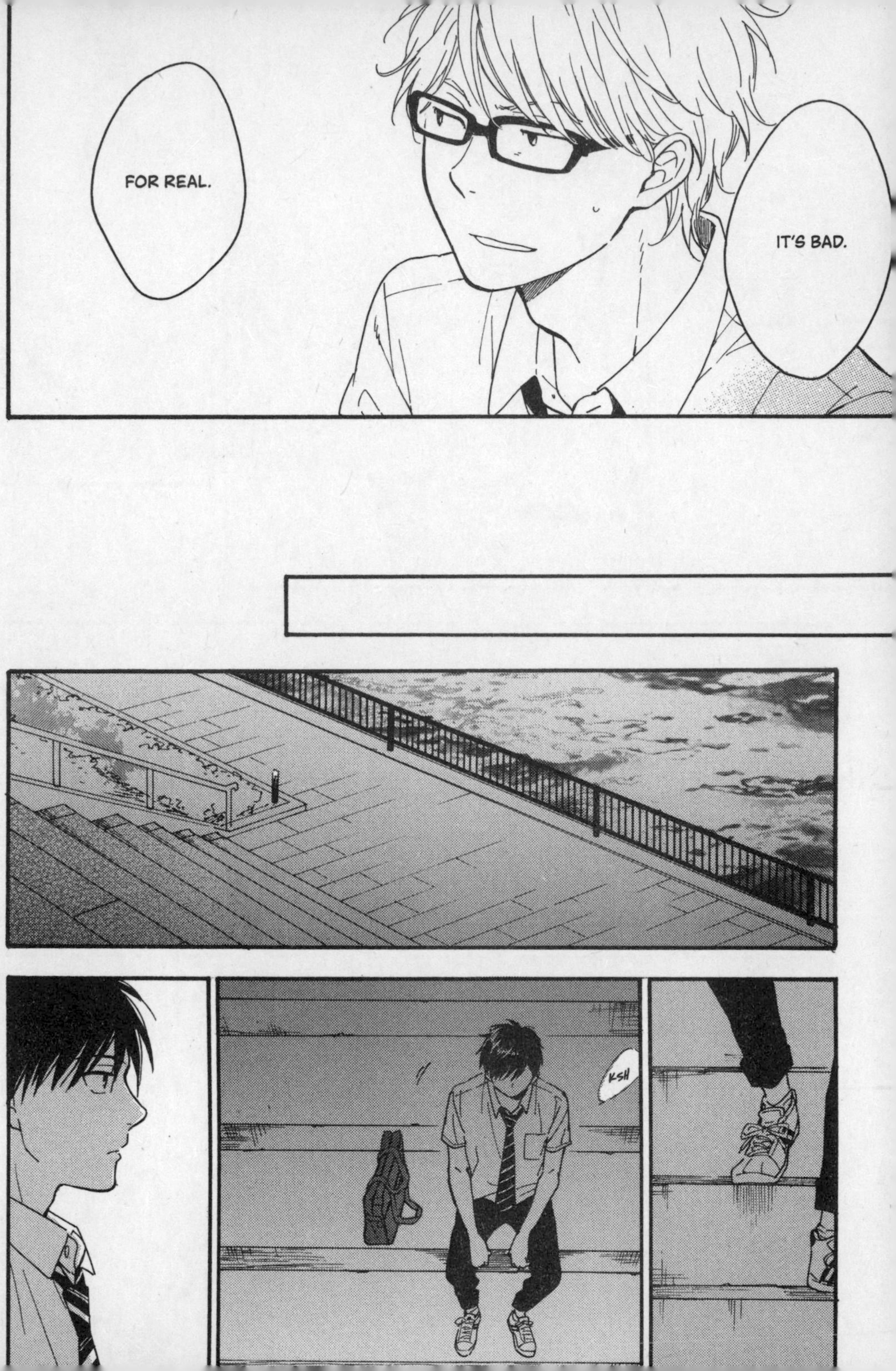
IT'S BAD.
FOR REAL.
KSH

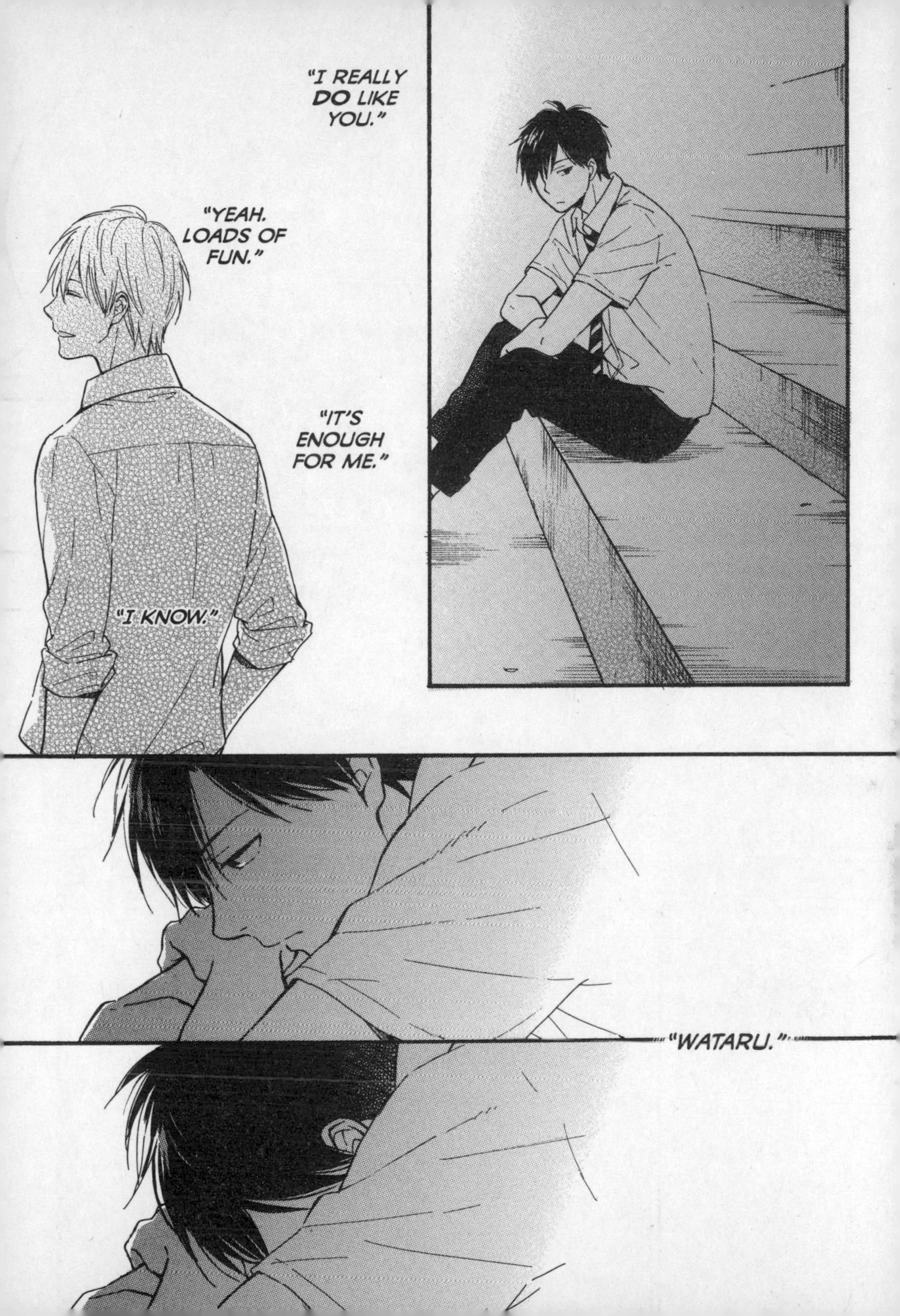
"I REALLY DO LIKE YOU."
"YEAH. LOADS OF FUN."
"IT'S ENOUGH FOR ME."
"I KNOW."
"WATARU."

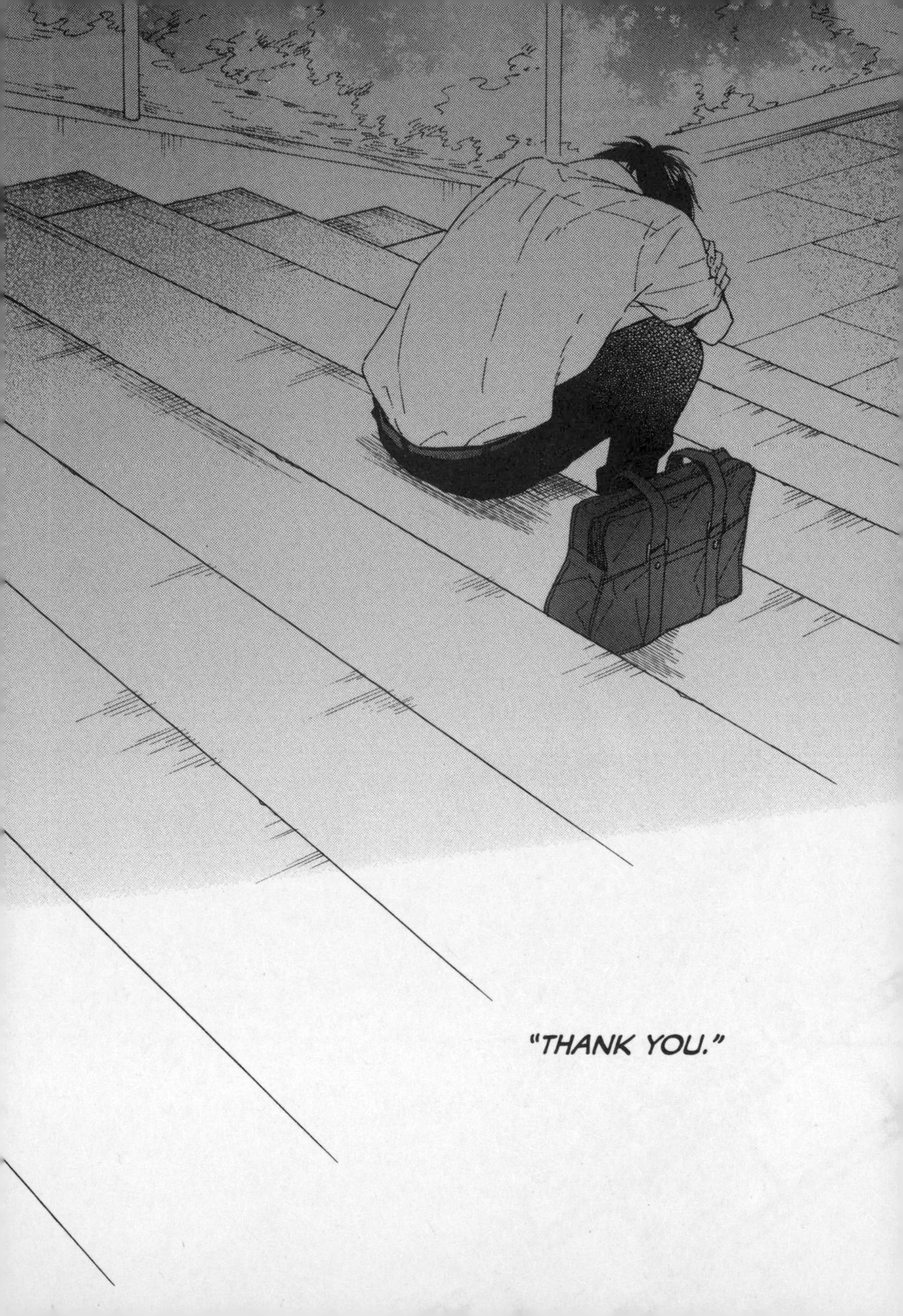
"THANK YOU."

MY SUMMER OF YOU

MY SUMMER OF YOU

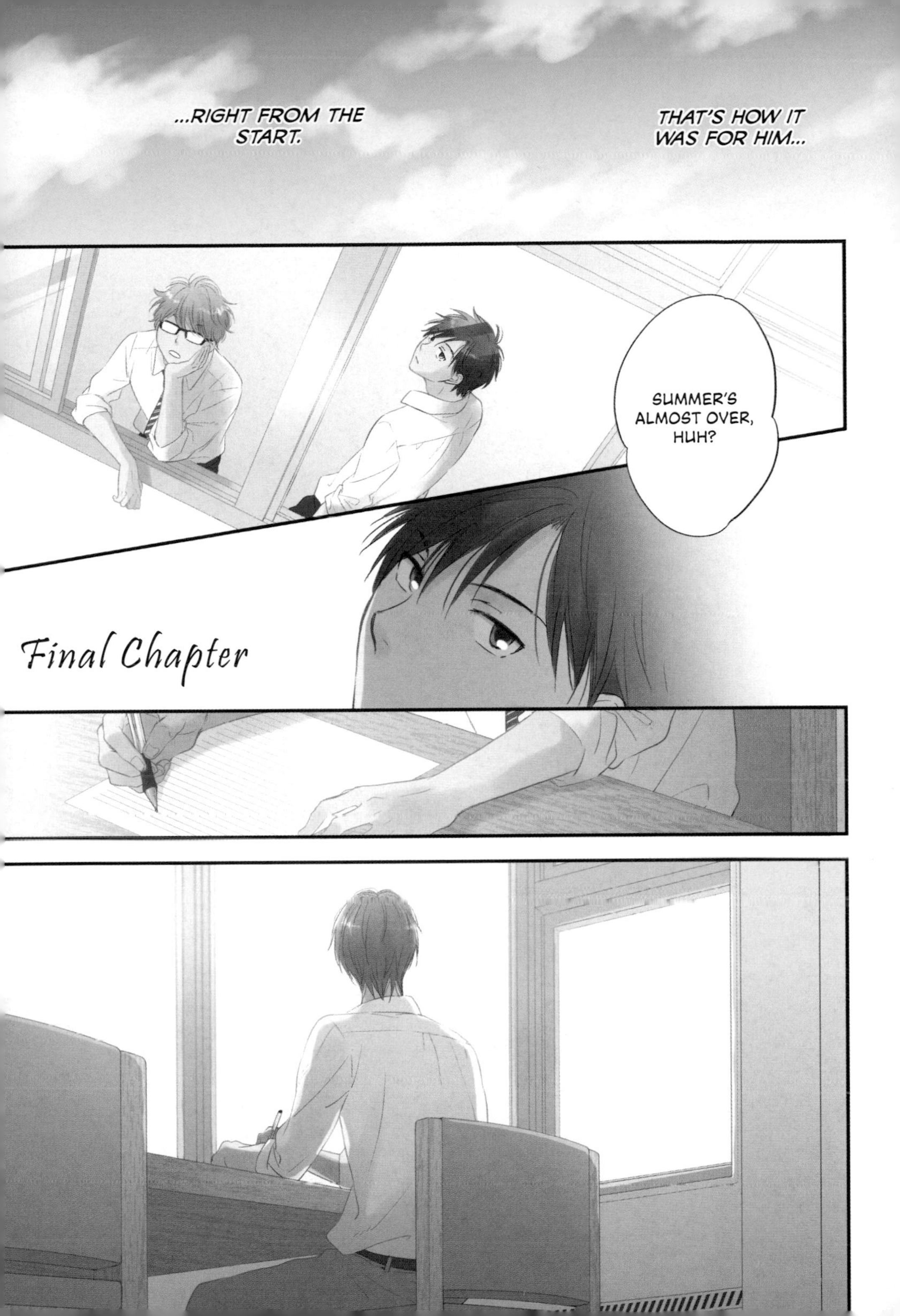
THAT'S HOW IT WAS FOR HIM...
...RIGHT FROM THE START.
SUMMER'S ALMOST OVER, HUH?
Final Chapter

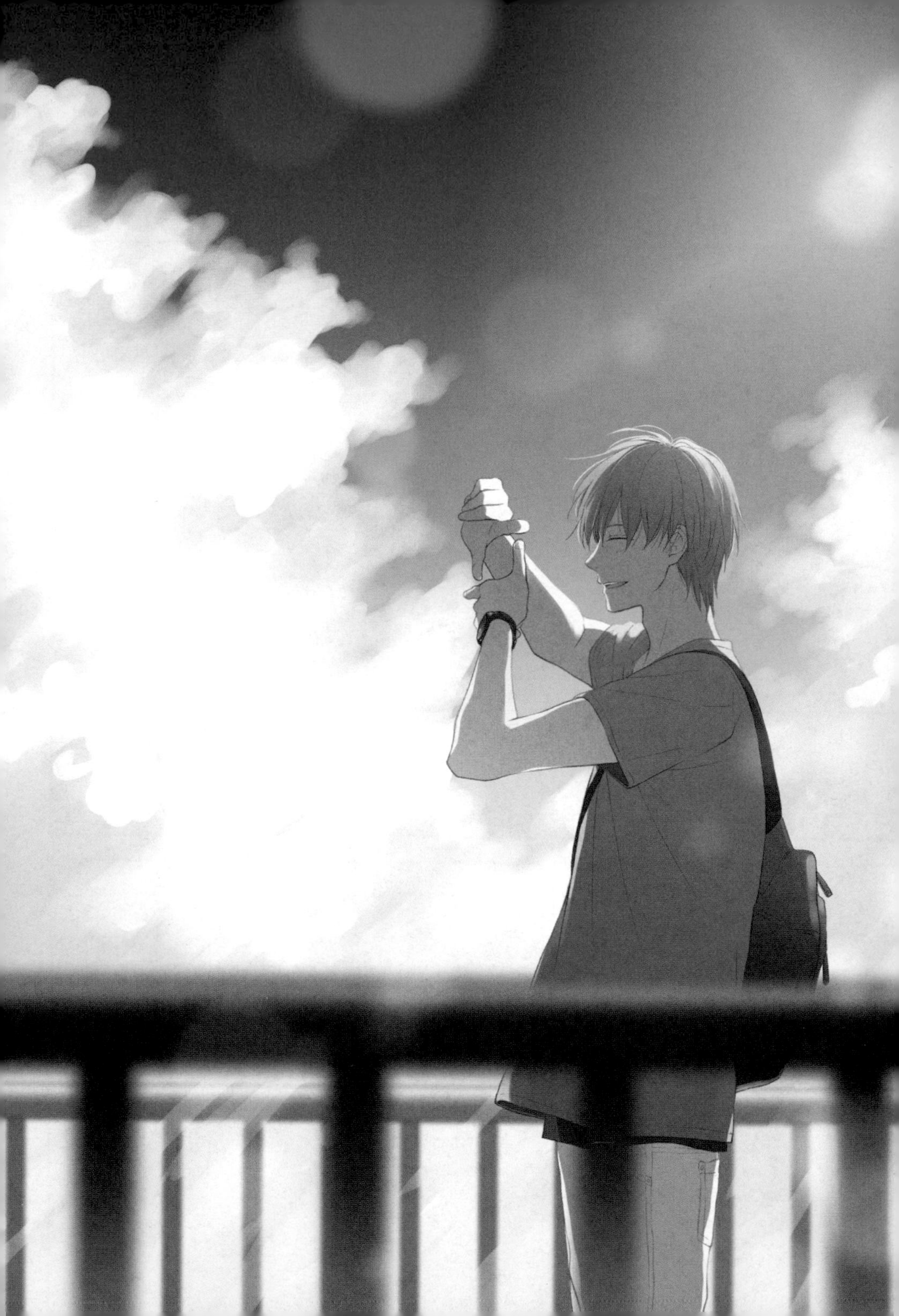

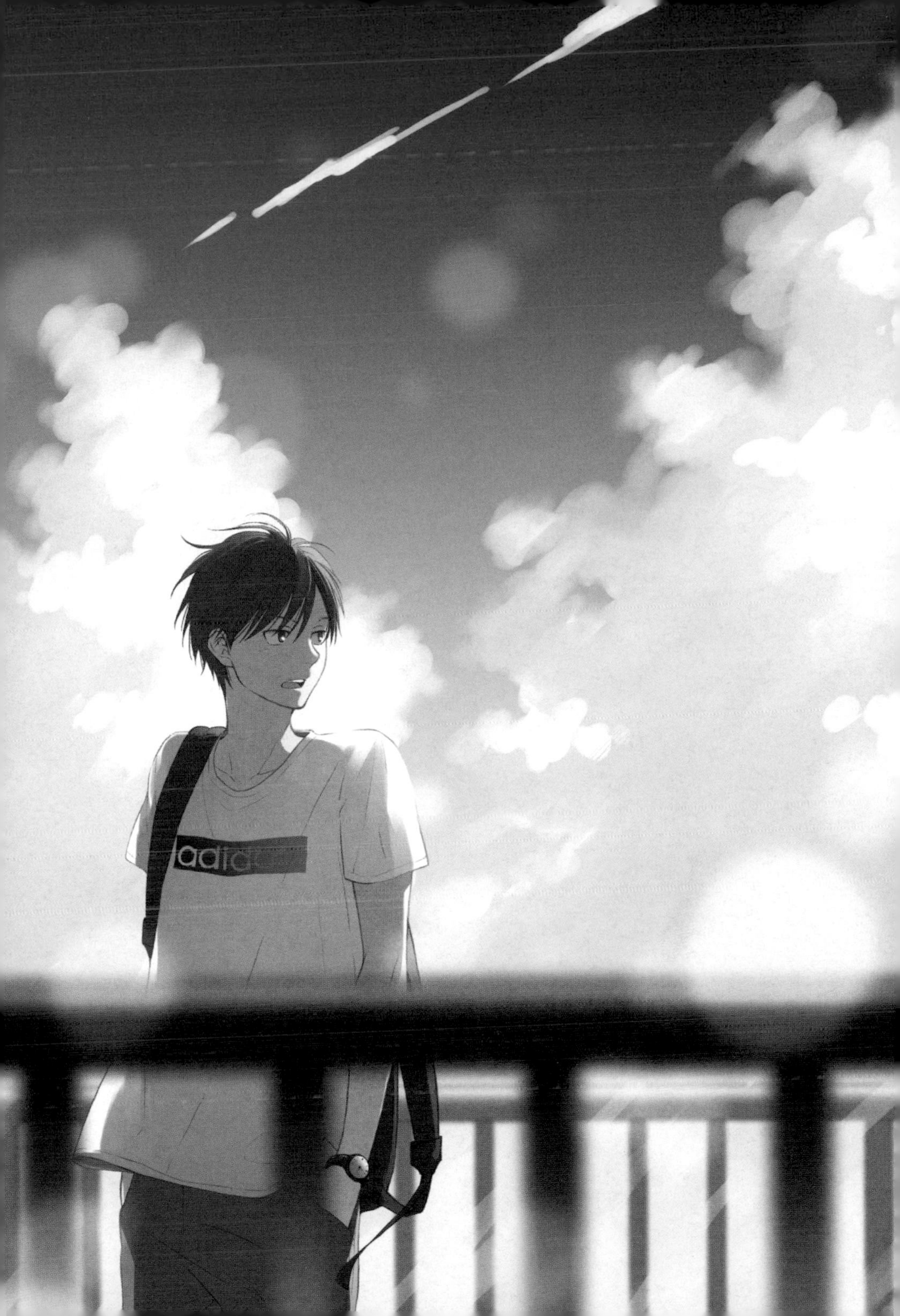

MY SUMMER OF YOU

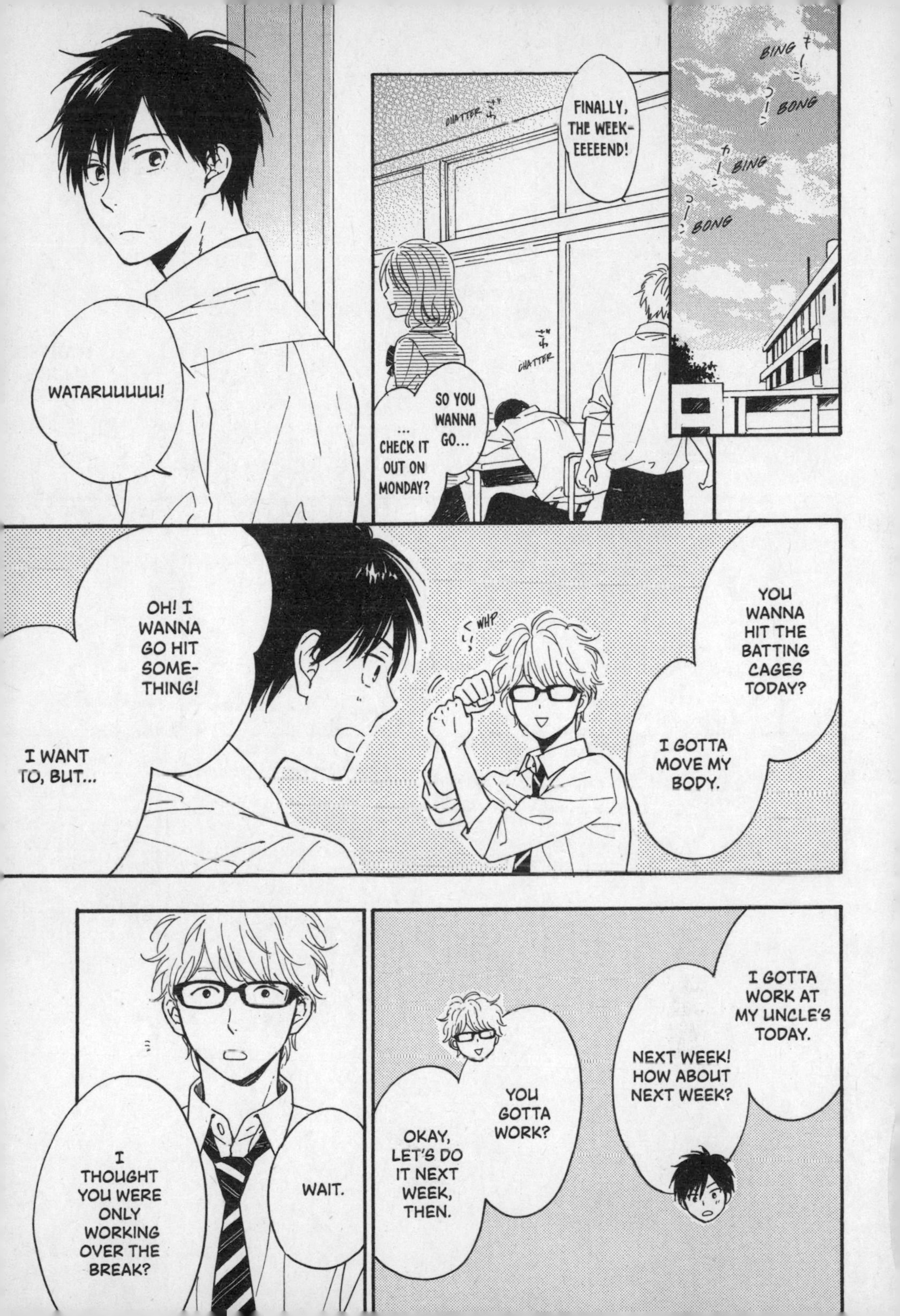
BING
BONG
BING
BONG
CHATTER
FINALLY, THE WEEK-EEEEEND!
CHATTER
SO YOU WANNA GO...
... CHECK IT OUT ON MONDAY?
WATARUUUUU!
YOU WANNA HIT THE BATTING CAGES TODAY?
I GOTTA MOVE MY BODY.
WHP
OH! I WANNA GO HIT SOME-THING!
I WANT TO, BUT...
I GOTTA WORK AT MY UNCLE'S TODAY.
NEXT WEEK! HOW ABOUT NEXT WEEK?
YOU GOTTA WORK?
OKAY, LET'S DO IT NEXT WEEK, THEN.
WAIT.
I THOUGHT YOU WERE ONLY WORKING OVER THE BREAK?

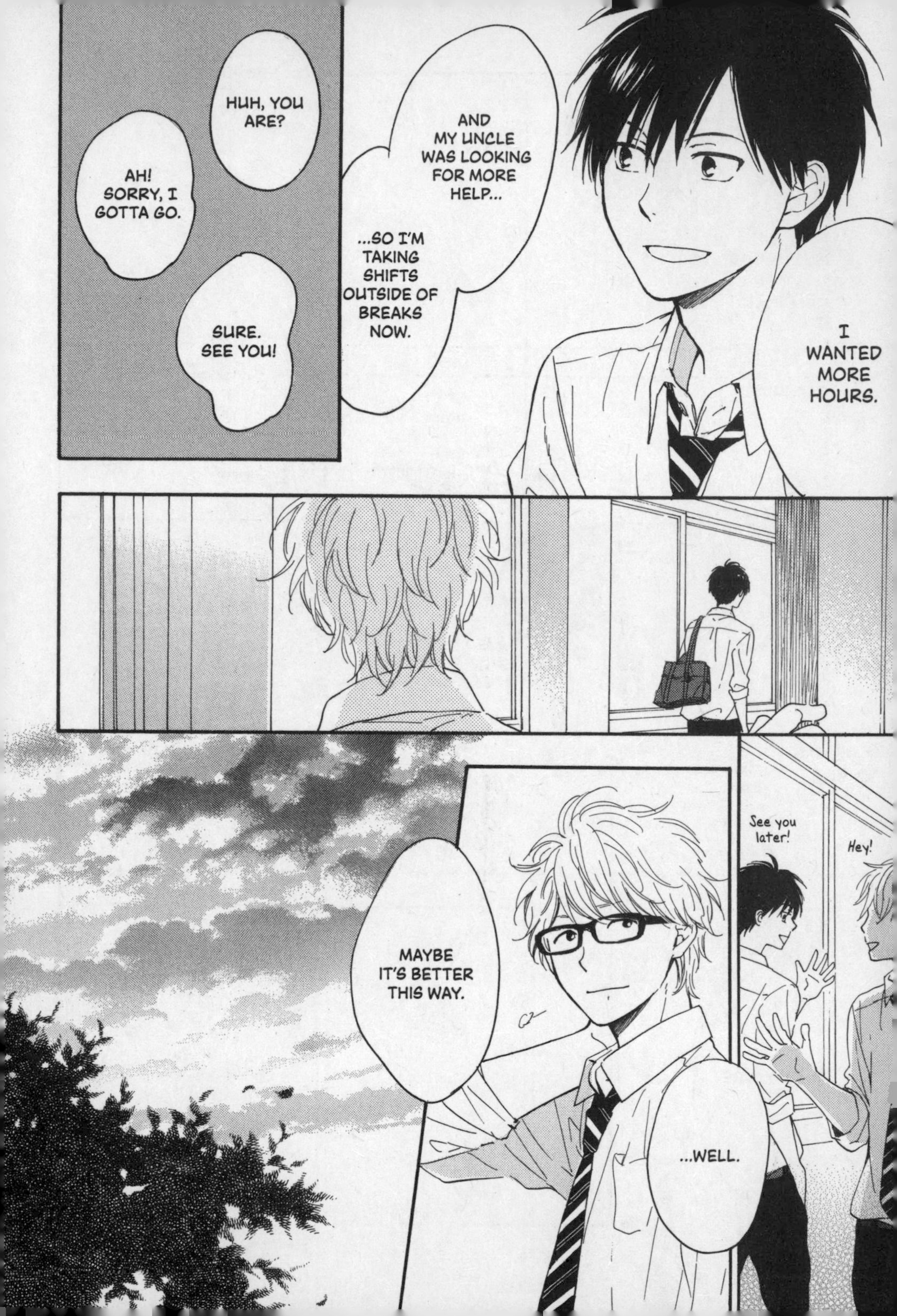
I WANTED MORE HOURS.
AND MY UNCLE WAS LOOKING FOR MORE HELP...
...SO I'M TAKING SHIFTS OUTSIDE OF BREAKS NOW.
HUH, YOU ARE?
AH! SORRY, I GOTTA GO.
SURE. SEE YOU!
Hey!
See you later!
...WELL.
MAYBE IT'S BETTER THIS WAY.

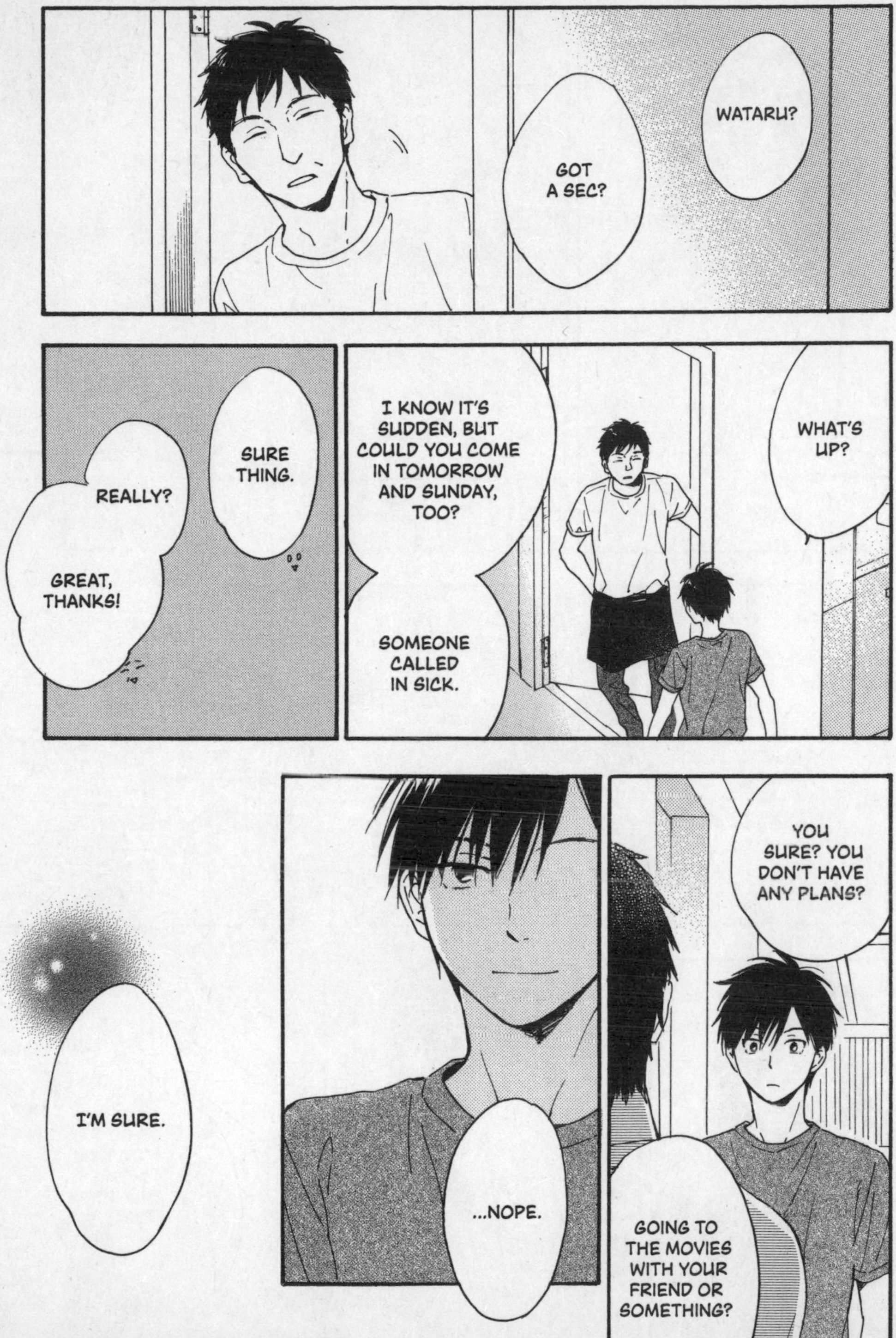
WATARU?
GOT A SEC?
WHAT'S UP?
I KNOW IT'S SUDDEN, BUT COULD YOU COME IN TOMORROW AND SUNDAY, TOO?
SOMEONE CALLED IN SICK.
SURE THING.
REALLY?
GREAT, THANKS!
YOU SURE? YOU DON'T HAVE ANY PLANS?
GOING TO THE MOVIES WITH YOUR FRIEND OR SOMETHING?
...NOPE.
I'M SURE.

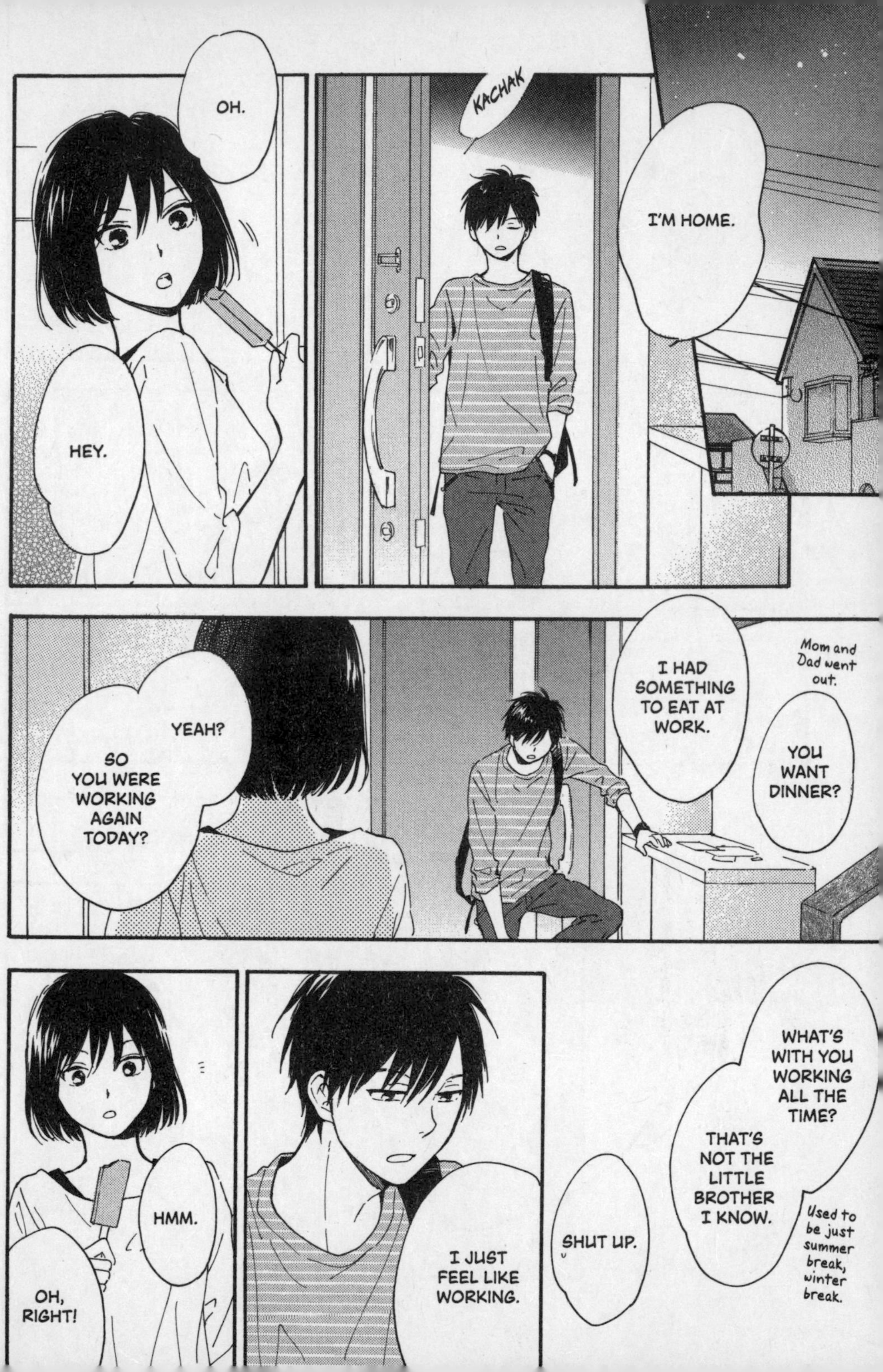
I'M HOME.
KACHAK
OH.
HEY.
Mom and Dad went out.
YOU WANT DINNER?
I HAD SOMETHING TO EAT AT WORK.
YEAH?
SO YOU WERE WORKING AGAIN TODAY?
WHAT'S WITH YOU WORKING ALL THE TIME?
THAT'S NOT THE LITTLE BROTHER I KNOW.
Used to be just summer break, winter break.
SHUT UP.
I JUST FEEL LIKE WORKING.
HMM.
OH, RIGHT!

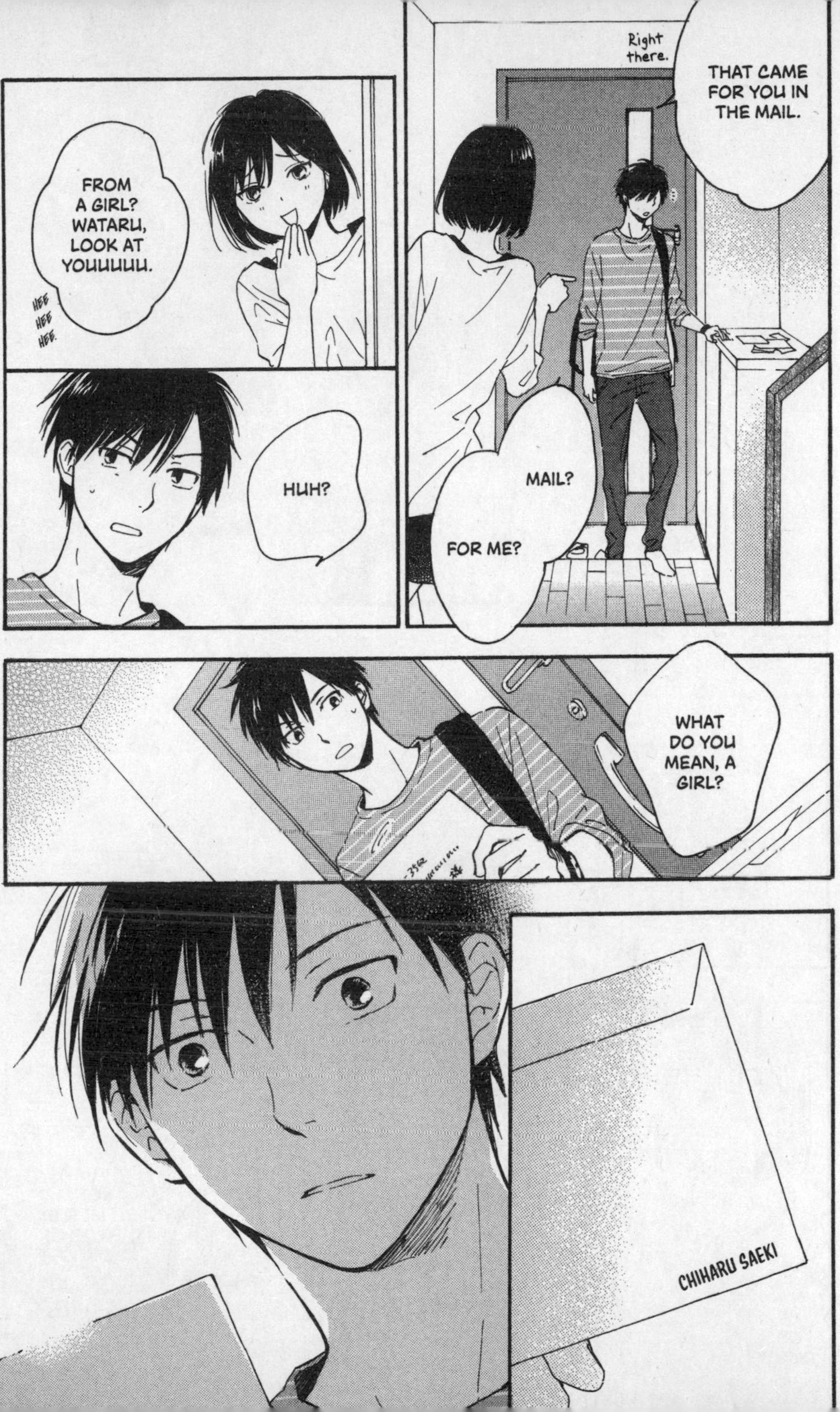
THAT CAME FOR YOU IN THE MAIL.
Right there.
MAIL?
FOR ME?
FROM A GIRL? WATARU, LOOK AT YOUUUUU.
HEE HEE HEE.
HUH?
WHAT DO YOU MEAN, A GIRL?
CHIHARU SAEKI

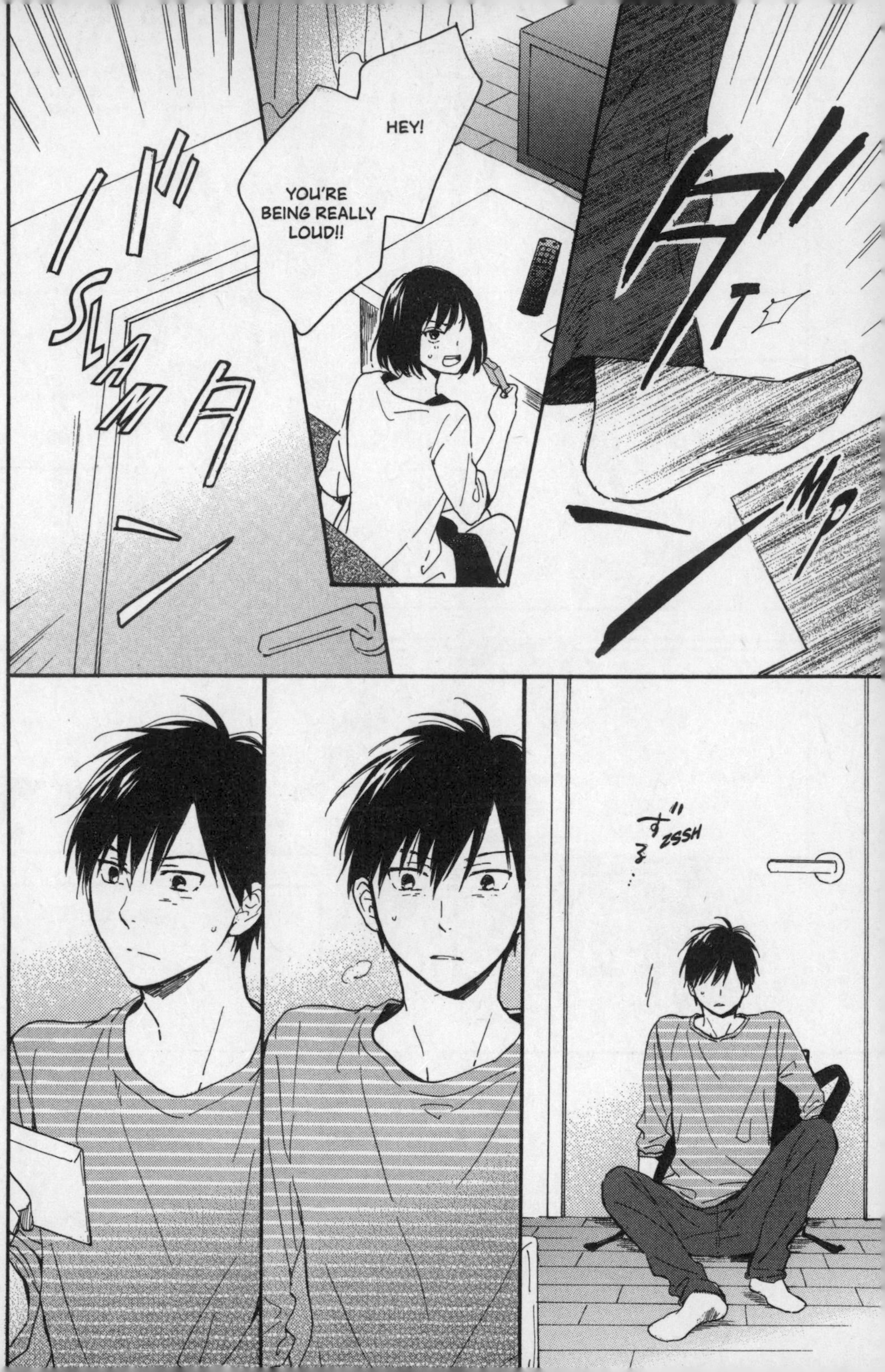
ダッ
T
MP
HEY!
YOU'RE BEING REALLY LOUD!!
バタン
SLAM
ずる…
ZSSH

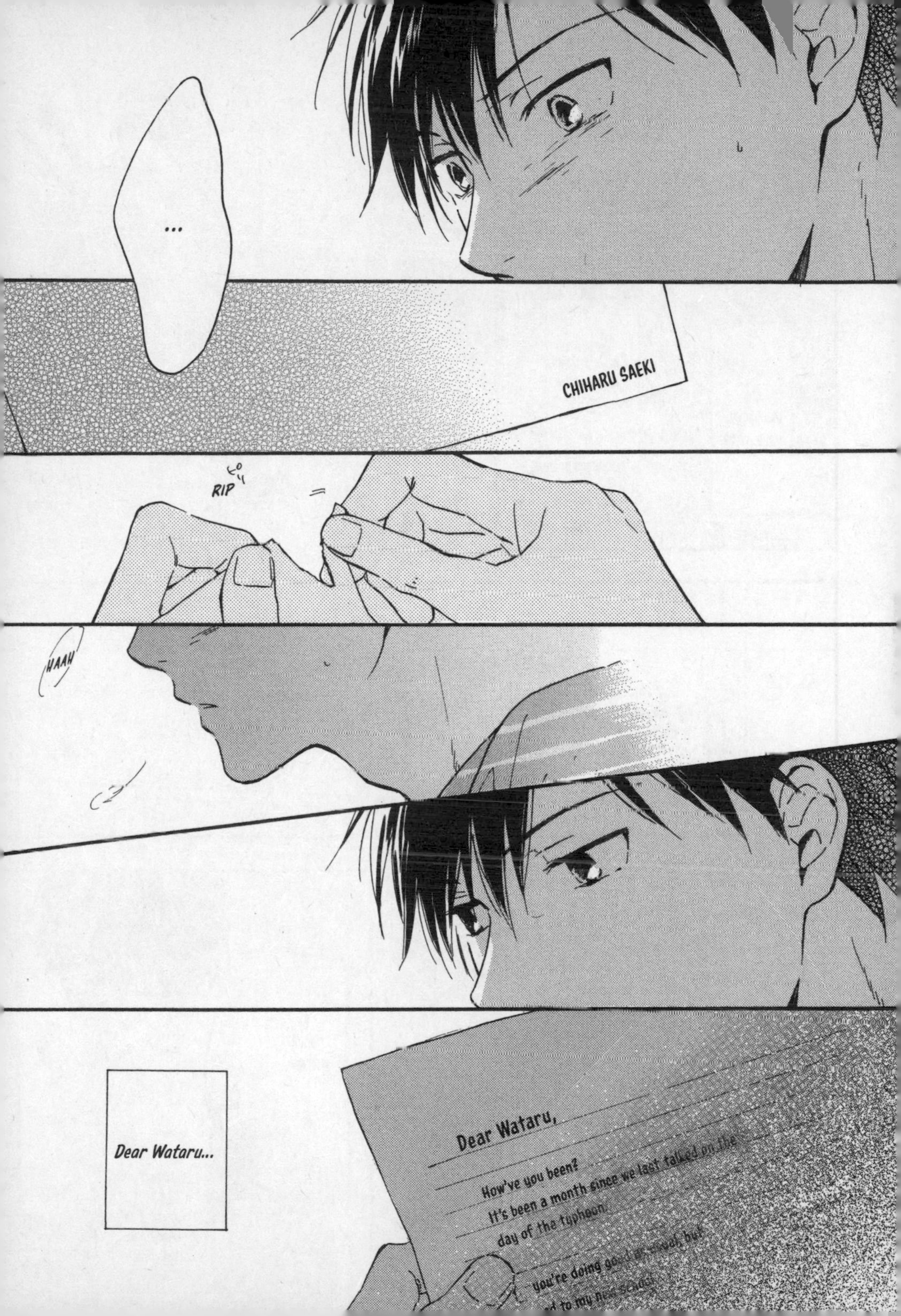
...
CHIHARU SAEKI
RIP
HAAH
Dear Wataru,
How've you been?
It's been a month since we last talked on the
day of the typhoon.
Dear Wataru...

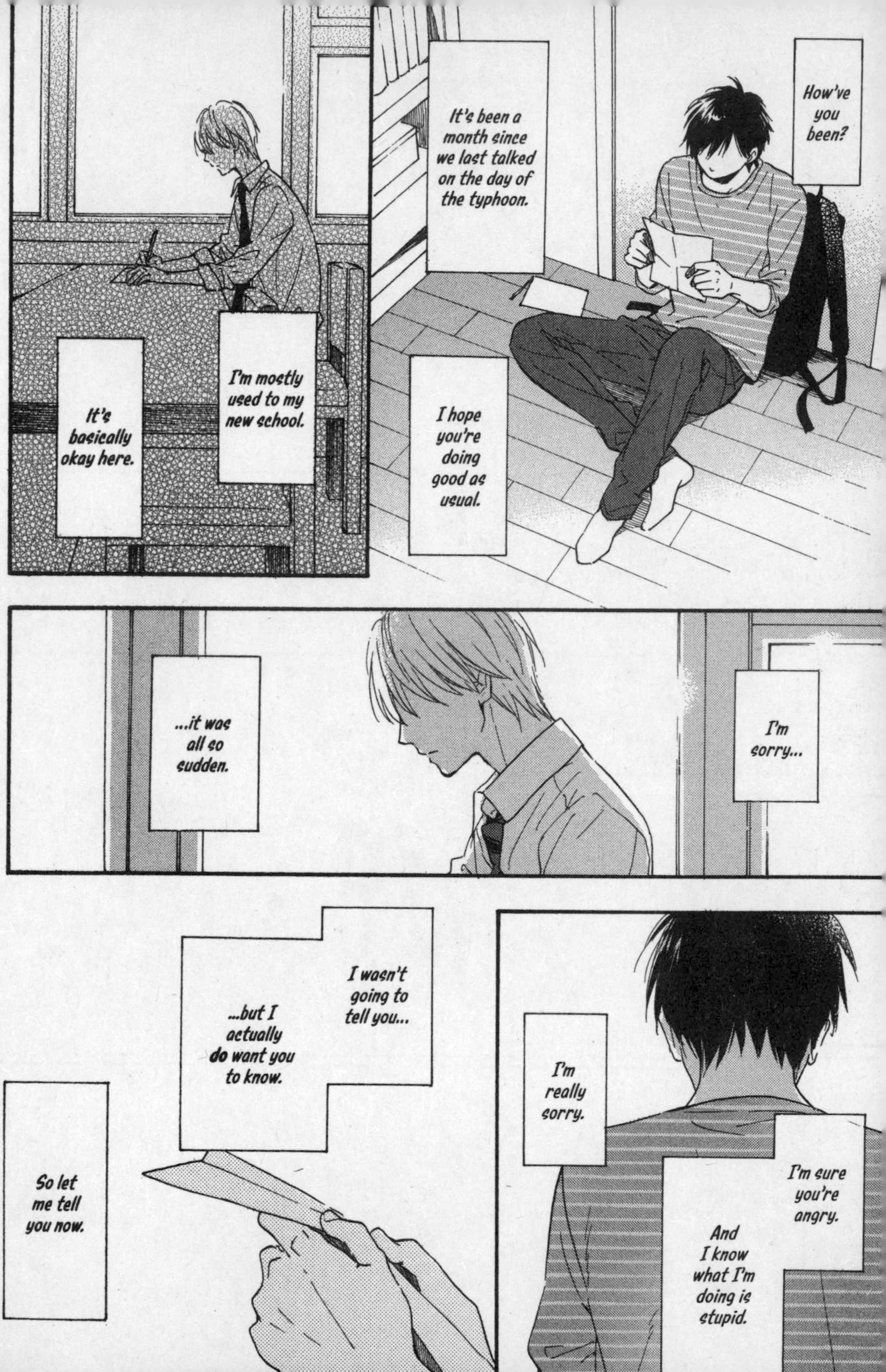
How've you been?
It's been a month since we last talked on the day of the typhoon.
I hope you're doing good as usual.
I'm mostly used to my new school.
It's basically okay here.
I'm sorry...
...it was all so sudden.
I'm sure you're angry.
And I know what I'm doing is stupid.
I'm really sorry.
I wasn't going to tell you...
...but I actually do want you to know.
So let me tell you now.

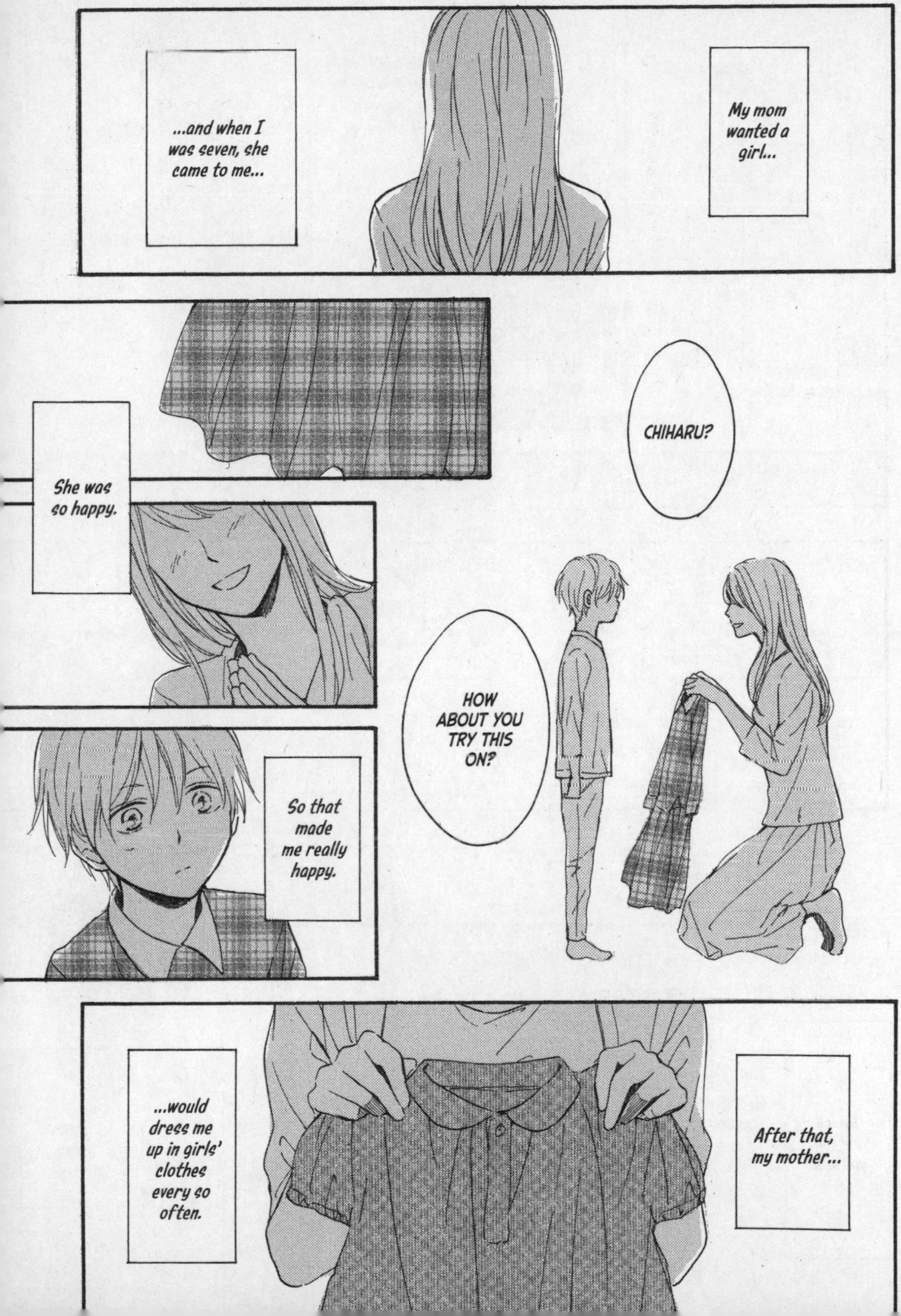
My mom wanted a girl...
...and when I was seven, she came to me...
CHIHARU?
HOW ABOUT YOU TRY THIS ON?
She was so happy.
So that made me really happy.
After that, my mother...
...would dress me up in girls' clothes every so often.

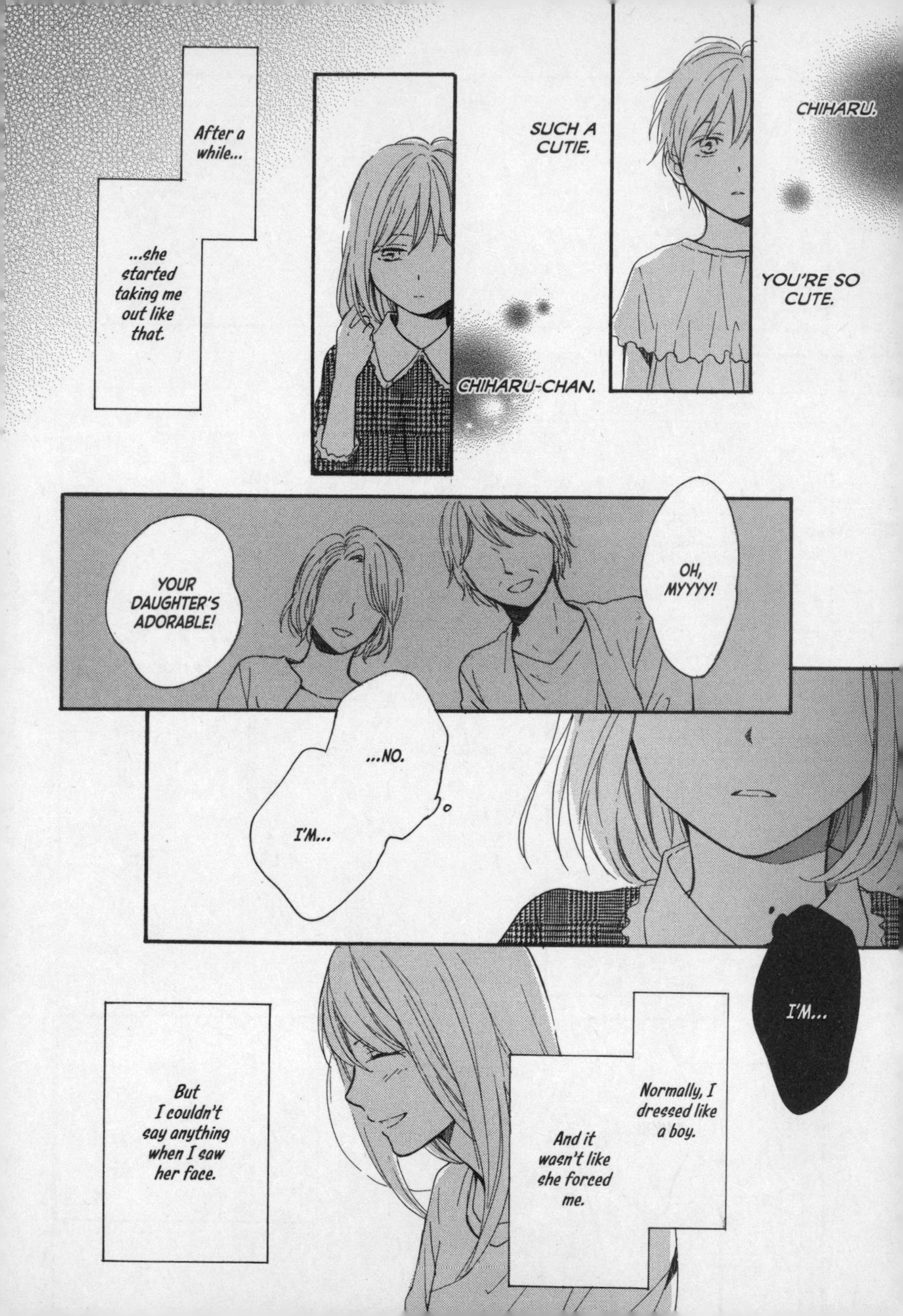
CHIHARU.
YOU'RE SO CUTE.
SUCH A CUTIE.
CHIHARU-CHAN.
After a while...
...she started taking me out like that.
OH, MYYYY!
YOUR DAUGHTER'S ADORABLE!
...NO.
I'M...
I'M...
Normally, I dressed like a boy.
And it wasn't like she forced me.
But I couldn't say anything when I saw her face.

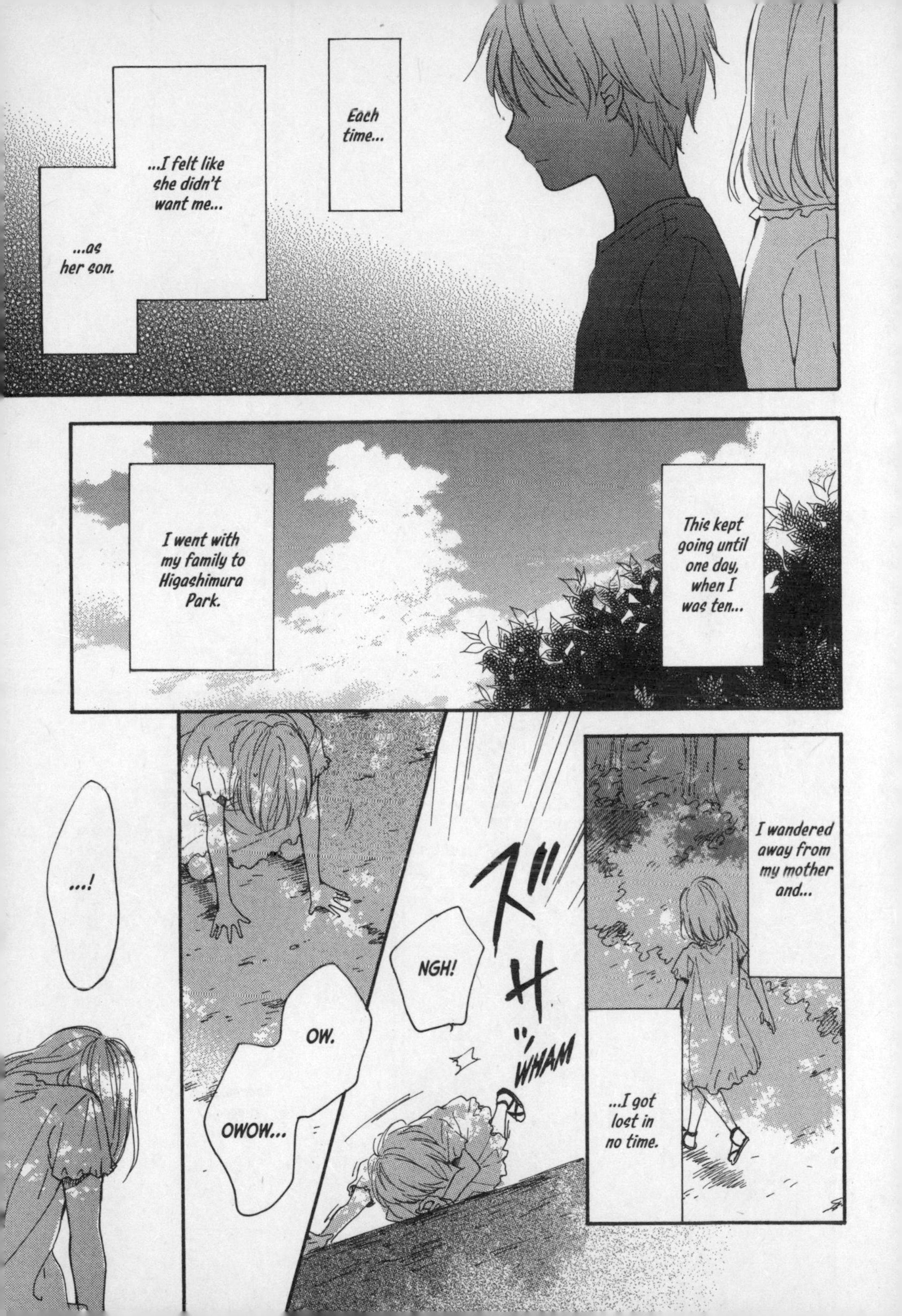

Each time...
...I felt like she didn't want me...
...as her son.
This kept going until one day, when I was ten...
I went with my family to Higashimura Park.
I wandered away from my mother and...
...I got lost in no time.
WHAM
NGH!
OW.
OWOW...
...!

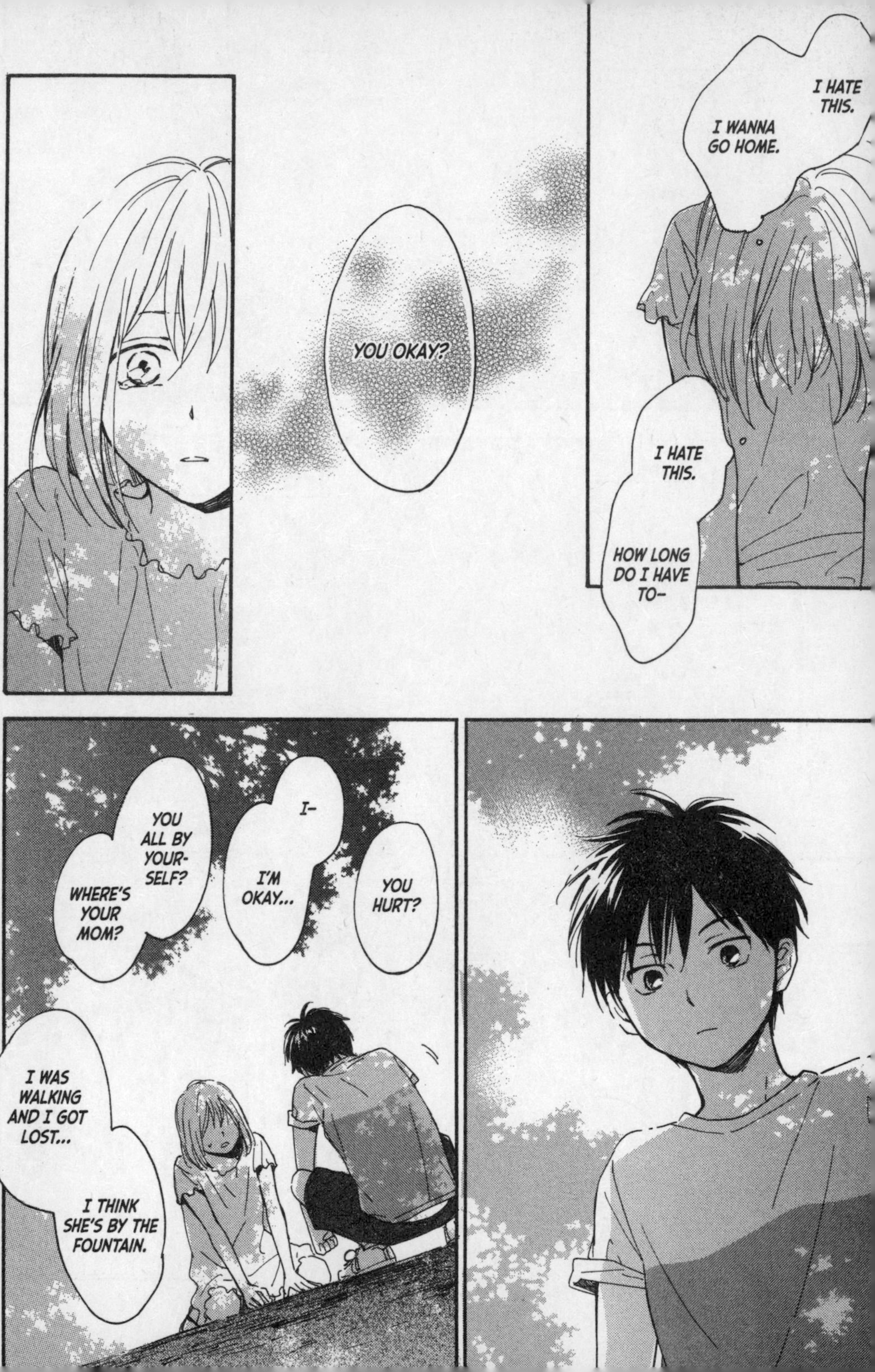
I HATE THIS.
I WANNA GO HOME.
I HATE THIS.
HOW LONG DO I HAVE TO–
YOU OKAY?
YOU HURT?
I–
I'M OKAY...
YOU ALL BY YOURSELF?
WHERE'S YOUR MOM?
I WAS WALKING AND I GOT LOST...
I THINK SHE'S BY THE FOUNTAIN.

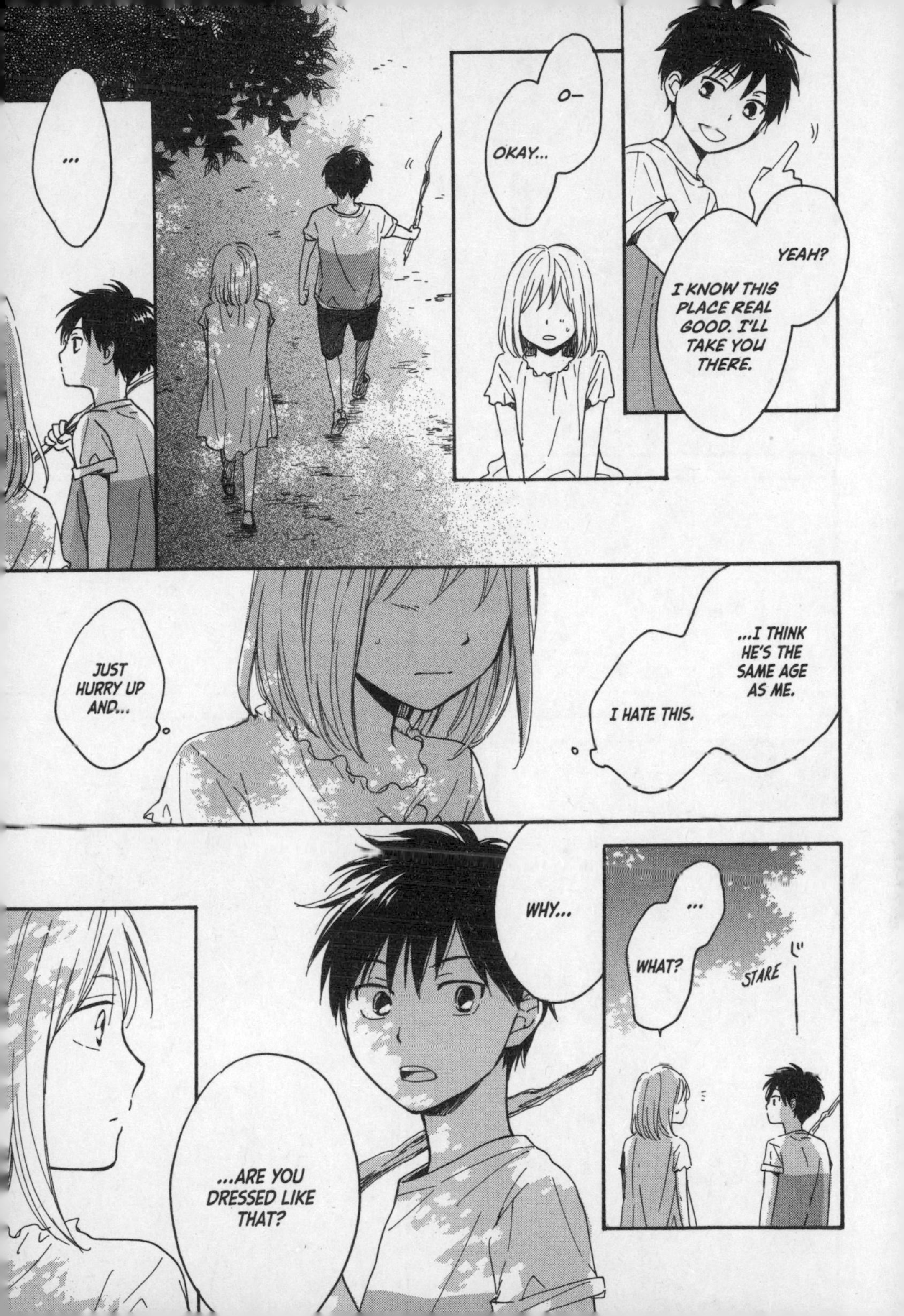
YEAH?
I KNOW THIS PLACE REAL GOOD. I'LL TAKE YOU THERE.
O—
OKAY...
...
...I THINK HE'S THE SAME AGE AS ME.
I HATE THIS.
JUST HURRY UP AND...
...
WHAT?
STARE
WHY...
...ARE YOU DRESSED LIKE THAT?

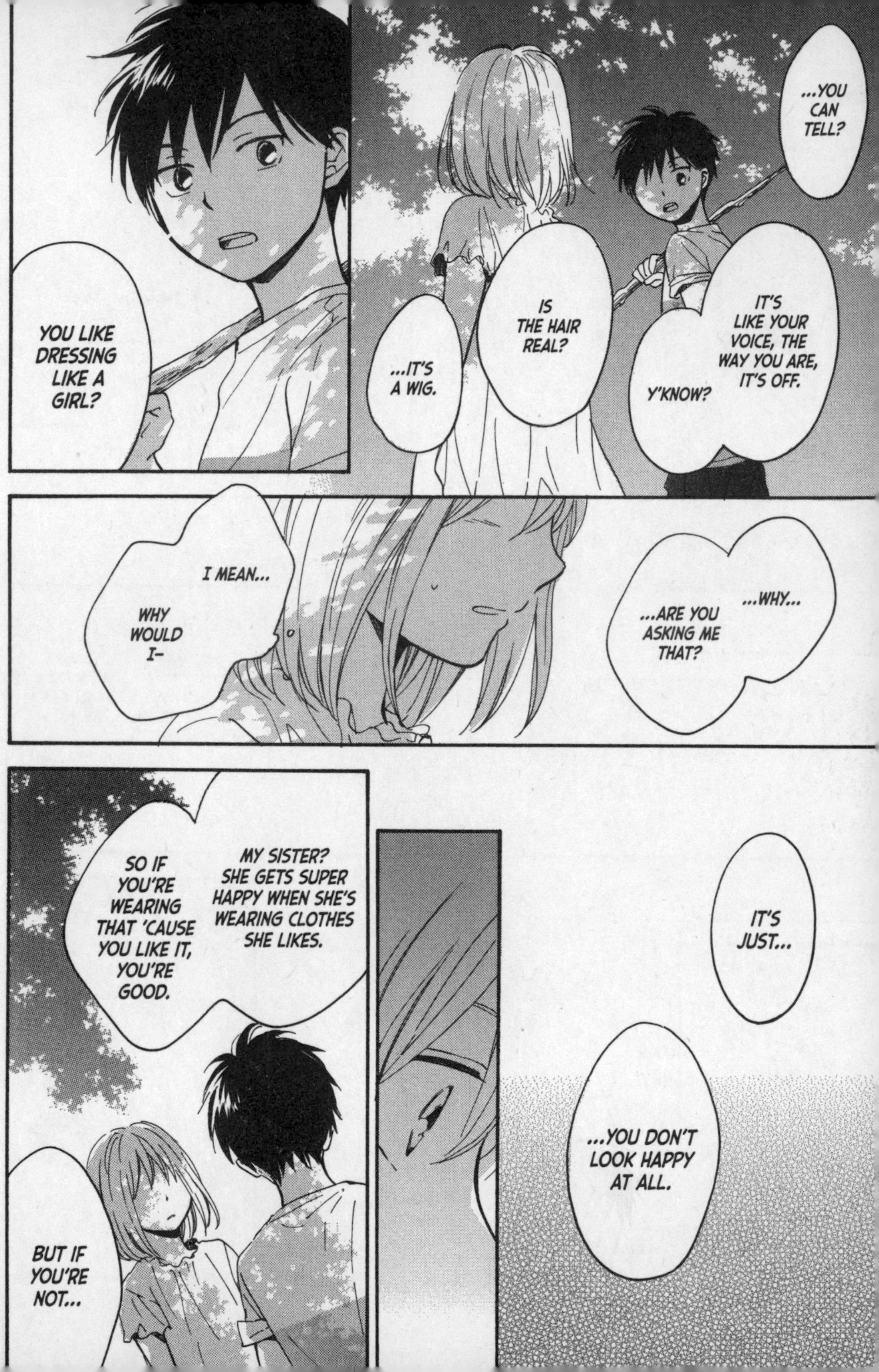
...YOU CAN TELL?
IT'S LIKE YOUR VOICE, THE WAY YOU ARE, IT'S OFF.
Y'KNOW?
IS THE HAIR REAL?
...IT'S A WIG.
YOU LIKE DRESSING LIKE A GIRL?
...WHY...
...ARE YOU ASKING ME THAT?
I MEAN...
WHY WOULD I–
IT'S JUST...
...YOU DON'T LOOK HAPPY AT ALL.
MY SISTER? SHE GETS SUPER HAPPY WHEN SHE'S WEARING CLOTHES SHE LIKES.
SO IF YOU'RE WEARING THAT 'CAUSE YOU LIKE IT, YOU'RE GOOD.
BUT IF YOU'RE NOT...

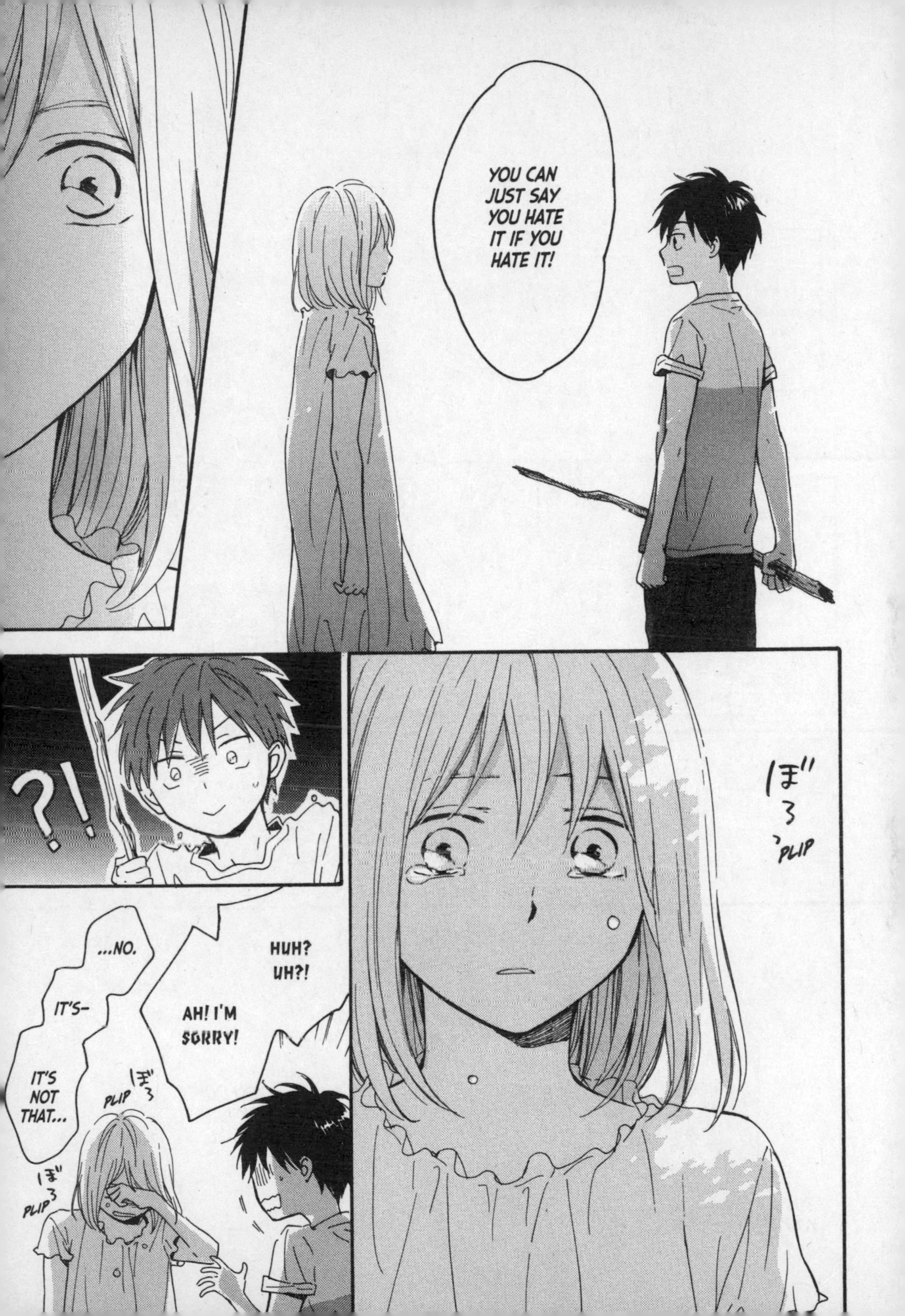
YOU CAN JUST SAY YOU HATE IT IF YOU HATE IT!
ぼろっ
PLIP
?!
HUH? UH?!
AH! I'M SORRY!
...NO.
IT'S-
ぼろ
PLIP
IT'S NOT THAT...
ぼろ
PLIP

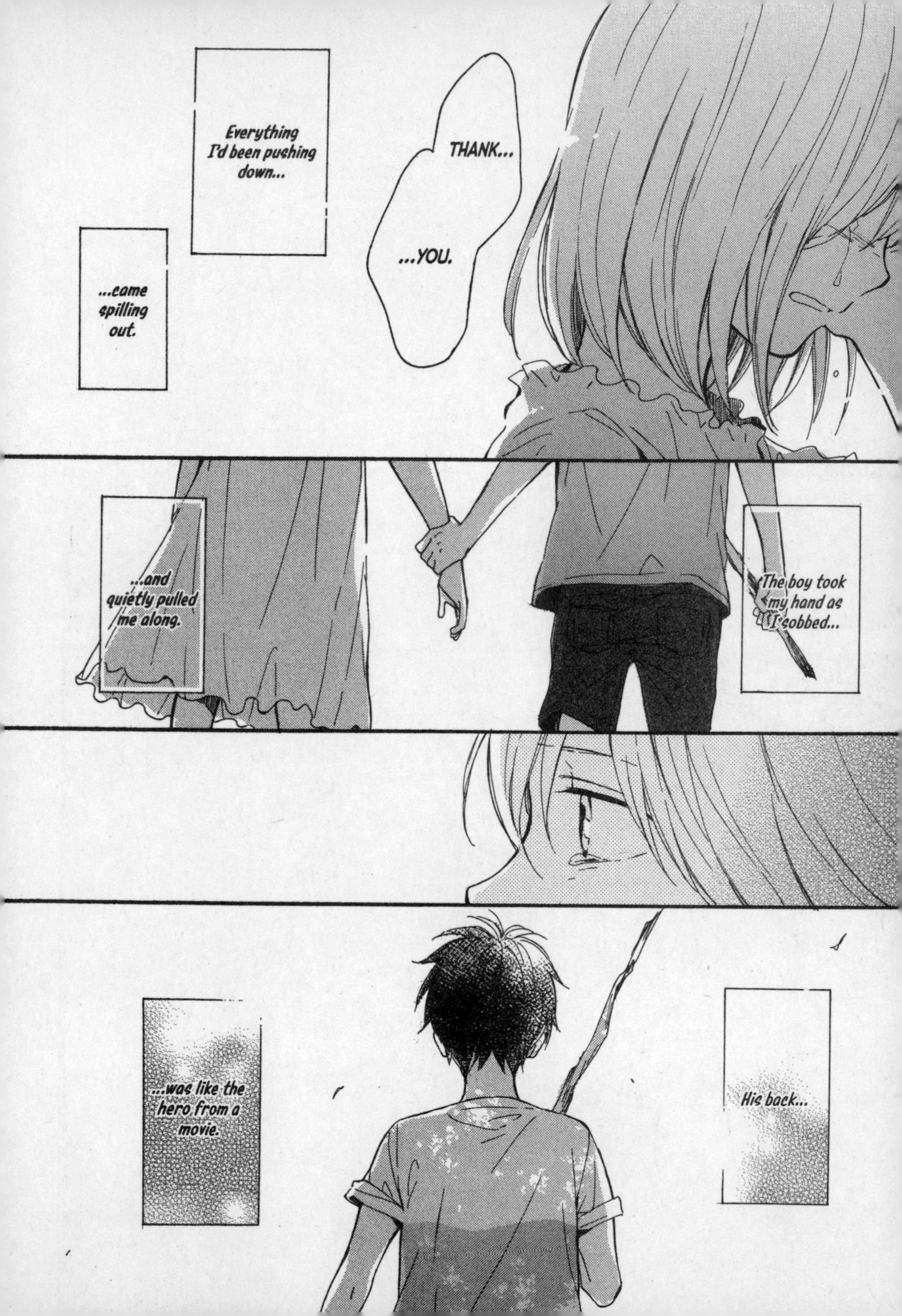
THANK...
...YOU.
Everything I'd been pushing down...
...came spilling out.
The boy took my hand as I sobbed...
...and quietly pulled me along.
His back...
...was like the hero from a movie.

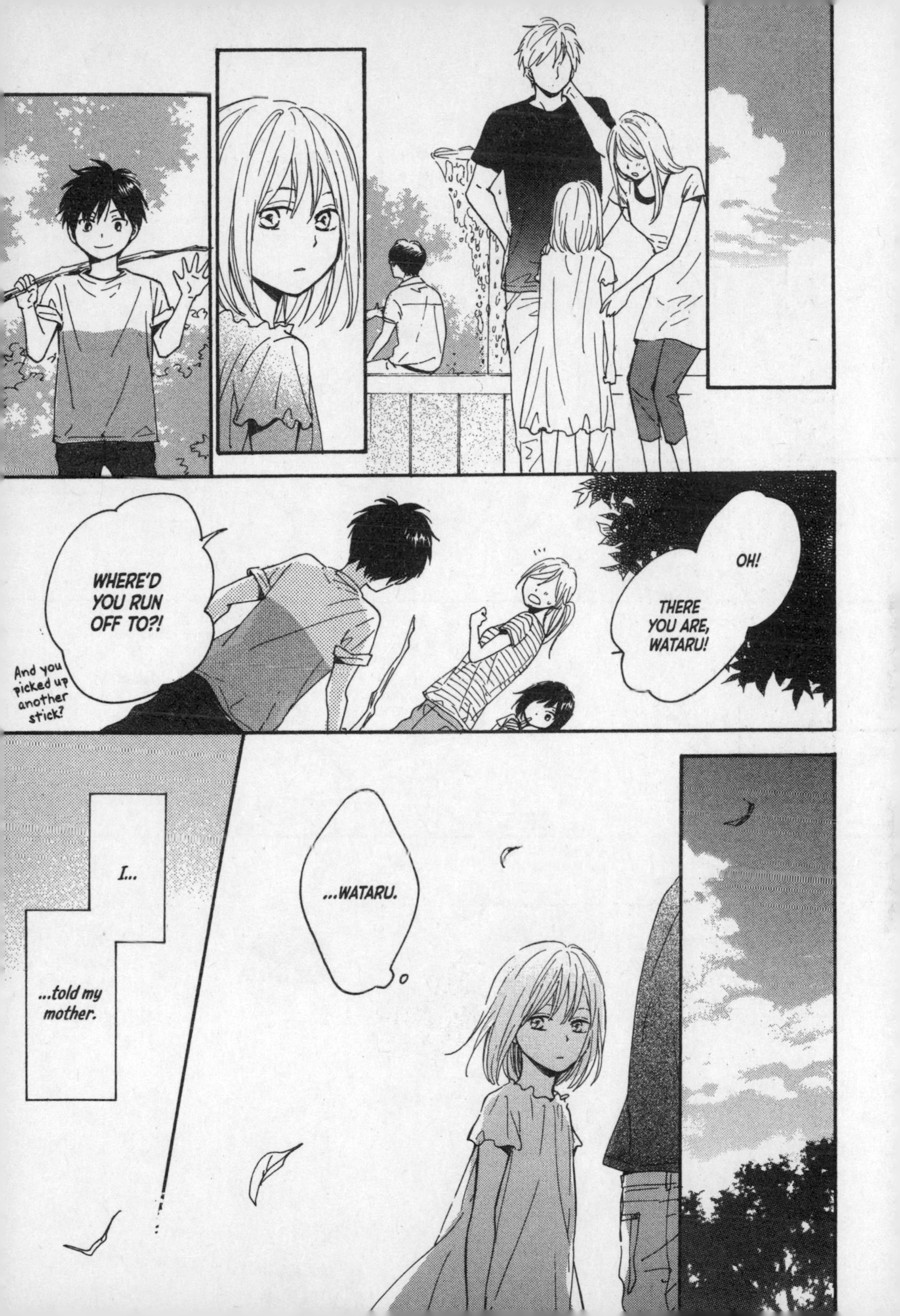
OH!
THERE YOU ARE, WATARU!
WHERE'D YOU RUN OFF TO?!
And you picked up another stick?
...WATARU.
I...
...told my mother.

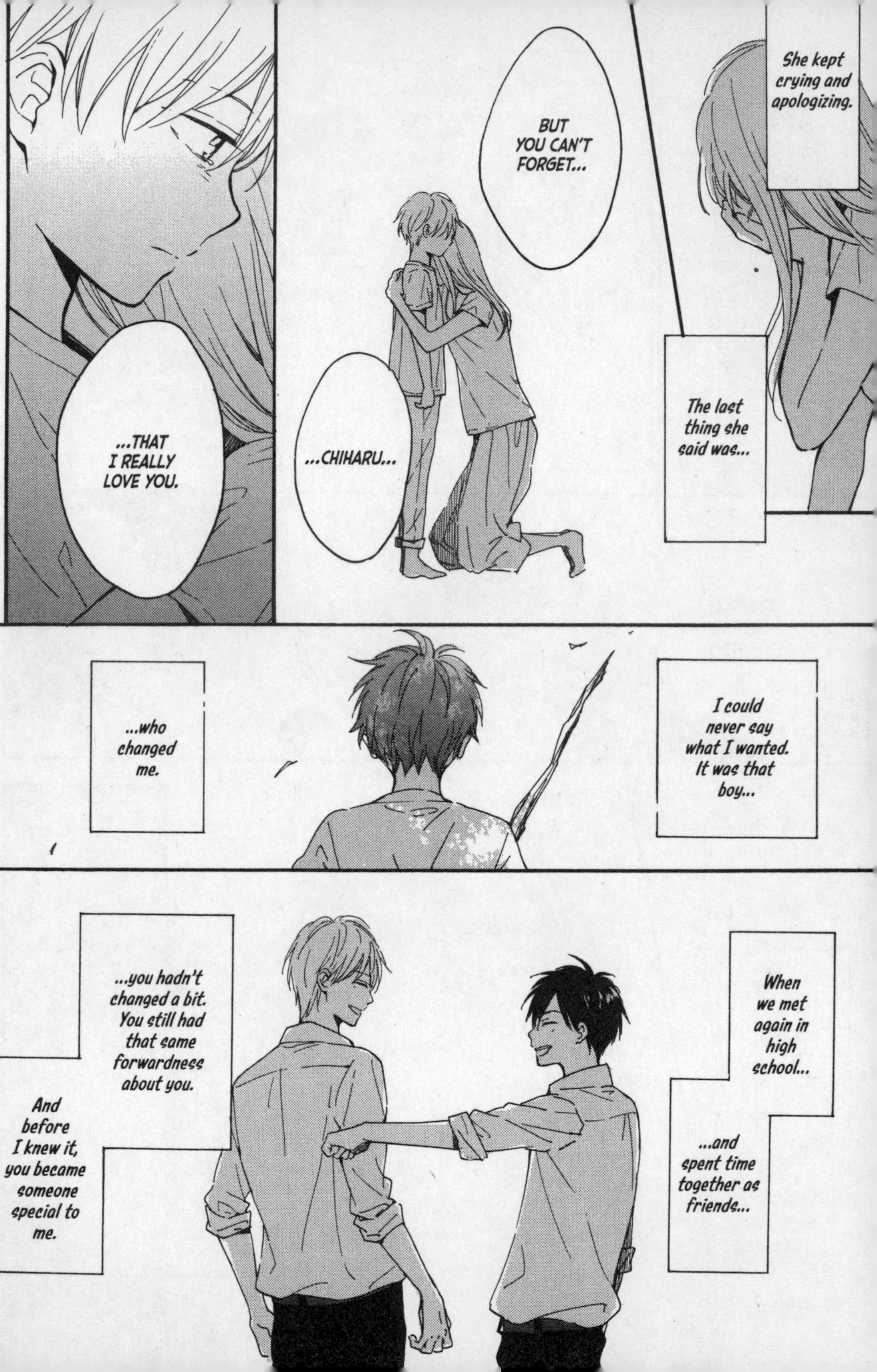
She kept crying and apologizing.
The last thing she said was...
BUT YOU CAN'T FORGET...
...CHIHARU...
...THAT I REALLY LOVE YOU.
I could never say what I wanted. It was that boy...
...who changed me.
When we met again in high school...
...and spent time together as friends...
...you hadn't changed a bit. You still had that same forwardness about you.
And before I knew it, you became someone special to me.

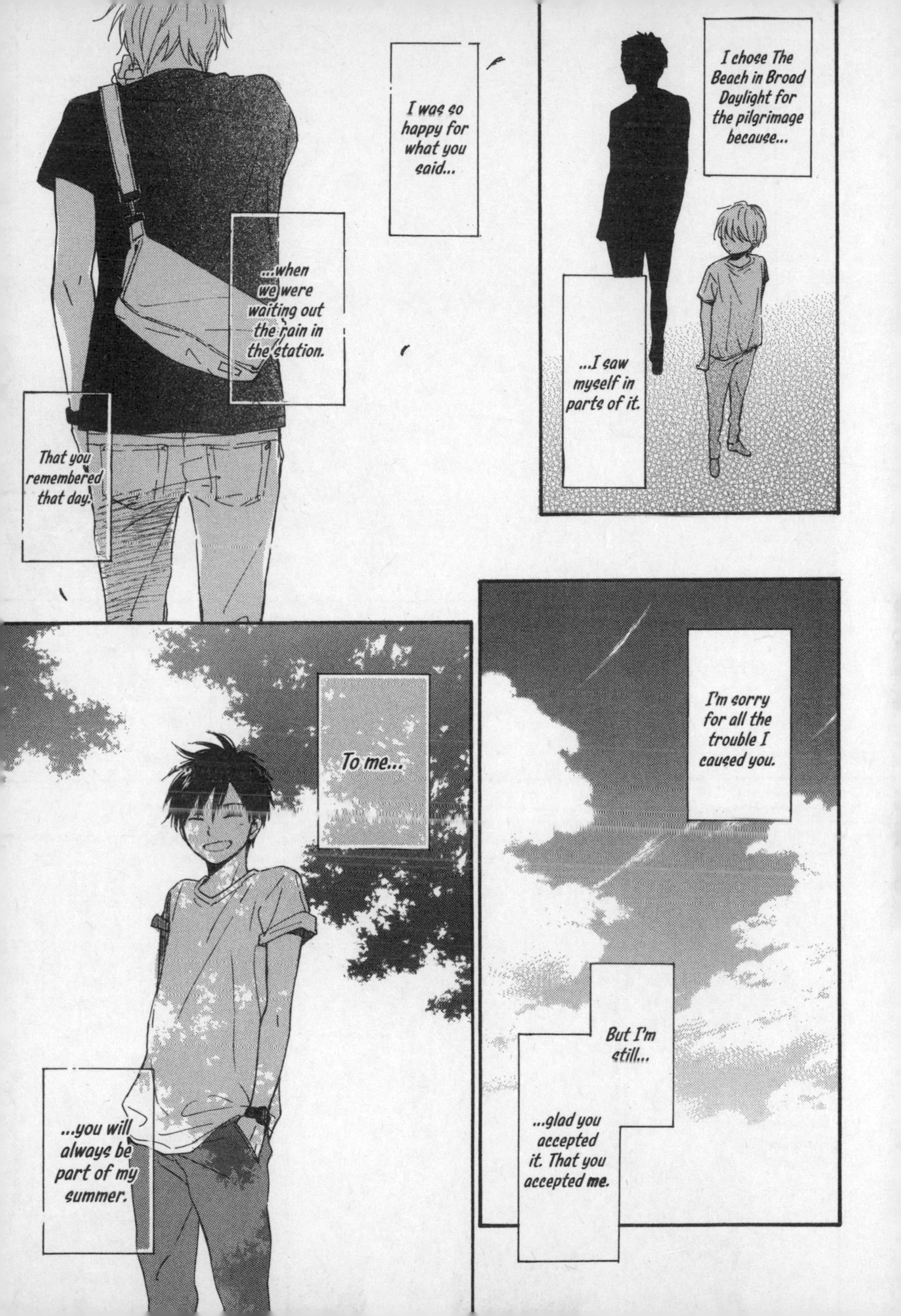
I chose The Beach in Broad Daylight for the pilgrimage because...
...I saw myself in parts of it.
I was so happy for what you said...
...when we were waiting out the rain in the station.
That you remembered that day.
I'm sorry for all the trouble I caused you.
But I'm still...
...glad you accepted it. That you accepted **me**.
To me...
...you will always be part of my summer.

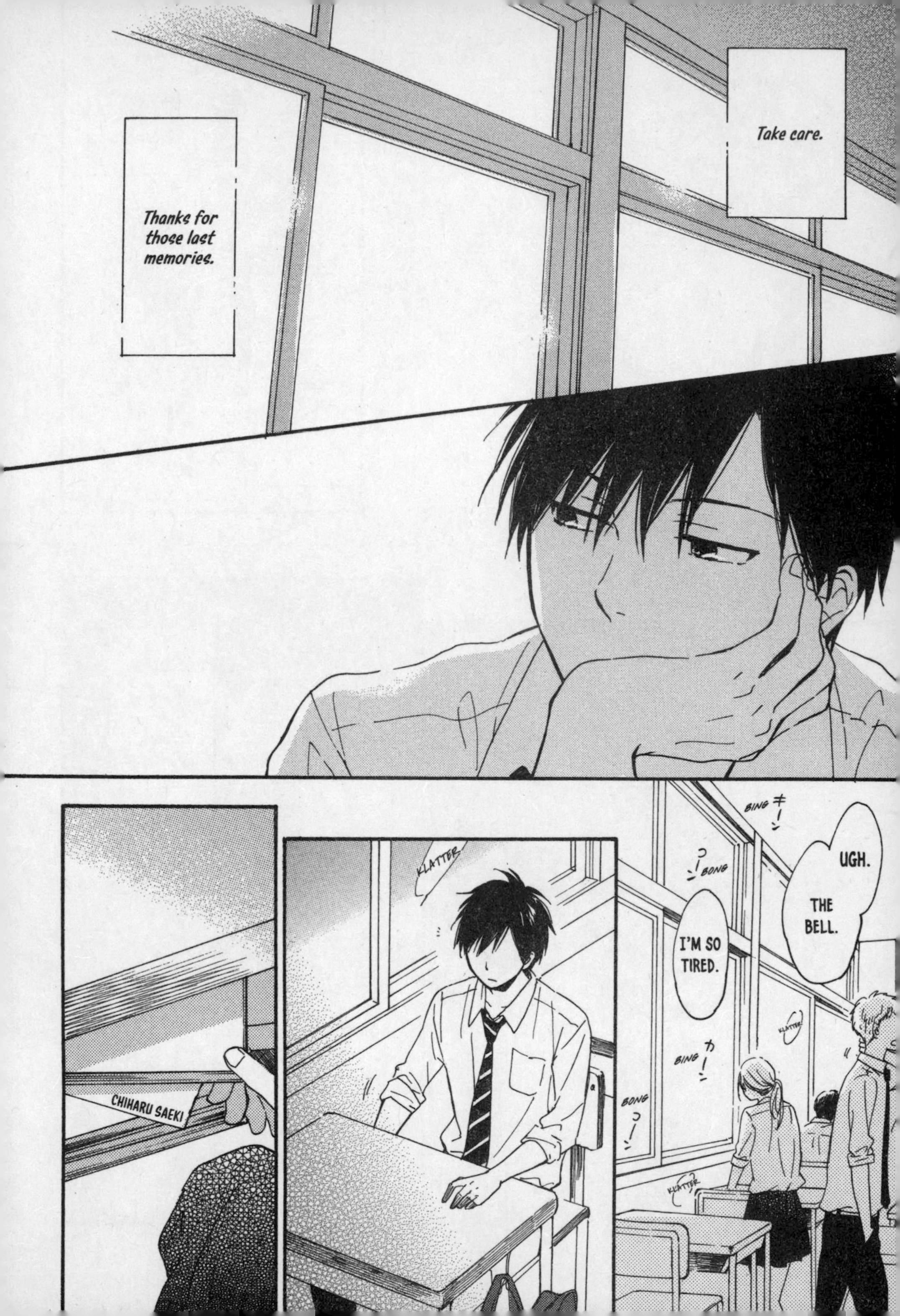
Take care.
Thanks for those last memories.
BING
UGH. THE BELL.
BONG
I'M SO TIRED.
KLATTER
BING
BONG
KLATTER
KLATTER
CHIHARU SAEKI

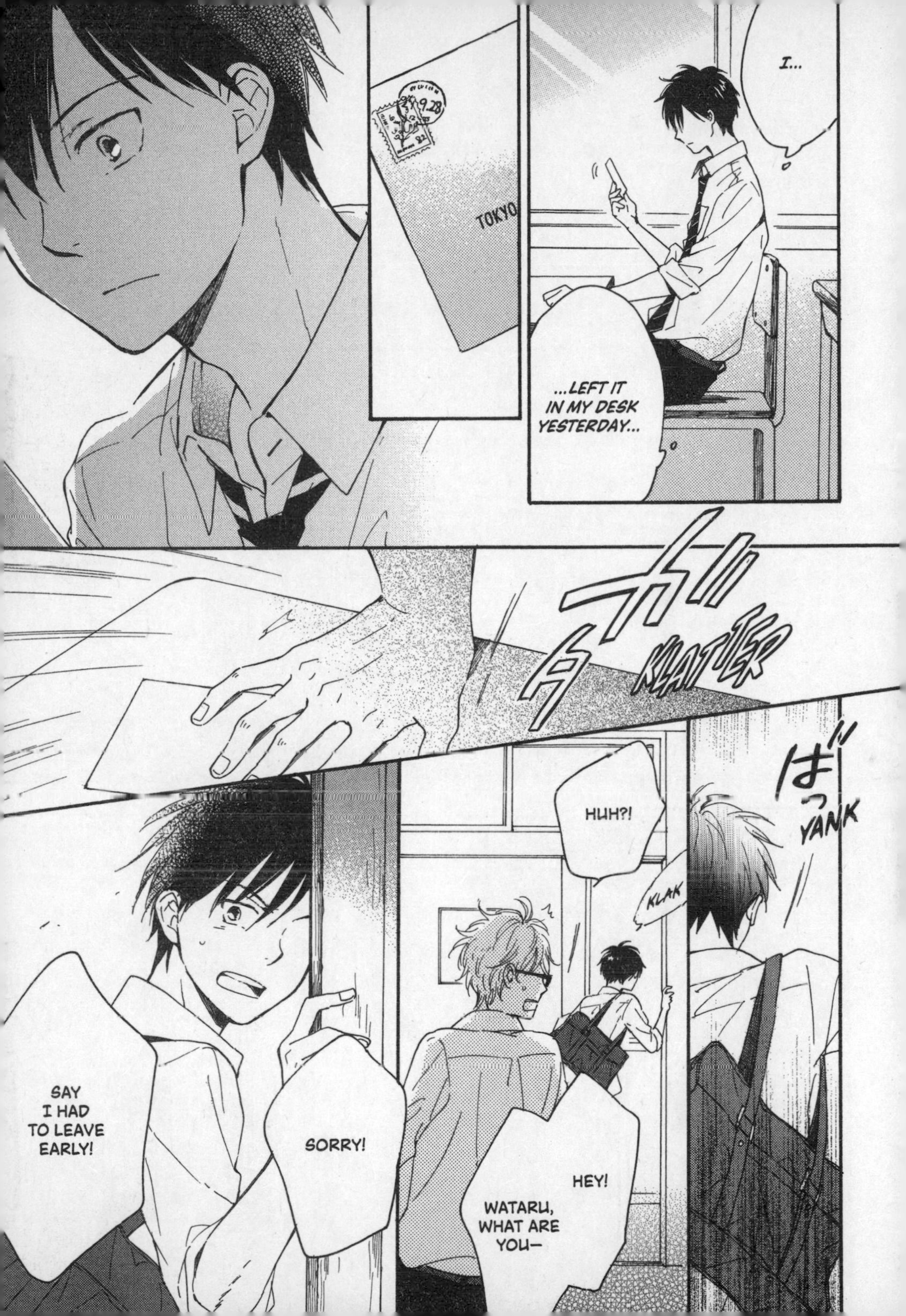
I...
...LEFT IT IN MY DESK YESTERDAY...
9.28
TOKYO
KLATTER
ばっ
YANK
HUH?!
KLAK
HEY!
WATARU, WHAT ARE YOU—
SORRY!
SAY I HAD TO LEAVE EARLY!

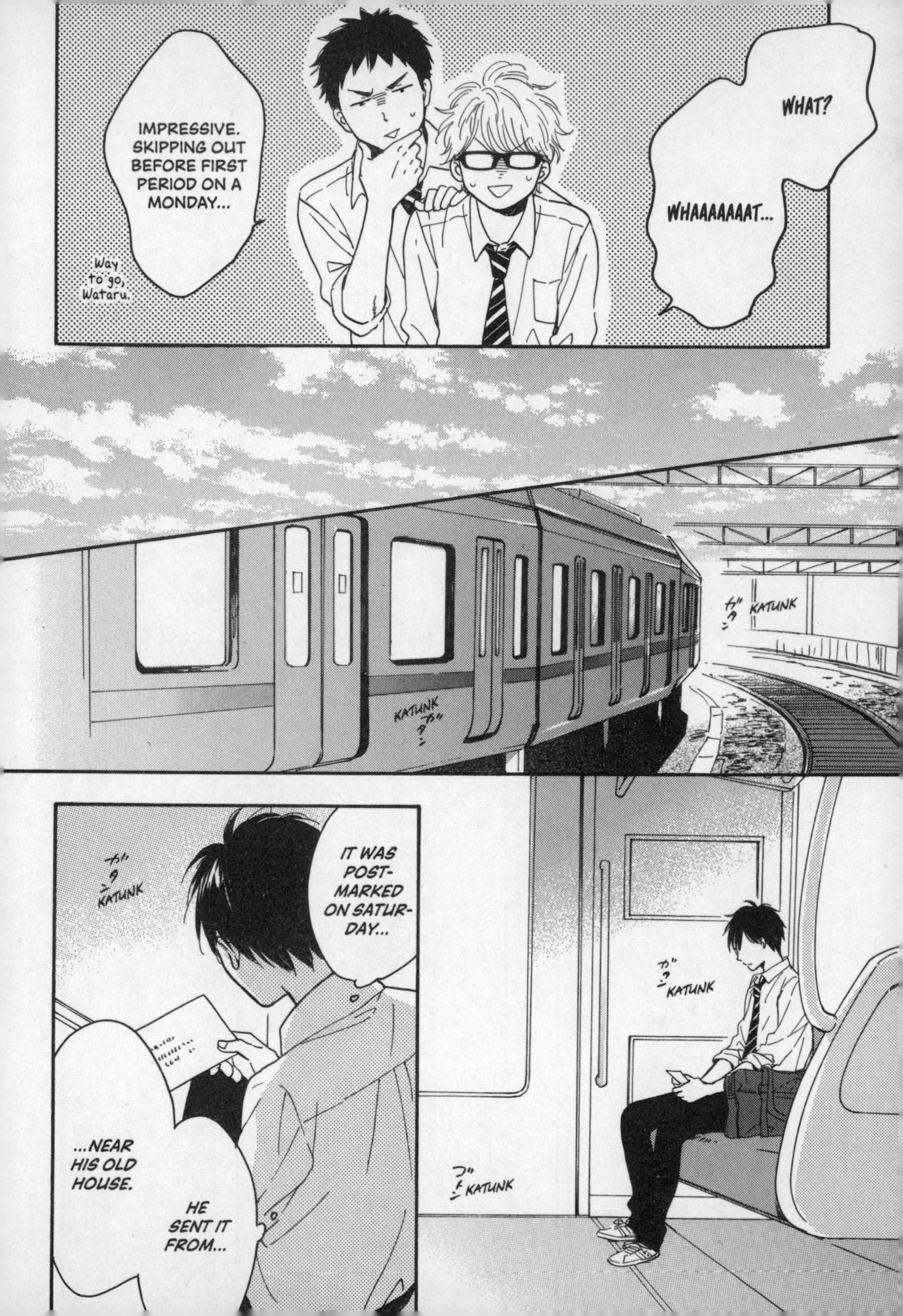
WHAT?
WHAAAAAAAT...
IMPRESSIVE. SKIPPING OUT BEFORE FIRST PERIOD ON A MONDAY...
Way to go, Wataru.
KATUNK
KATUNK
KATUNK
KATUNK
IT WAS POST-MARKED ON SATUR-DAY...
KATUNK
HE SENT IT FROM...
...NEAR HIS OLD HOUSE.

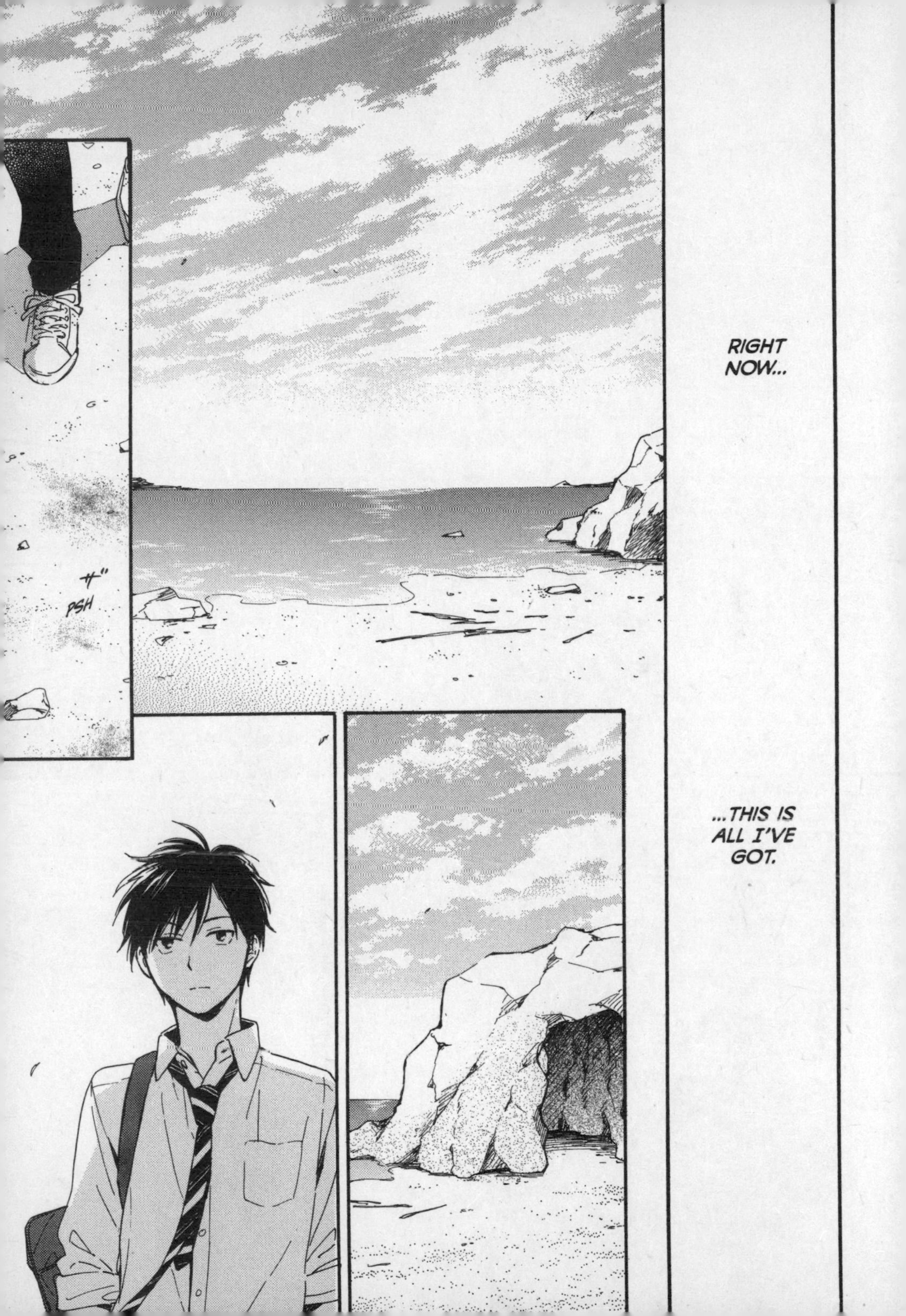
RIGHT NOW...
...THIS IS ALL I'VE GOT.
PSH

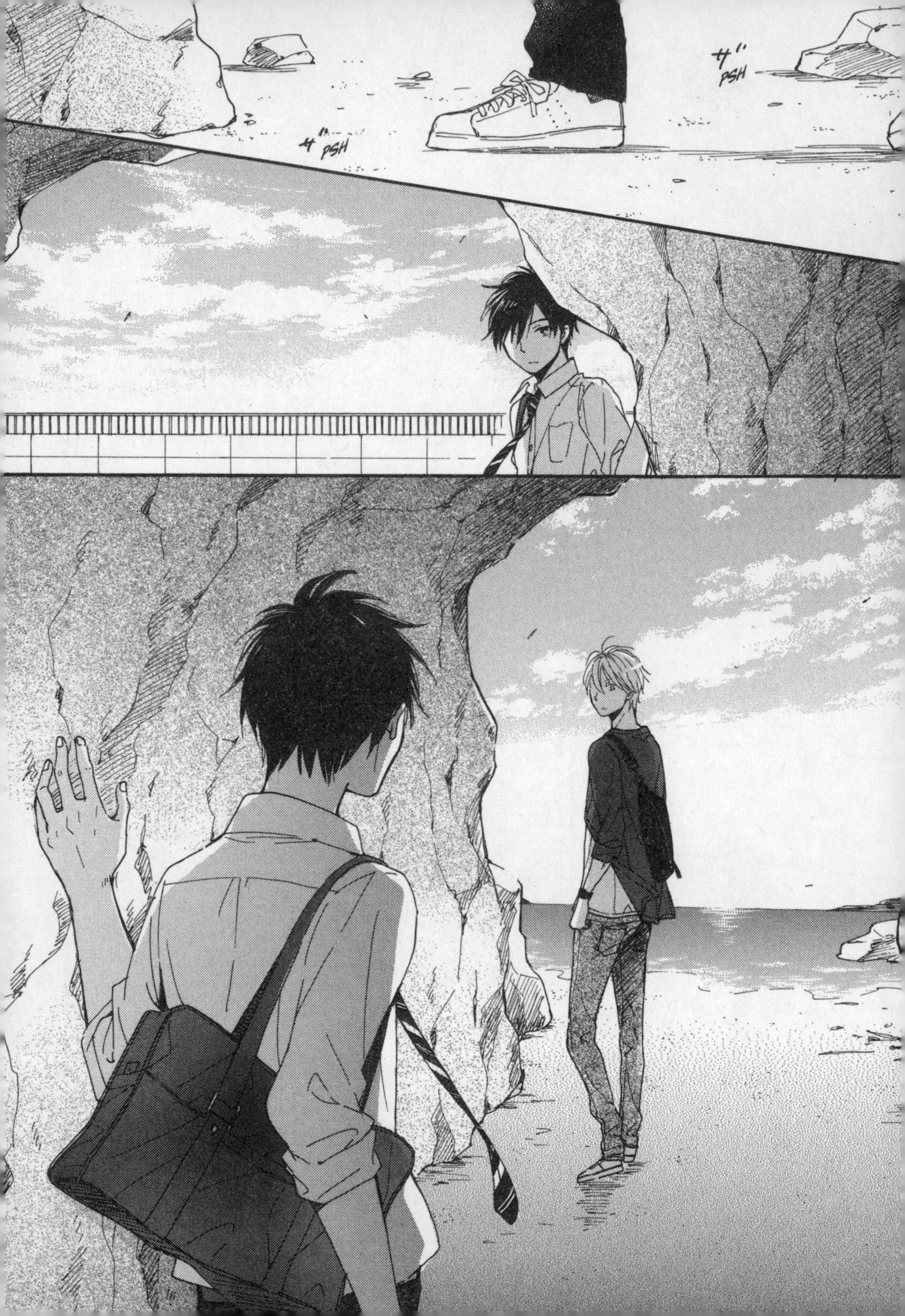
ザ
PSH
ザ
PSH

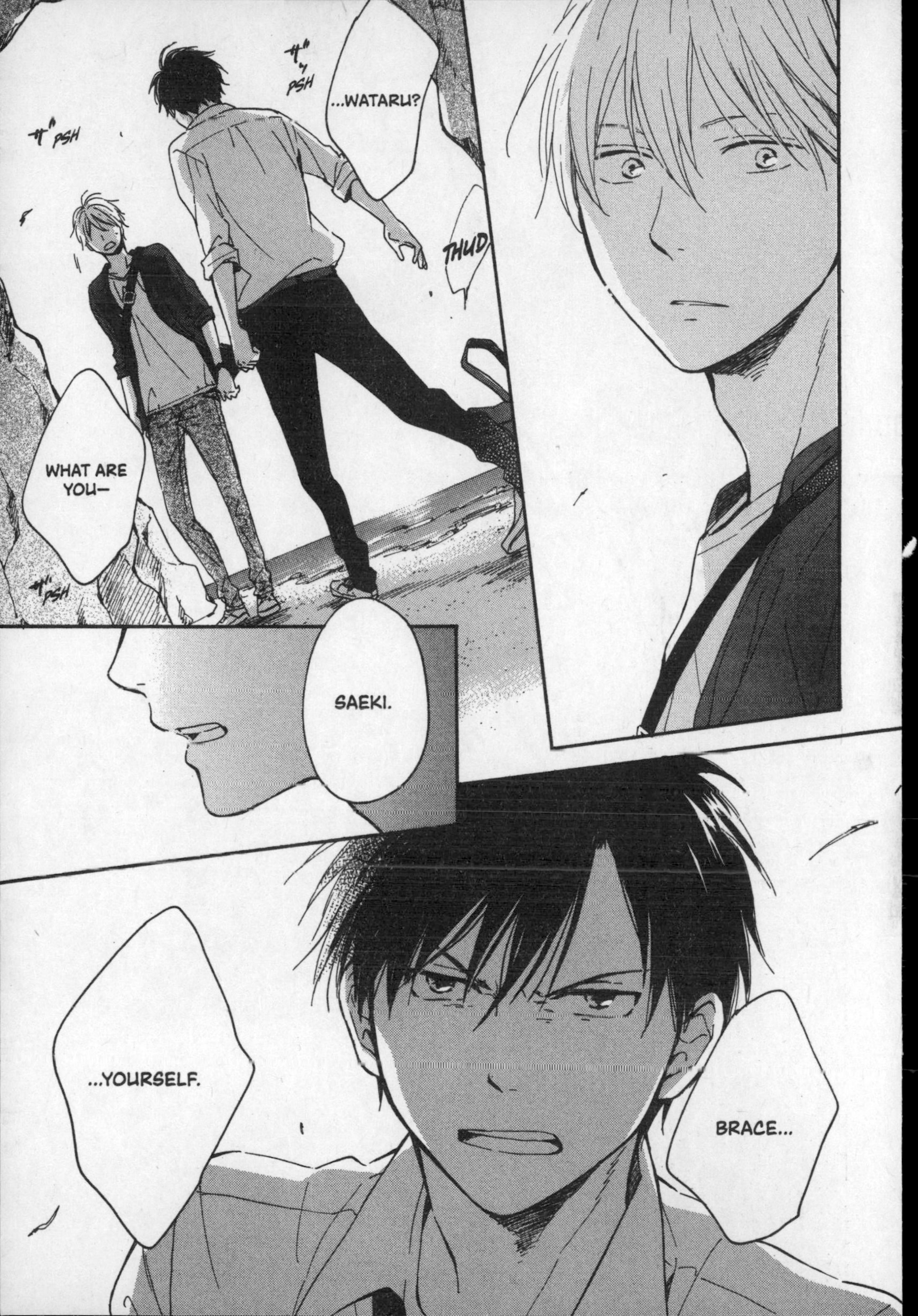

...WATARU?
PSH
THUD
PSH
WHAT ARE YOU—
PSH
SAEKI.
BRACE...
...YOURSELF.

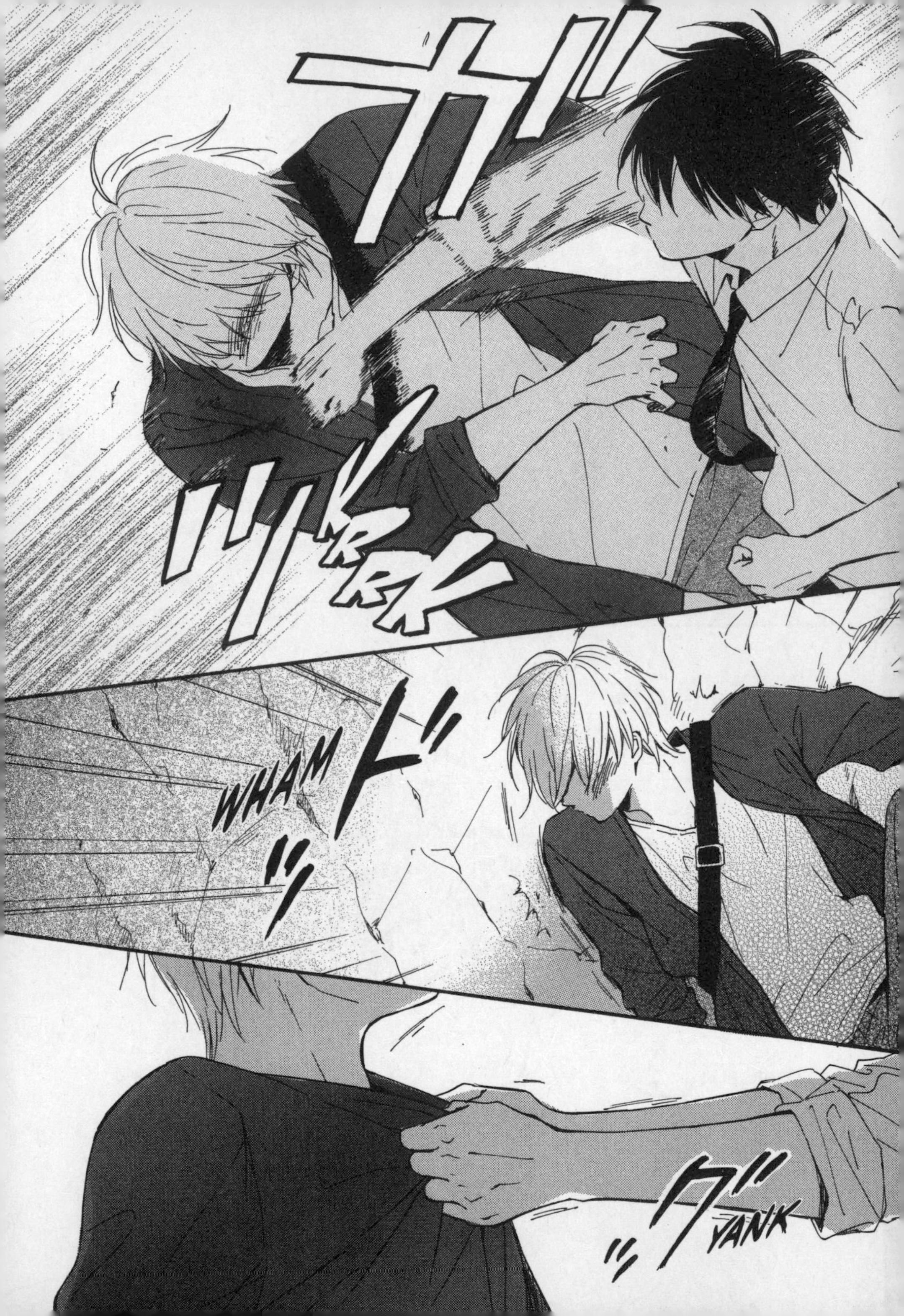
ガッ
JERK
ドッ
WHAM
グッ
YANK

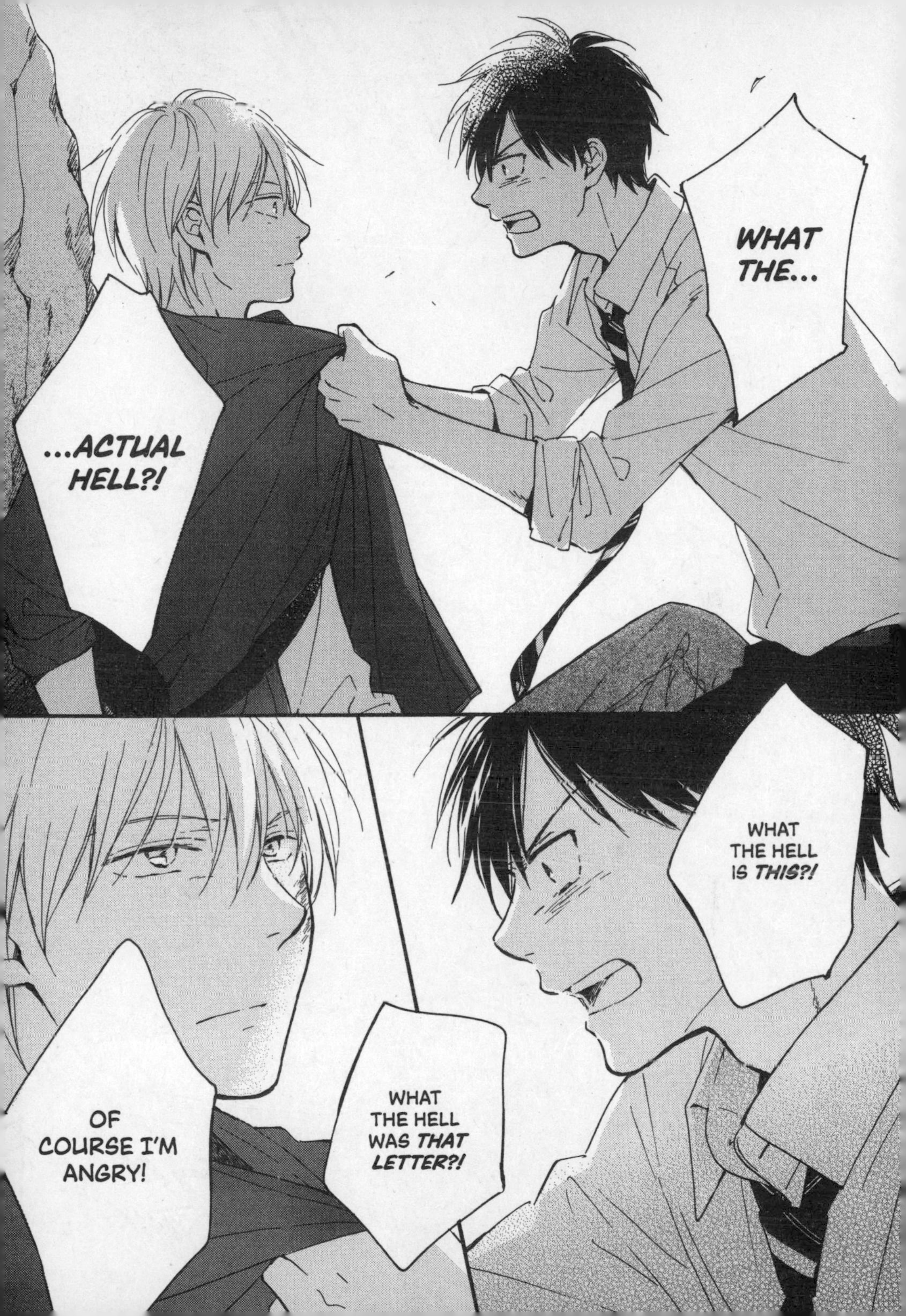
WHAT THE...
...ACTUAL HELL?!
WHAT THE HELL IS THIS?!
WHAT THE HELL WAS THAT LETTER?!
OF COURSE I'M ANGRY!

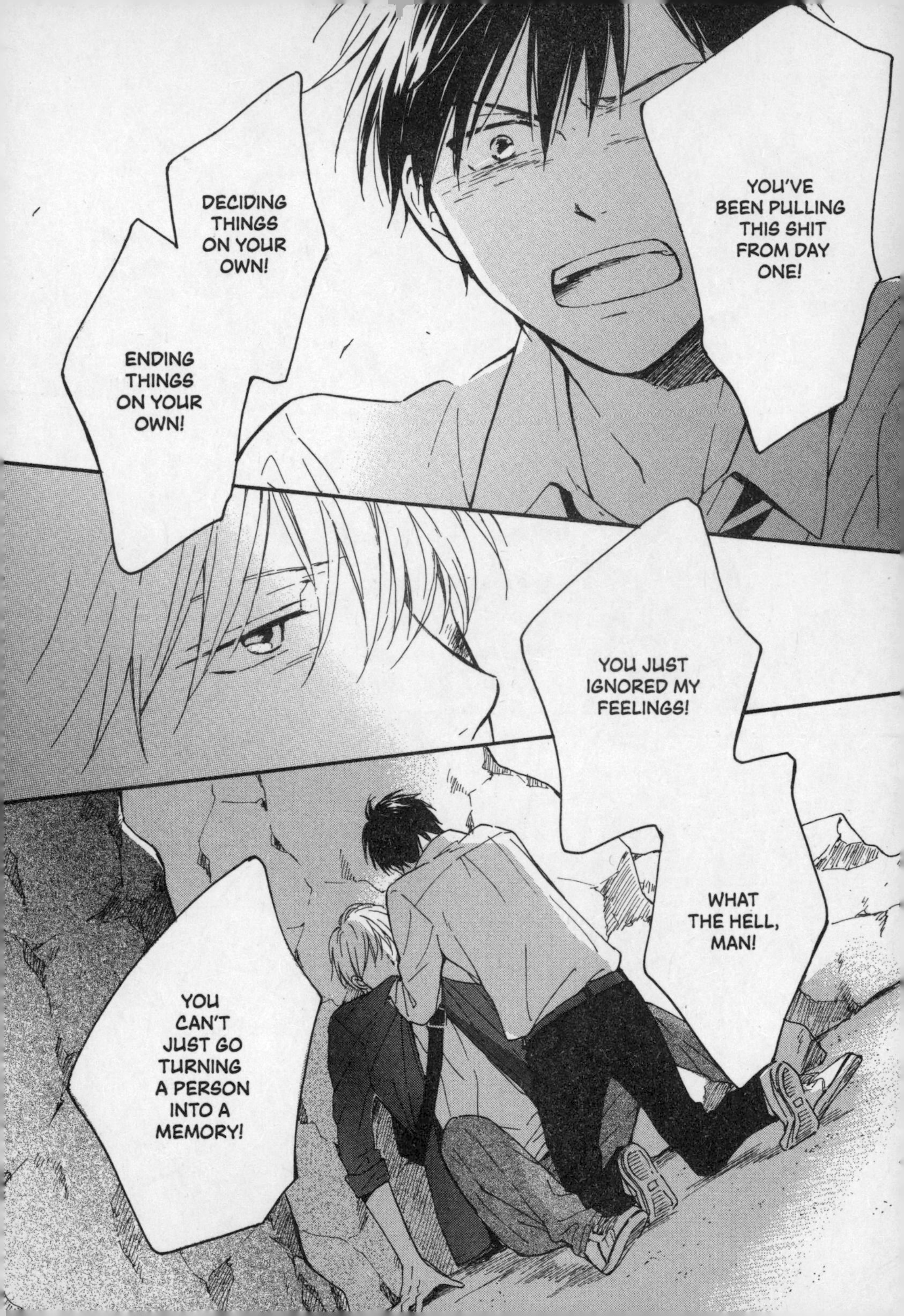
YOU'VE BEEN PULLING THIS SHIT FROM DAY ONE!
DECIDING THINGS ON YOUR OWN!
ENDING THINGS ON YOUR OWN!
YOU JUST IGNORED MY FEELINGS!
WHAT THE HELL, MAN!
YOU CAN'T JUST GO TURNING A PERSON INTO A MEMORY!

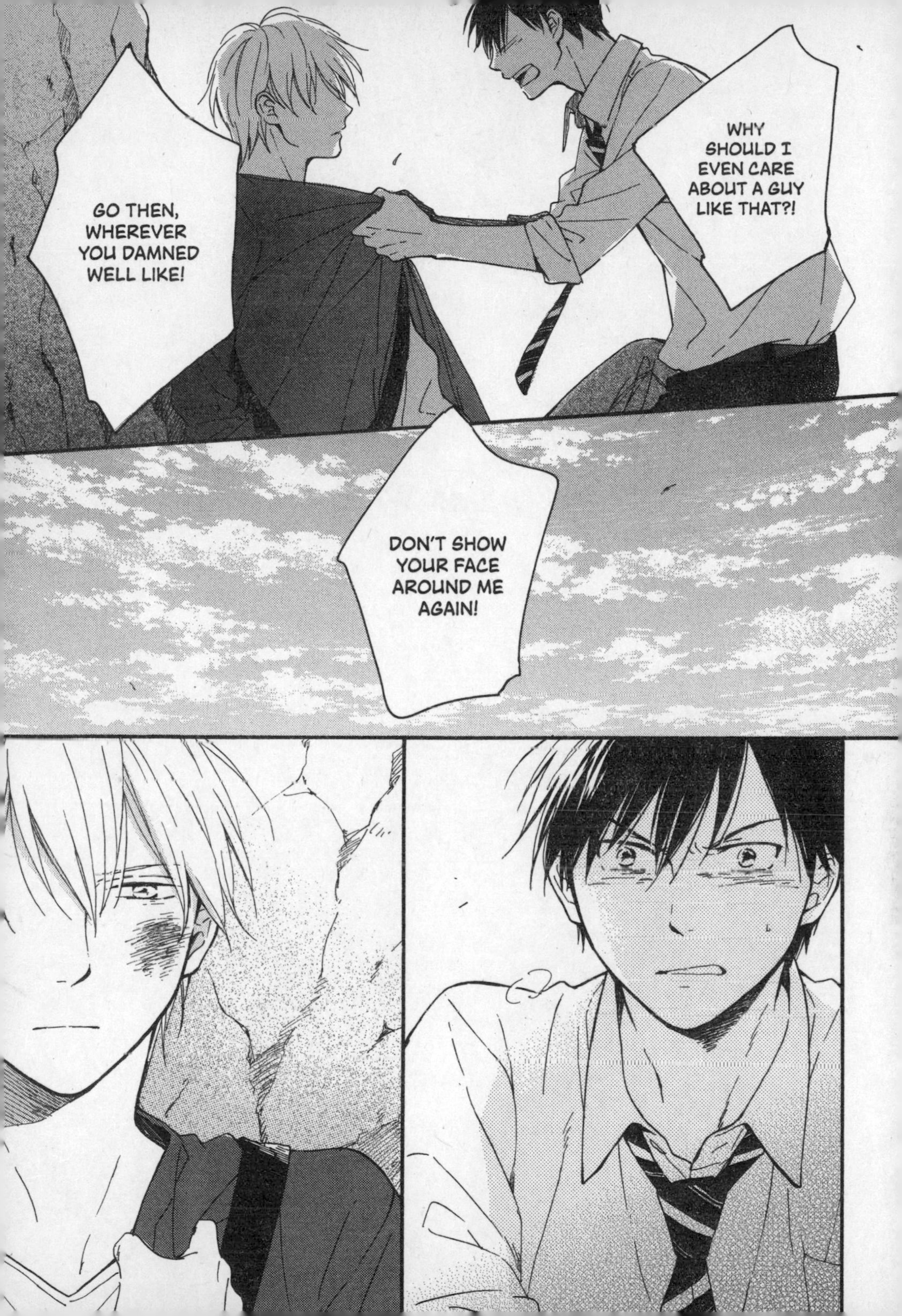
WHY SHOULD I EVEN CARE ABOUT A GUY LIKE THAT?!
GO THEN, WHEREVER YOU DAMNED WELL LIKE!
DON'T SHOW YOUR FACE AROUND ME AGAIN!

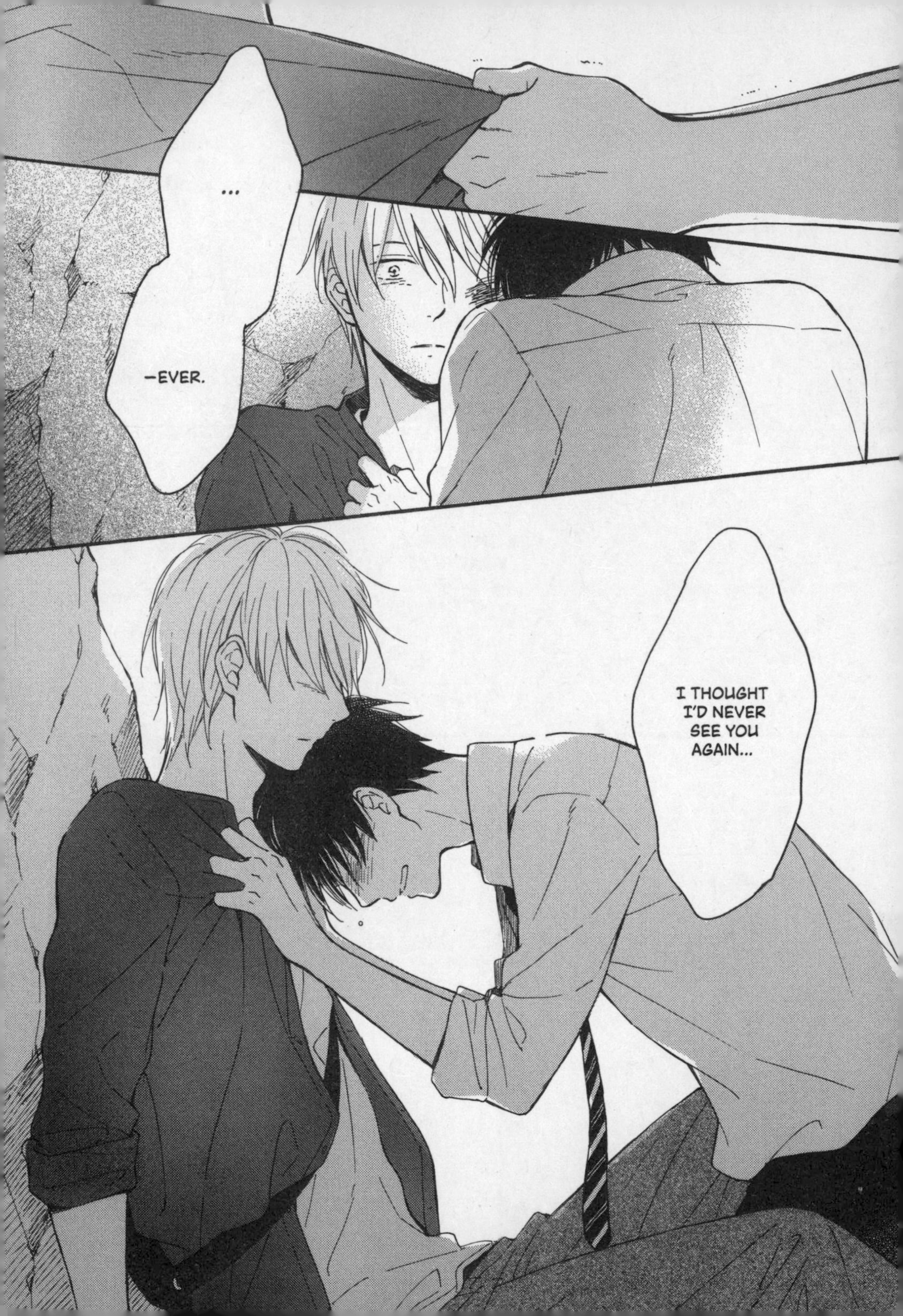
...
—EVER.
I THOUGHT I'D NEVER SEE YOU AGAIN...

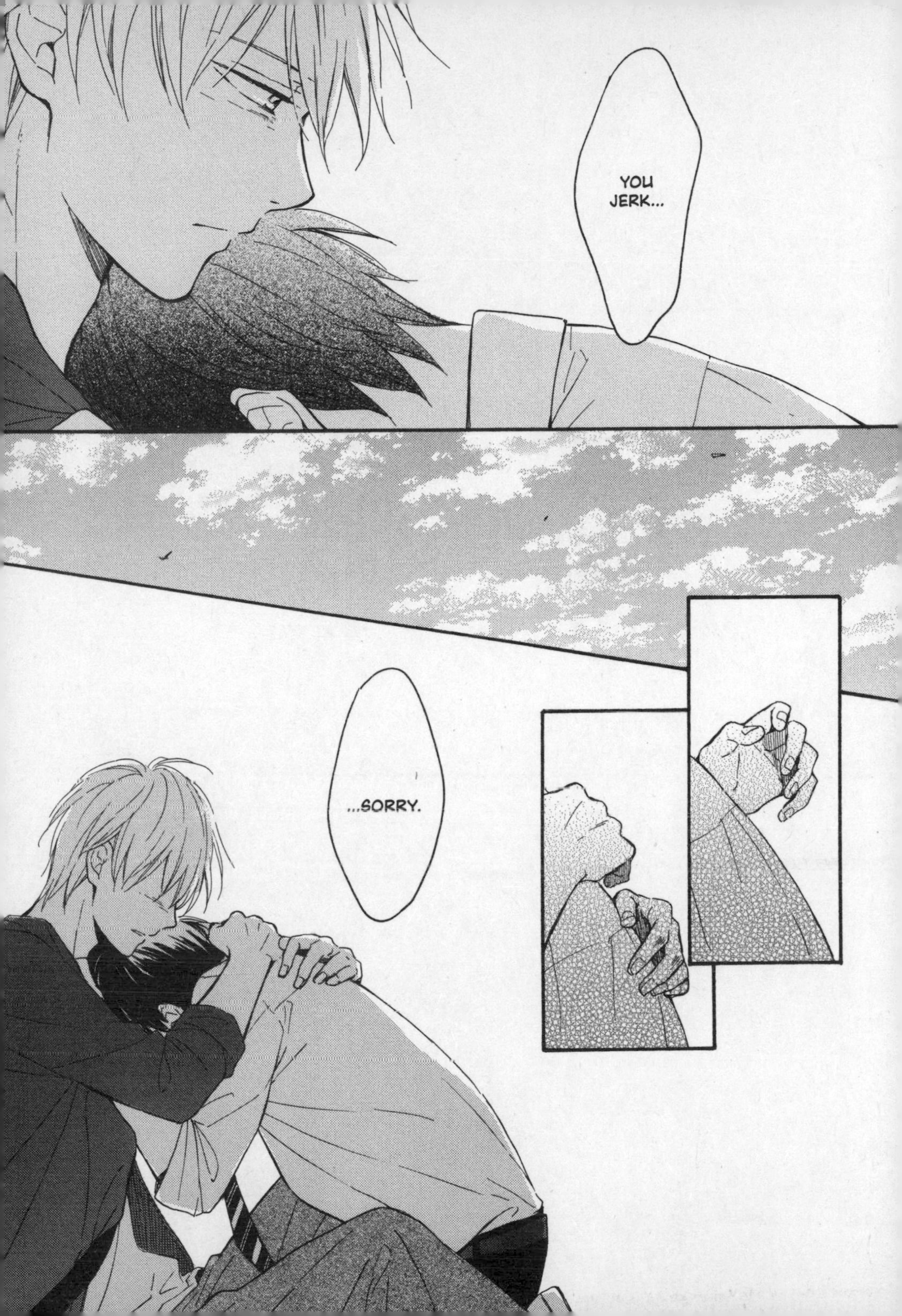
YOU JERK...
...SORRY.

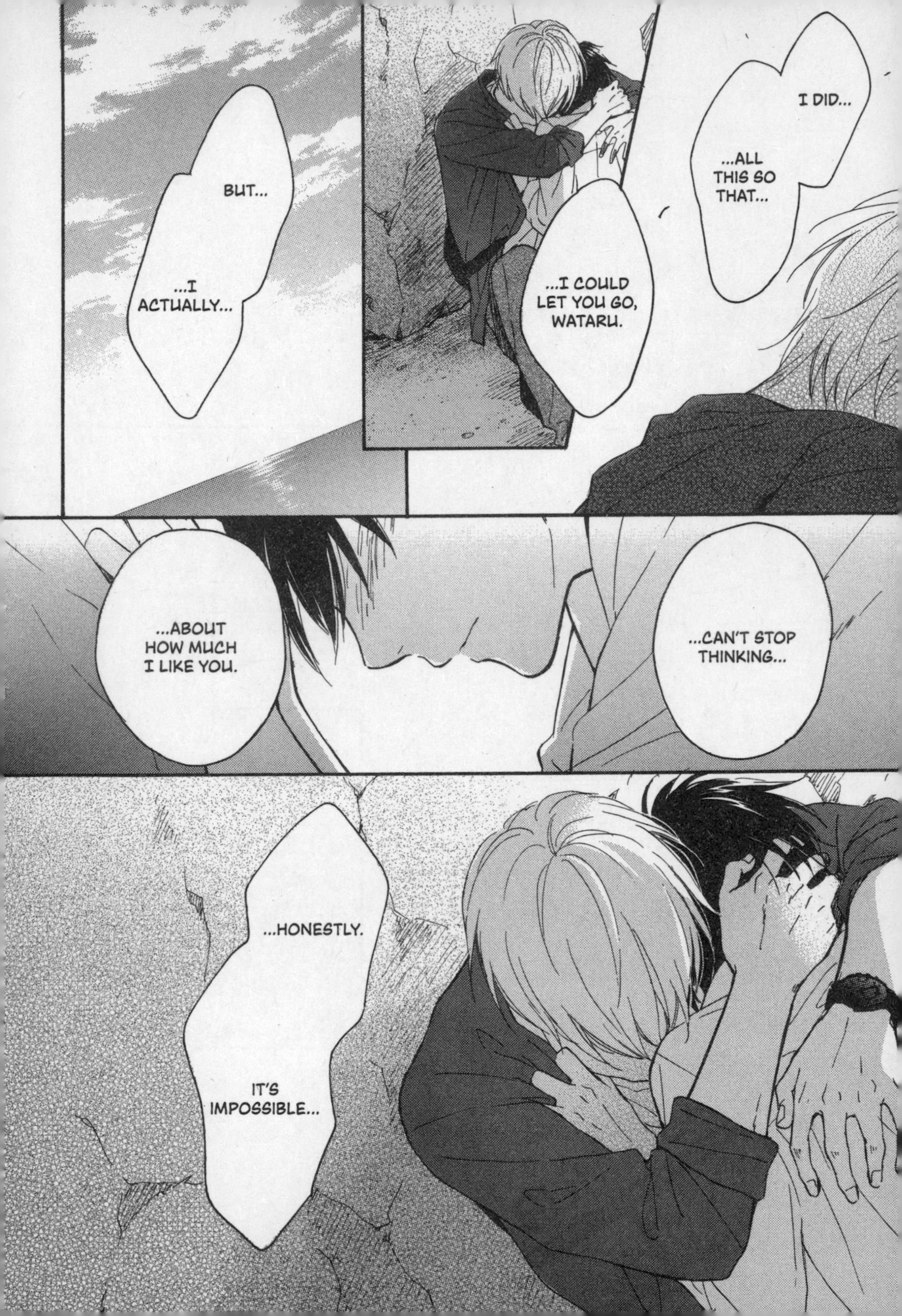
I DID...
...ALL THIS SO THAT...
...I COULD LET YOU GO, WATARU.
BUT...
...I ACTUALLY...
...CAN'T STOP THINKING...
...ABOUT HOW MUCH I LIKE YOU.
...HONESTLY.
IT'S IMPOSSIBLE...

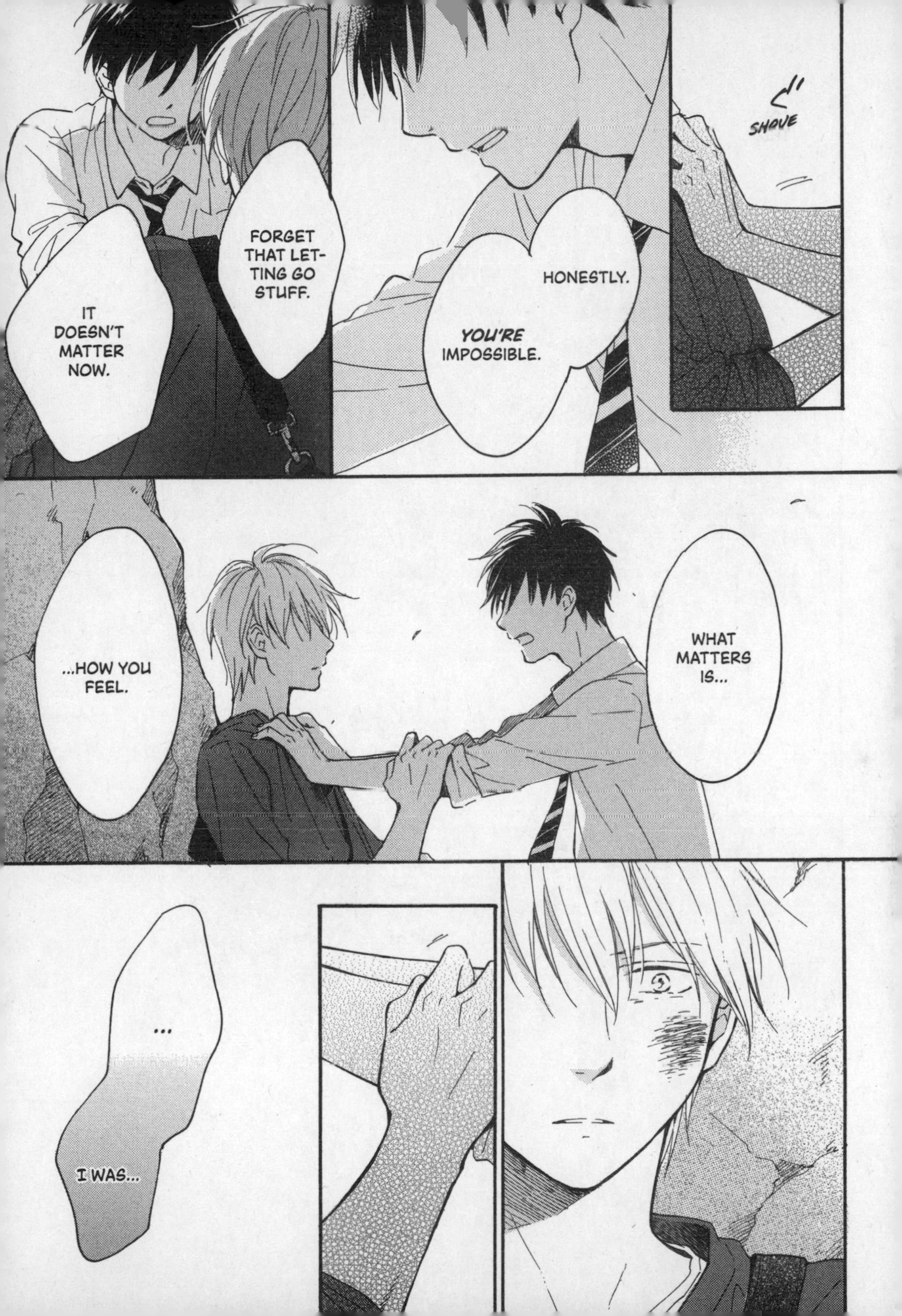
SHOVE
HONESTLY. YOU'RE IMPOSSIBLE.
FORGET THAT LETTING GO STUFF.
IT DOESN'T MATTER NOW.
WHAT MATTERS IS...
...HOW YOU FEEL.
...
I WAS...

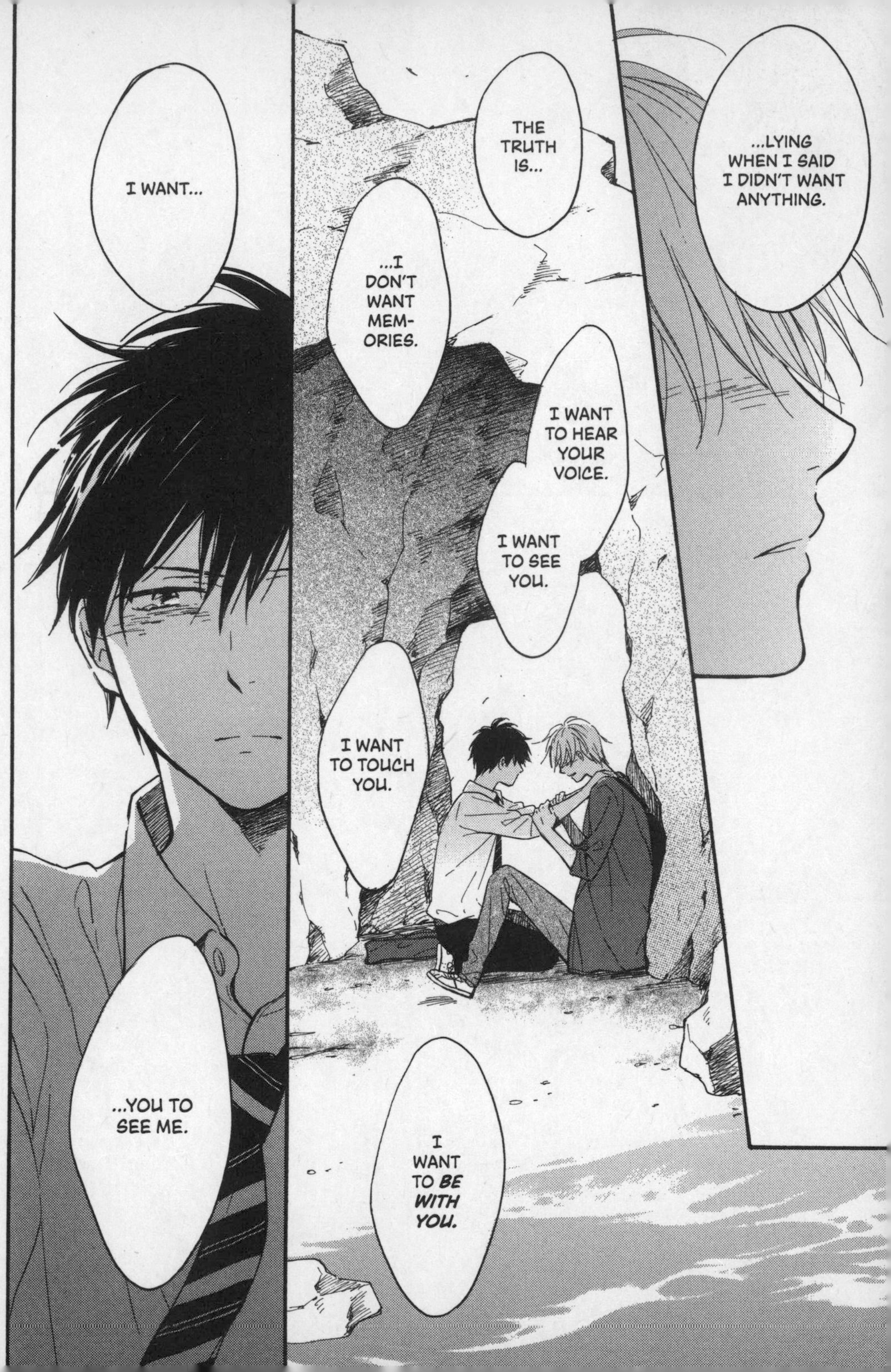
...LYING WHEN I SAID I DIDN'T WANT ANYTHING.
THE TRUTH IS...
...I DON'T WANT MEM-ORIES.
I WANT TO HEAR YOUR VOICE.
I WANT TO SEE YOU.
I WANT TO TOUCH YOU.
I WANT TO *BE WITH YOU.*
I WANT...
...YOU TO SEE ME.

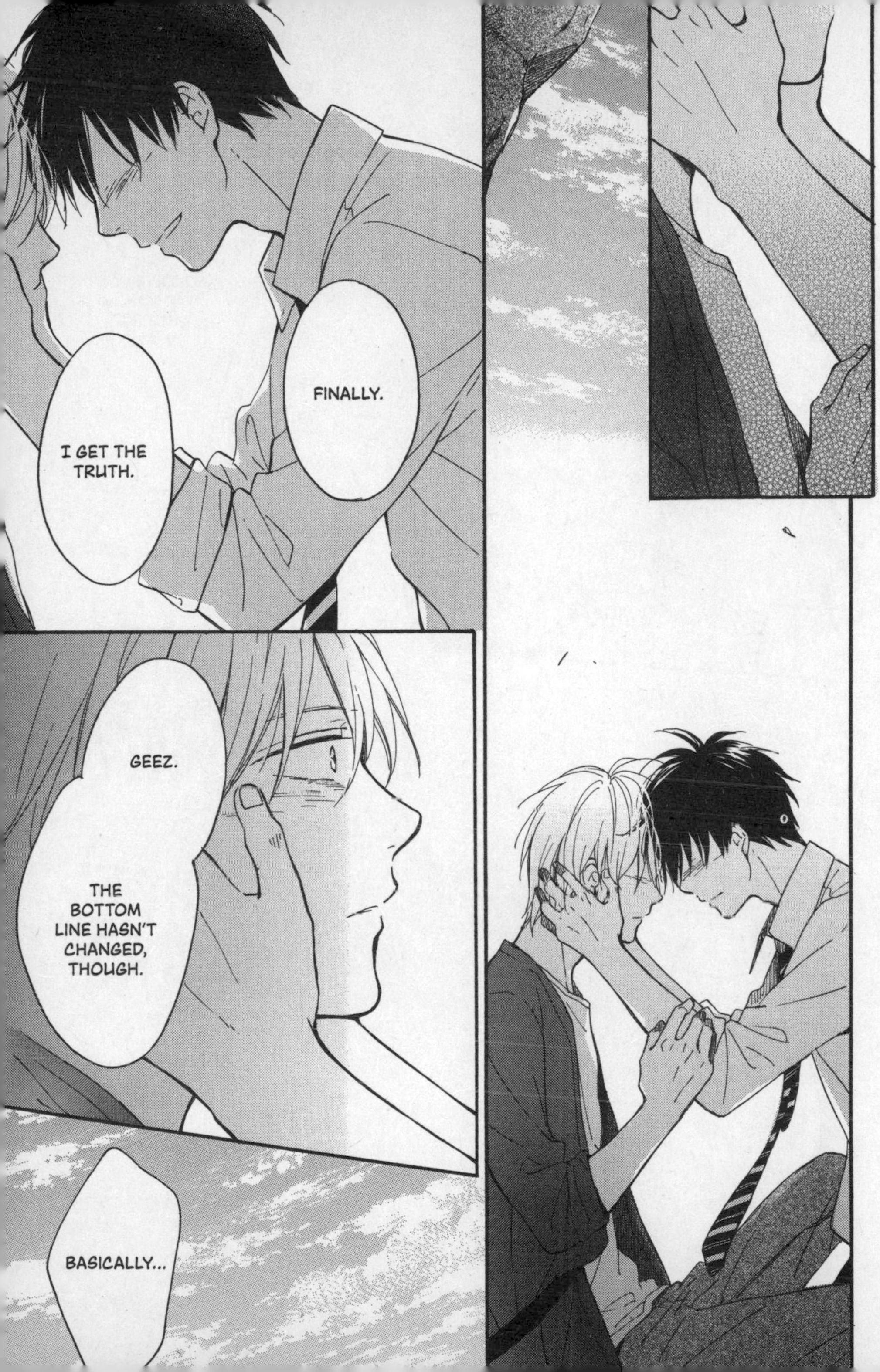
FINALLY.
I GET THE TRUTH.
GEEZ.
THE BOTTOM LINE HASN'T CHANGED, THOUGH.
BASICALLY...

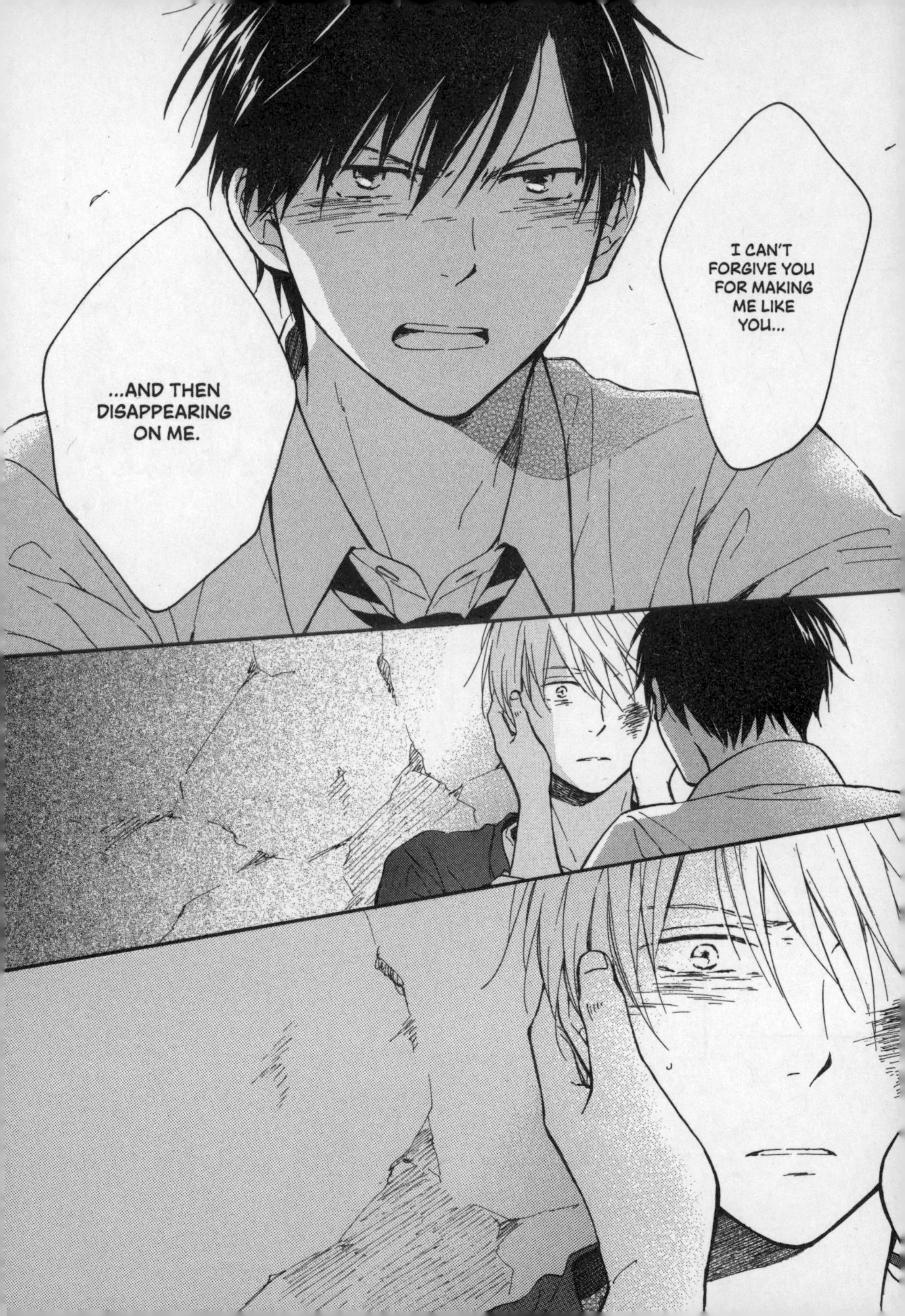
I CAN'T FORGIVE YOU FOR MAKING ME LIKE YOU...
...AND THEN DISAPPEARING ON ME.

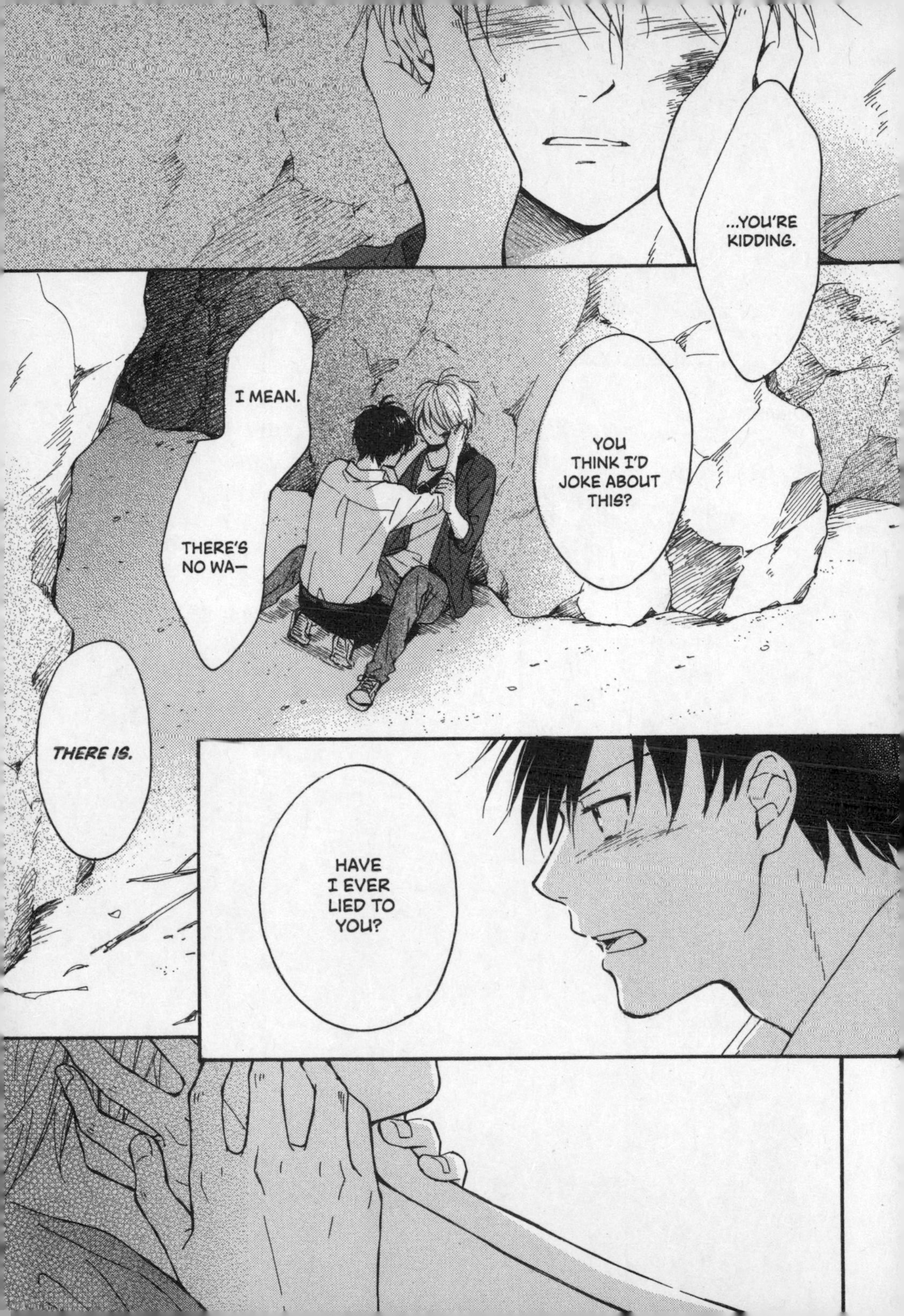
...YOU'RE KIDDING.
YOU THINK I'D JOKE ABOUT THIS?
I MEAN.
THERE'S NO WA—
THERE IS.
HAVE I EVER LIED TO YOU?

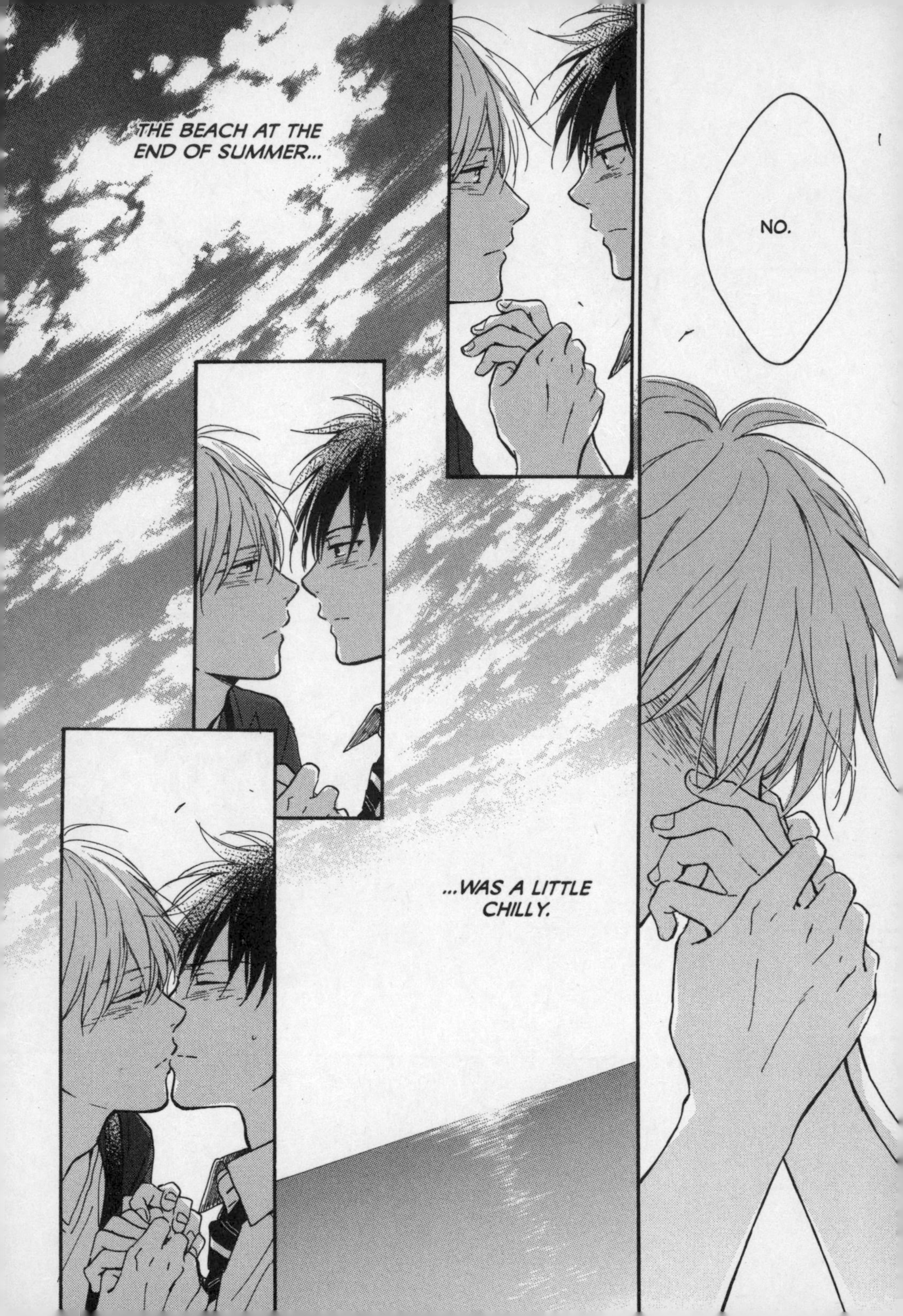
NO.
THE BEACH AT THE END OF SUMMER...
...WAS A LITTLE CHILLY.

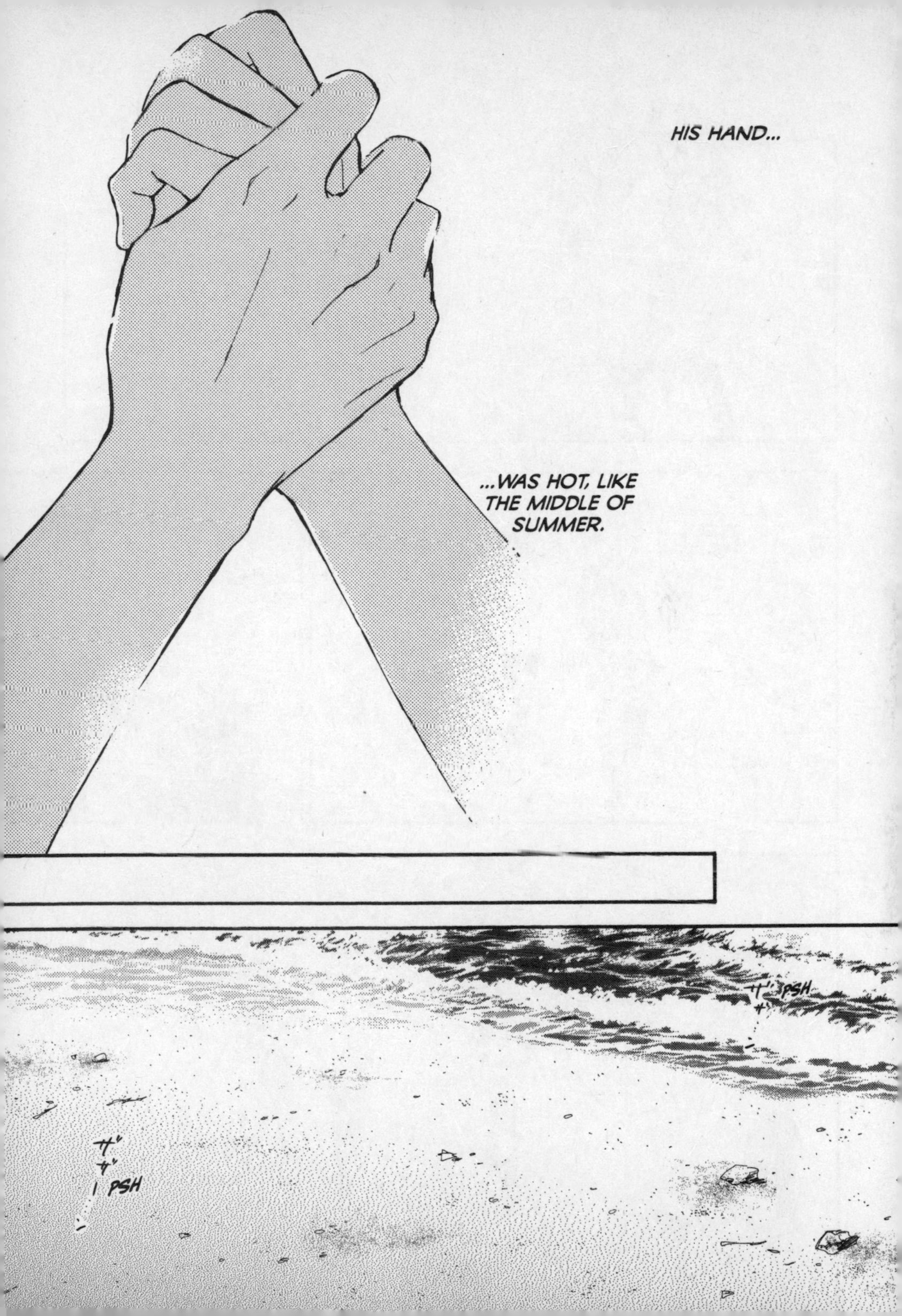
HIS HAND...
...WAS HOT, LIKE THE MIDDLE OF SUMMER.
PSH
PSH

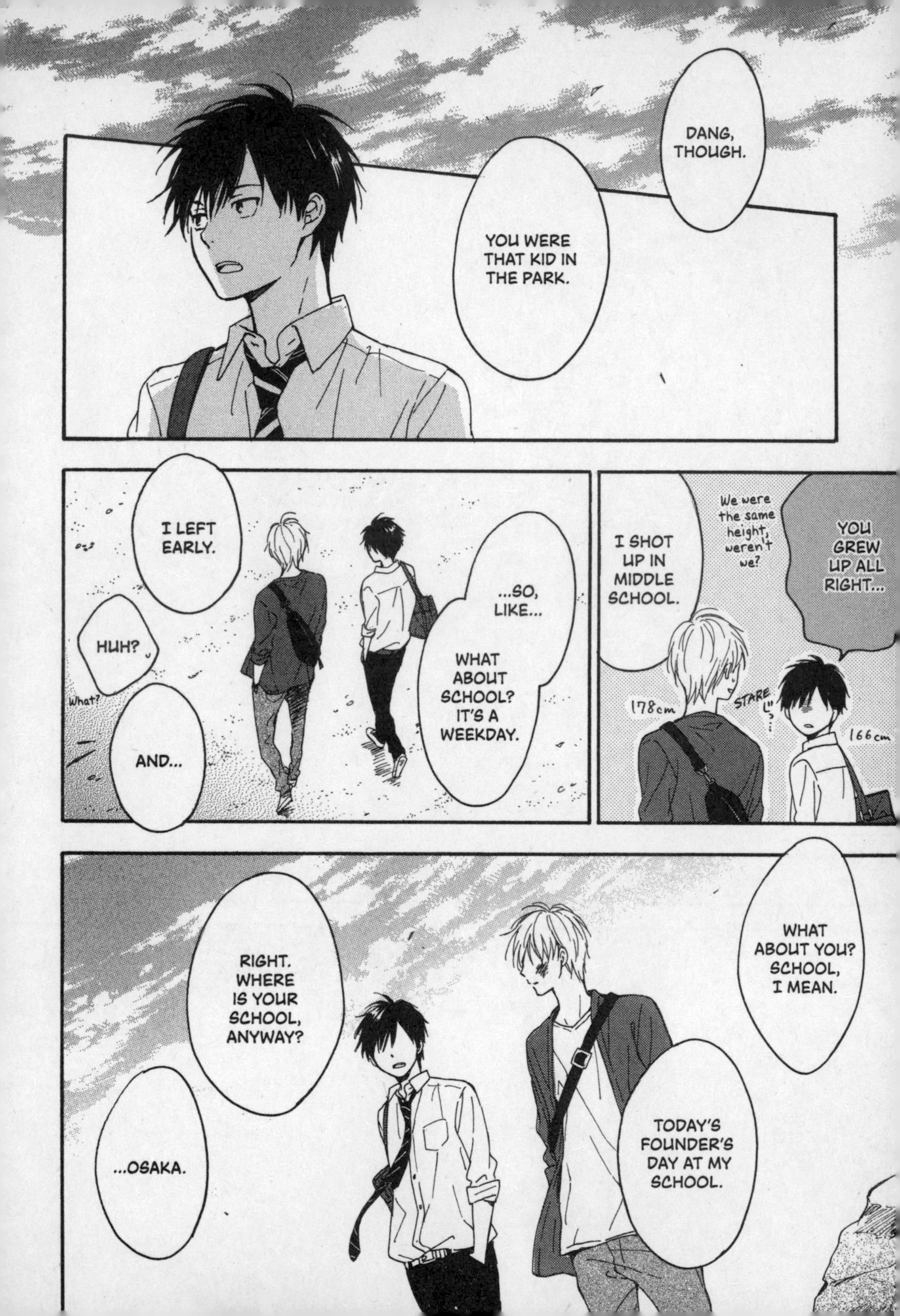
DANG, THOUGH.
YOU WERE THAT KID IN THE PARK.
YOU GREW UP ALL RIGHT...
We were the same height, weren't we?
I SHOT UP IN MIDDLE SCHOOL.
178cm
STARE
166cm
...SO, LIKE...
WHAT ABOUT SCHOOL? IT'S A WEEKDAY.
I LEFT EARLY.
HUH?
What?
AND...
WHAT ABOUT YOU? SCHOOL, I MEAN.
TODAY'S FOUNDER'S DAY AT MY SCHOOL.
RIGHT. WHERE IS YOUR SCHOOL, ANYWAY?
...OSAKA.

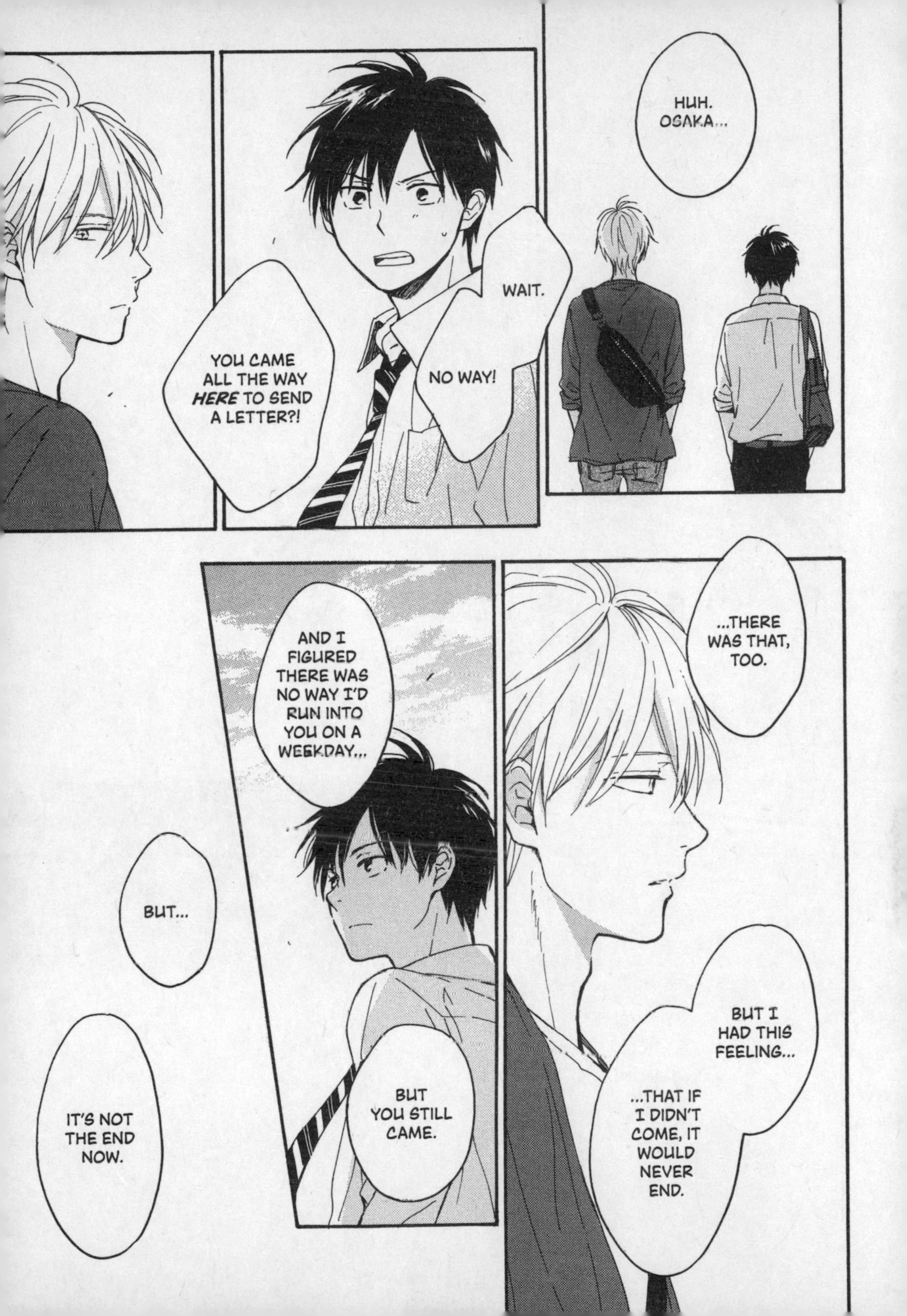
HUH. OSAKA...
WAIT.
NO WAY!
YOU CAME ALL THE WAY *HERE* TO SEND A LETTER?!
...THERE WAS THAT, TOO.
BUT I HAD THIS FEELING...
...THAT IF I DIDN'T COME, IT WOULD NEVER END.
AND I FIGURED THERE WAS NO WAY I'D RUN INTO YOU ON A WEEKDAY...
BUT YOU STILL CAME.
BUT...
IT'S NOT THE END NOW.

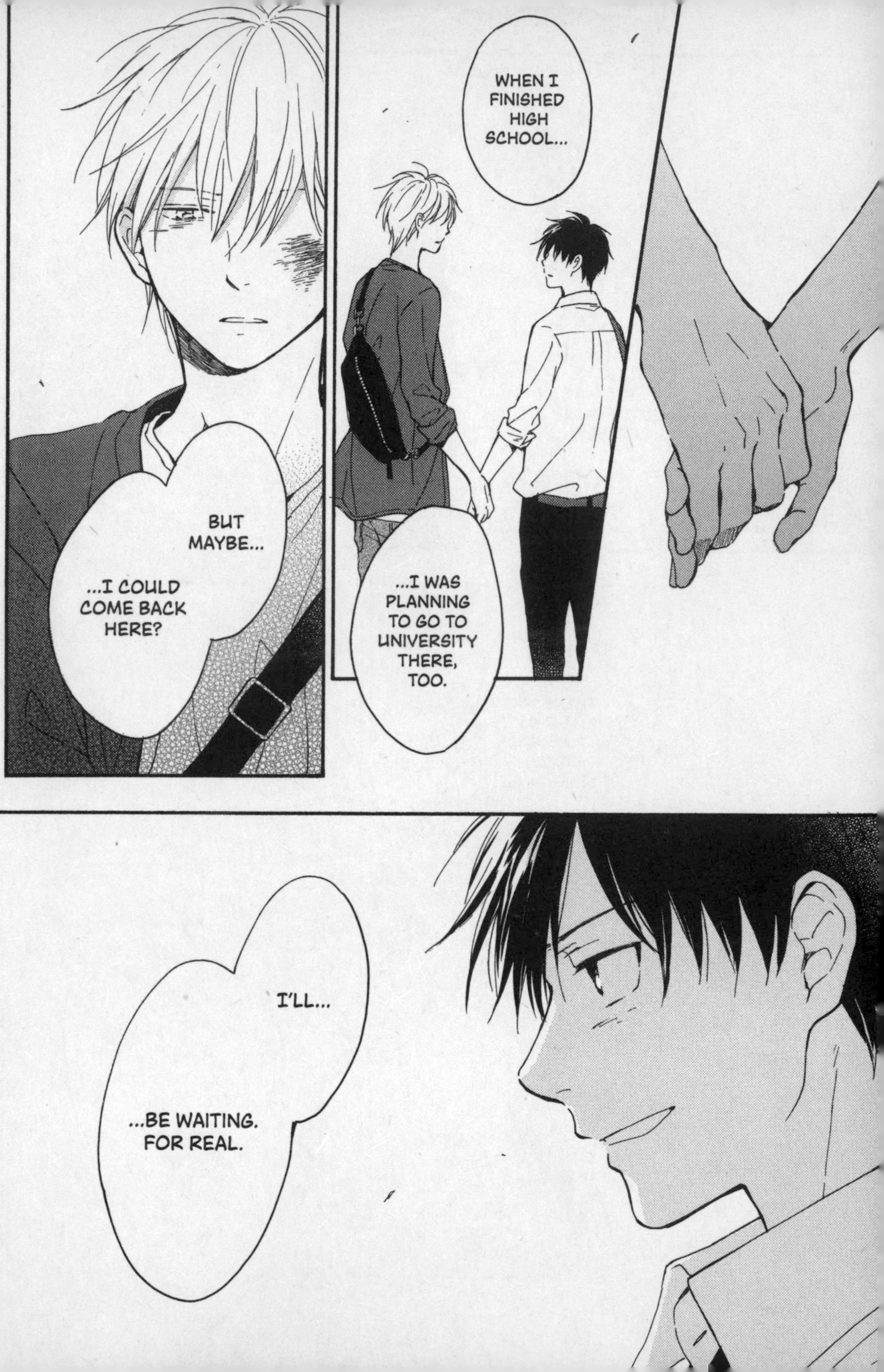
WHEN I FINISHED HIGH SCHOOL...
...I WAS PLANNING TO GO TO UNIVERSITY THERE, TOO.
BUT MAYBE...
...I COULD COME BACK HERE?
I'LL...
...BE WAITING. FOR REAL.

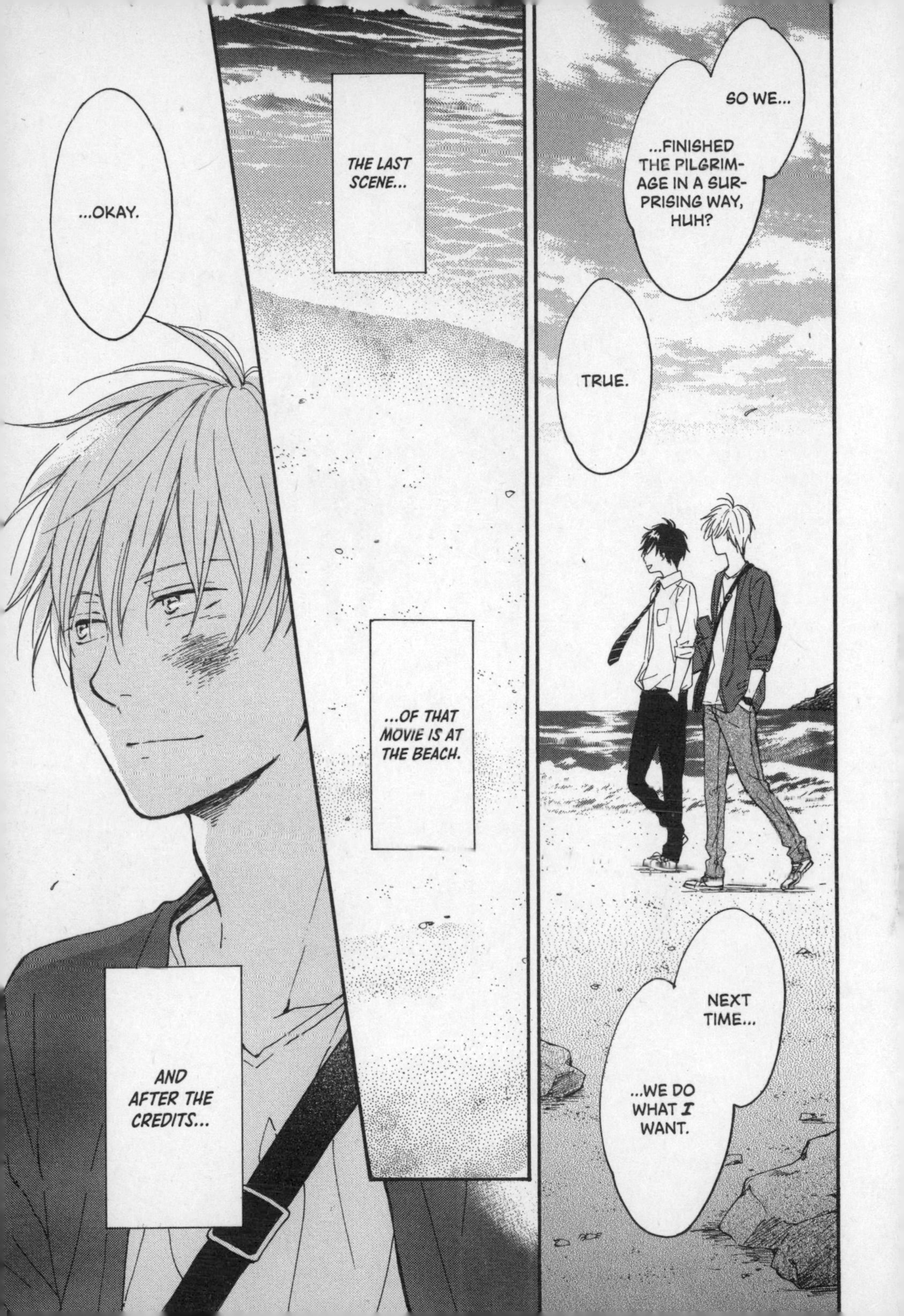
SO WE...
...FINISHED THE PILGRIMAGE IN A SURPRISING WAY, HUH?
TRUE.
NEXT TIME...
...WE DO WHAT I WANT.
THE LAST SCENE...
...OF THAT MOVIE IS AT THE BEACH.
...OKAY.
AND AFTER THE CREDITS...

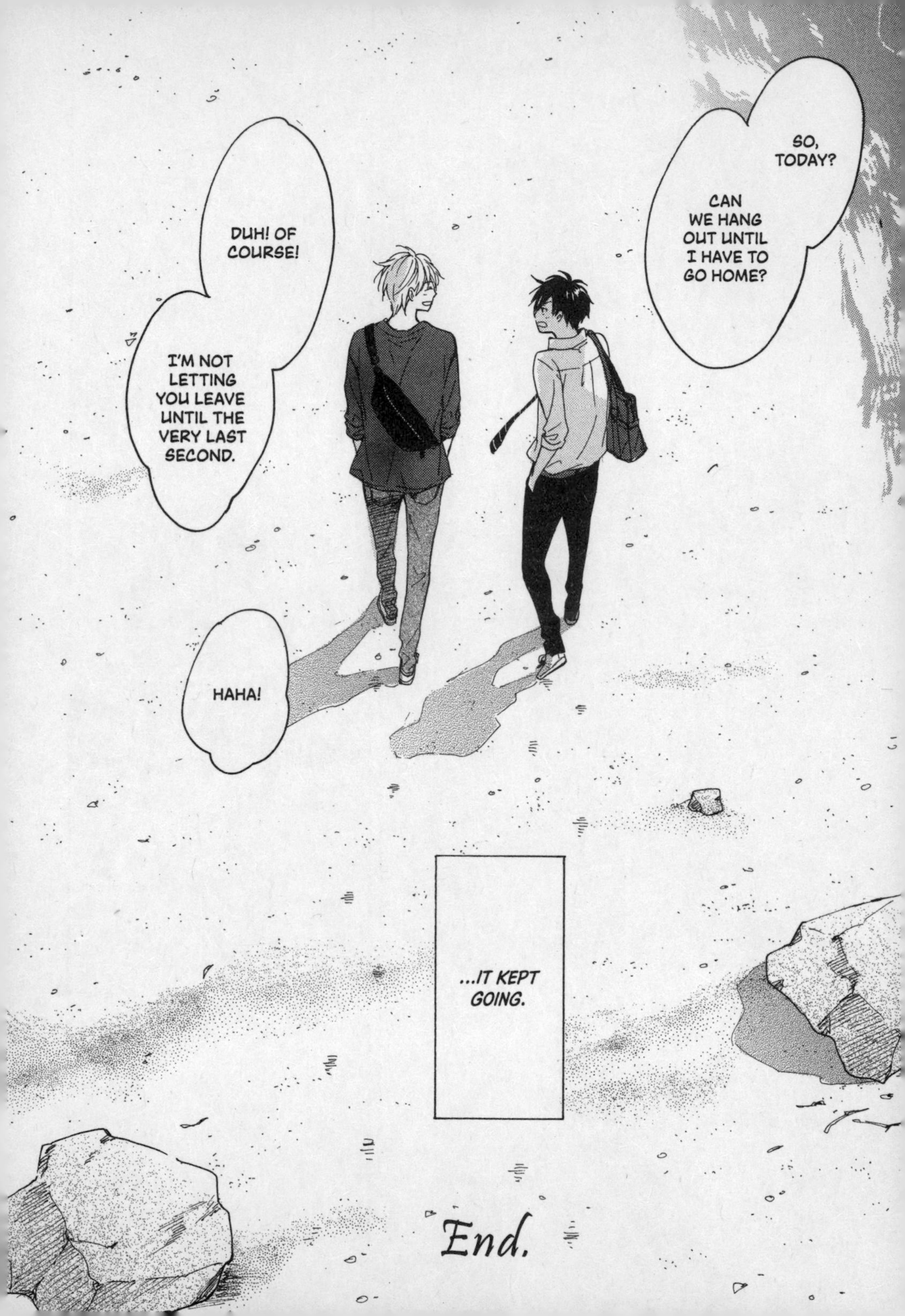
SO, TODAY?
CAN WE HANG OUT UNTIL I HAVE TO GO HOME?
DUH! OF COURSE!
I'M NOT LETTING YOU LEAVE UNTIL THE VERY LAST SECOND.
HAHA!
...IT KEPT GOING.
End.

First Published

Chapter 1	*gateau*	Sept. 2016
Chapter 2	*gateau*	Nov. 2016
Chapter 3	*gateau*	Feb. 2017
Chapter 4	*gateau*	May 2017
Final Chapter	*gateau*	July 2017

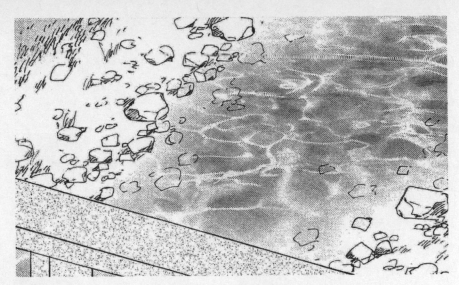

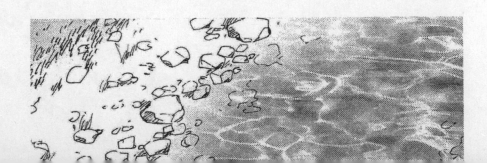

MY **SUMMER** OF **YOU**

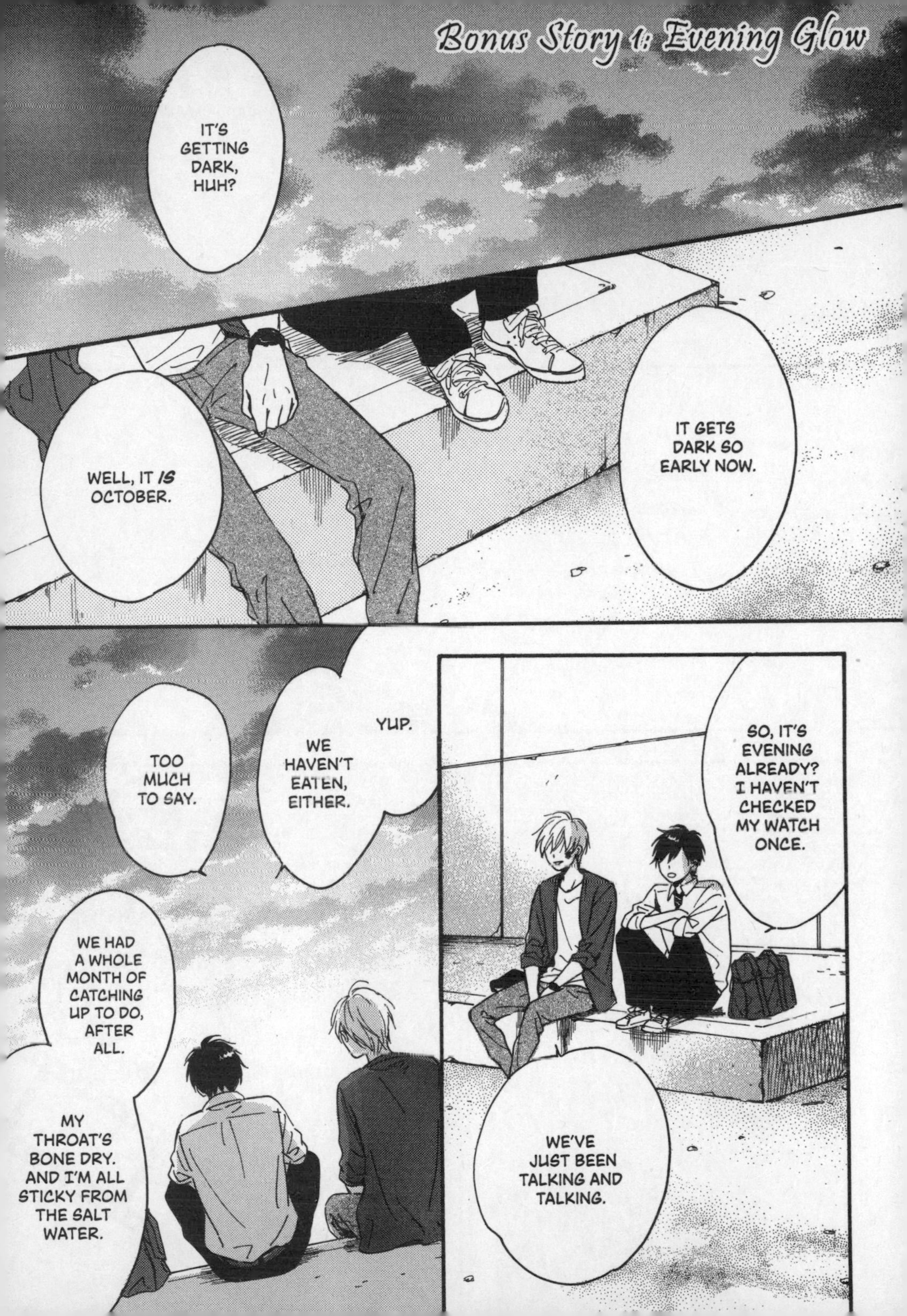
Bonus Story 1: Evening Glow
IT'S GETTING DARK, HUH?
IT GETS DARK SO EARLY NOW.
WELL, IT *IS* OCTOBER.
SO, IT'S EVENING ALREADY? I HAVEN'T CHECKED MY WATCH ONCE.
WE'VE JUST BEEN TALKING AND TALKING.
YUP.
WE HAVEN'T EATEN, EITHER.
TOO MUCH TO SAY.
WE HAD A WHOLE MONTH OF CATCHING UP TO DO, AFTER ALL.
MY THROAT'S BONE DRY. AND I'M ALL STICKY FROM THE SALT WATER.

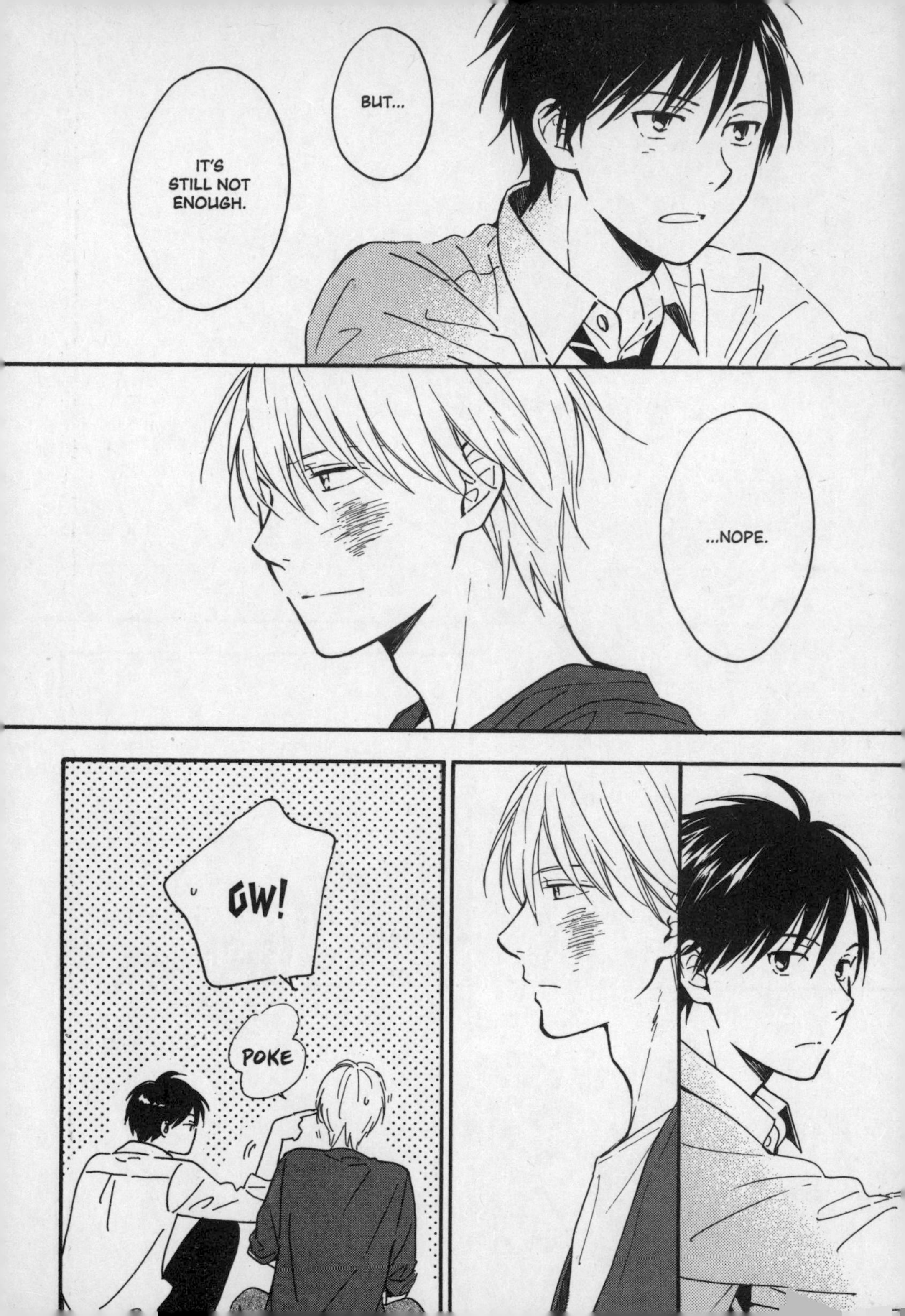
BUT...
IT'S STILL NOT ENOUGH.
...NOPE.
OW!
POKE

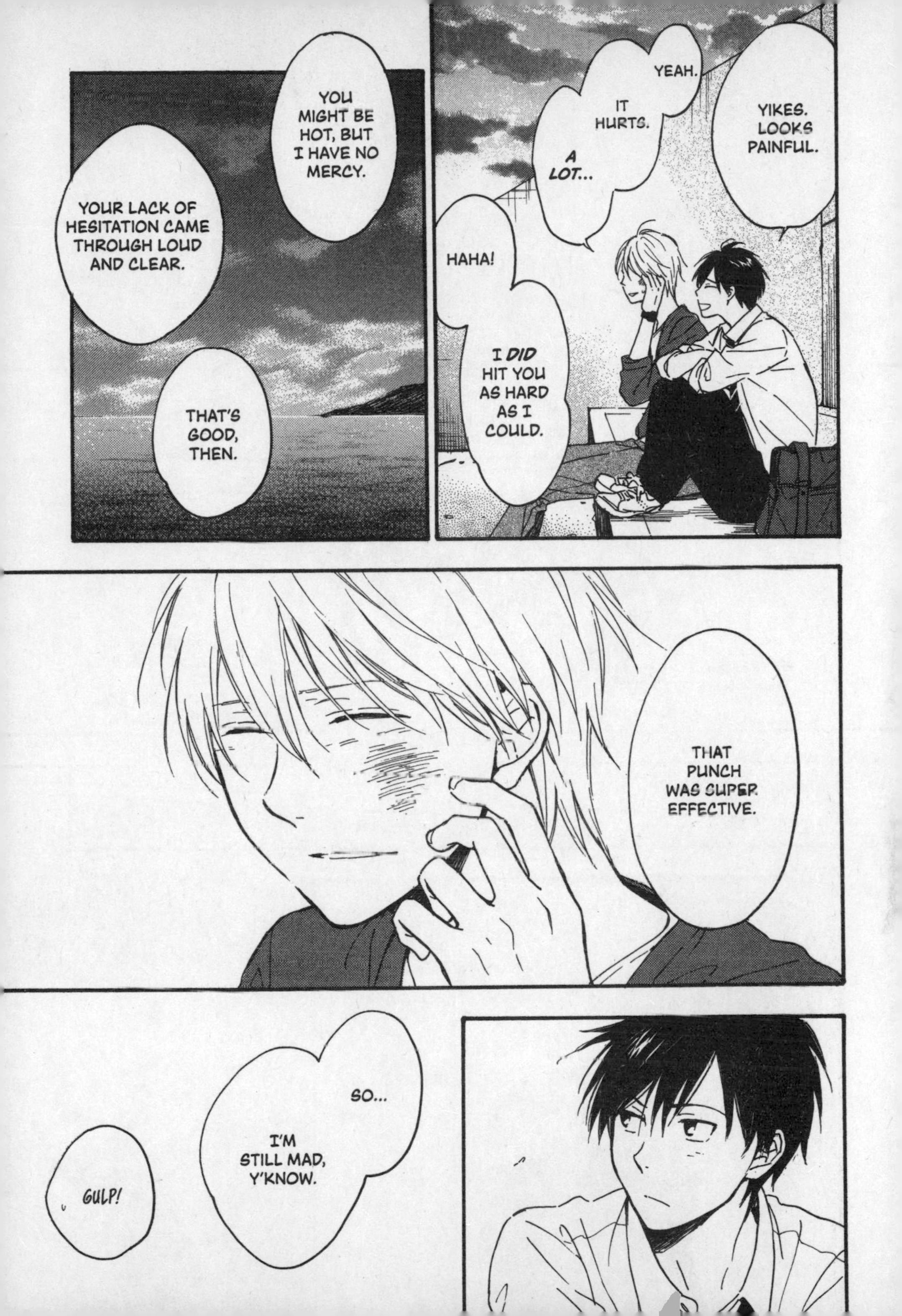
YIKES. LOOKS PAINFUL.
YEAH.
IT HURTS.
A LOT...
HAHA!
I DID HIT YOU AS HARD AS I COULD.
YOU MIGHT BE HOT, BUT I HAVE NO MERCY.
YOUR LACK OF HESITATION CAME THROUGH LOUD AND CLEAR.
THAT'S GOOD, THEN.
THAT PUNCH WAS SUPER EFFECTIVE.
SO...
I'M STILL MAD, Y'KNOW.
GULP!

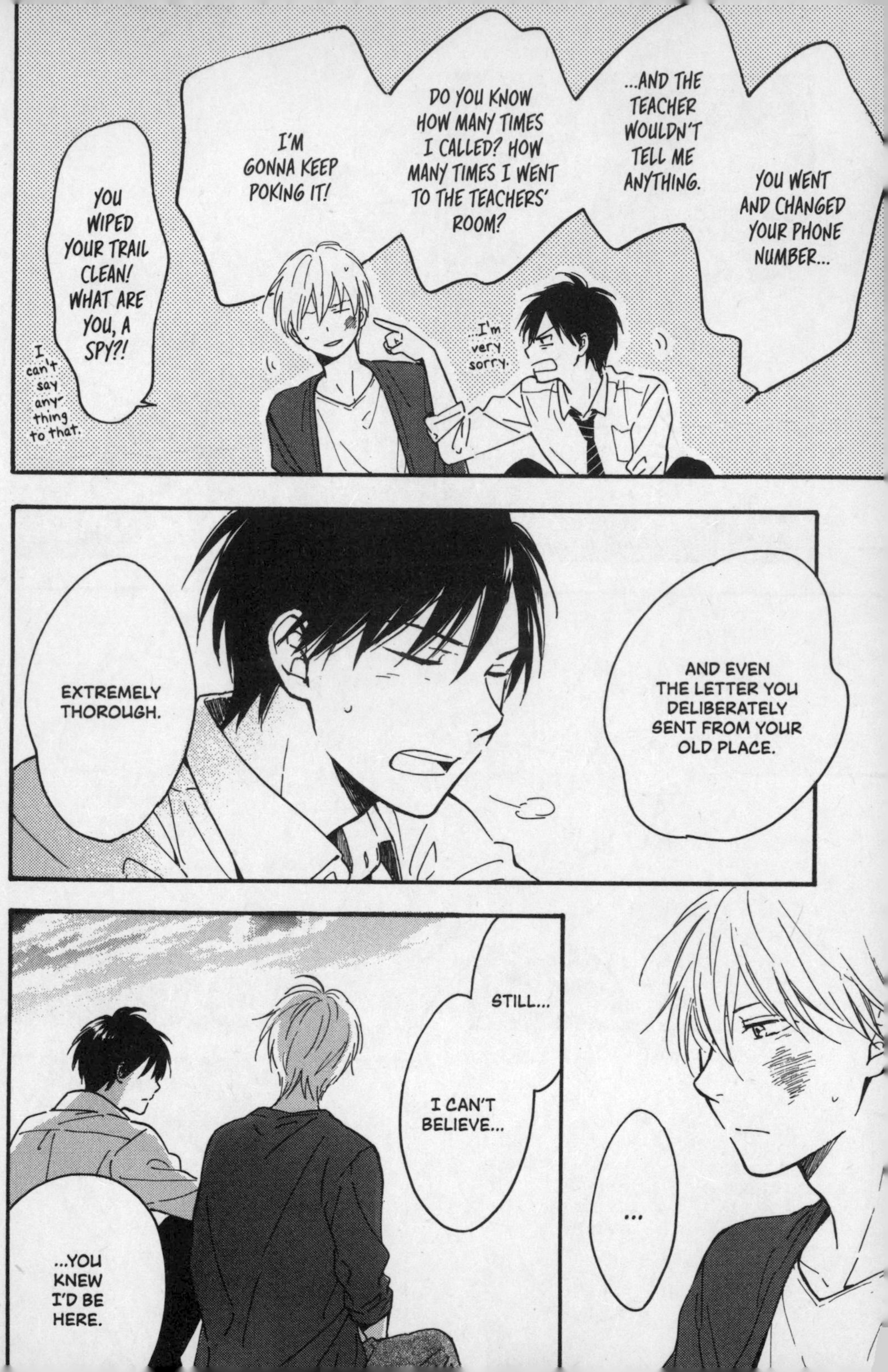
YOU WENT AND CHANGED YOUR PHONE NUMBER...
...AND THE TEACHER WOULDN'T TELL ME ANYTHING.
DO YOU KNOW HOW MANY TIMES I CALLED? HOW MANY TIMES I WENT TO THE TEACHERS' ROOM?
I'M GONNA KEEP POKING IT!
...I'm very sorry.
YOU WIPED YOUR TRAIL CLEAN! WHAT ARE YOU, A SPY?!
I can't say anything to that.
AND EVEN THE LETTER YOU DELIBERATELY SENT FROM YOUR OLD PLACE.
EXTREMELY THOROUGH.
...
STILL...
I CAN'T BELIEVE...
...YOU KNEW I'D BE HERE.

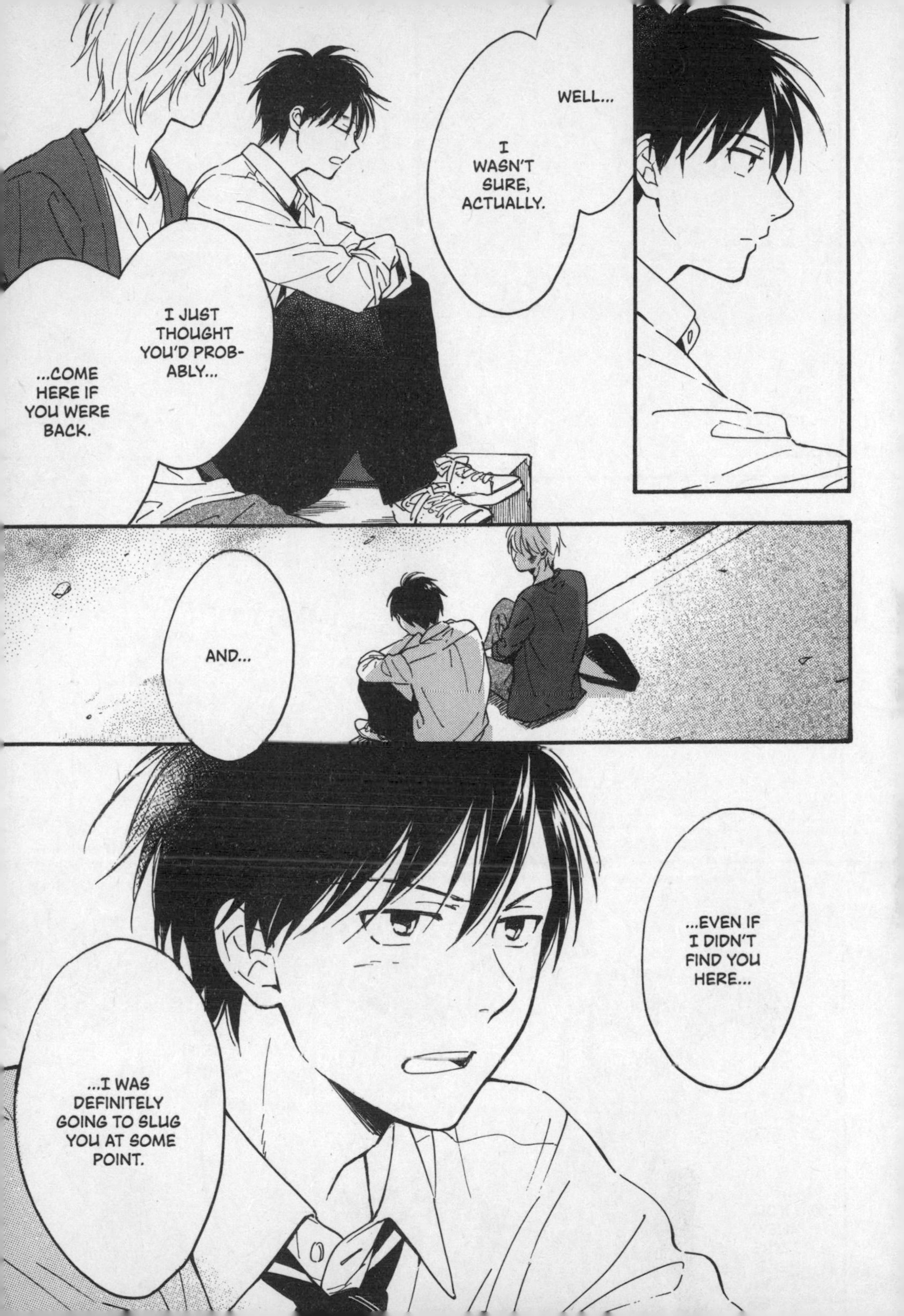
WELL...
I WASN'T SURE, ACTUALLY.
I JUST THOUGHT YOU'D PROB-ABLY...
...COME HERE IF YOU WERE BACK.
AND...
...EVEN IF I DIDN'T FIND YOU HERE...
...I WAS DEFINITELY GOING TO SLUG YOU AT SOME POINT.

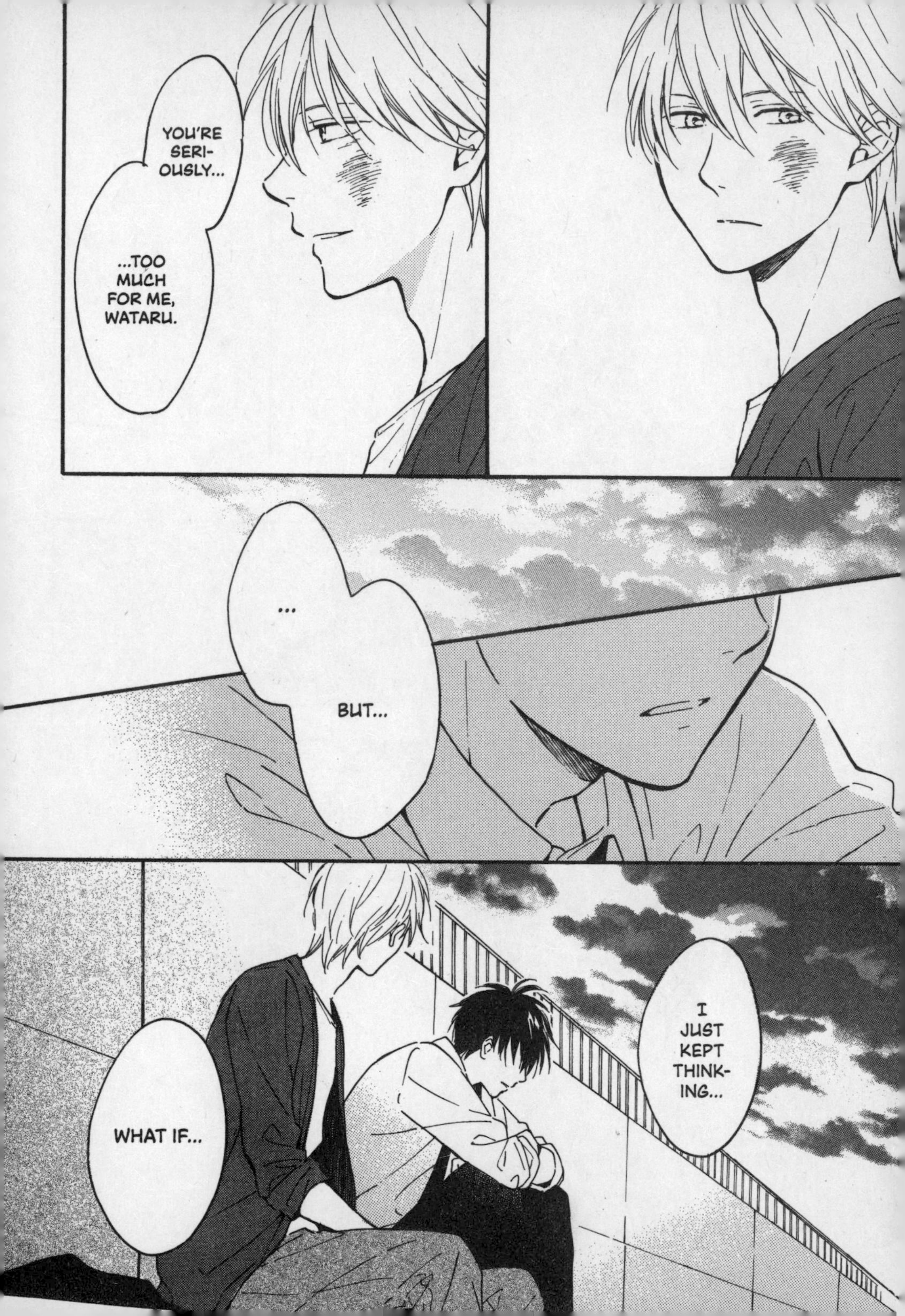
YOU'RE SERI-OUSLY...
...TOO MUCH FOR ME, WATARU.
...
BUT...
I JUST KEPT THINK-ING...
WHAT IF...

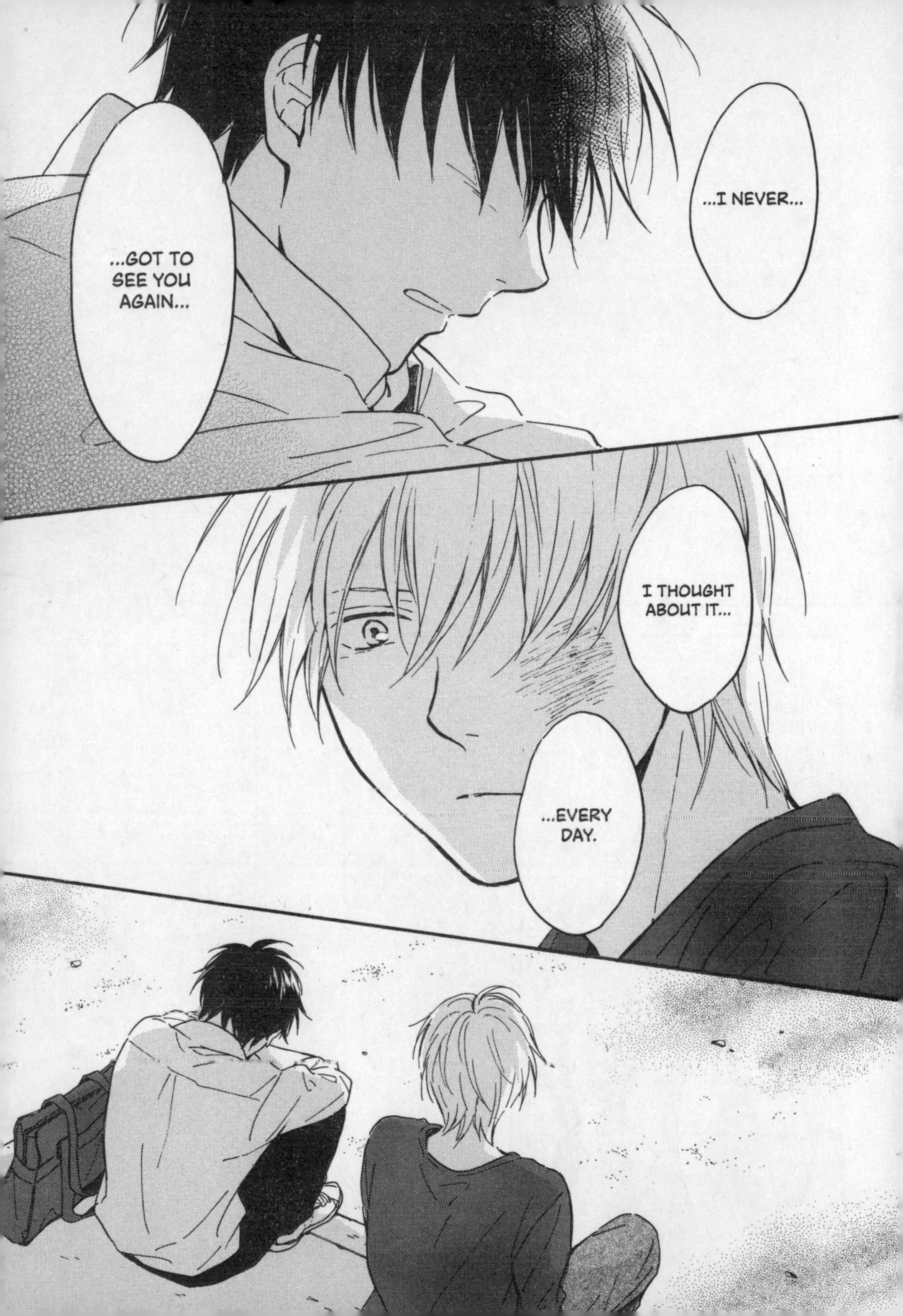
...I NEVER...
...GOT TO SEE YOU AGAIN...
I THOUGHT ABOUT IT...
...EVERY DAY.

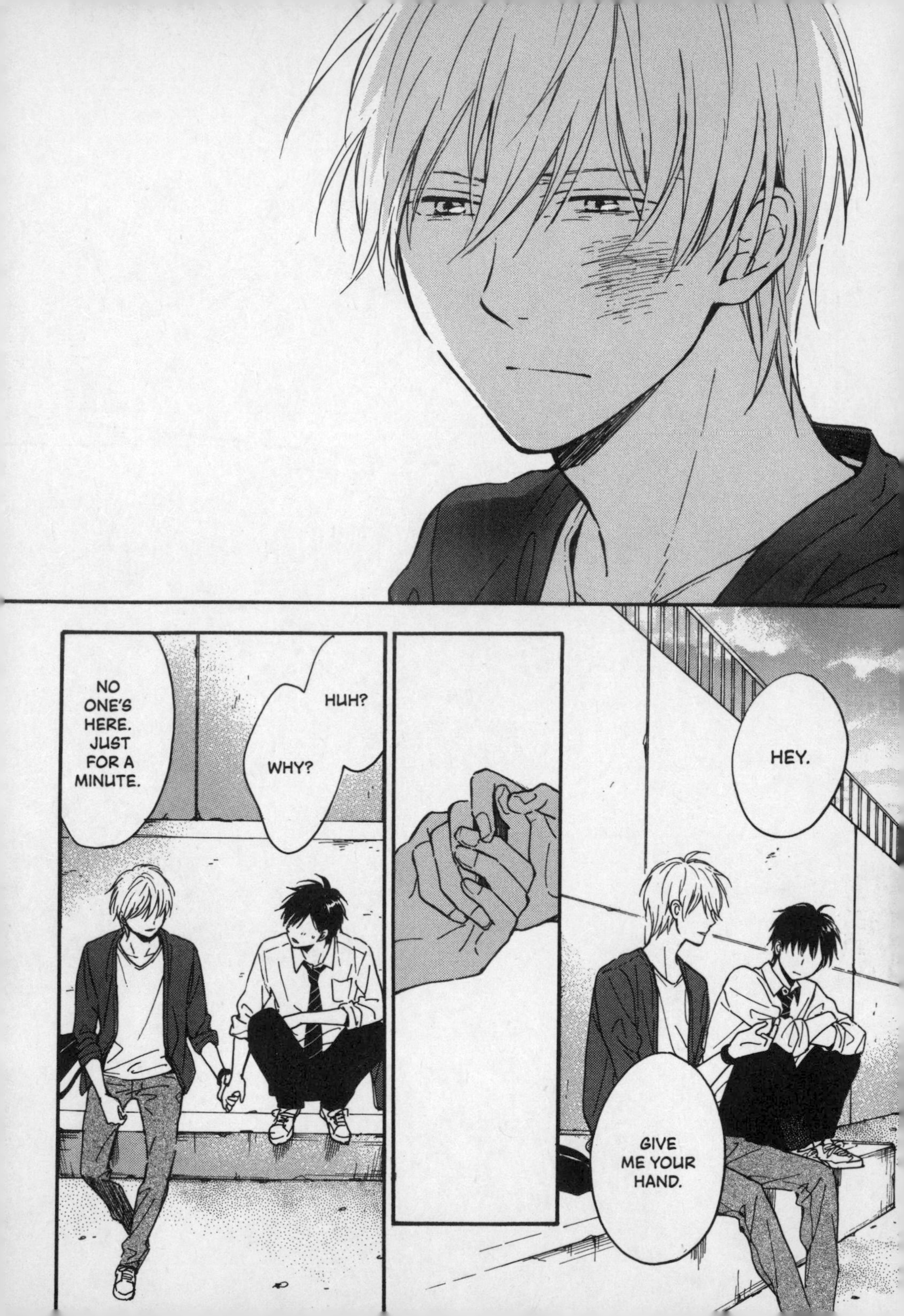
HEY.
GIVE ME YOUR HAND.
HUH?
WHY?
NO ONE'S HERE. JUST FOR A MINUTE.

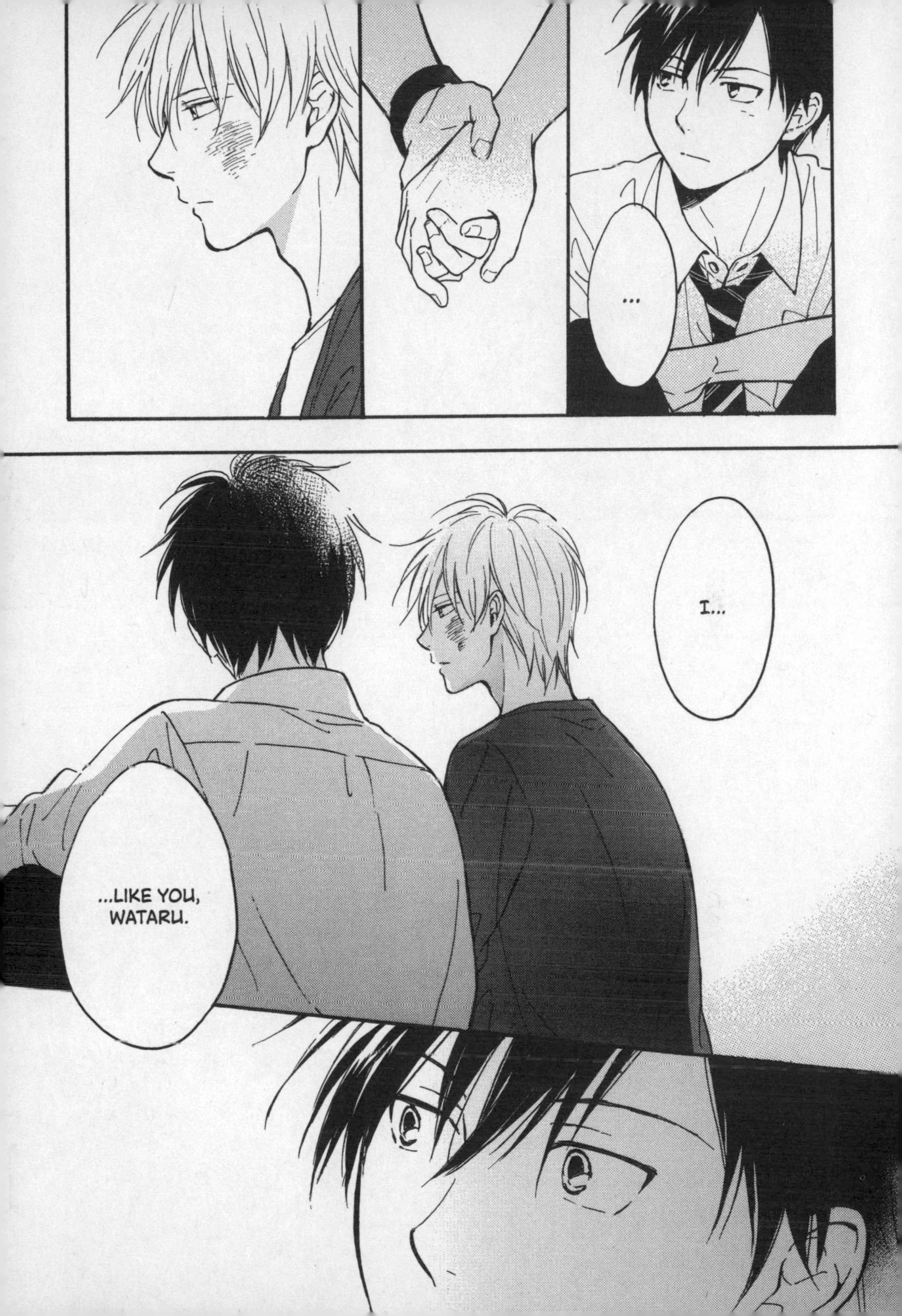
...
I...
...LIKE YOU, WATARU.

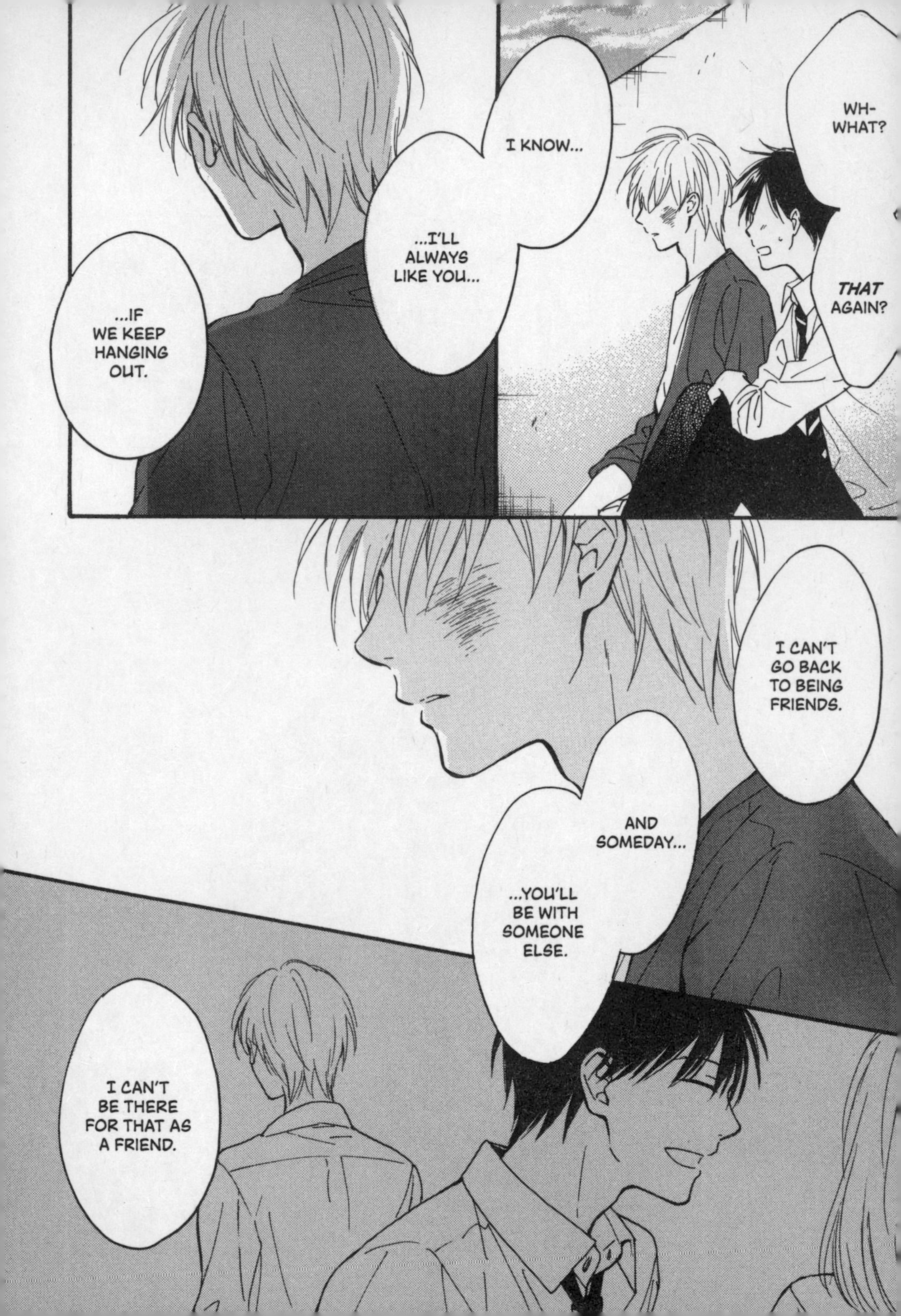
WH-
WHAT?
THAT AGAIN?
I KNOW...
...I'LL ALWAYS LIKE YOU...
...IF WE KEEP HANGING OUT.
I CAN'T GO BACK TO BEING FRIENDS.
AND SOMEDAY...
...YOU'LL BE WITH SOMEONE ELSE.
I CAN'T BE THERE FOR THAT AS A FRIEND.

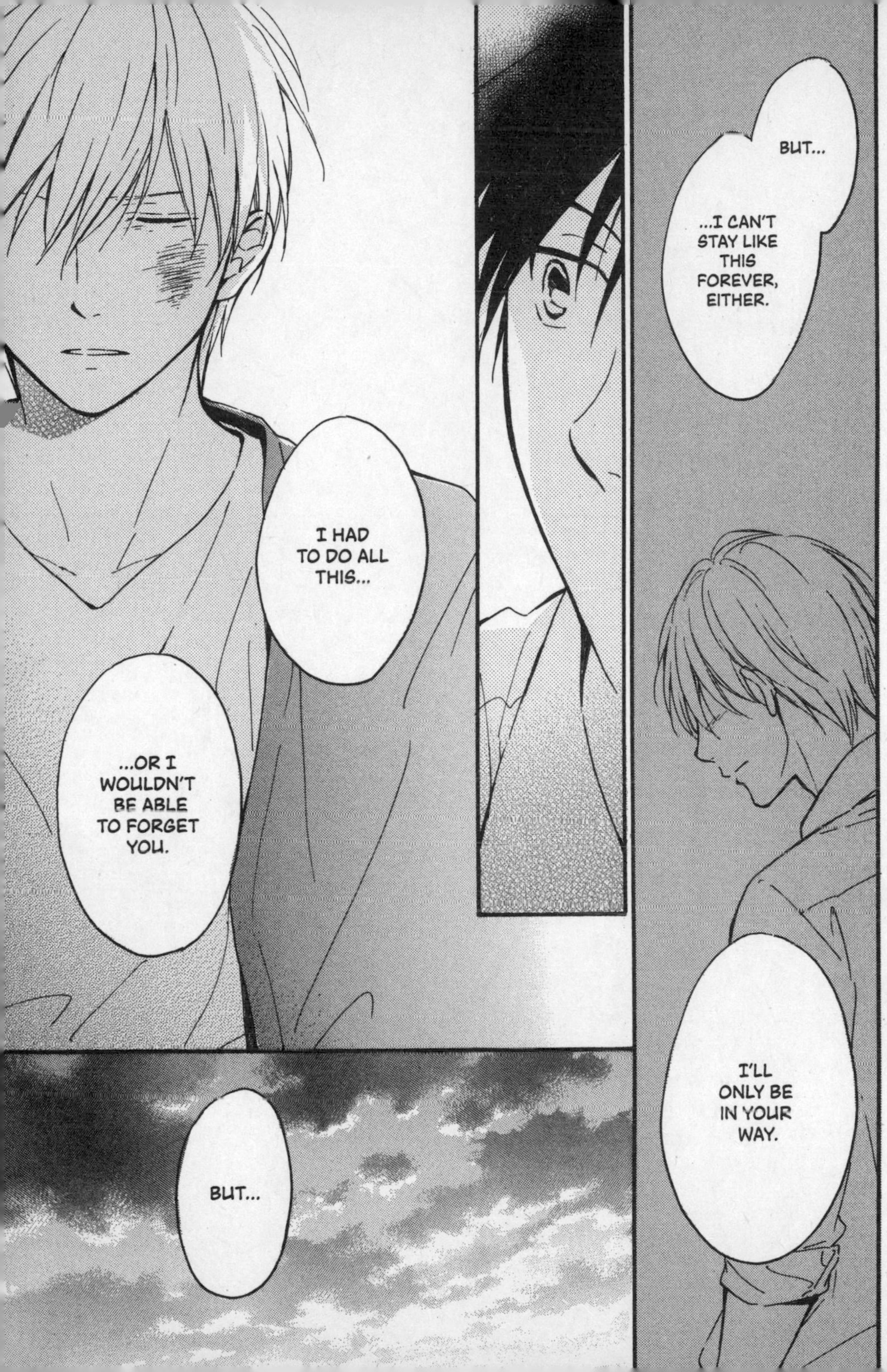
BUT...
...I CAN'T STAY LIKE THIS FOREVER, EITHER.
I'LL ONLY BE IN YOUR WAY.
I HAD TO DO ALL THIS...
...OR I WOULDN'T BE ABLE TO FORGET YOU.
BUT...

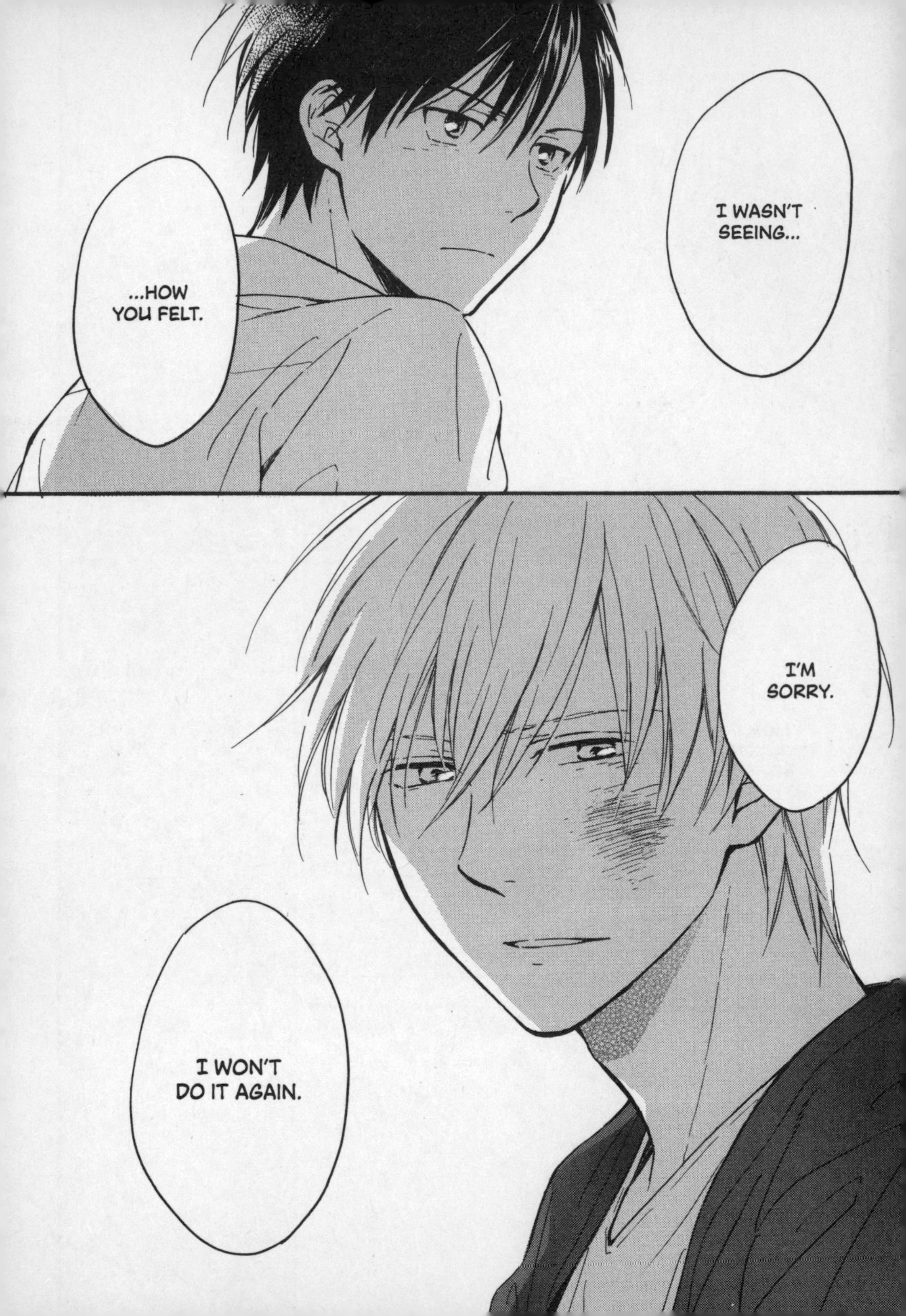
I WASN'T SEEING...
...HOW YOU FELT.
I'M SORRY.
I WON'T DO IT AGAIN.

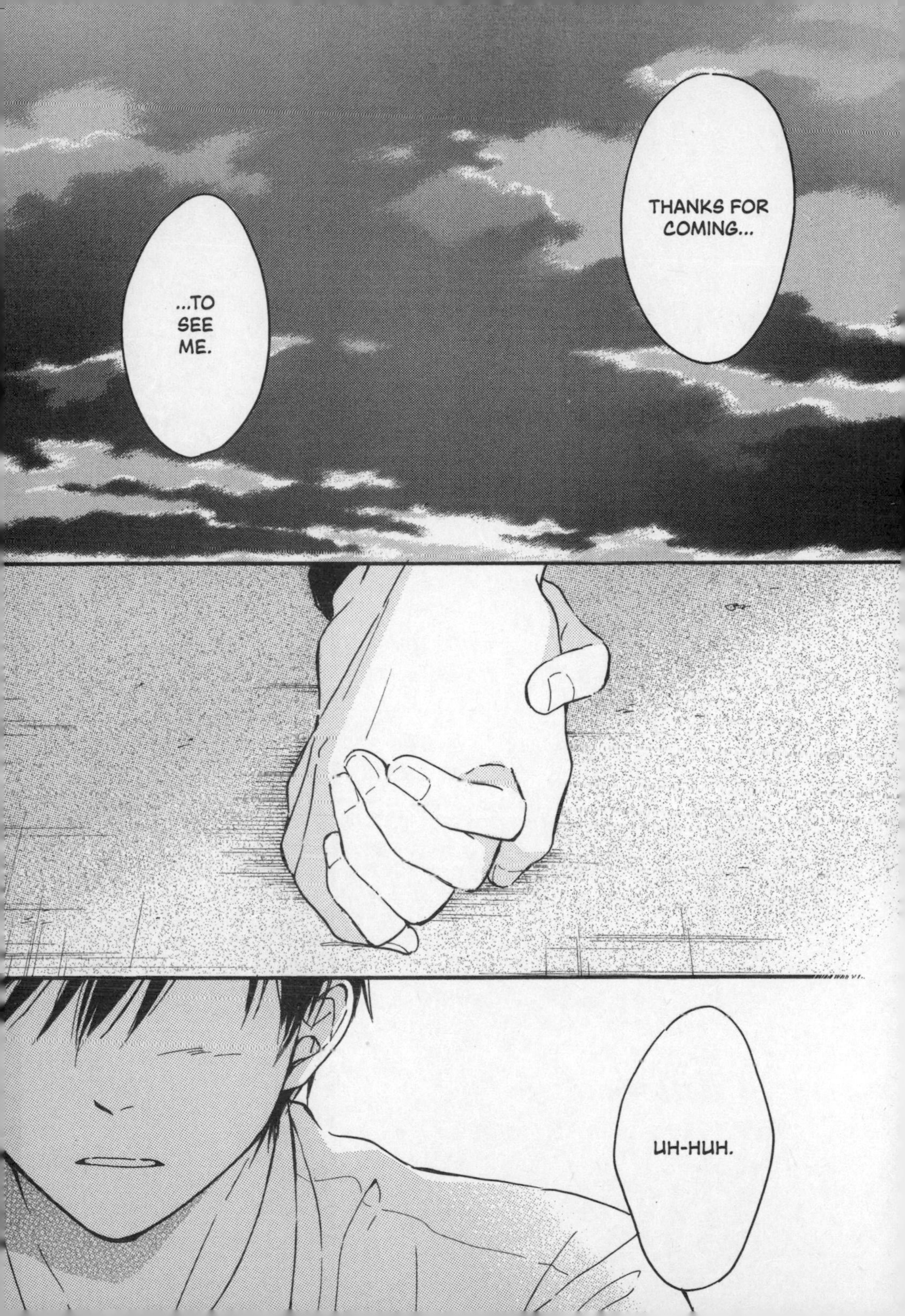
THANKS FOR COMING...
...TO SEE ME.
UH-HUH.

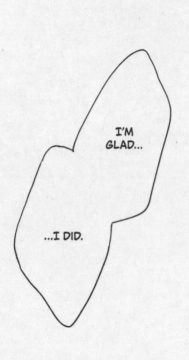

I'M GLAD...

...I DID.

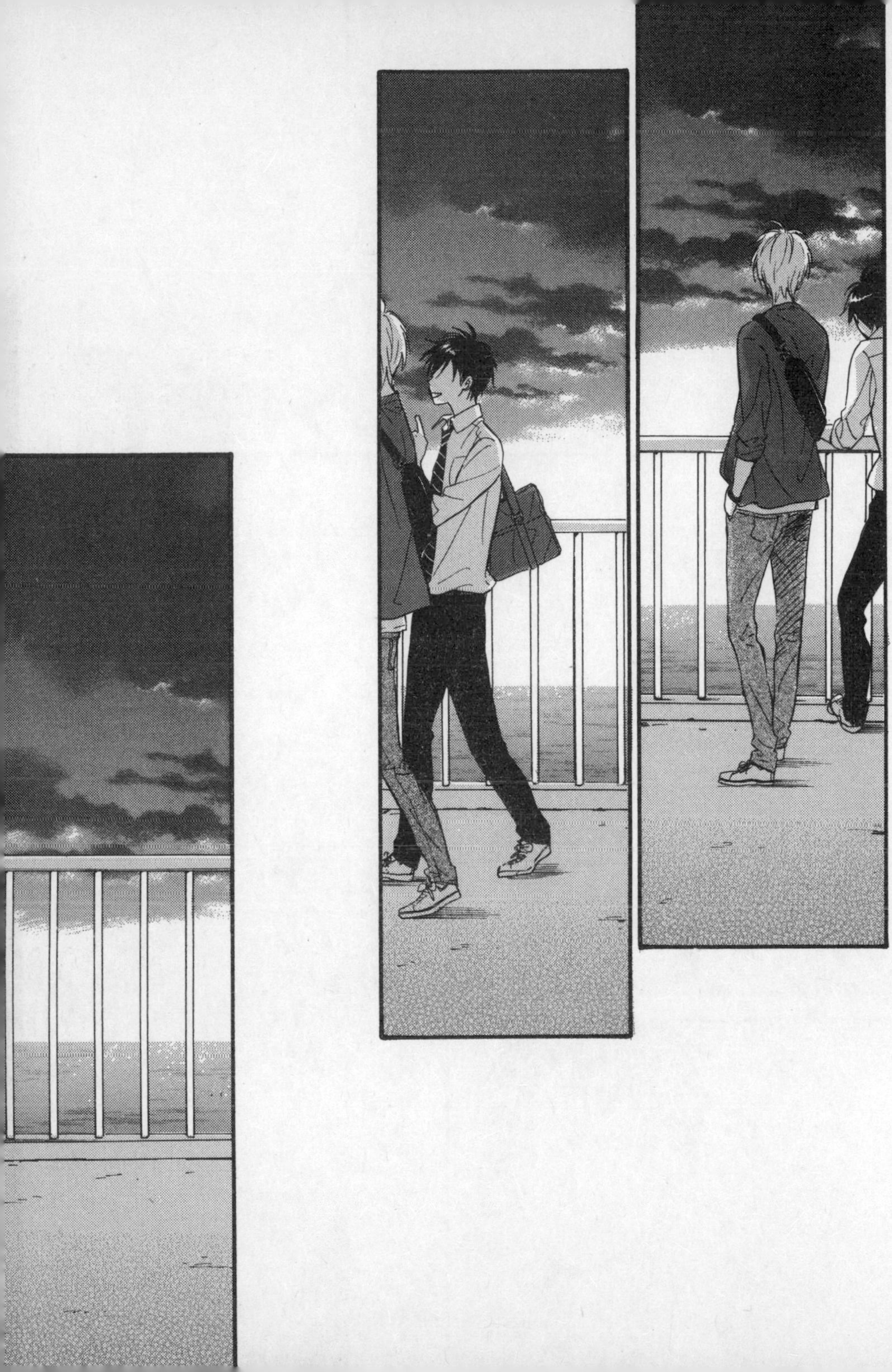

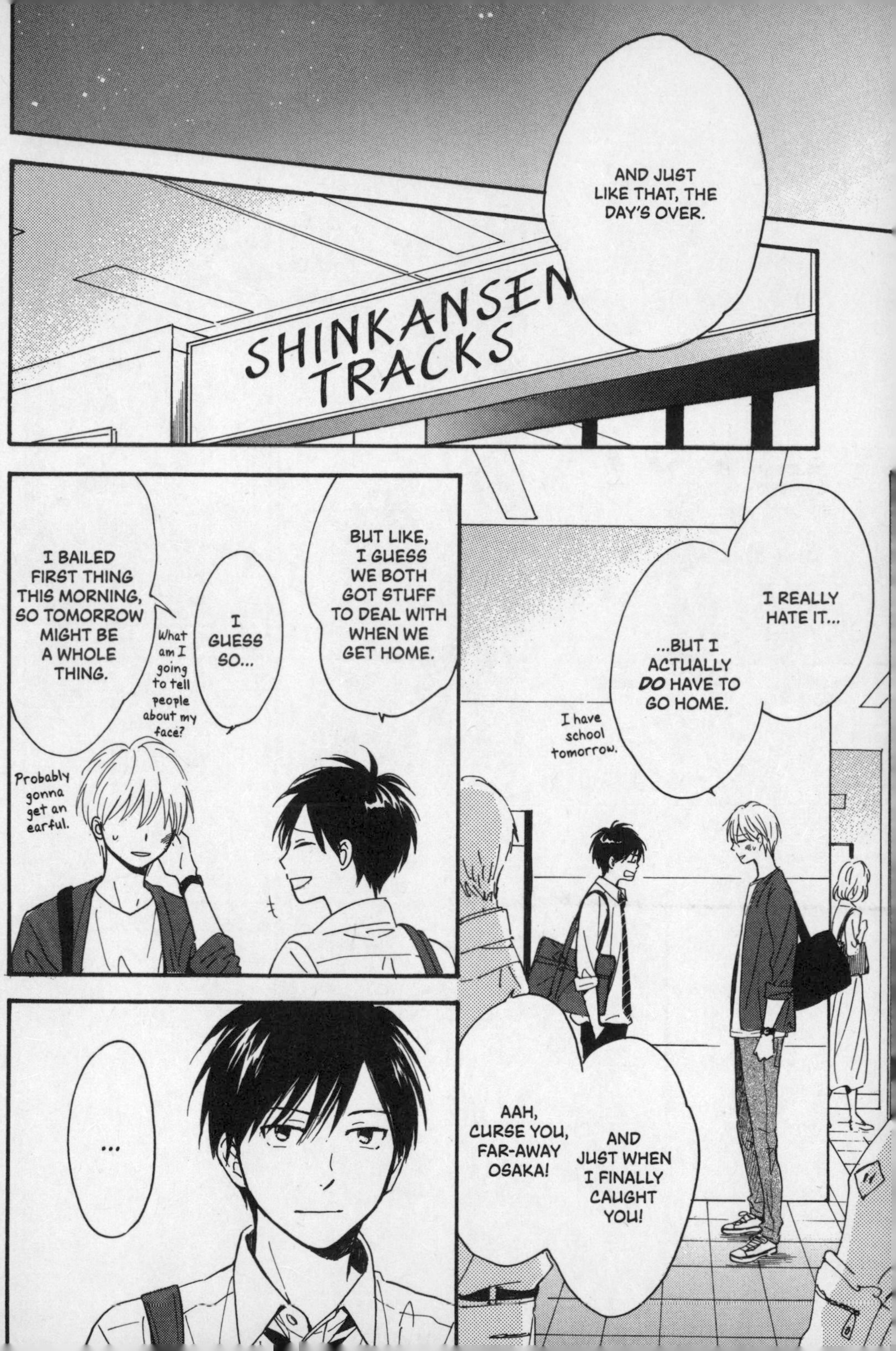
AND JUST LIKE THAT, THE DAY'S OVER.
SHINKANSEN TRACKS
I REALLY HATE IT...
...BUT I ACTUALLY DO HAVE TO GO HOME.
I have school tomorrow.
AND JUST WHEN I FINALLY CAUGHT YOU!
AAH, CURSE YOU, FAR-AWAY OSAKA!
BUT LIKE, I GUESS WE BOTH GOT STUFF TO DEAL WITH WHEN WE GET HOME.
I GUESS SO...
What am I going to tell people about my face?
I BAILED FIRST THING THIS MORNING, SO TOMORROW MIGHT BE A WHOLE THING.
Probably gonna get an earful.
...

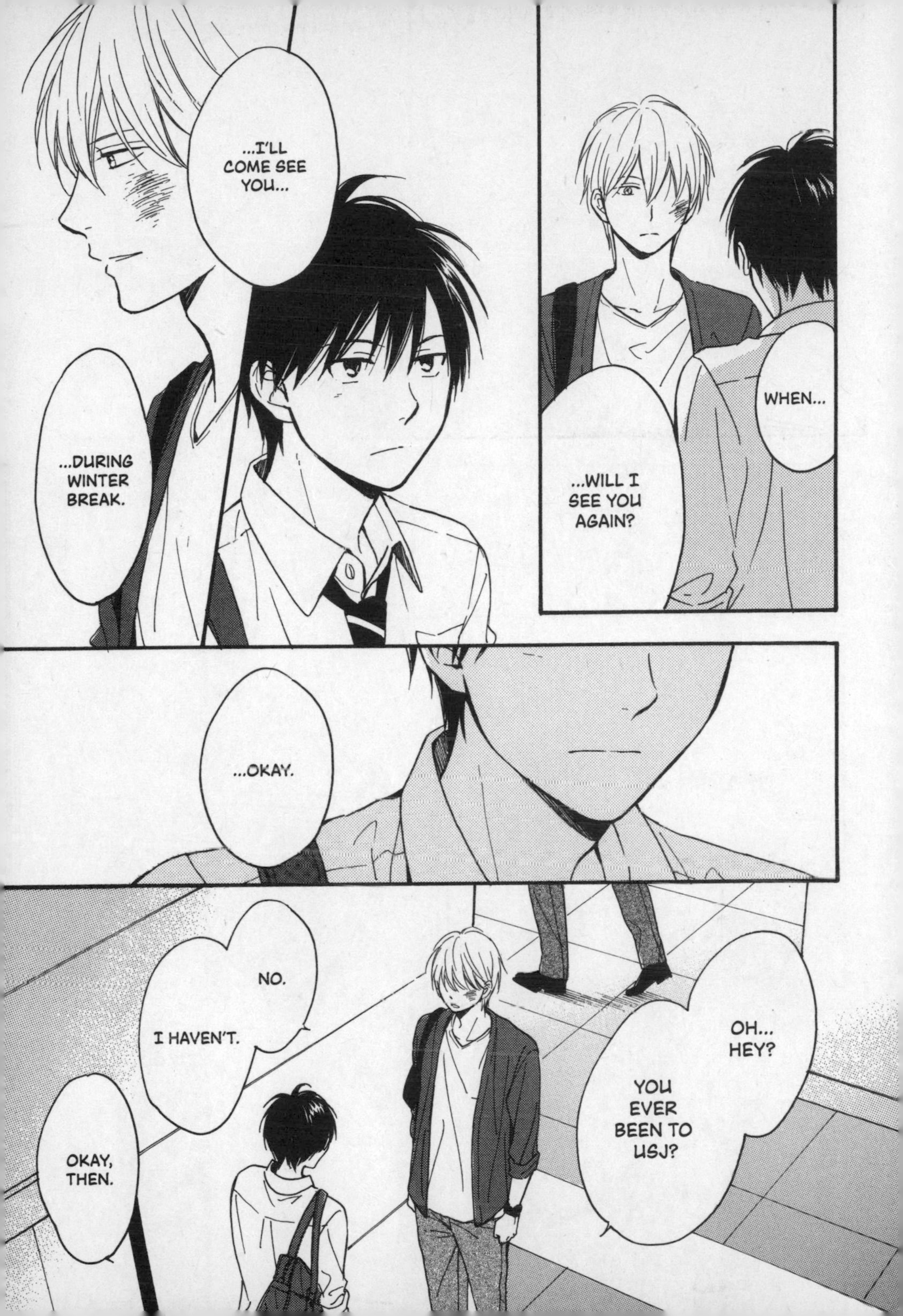
WHEN...
...WILL I SEE YOU AGAIN?
...I'LL COME SEE YOU...
...DURING WINTER BREAK.
...OKAY.
OH... HEY?
YOU EVER BEEN TO USJ?
NO.
I HAVEN'T.
OKAY, THEN.

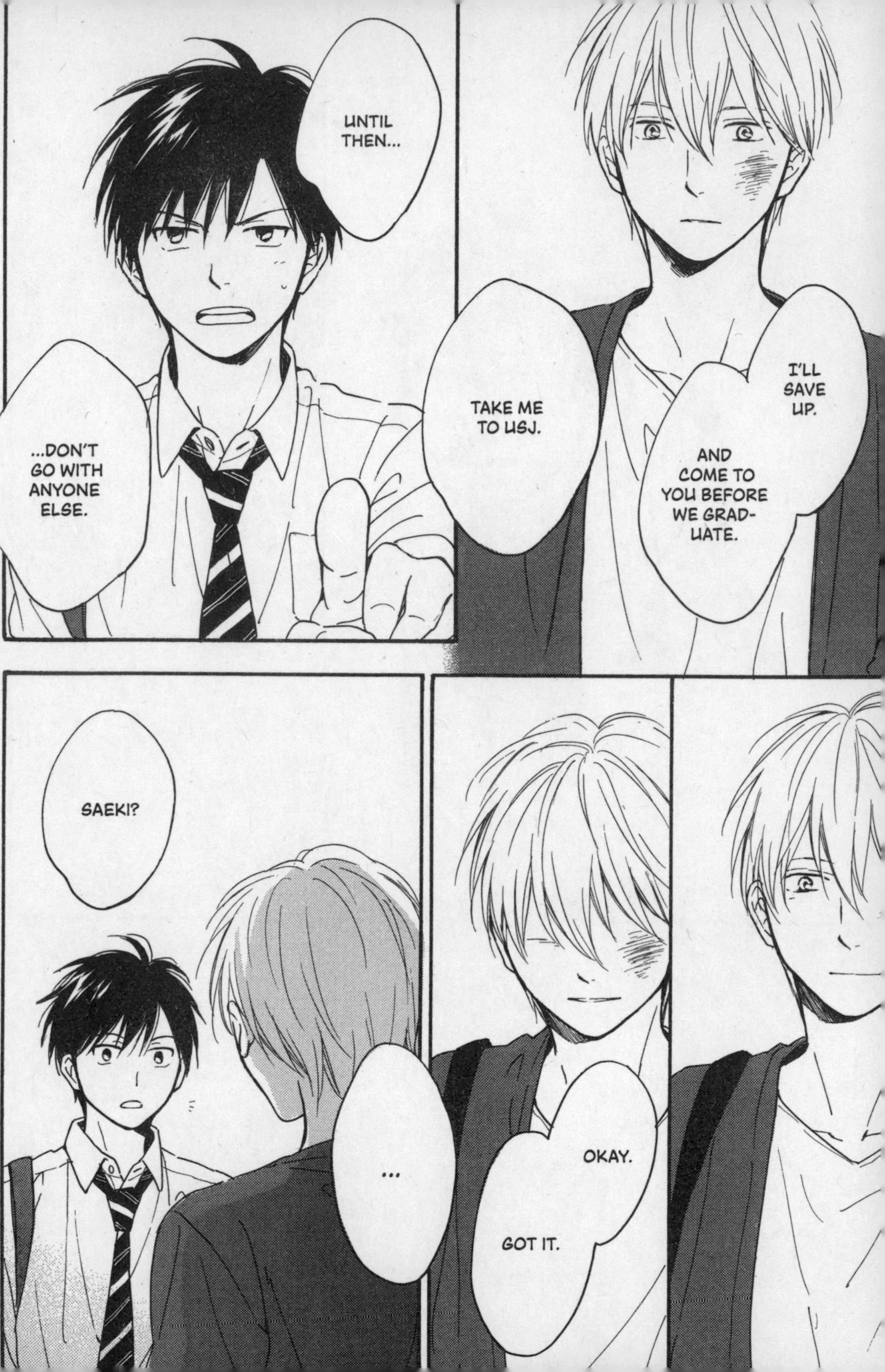
TAKE ME TO USJ.
I'LL SAVE UP.
AND COME TO YOU BEFORE WE GRAD-UATE.
UNTIL THEN...
...DON'T GO WITH ANYONE ELSE.
OKAY.
GOT IT.
SAEKI?
...

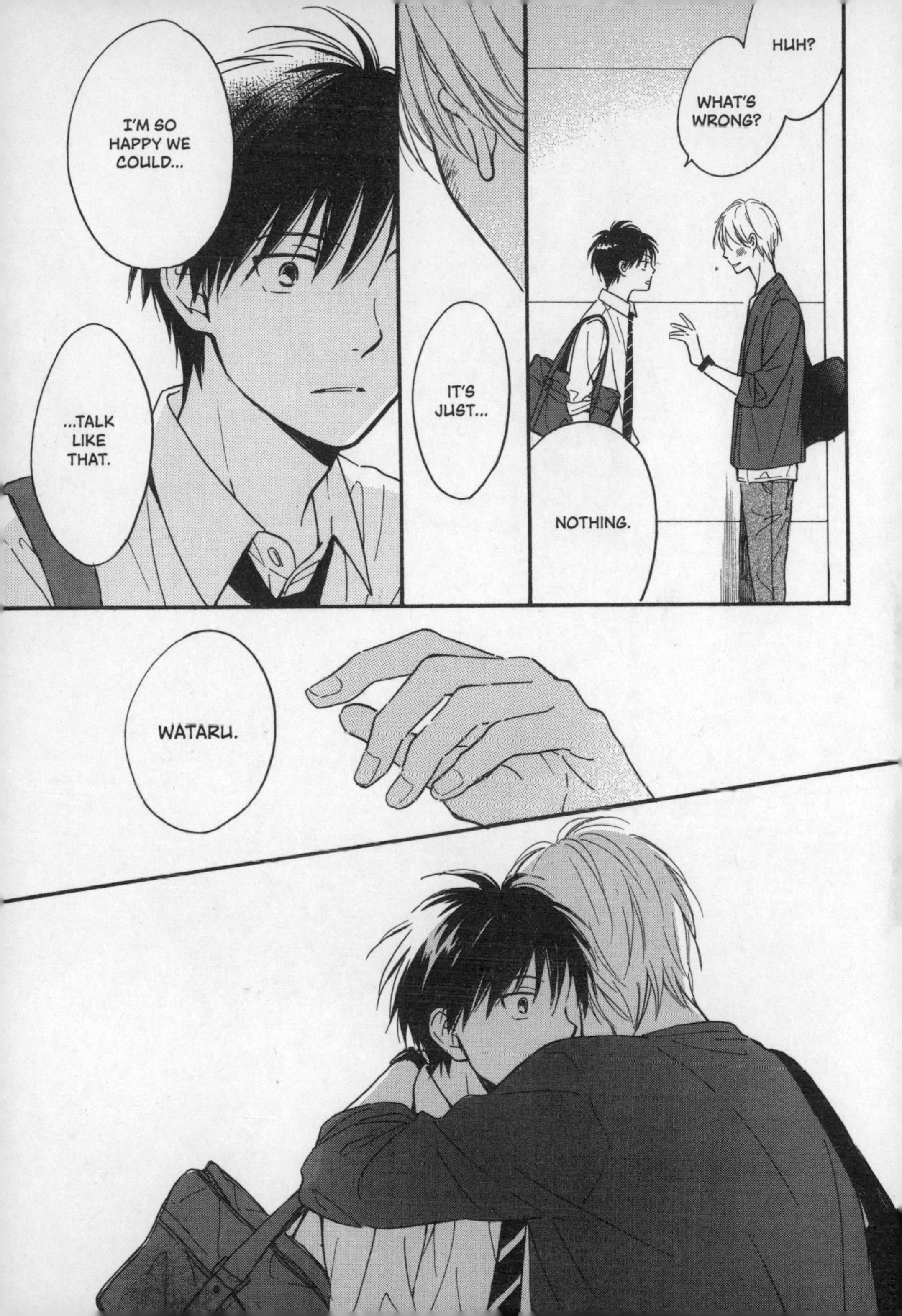
HUH?
WHAT'S WRONG?
NOTHING.
IT'S JUST...
I'M SO HAPPY WE COULD...
...TALK LIKE THAT.
WATARU.

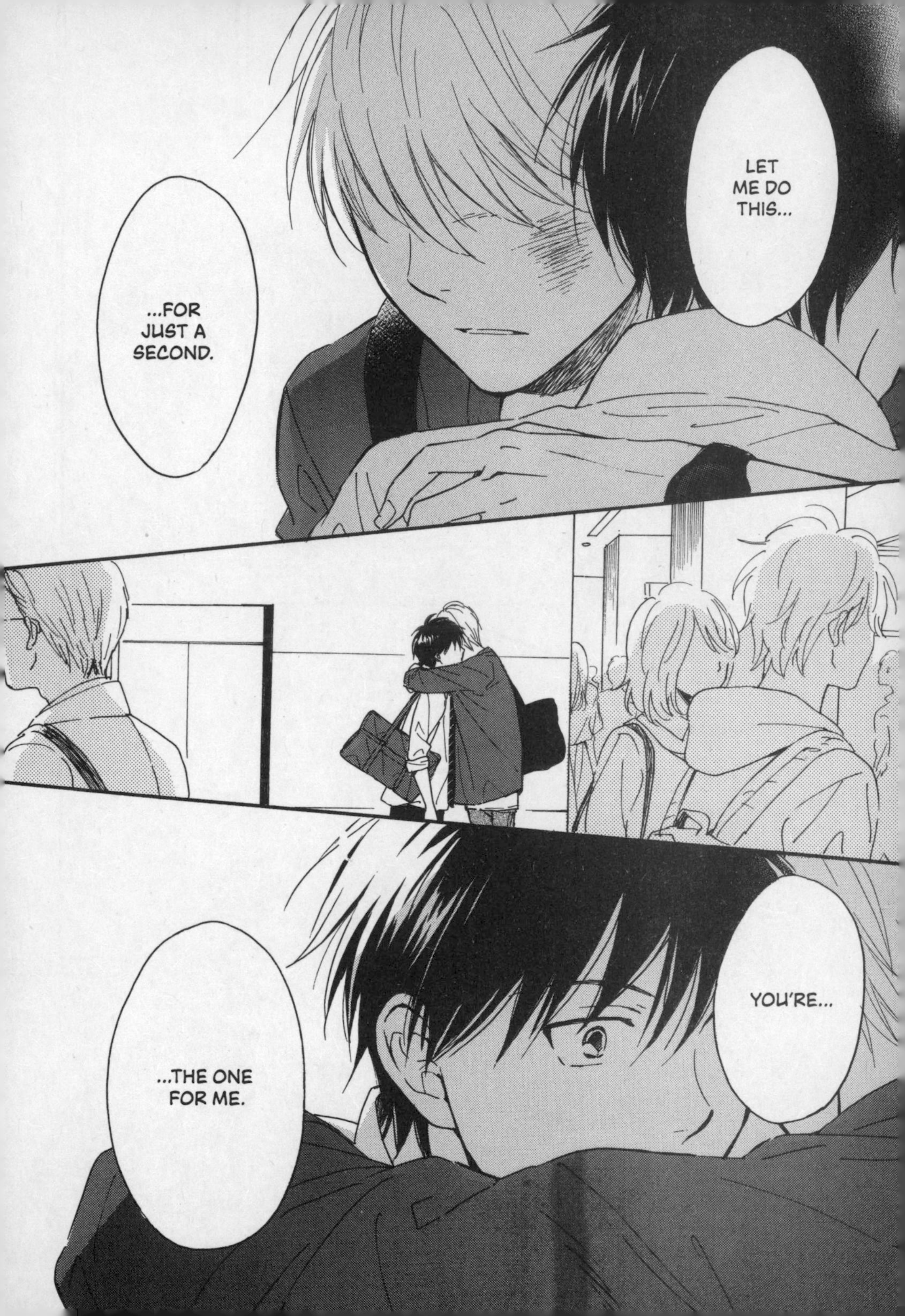
LET ME DO THIS...
...FOR JUST A SECOND.
YOU'RE...
...THE ONE FOR ME.

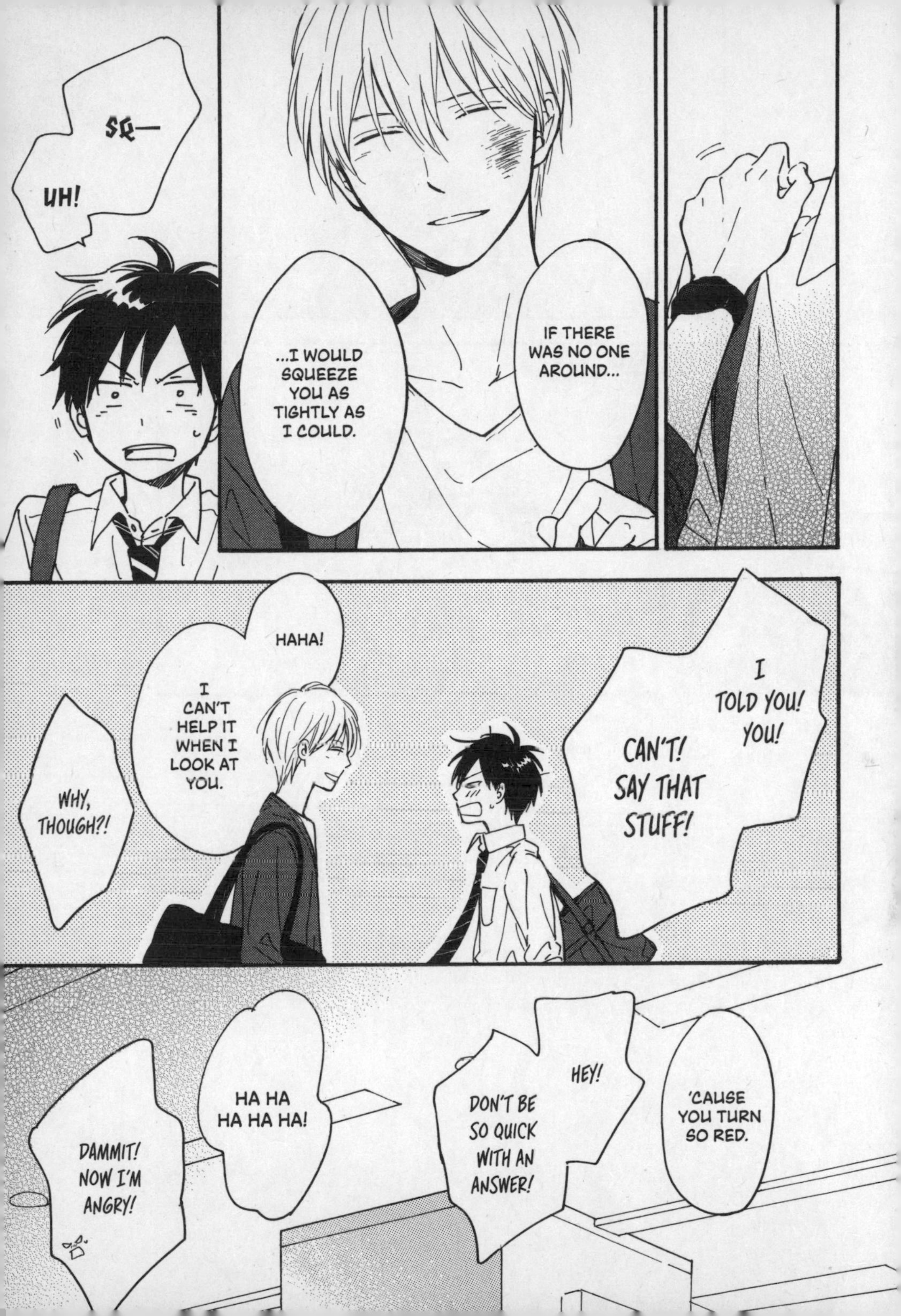
IF THERE WAS NO ONE AROUND...
...I WOULD SQUEEZE YOU AS TIGHTLY AS I COULD.
SQ— UH!
I TOLD YOU! YOU!
CAN'T! SAY THAT STUFF!
HAHA!
I CAN'T HELP IT WHEN I LOOK AT YOU.
WHY, THOUGH?!
'CAUSE YOU TURN SO RED.
HEY!
DON'T BE SO QUICK WITH AN ANSWER!
HA HA HA HA HA!
DAMMIT! NOW I'M ANGRY!

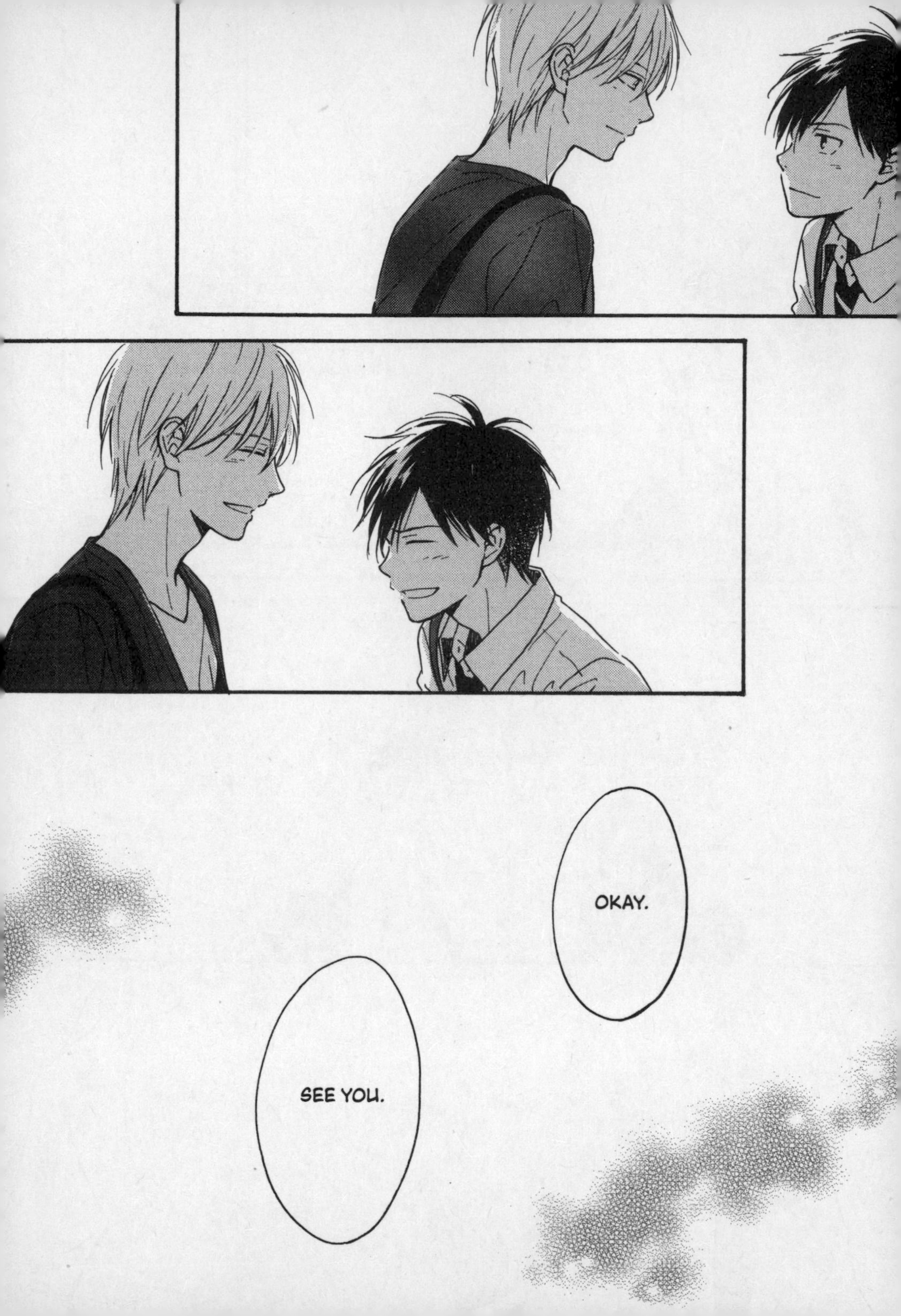
OKAY.
SEE YOU.

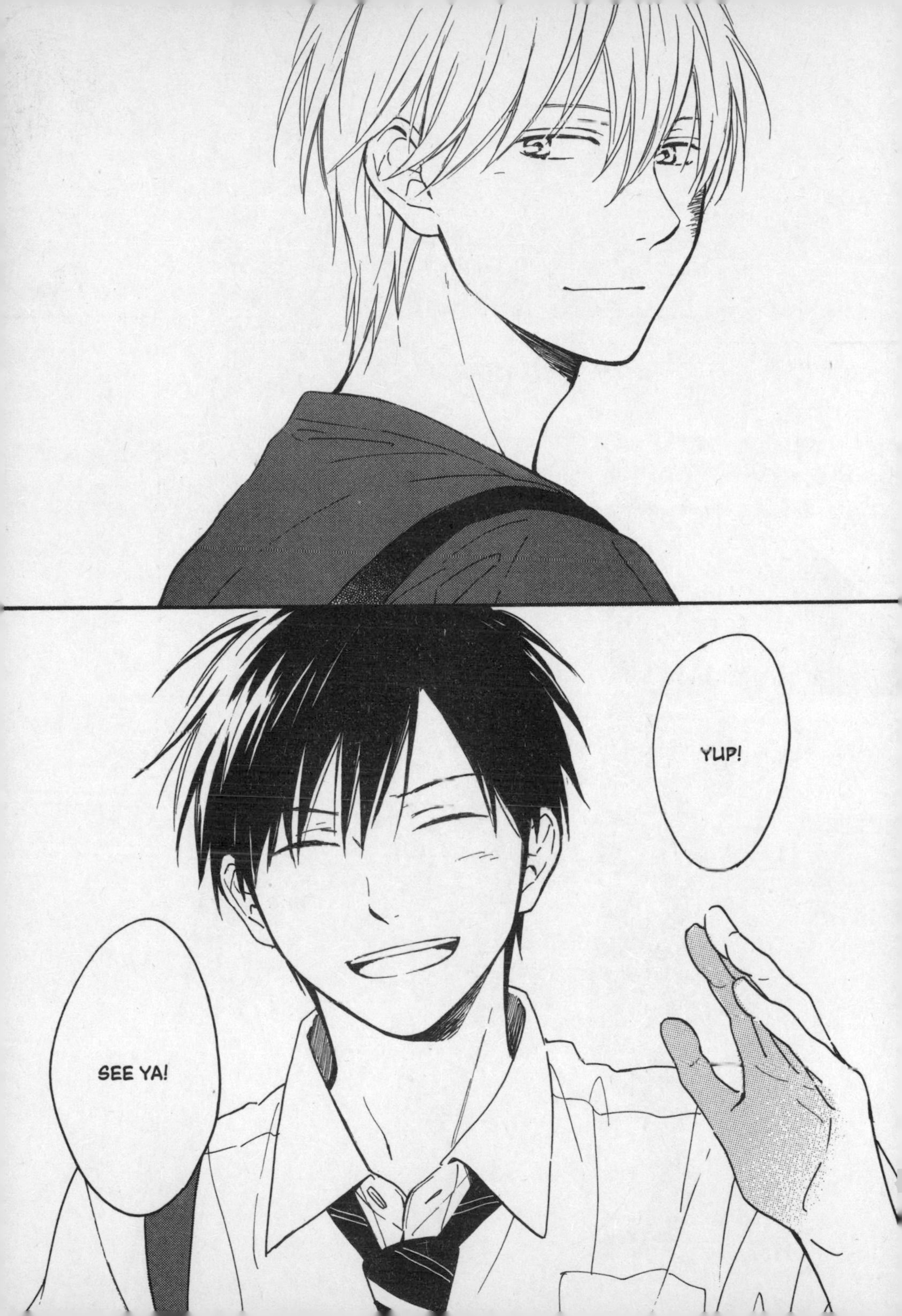
YUP!
SEE YA!

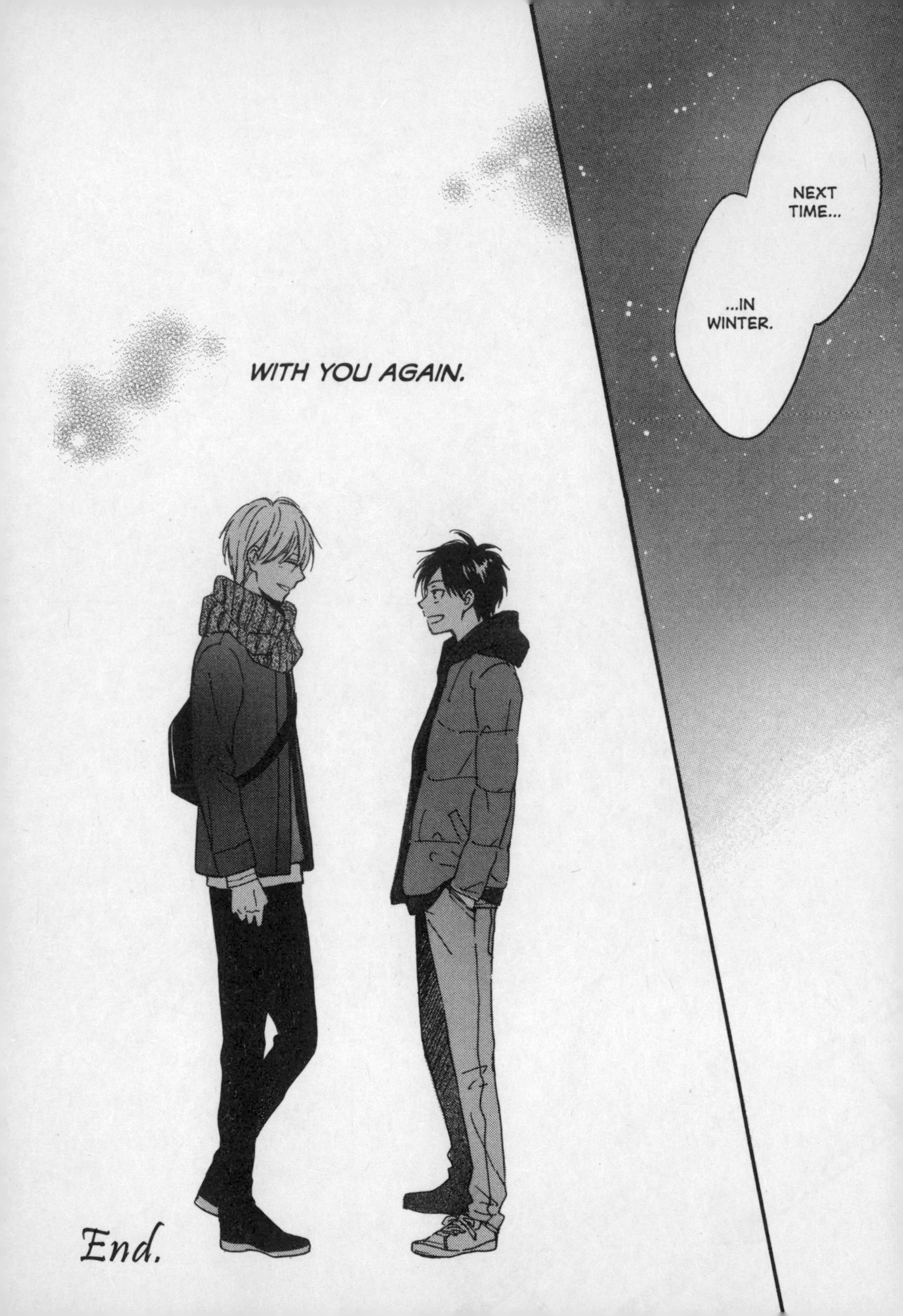
NEXT TIME...
...IN WINTER.
WITH YOU AGAIN.
End.

MY SUMMER OF YOU

MY SUMMER OF YOU

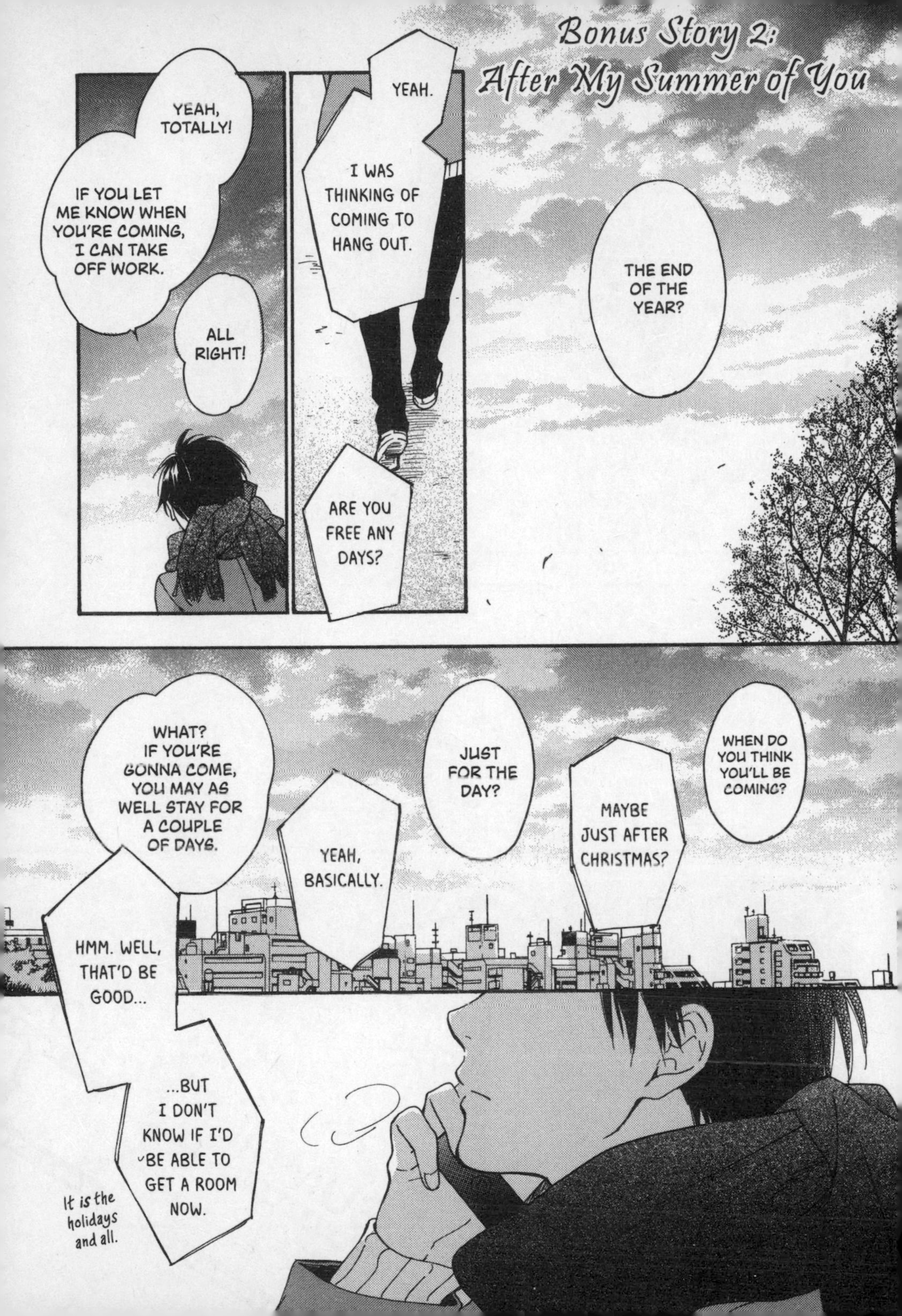
Bonus Story 2:
After My Summer of You
THE END OF THE YEAR?
YEAH.
I WAS THINKING OF COMING TO HANG OUT.
ARE YOU FREE ANY DAYS?
YEAH, TOTALLY!
IF YOU LET ME KNOW WHEN YOU'RE COMING, I CAN TAKE OFF WORK.
ALL RIGHT!
WHEN DO YOU THINK YOU'LL BE COMING?
MAYBE JUST AFTER CHRISTMAS?
JUST FOR THE DAY?
YEAH, BASICALLY.
WHAT? IF YOU'RE GONNA COME, YOU MAY AS WELL STAY FOR A COUPLE OF DAYS.
HMM. WELL, THAT'D BE GOOD...
...BUT I DON'T KNOW IF I'D BE ABLE TO GET A ROOM NOW.
It is the holidays and all.

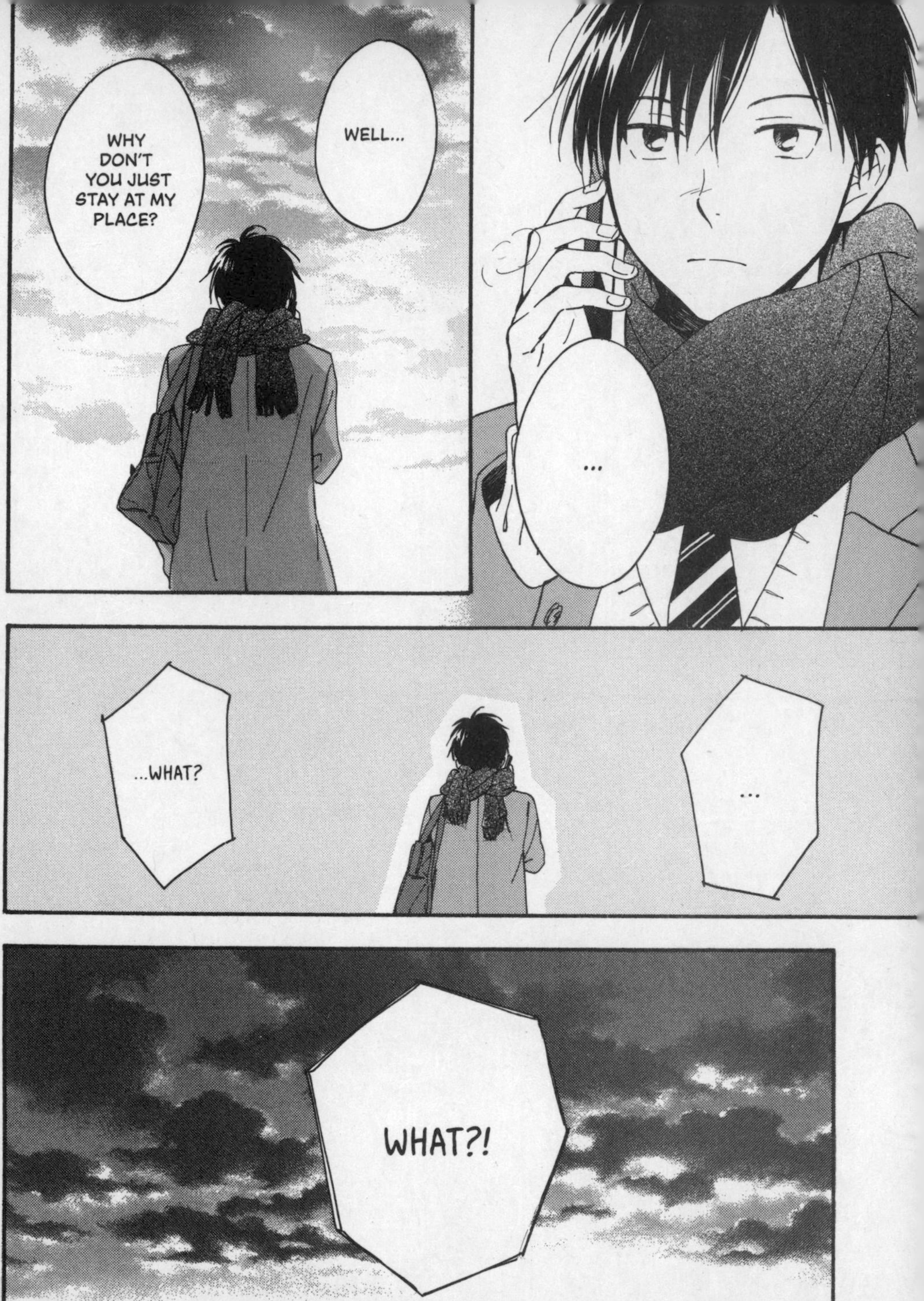
...
WELL...
WHY DON'T YOU JUST STAY AT MY PLACE?
...
...WHAT?
WHAT?!

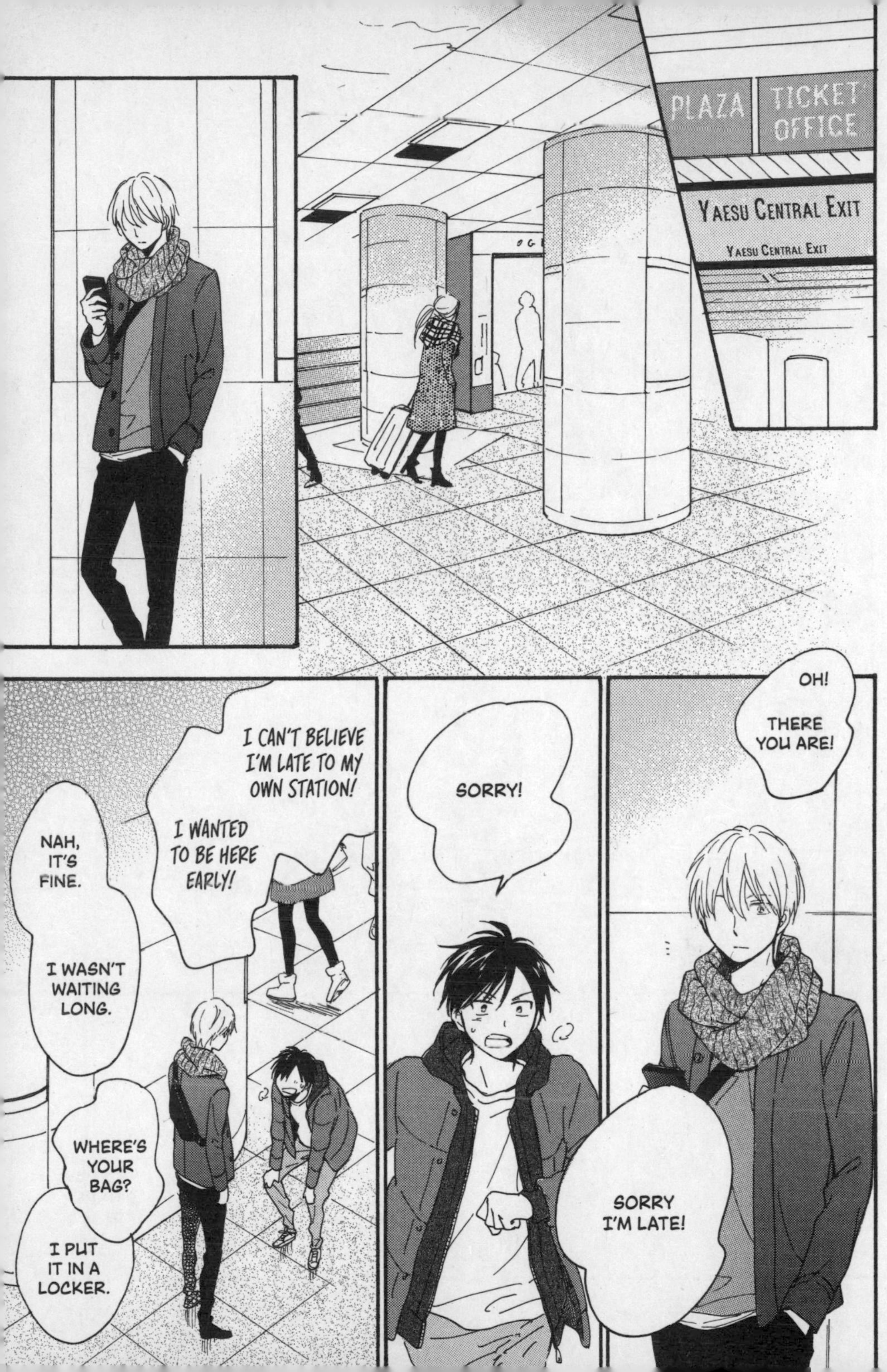
PLAZA
TICKET OFFICE
YAESU CENTRAL EXIT
YAESU CENTRAL EXIT
OH!
THERE YOU ARE!
SORRY I'M LATE!
SORRY!
I CAN'T BELIEVE I'M LATE TO MY OWN STATION!
I WANTED TO BE HERE EARLY!
NAH, IT'S FINE.
I WASN'T WAITING LONG.
WHERE'S YOUR BAG?
I PUT IT IN A LOCKER.

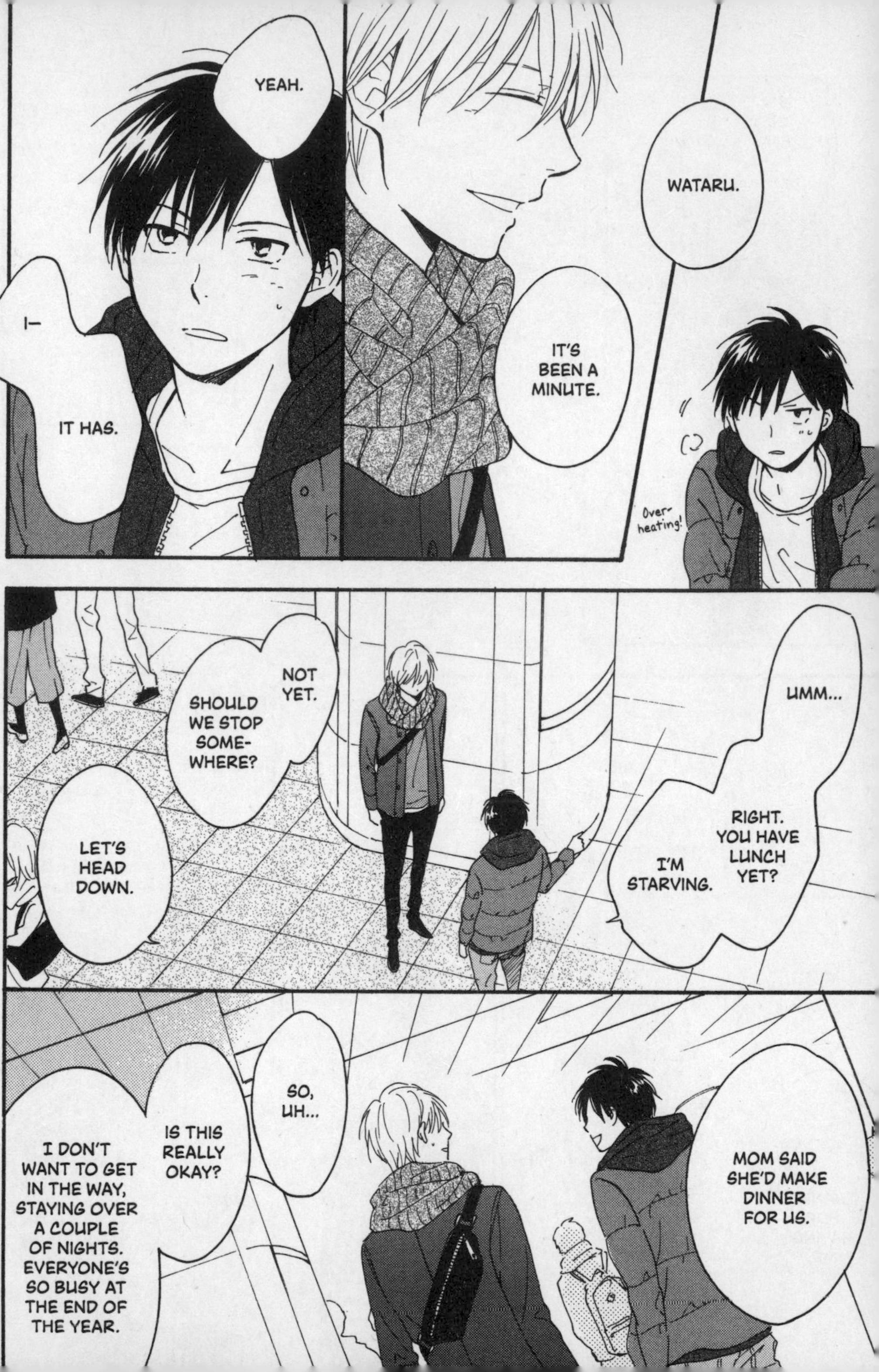
WATARU.
Over-heating!
IT'S BEEN A MINUTE.
YEAH.
I—
IT HAS.
UMM...
RIGHT. YOU HAVE LUNCH YET?
I'M STARVING.
NOT YET.
SHOULD WE STOP SOME-WHERE?
LET'S HEAD DOWN.
MOM SAID SHE'D MAKE DINNER FOR US.
SO, UH...
IS THIS REALLY OKAY?
I DON'T WANT TO GET IN THE WAY, STAYING OVER A COUPLE OF NIGHTS. EVERYONE'S SO BUSY AT THE END OF THE YEAR.

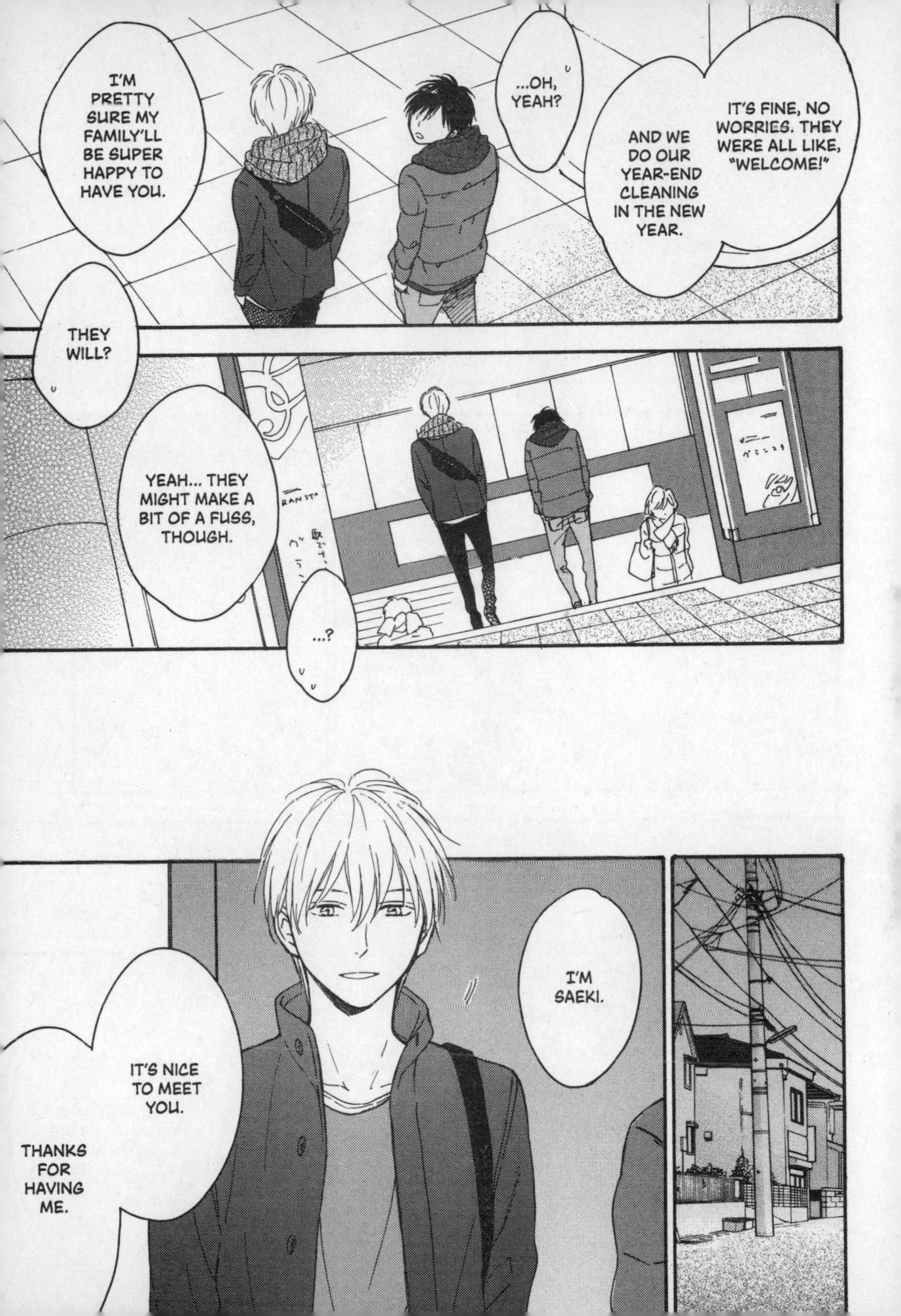
IT'S FINE, NO WORRIES. THEY WERE ALL LIKE, "WELCOME!"
AND WE DO OUR YEAR-END CLEANING IN THE NEW YEAR.
...OH, YEAH?
I'M PRETTY SURE MY FAMILY'LL BE SUPER HAPPY TO HAVE YOU.
THEY WILL?
YEAH... THEY MIGHT MAKE A BIT OF A FUSS, THOUGH.
...?
I'M SAEKI.
IT'S NICE TO MEET YOU.
THANKS FOR HAVING ME.

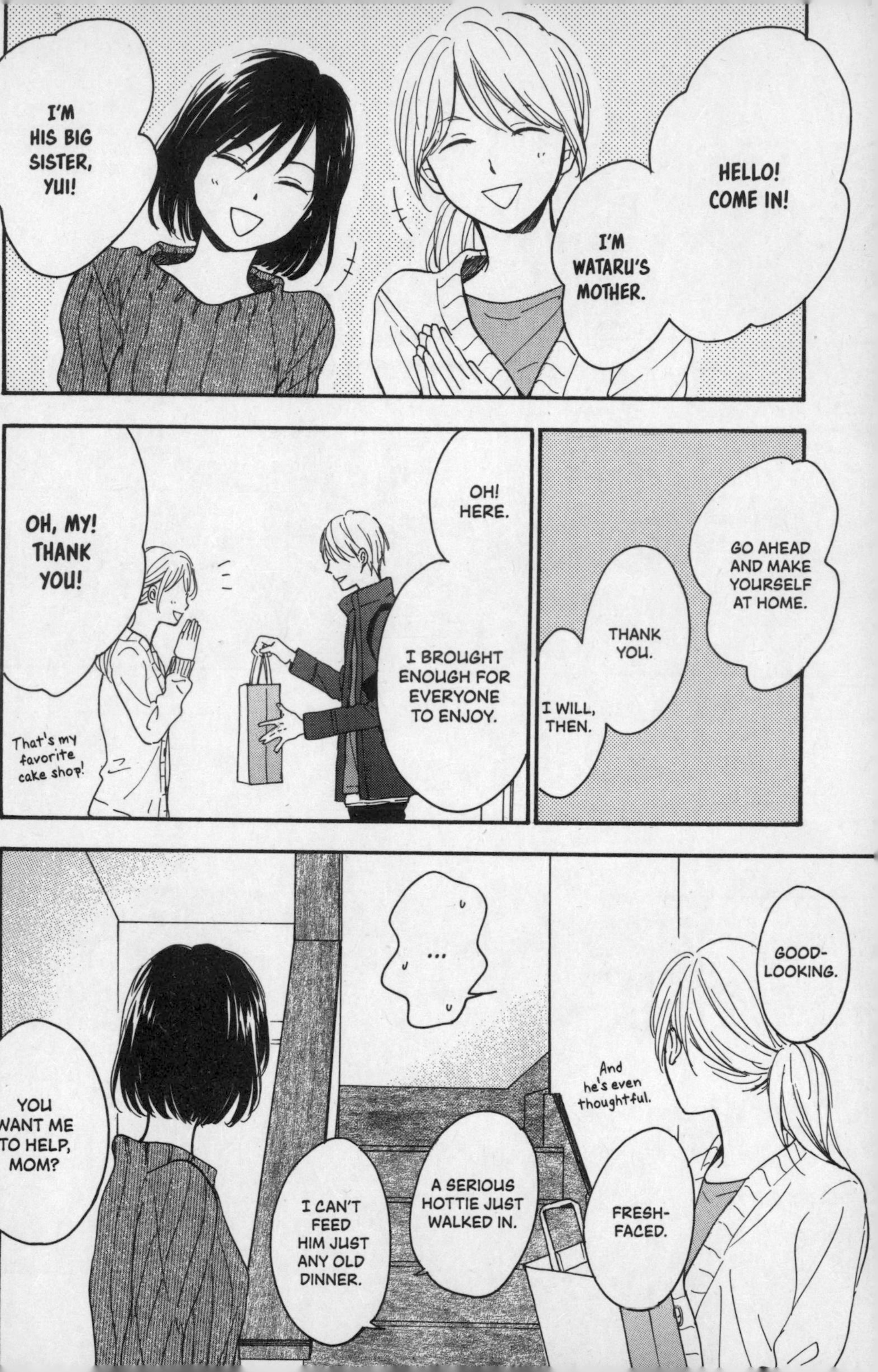
HELLO! COME IN!
I'M WATARU'S MOTHER.
I'M HIS BIG SISTER, YUI!
GO AHEAD AND MAKE YOURSELF AT HOME.
THANK YOU.
I WILL, THEN.
OH! HERE.
I BROUGHT ENOUGH FOR EVERYONE TO ENJOY.
OH, MY! THANK YOU!
That's my favorite cake shop!
GOOD-LOOKING.
...
And he's even thoughtful.
FRESH-FACED.
A SERIOUS HOTTIE JUST WALKED IN.
I CAN'T FEED HIM JUST ANY OLD DINNER.
YOU WANT ME TO HELP, MOM?

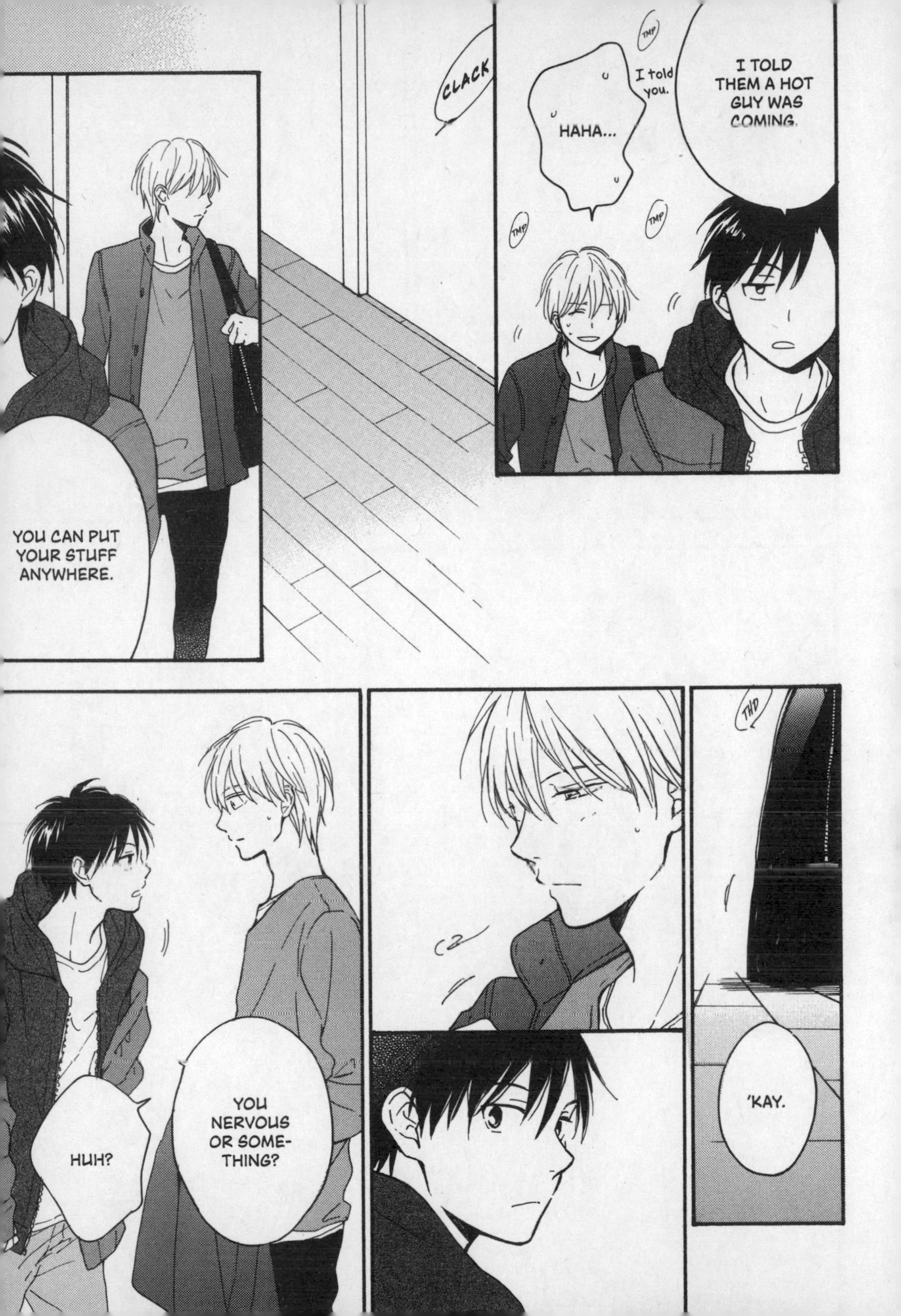
I TOLD THEM A HOT GUY WAS COMING.
I told you.
TMP
HAHA...
TMP
TMP
CLACK
YOU CAN PUT YOUR STUFF ANYWHERE.
THD
'KAY.
YOU NERVOUS OR SOME-THING?
HUH?

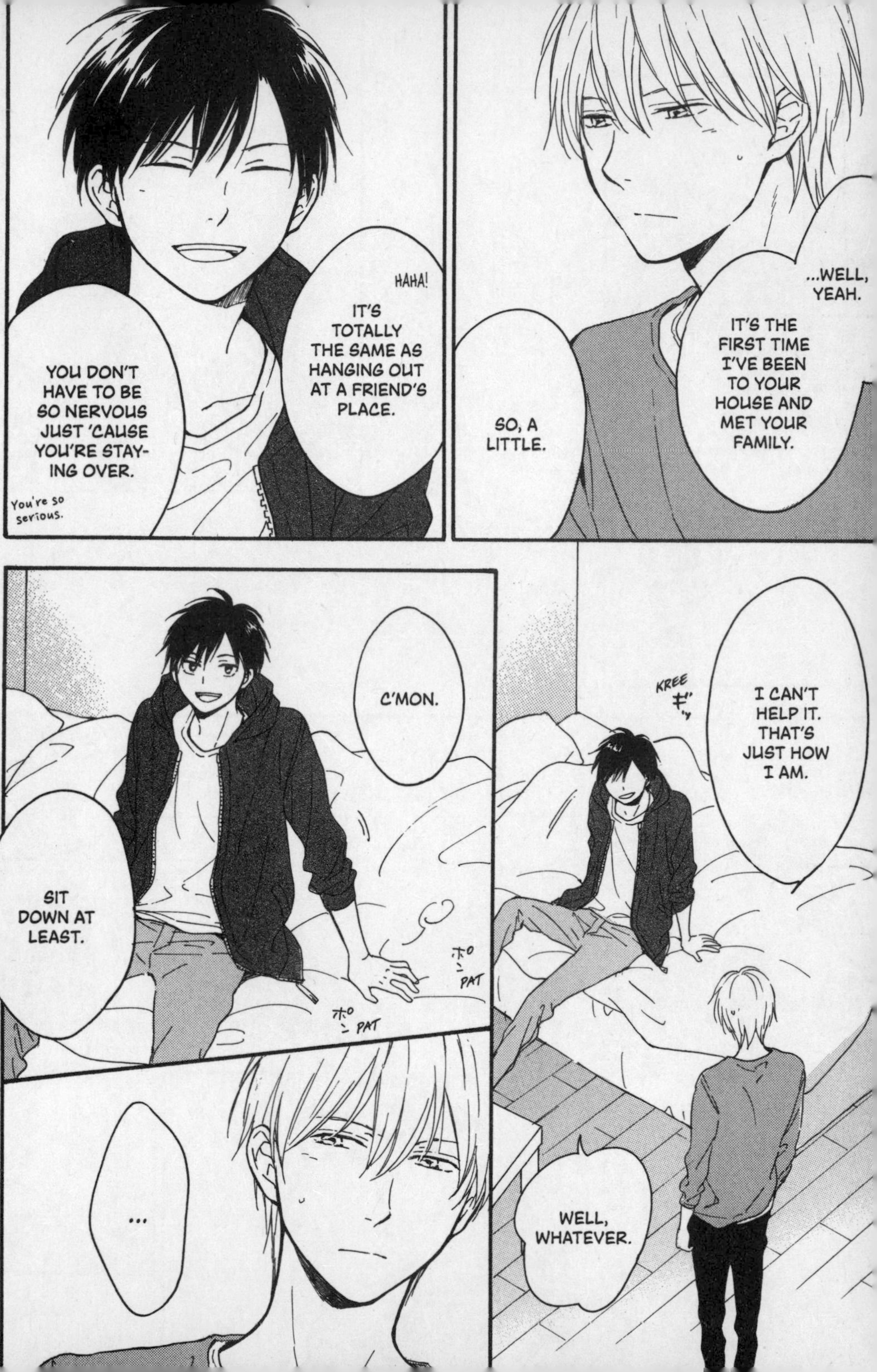
...WELL, YEAH.
IT'S THE FIRST TIME I'VE BEEN TO YOUR HOUSE AND MET YOUR FAMILY.
SO, A LITTLE.
HAHA!
IT'S TOTALLY THE SAME AS HANGING OUT AT A FRIEND'S PLACE.
YOU DON'T HAVE TO BE SO NERVOUS JUST 'CAUSE YOU'RE STAYING OVER.
You're so serious.
KREE
I CAN'T HELP IT. THAT'S JUST HOW I AM.
WELL, WHATEVER.
C'MON.
SIT DOWN AT LEAST.
PAT
PAT
...

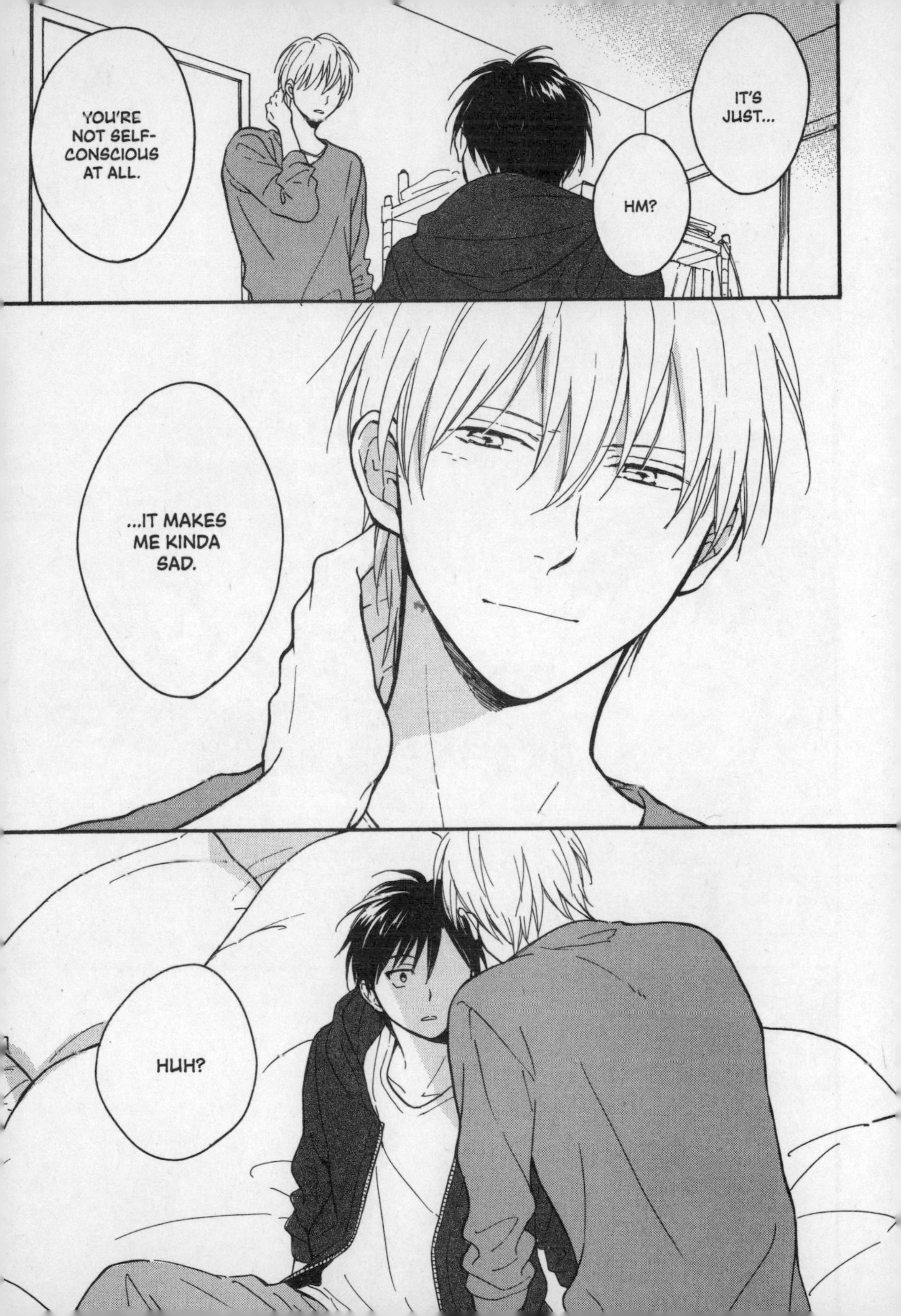
YOU'RE NOT SELF-CONSCIOUS AT ALL.
HM?
IT'S JUST...
...IT MAKES ME KINDA SAD.
HUH?

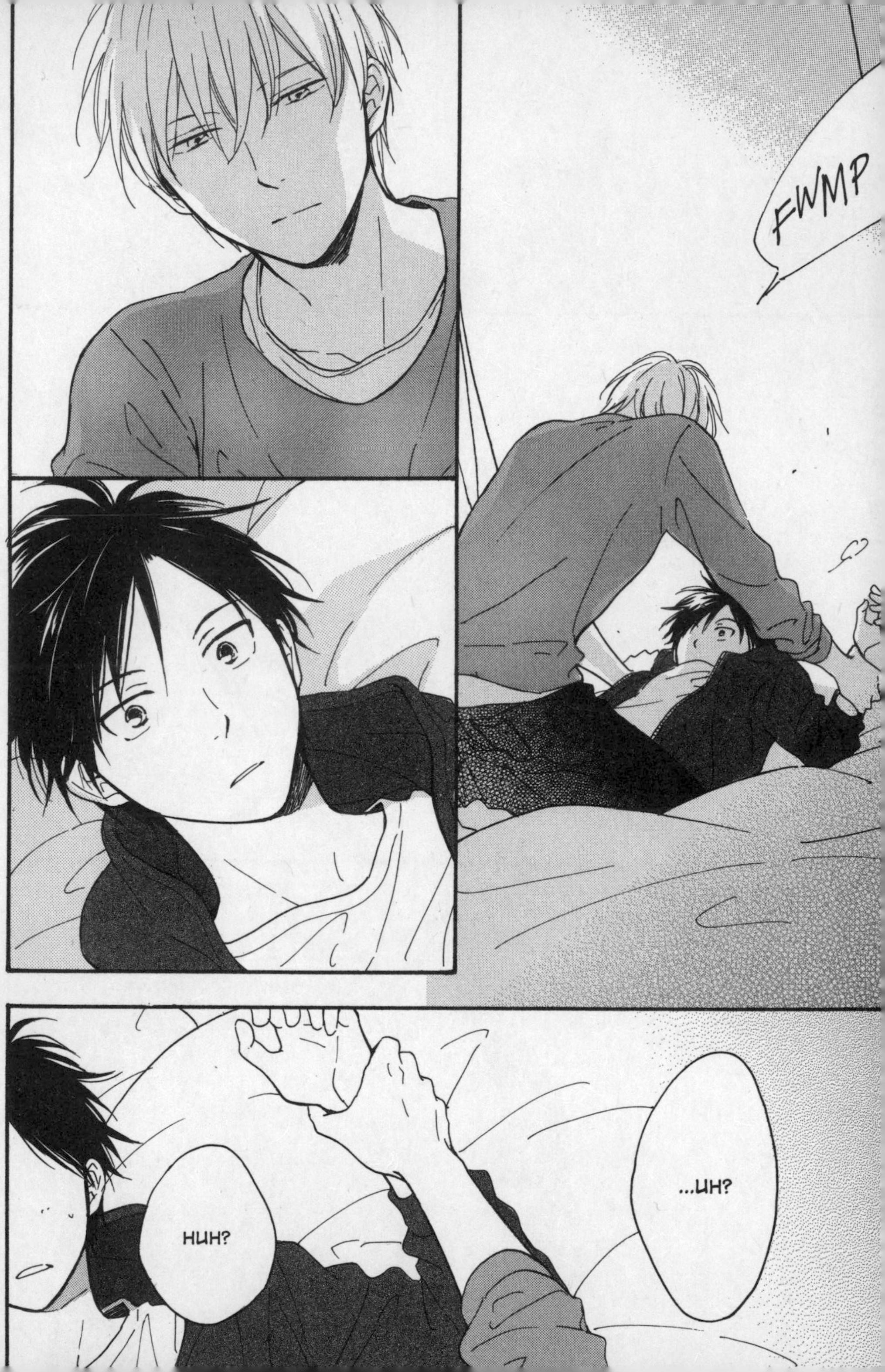
FWMP
...UH?
HUH?

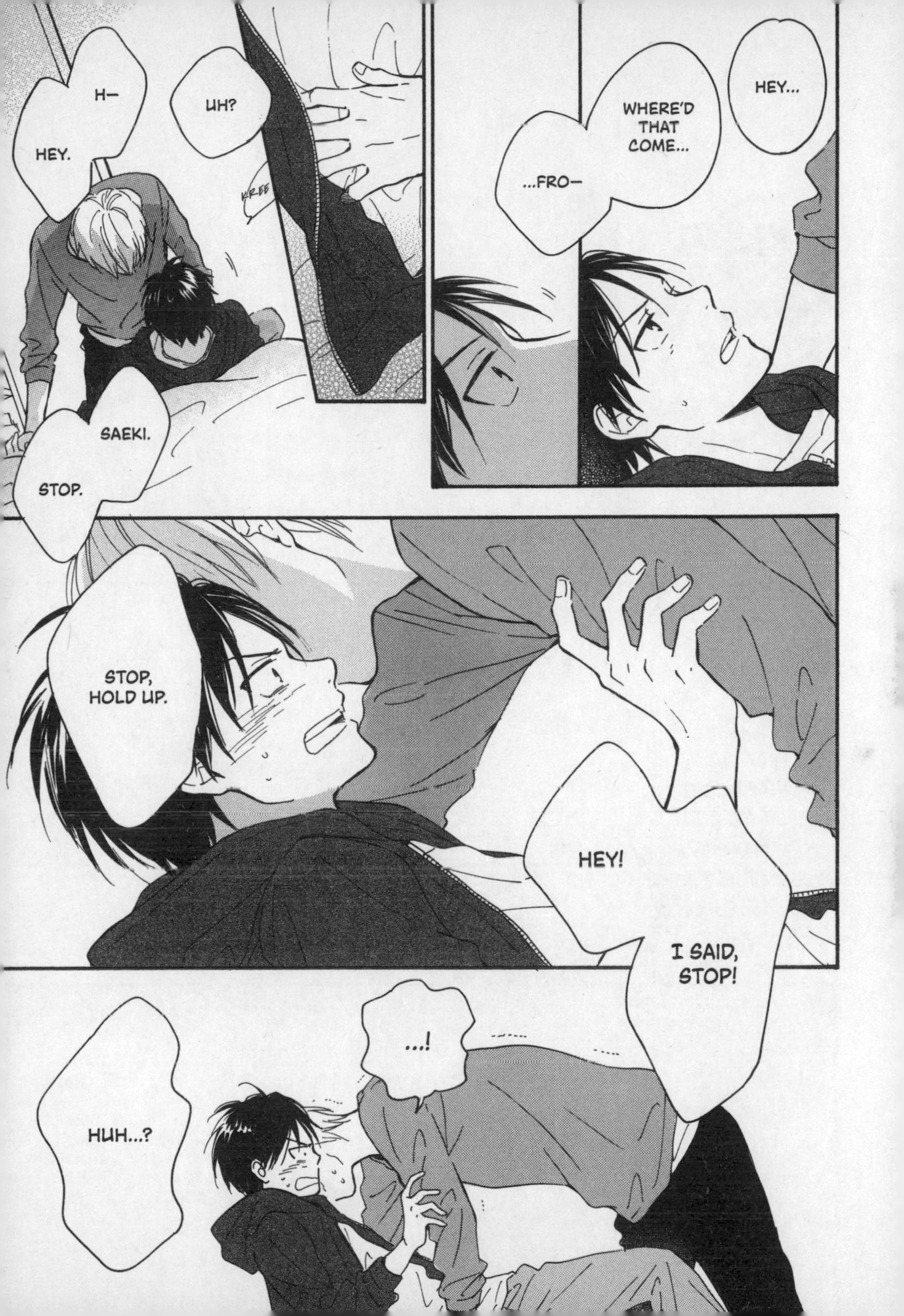
HEY...
WHERE'D THAT COME...
...FRO—
KREE
UH?
H—
HEY.
SAEKI.
STOP.
STOP, HOLD UP.
HEY!
I SAID, STOP!
...!
HUH...?

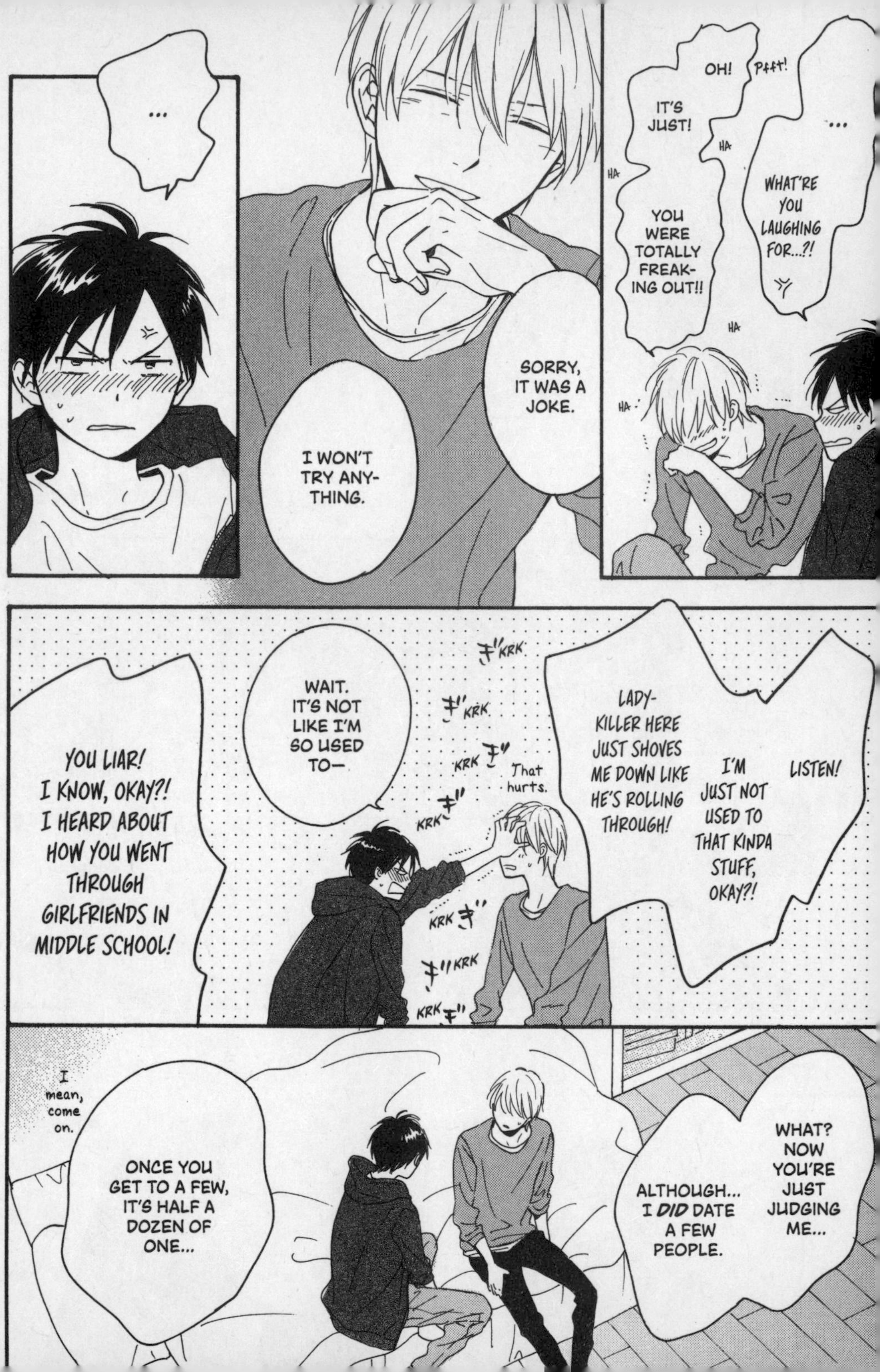
Pfft!
...
WHAT'RE YOU LAUGHING FOR...?!
OH!
IT'S JUST!
HA
HA
YOU WERE TOTALLY FREAK-ING OUT!!
HA
HA
SORRY, IT WAS A JOKE.
I WON'T TRY ANY-THING.
...
LISTEN!
I'M JUST NOT USED TO THAT KINDA STUFF, OKAY?!
LADY-KILLER HERE JUST SHOVES ME DOWN LIKE HE'S ROLLING THROUGH!
KRK
KRK
KRK
That hurts.
KRK
KRK
KRK
KRK
WAIT. IT'S NOT LIKE I'M SO USED TO—
YOU LIAR! I KNOW, OKAY?! I HEARD ABOUT HOW YOU WENT THROUGH GIRLFRIENDS IN MIDDLE SCHOOL!
WHAT? NOW YOU'RE JUST JUDGING ME...
ALTHOUGH... I *DID* DATE A FEW PEOPLE.
I mean, come on.
ONCE YOU GET TO A FEW, IT'S HALF A DOZEN OF ONE...

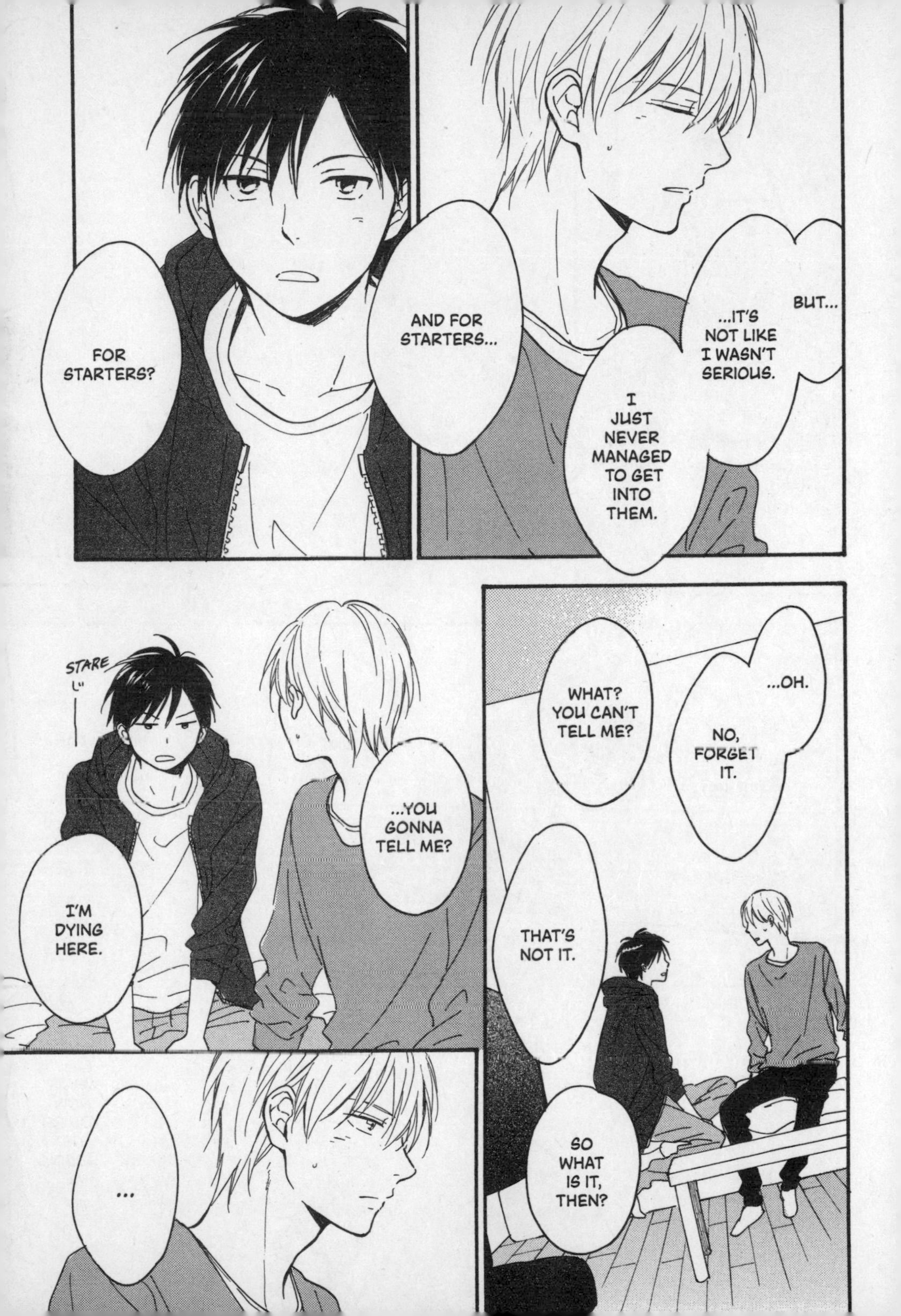
BUT...
...IT'S NOT LIKE I WASN'T SERIOUS.
I JUST NEVER MANAGED TO GET INTO THEM.
AND FOR STARTERS...
FOR STARTERS?
...OH.
NO, FORGET IT.
WHAT? YOU CAN'T TELL ME?
THAT'S NOT IT.
SO WHAT IS IT, THEN?
STARE
じー
...YOU GONNA TELL ME?
I'M DYING HERE.
...

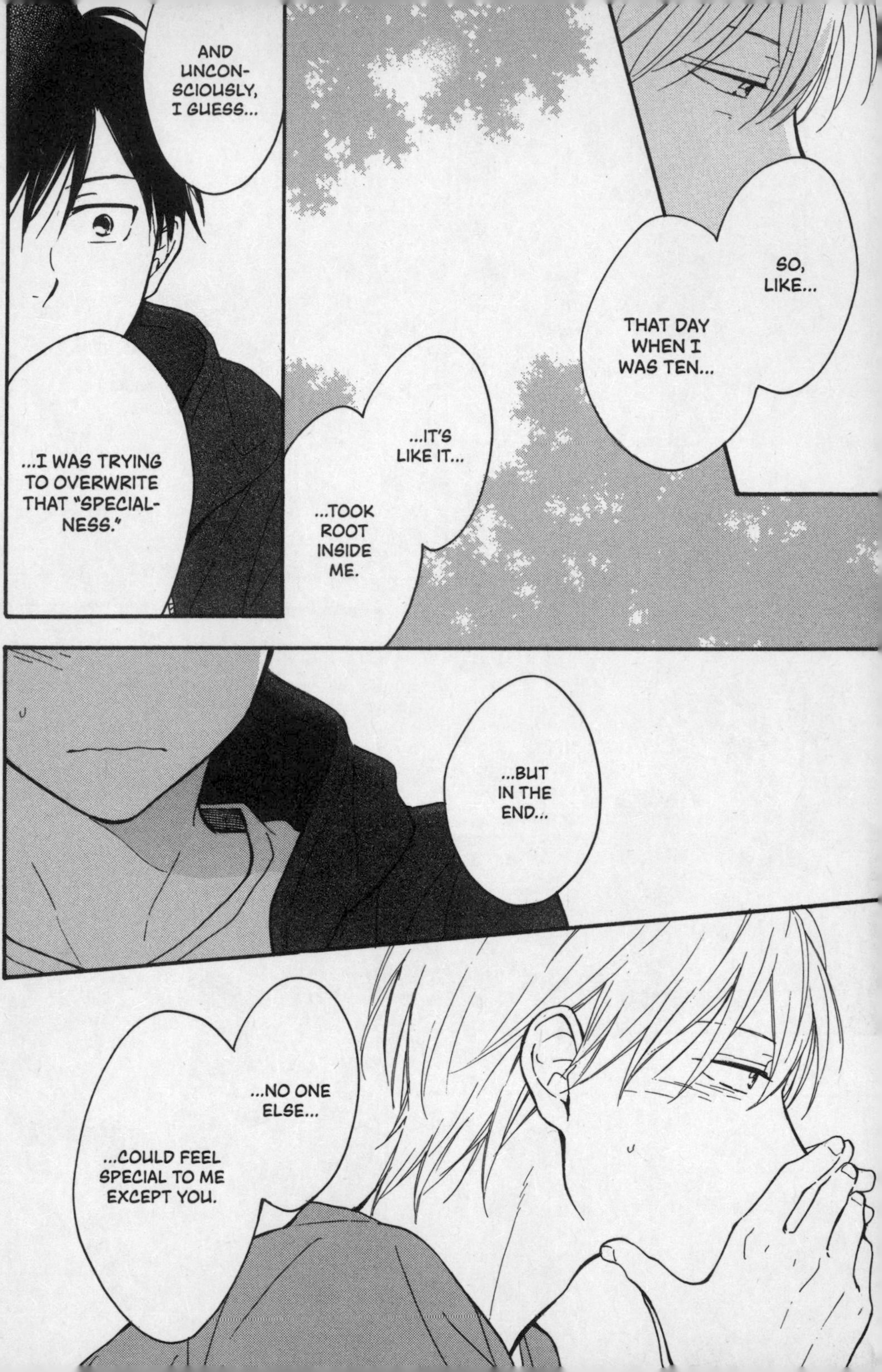
SO, LIKE...
THAT DAY WHEN I WAS TEN...
...IT'S LIKE IT...
...TOOK ROOT INSIDE ME.
AND UNCON-SCIOUSLY, I GUESS...
...I WAS TRYING TO OVERWRITE THAT "SPECIAL-NESS."
...BUT IN THE END...
...NO ONE ELSE...
...COULD FEEL SPECIAL TO ME EXCEPT YOU.

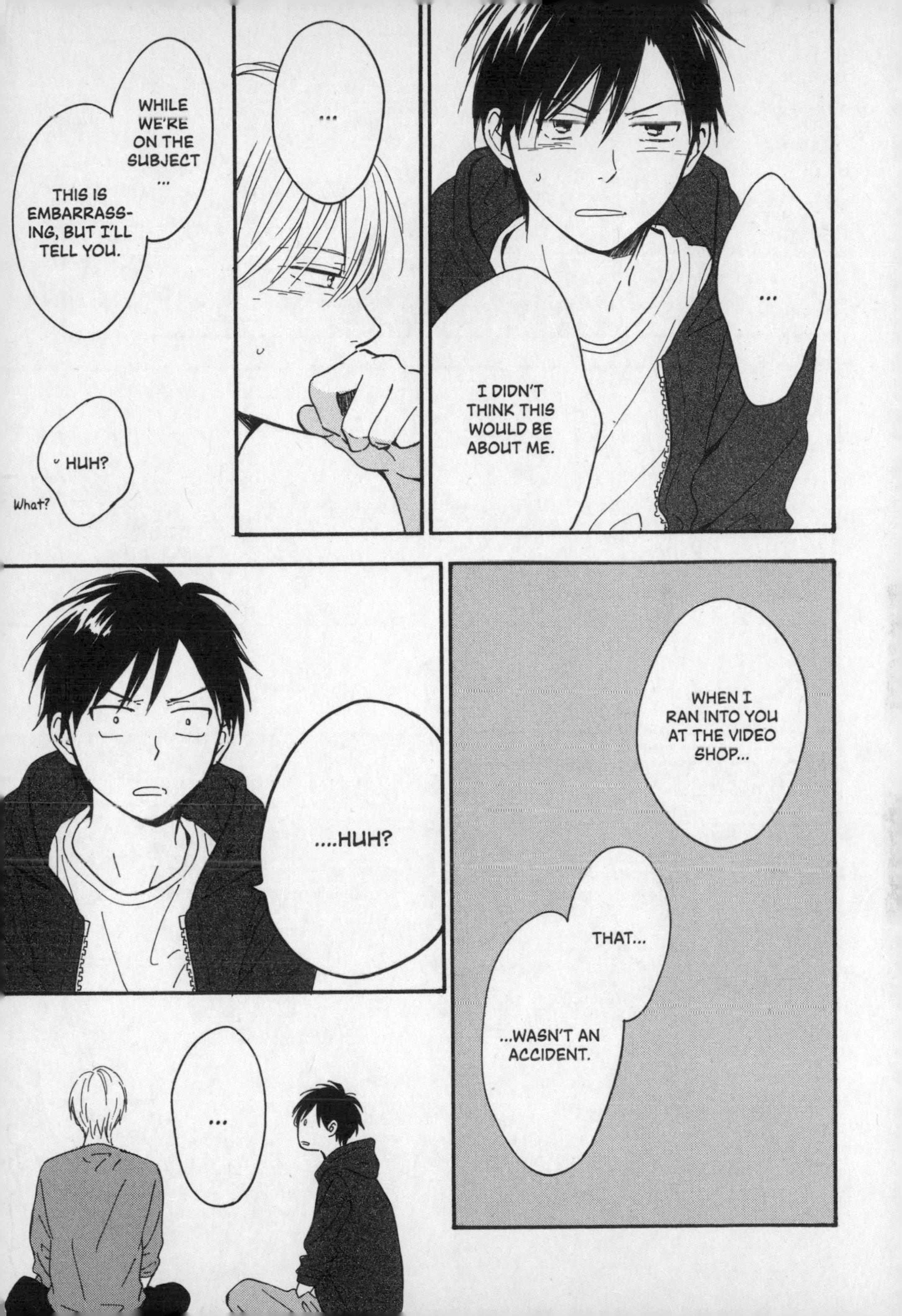
...
I DIDN'T THINK THIS WOULD BE ABOUT ME.
...
WHILE WE'RE ON THE SUBJECT ...
THIS IS EMBARRASSING, BUT I'LL TELL YOU.
HUH?
What?
WHEN I RAN INTO YOU AT THE VIDEO SHOP...
THAT...
...WASN'T AN ACCIDENT.
....HUH?
...

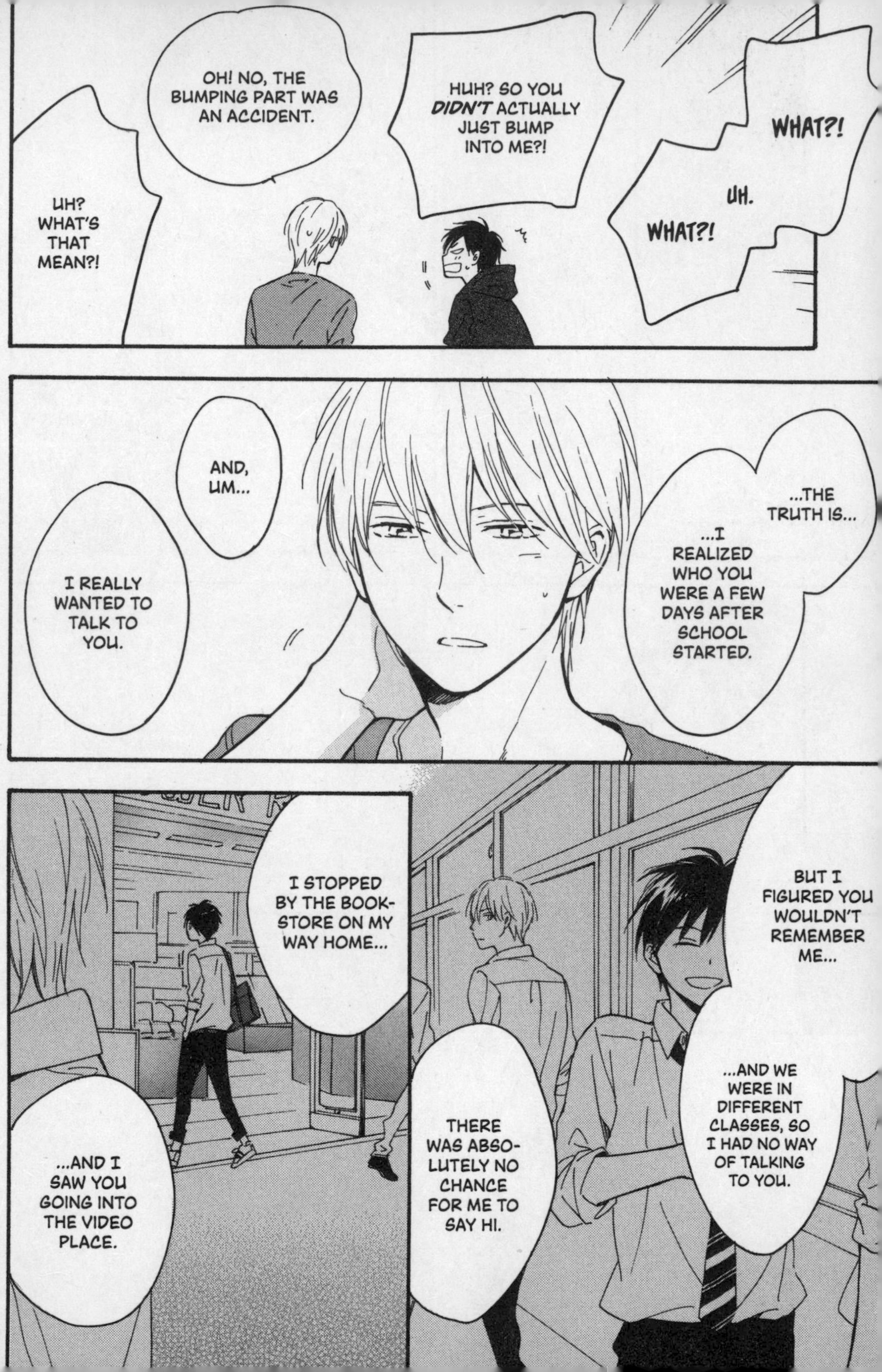
WHAT?!
UH.
WHAT?!
HUH? SO YOU *DIDN'T* ACTUALLY JUST BUMP INTO ME?!
OH! NO, THE BUMPING PART WAS AN ACCIDENT.
UH? WHAT'S THAT MEAN?!
...THE TRUTH IS...
...I REALIZED WHO YOU WERE A FEW DAYS AFTER SCHOOL STARTED.
AND, UM...
I REALLY WANTED TO TALK TO YOU.
BUT I FIGURED YOU WOULDN'T REMEMBER ME...
...AND WE WERE IN DIFFERENT CLASSES, SO I HAD NO WAY OF TALKING TO YOU.
THERE WAS ABSOLUTELY NO CHANCE FOR ME TO SAY HI.
I STOPPED BY THE BOOKSTORE ON MY WAY HOME...
...AND I SAW YOU GOING INTO THE VIDEO PLACE.

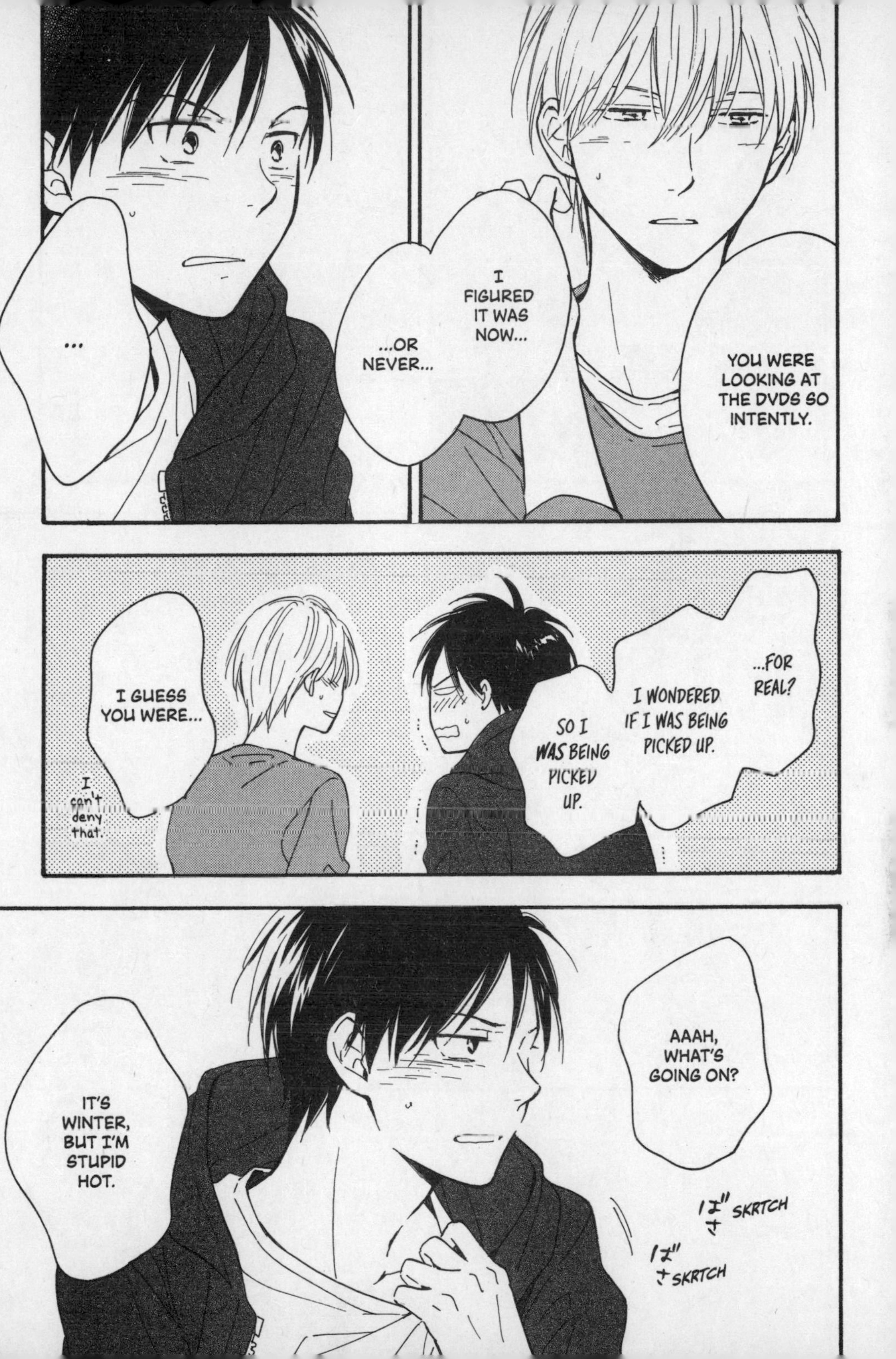
YOU WERE LOOKING AT THE DVDS SO INTENTLY.
I FIGURED IT WAS NOW...
...OR NEVER...
...
...FOR REAL?
I WONDERED IF I WAS BEING PICKED UP.
SO I WAS BEING PICKED UP.
I GUESS YOU WERE...
I can't deny that.
AAAH, WHAT'S GOING ON?
ばさ SKRTCH
ばさ SKRTCH
IT'S WINTER, BUT I'M STUPID HOT.

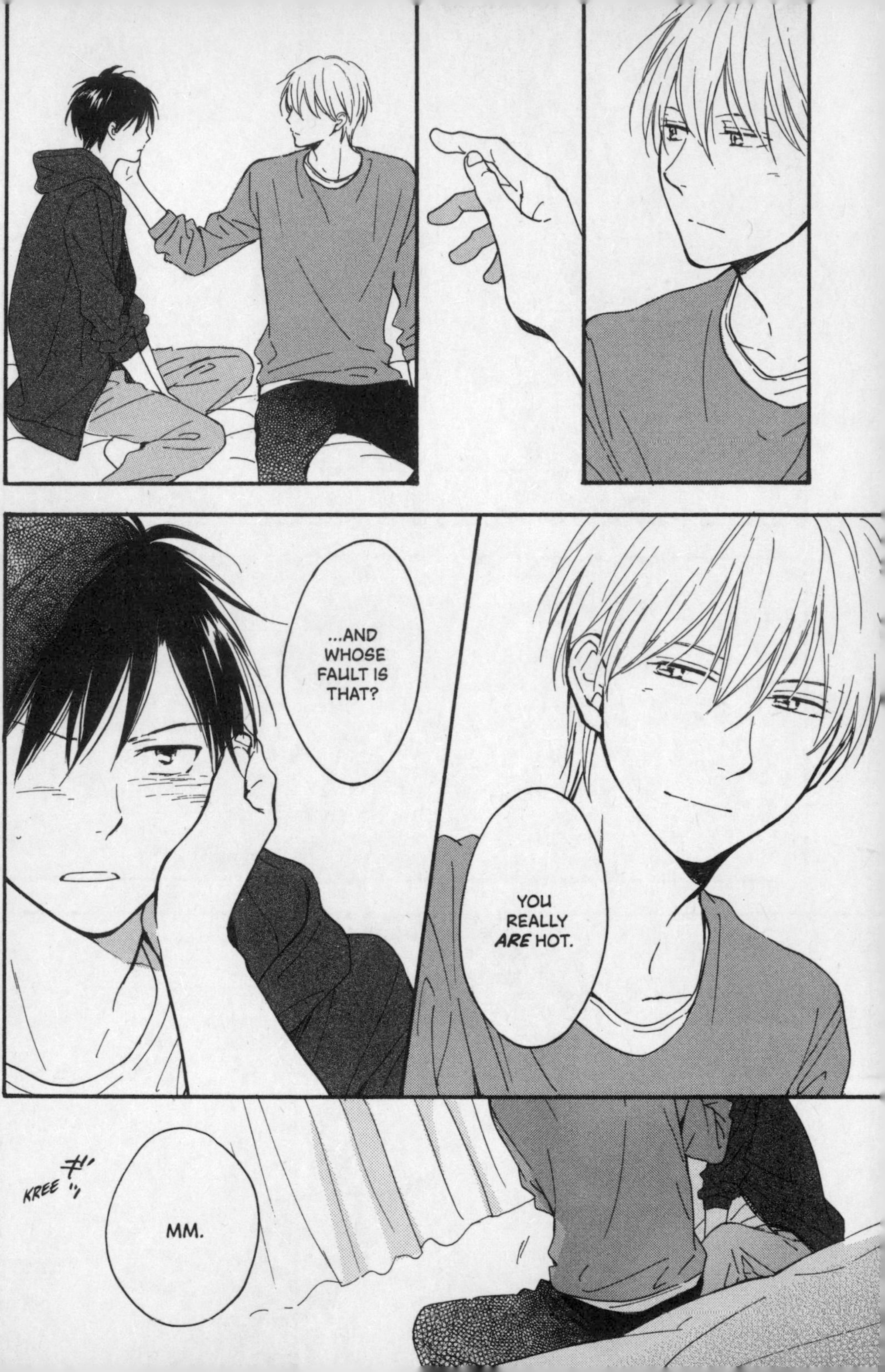
YOU REALLY *ARE* HOT.
...AND WHOSE FAULT IS THAT?
MM.
KREE

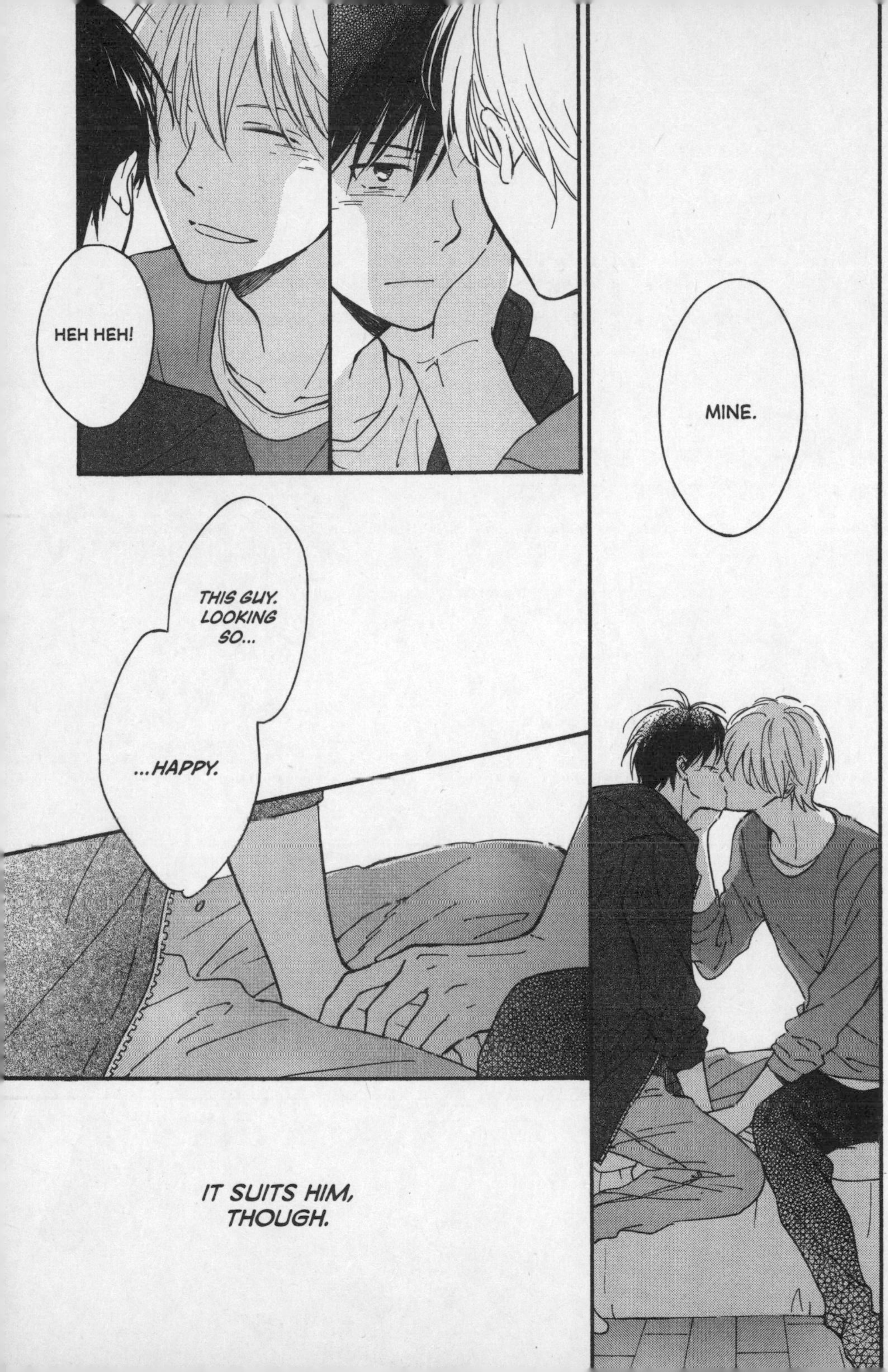
MINE.
HEH HEH!
THIS GUY. LOOKING SO...
...HAPPY.
IT SUITS HIM, THOUGH.

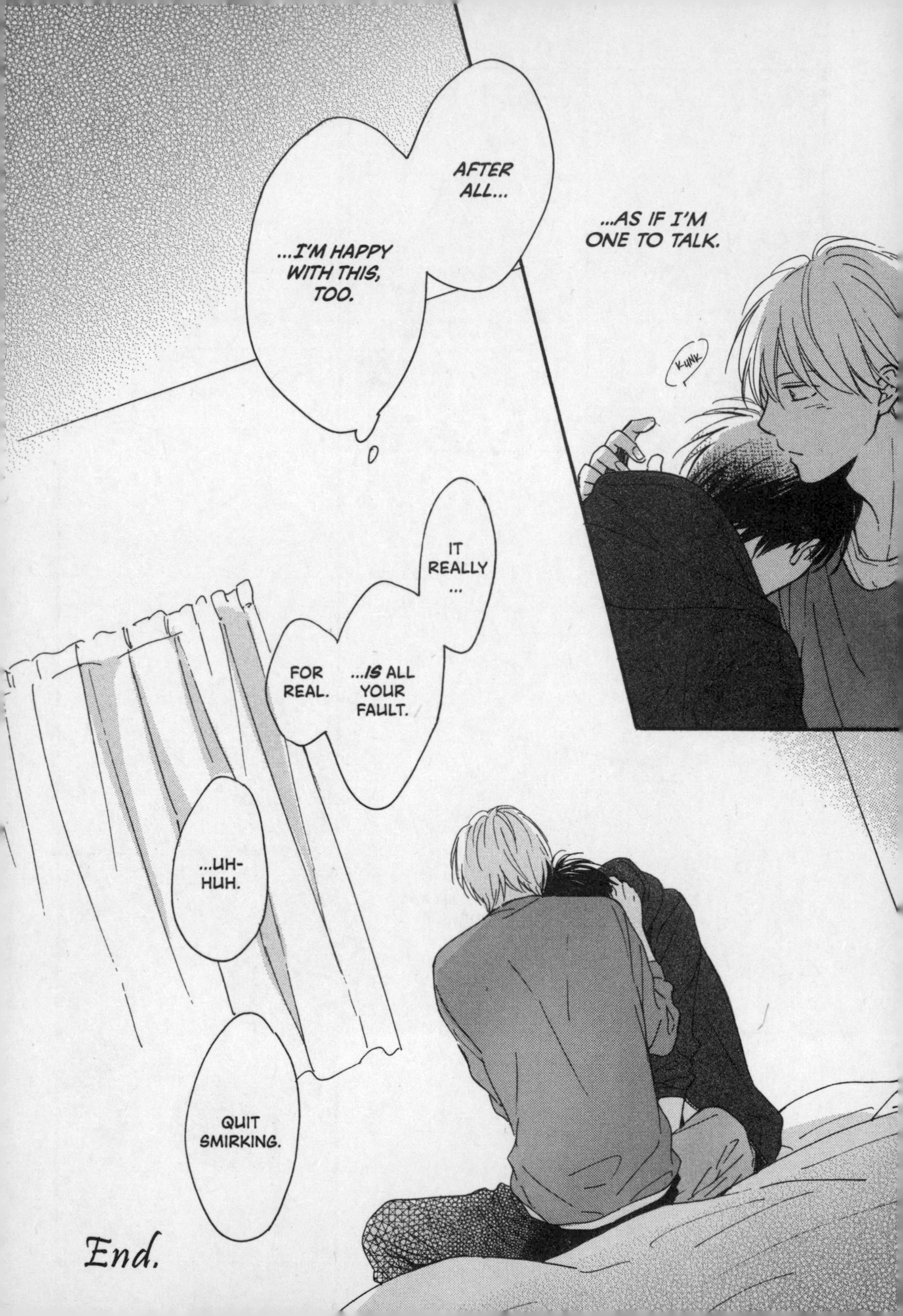
...AS IF I'M ONE TO TALK.
KUNK
AFTER ALL...
...I'M HAPPY WITH THIS, TOO.
IT REALLY...
...*IS* ALL YOUR FAULT.
FOR REAL.
...UH-HUH.
QUIT SMIRKING.
End.

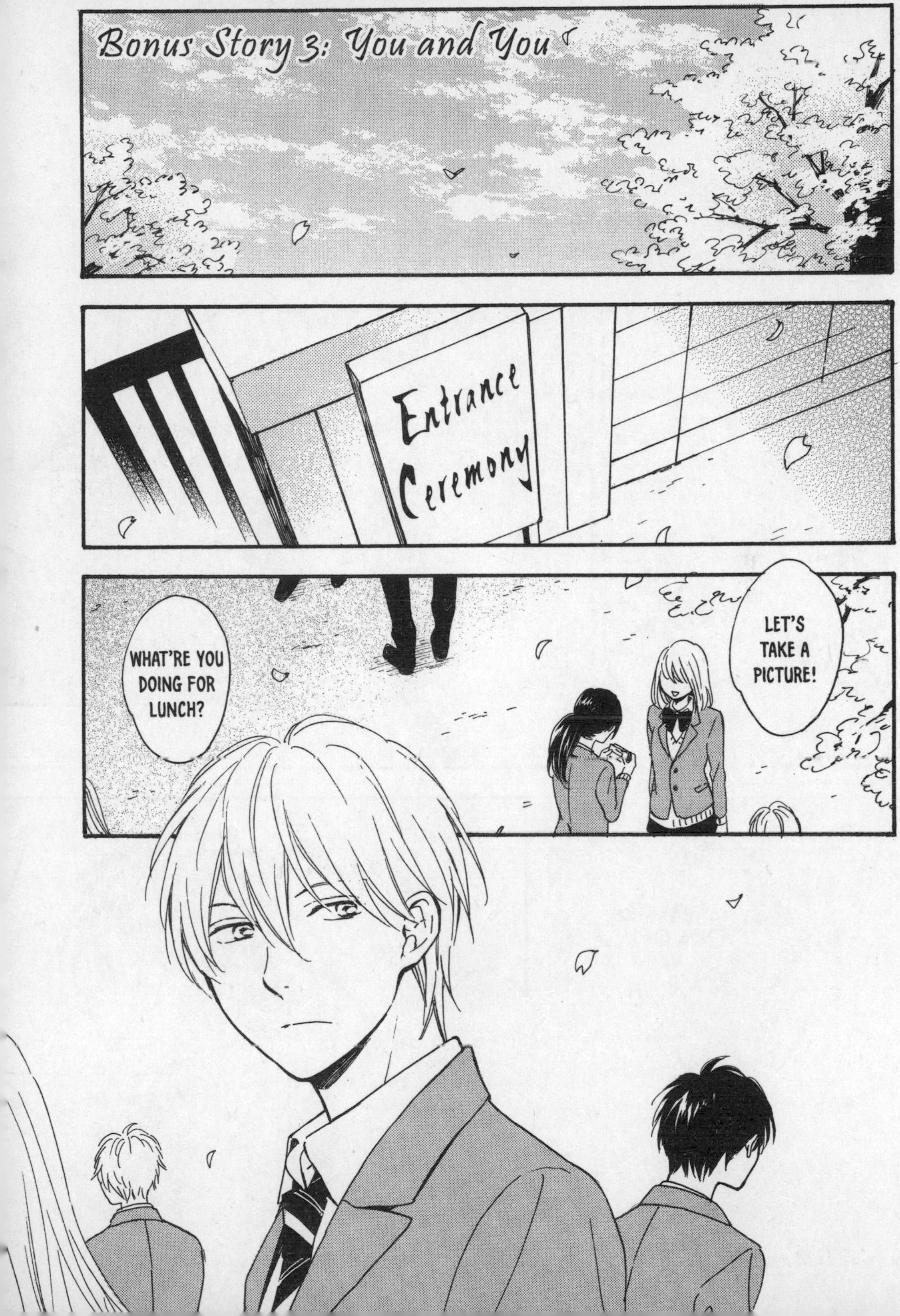
Bonus Story 3: You and You
Entrance Ceremony
LET'S TAKE A PICTURE!
WHAT'RE YOU DOING FOR LUNCH?

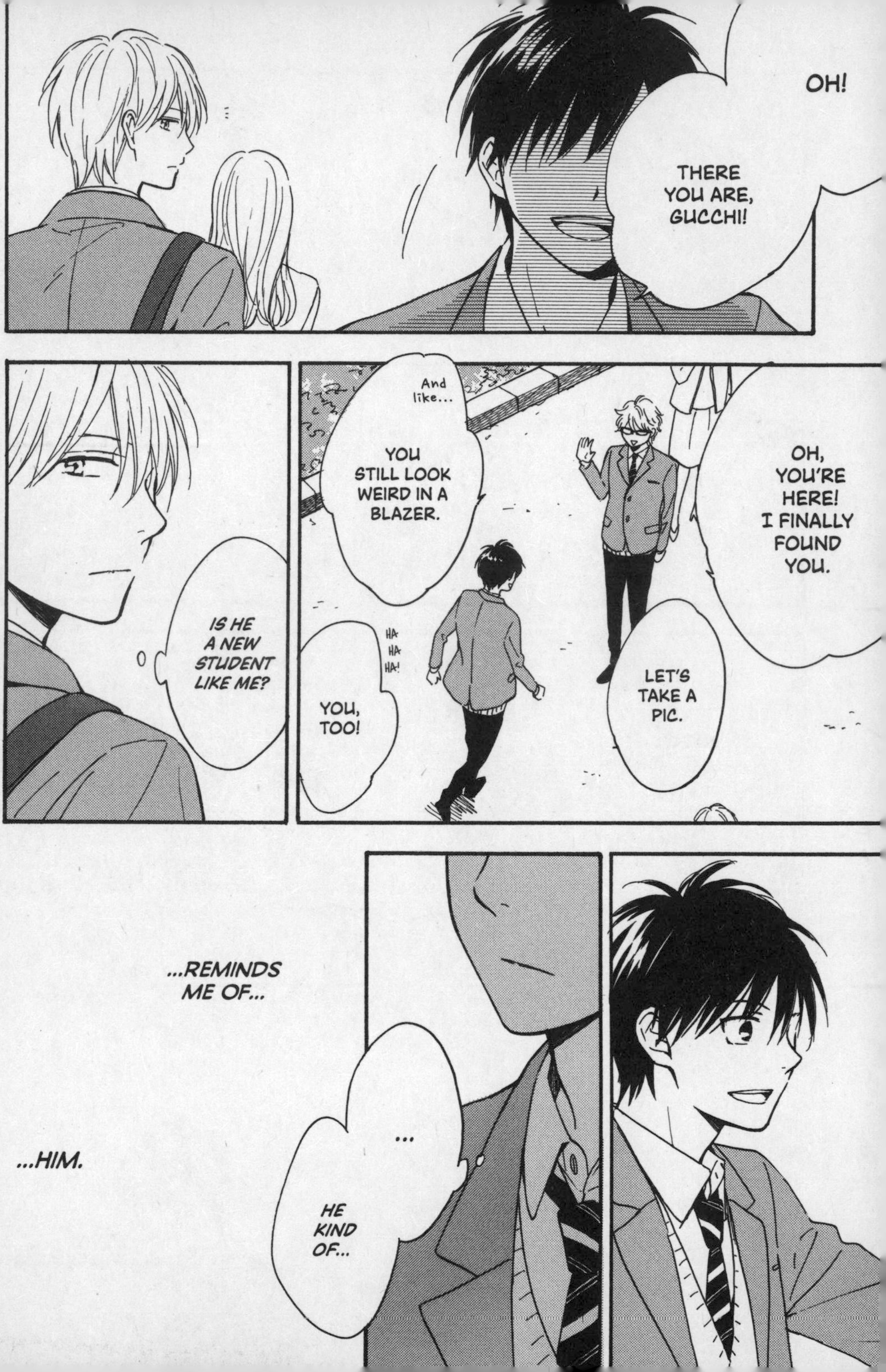
OH!
THERE YOU ARE, GUCCHI!
OH, YOU'RE HERE! I FINALLY FOUND YOU.
LET'S TAKE A PIC.
And like...
YOU STILL LOOK WEIRD IN A BLAZER.
HA HA HA!
YOU, TOO!
IS HE A NEW STUDENT LIKE ME?
...
HE KIND OF...
...REMINDS ME OF...
...HIM.

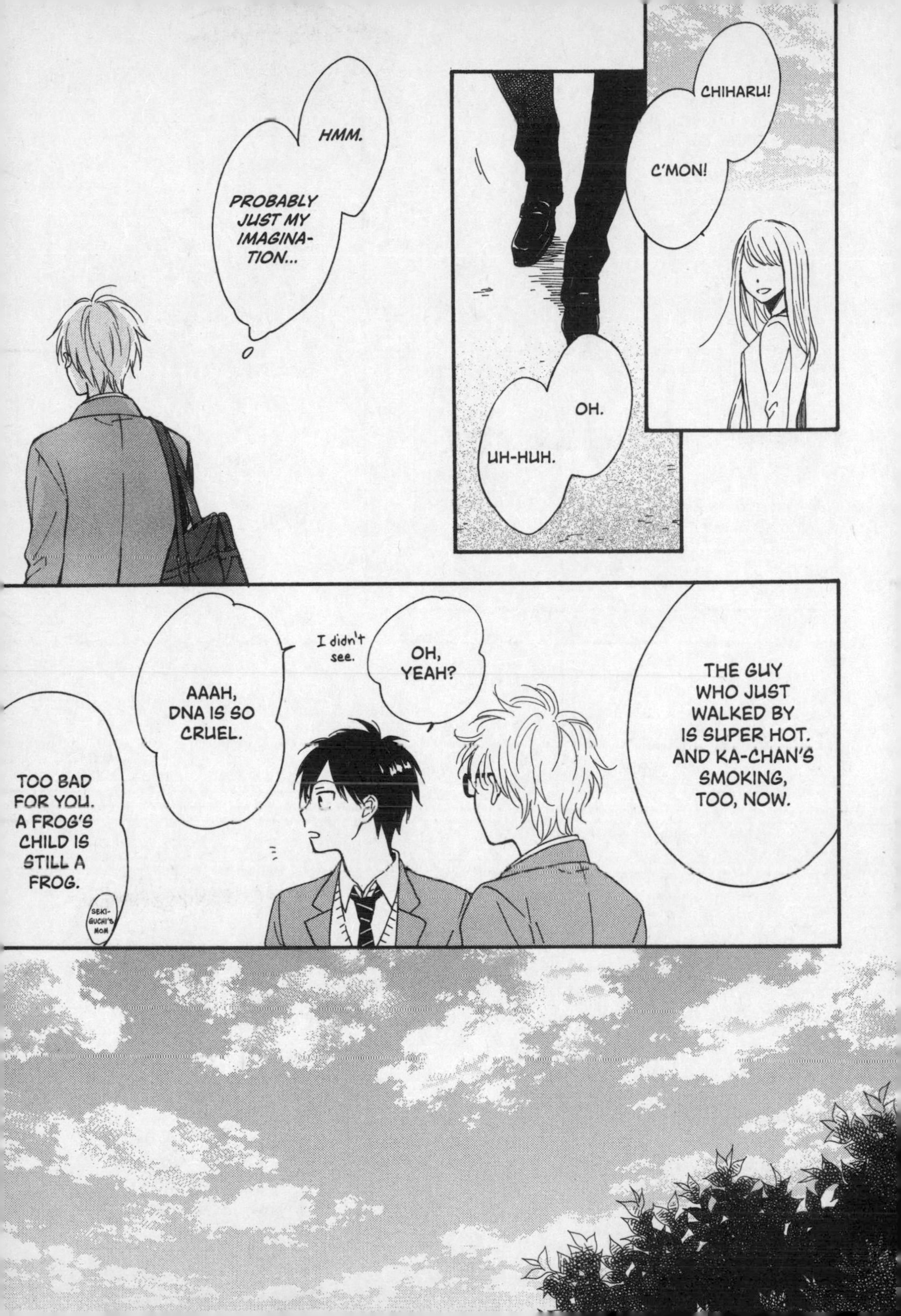
CHIHARU!
C'MON!
OH.
UH-HUH.
HMM.
PROBABLY JUST MY IMAGINATION...
THE GUY WHO JUST WALKED BY IS SUPER HOT. AND KA-CHAN'S SMOKING, TOO, NOW.
OH, YEAH?
I didn't see.
AAAH, DNA IS SO CRUEL.
TOO BAD FOR YOU. A FROG'S CHILD IS STILL A FROG.
SEKI-GUCHI'S MOM

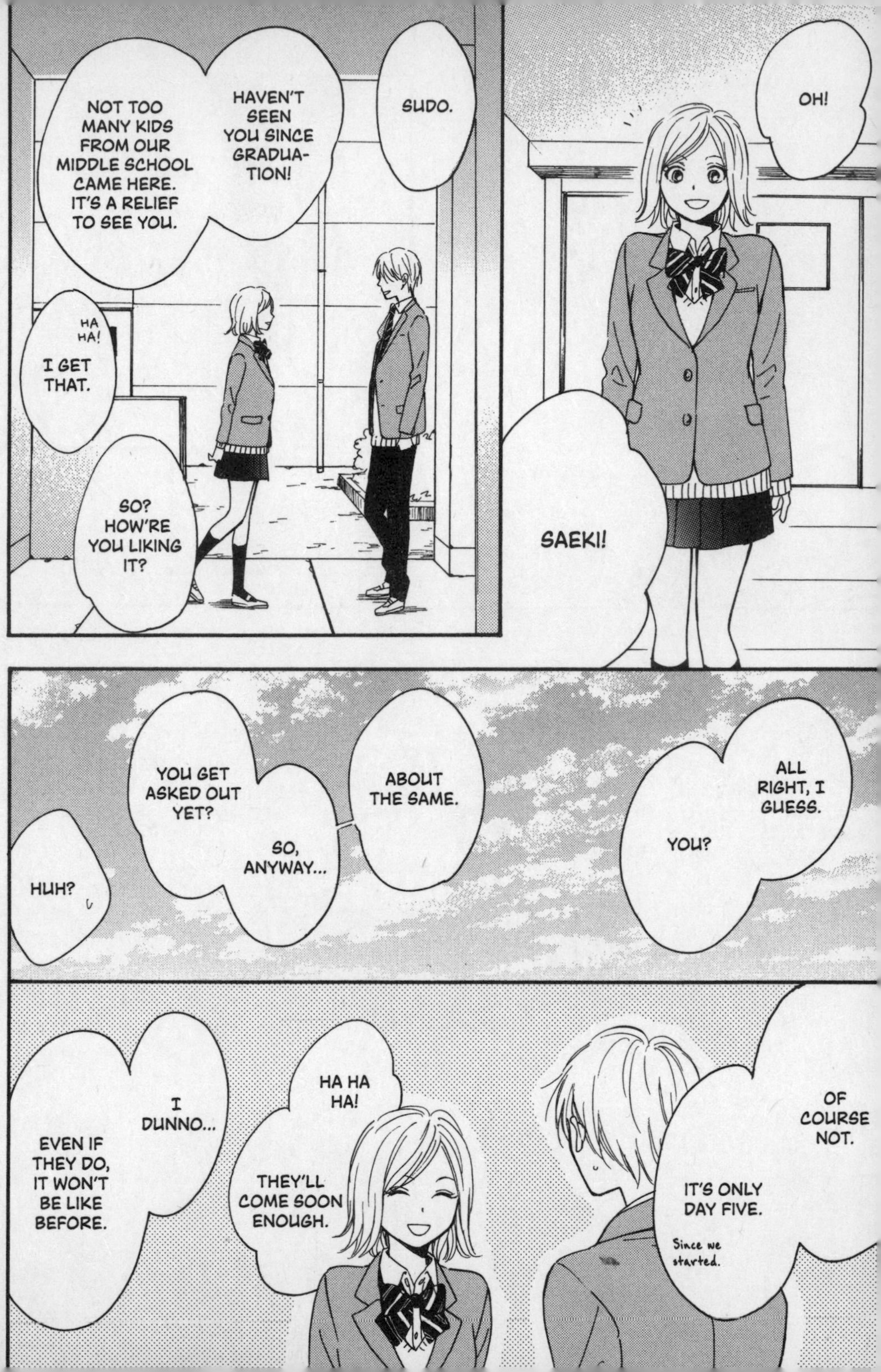
OH!
SAEKI!
SUDO.
HAVEN'T SEEN YOU SINCE GRADUATION!
NOT TOO MANY KIDS FROM OUR MIDDLE SCHOOL CAME HERE. IT'S A RELIEF TO SEE YOU.
HA HA!
I GET THAT.
SO? HOW'RE YOU LIKING IT?
ALL RIGHT, I GUESS.
YOU?
ABOUT THE SAME.
SO, ANYWAY...
YOU GET ASKED OUT YET?
HUH?
OF COURSE NOT.
IT'S ONLY DAY FIVE.
Since we started.
HA HA HA!
THEY'LL COME SOON ENOUGH.
I DUNNO...
EVEN IF THEY DO, IT WON'T BE LIKE BEFORE.

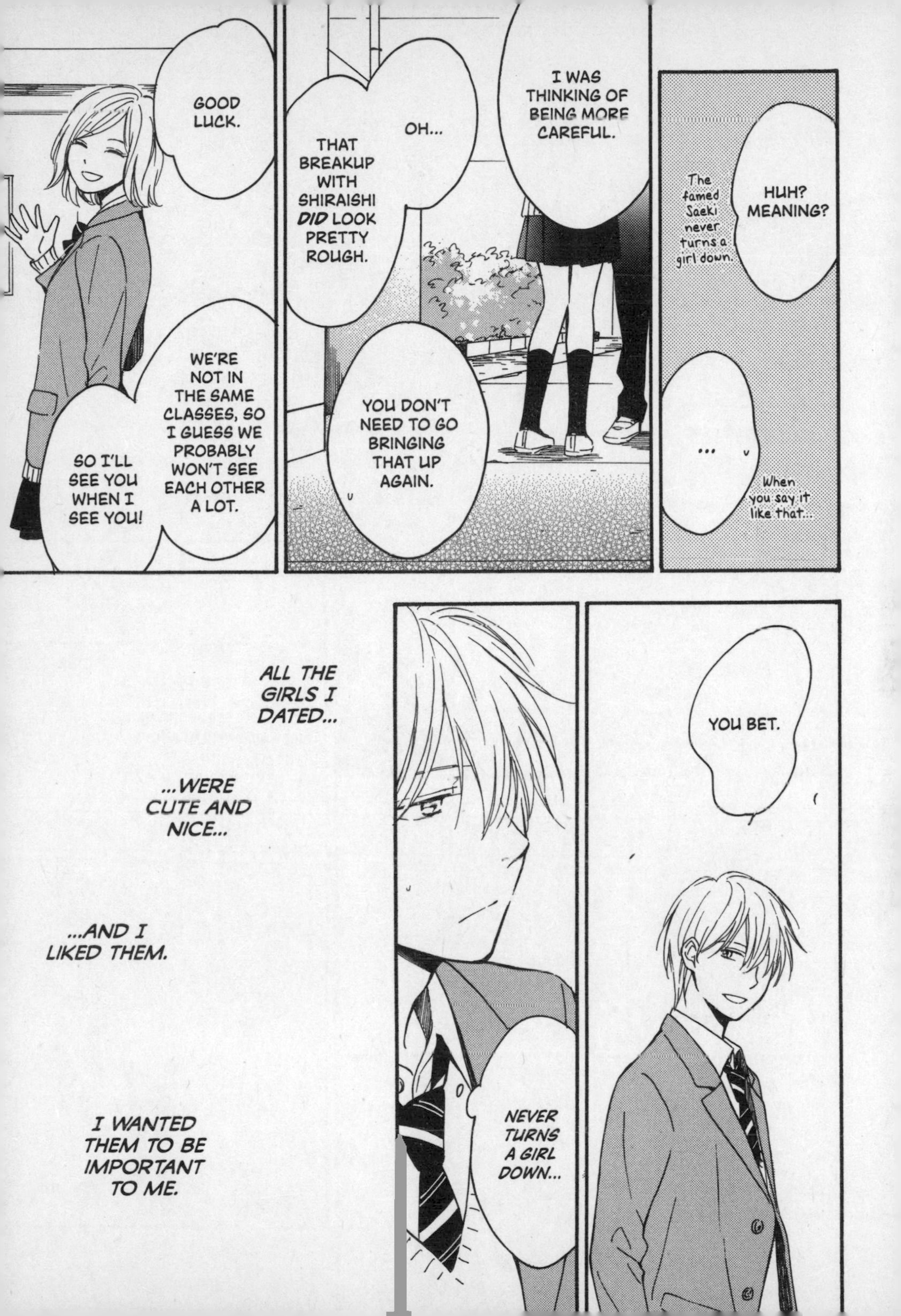
HUH? MEANING?
The famed Saeki never turns a girl down.
...
When you say it like that...
I WAS THINKING OF BEING MORE CAREFUL.
OH...
THAT BREAKUP WITH SHIRAISHI DID LOOK PRETTY ROUGH.
YOU DON'T NEED TO GO BRINGING THAT UP AGAIN.
GOOD LUCK.
WE'RE NOT IN THE SAME CLASSES, SO I GUESS WE PROBABLY WON'T SEE EACH OTHER A LOT.
SO I'LL SEE YOU WHEN I SEE YOU!
YOU BET.
NEVER TURNS A GIRL DOWN...
ALL THE GIRLS I DATED...
...WERE CUTE AND NICE...
...AND I LIKED THEM.
I WANTED THEM TO BE IMPORTANT TO ME.

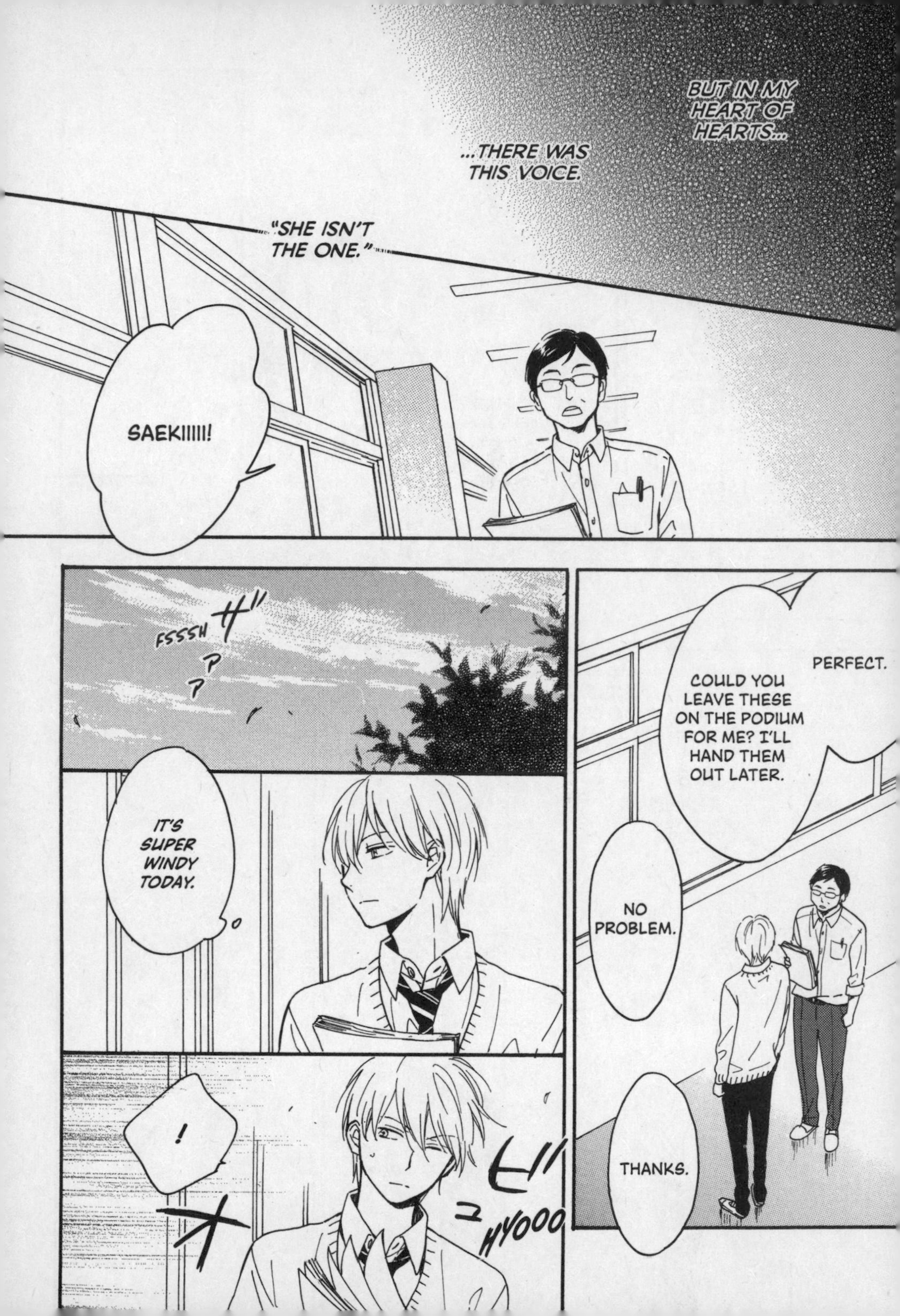
BUT IN MY HEART OF HEARTS...
...THERE WAS THIS VOICE.
..."SHE ISN'T THE ONE."...
SAEKIIIII!
PERFECT.
COULD YOU LEAVE THESE ON THE PODIUM FOR ME? I'LL HAND THEM OUT LATER.
NO PROBLEM.
THANKS.
FSSSH
ザァァ
IT'S SUPER WINDY TODAY.
!
ヒュー
HYOOO

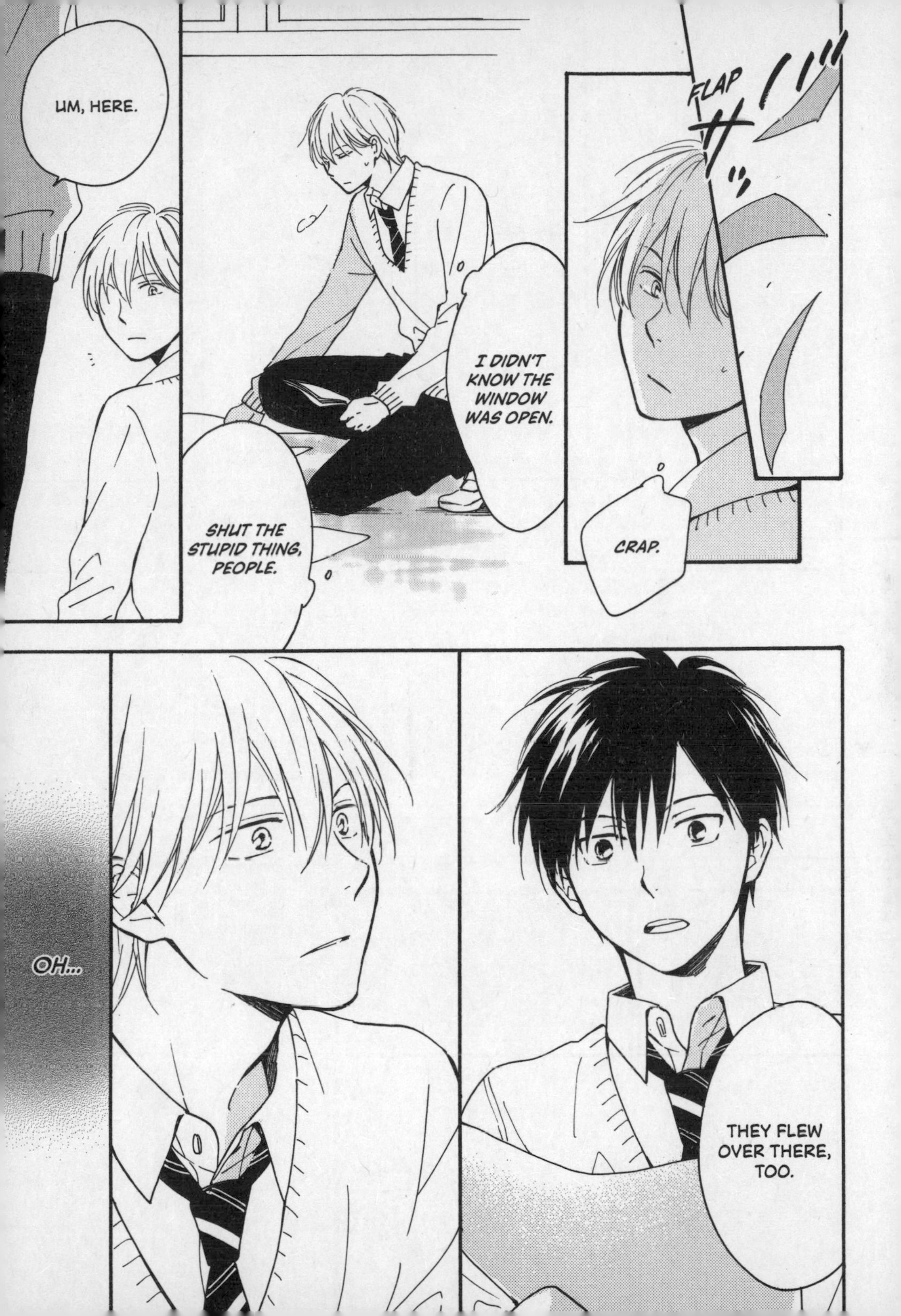
FLAP
CRAP.
I DIDN'T KNOW THE WINDOW WAS OPEN.
SHUT THE STUPID THING, PEOPLE.
UM, HERE.
THEY FLEW OVER THERE, TOO.
OH...

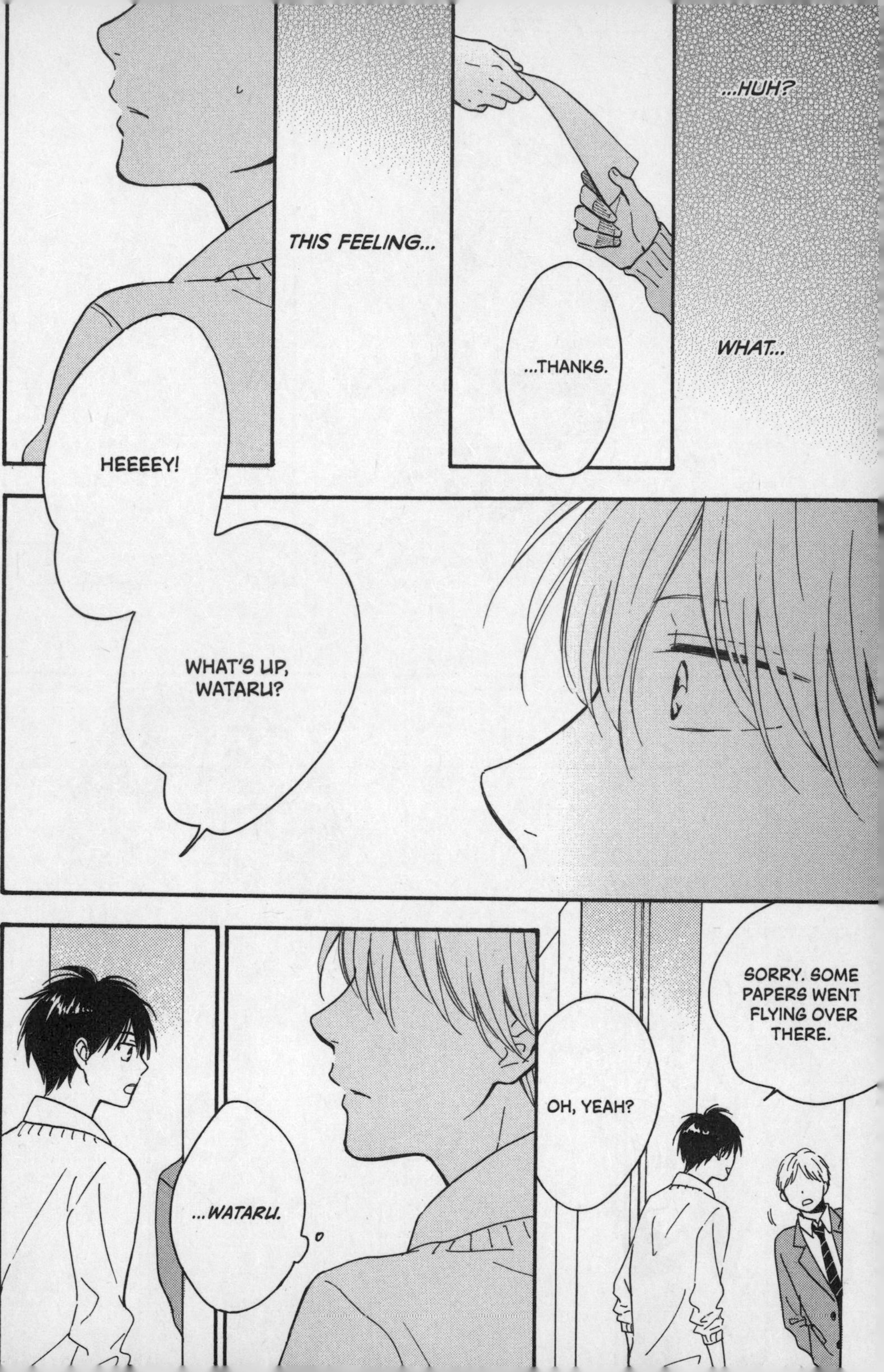
...HUH?
WHAT...
...THANKS.
THIS FEELING...
HEEEEY!
WHAT'S UP, WATARU?
SORRY. SOME PAPERS WENT FLYING OVER THERE.
OH, YEAH?
...WATARU.

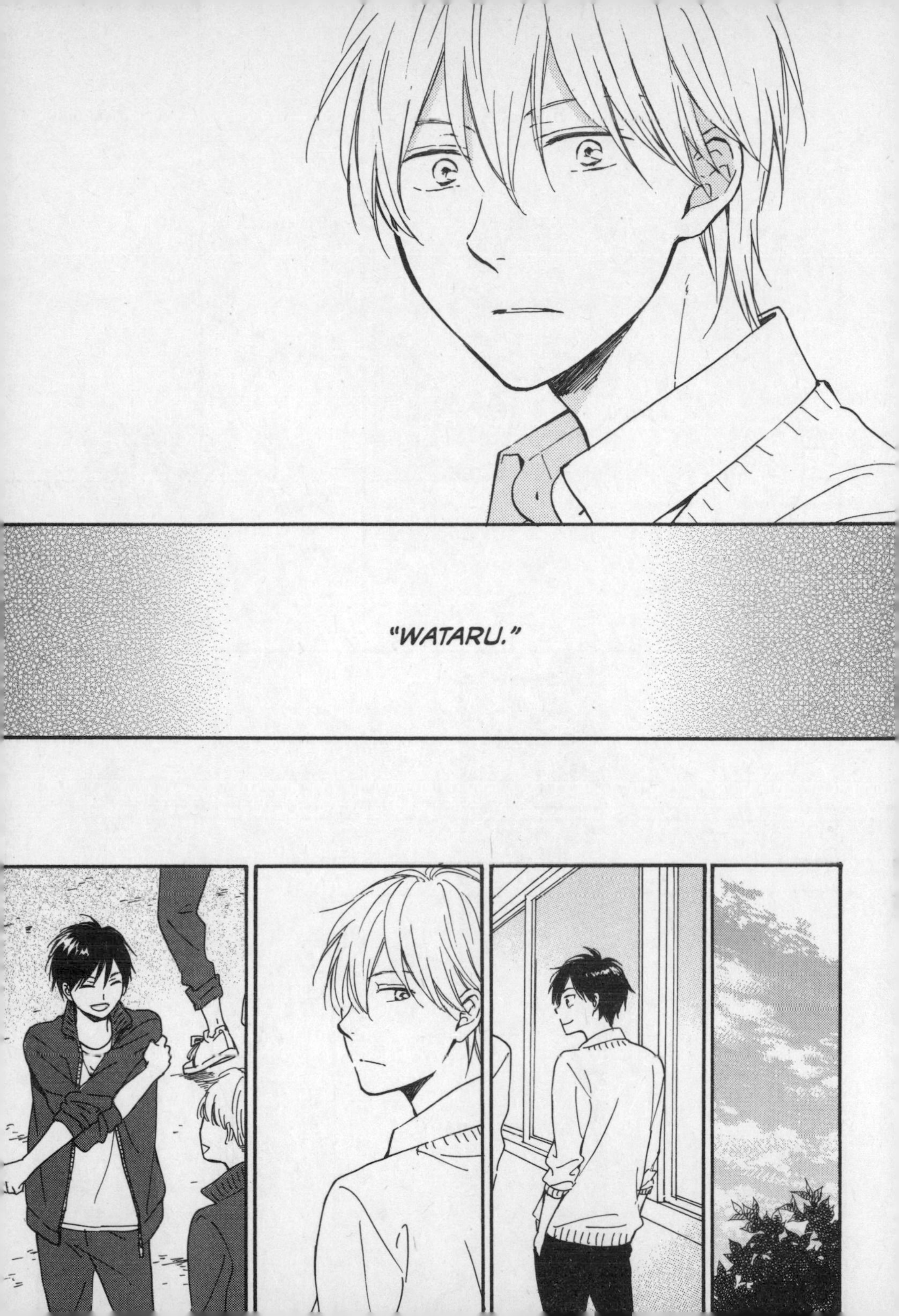
"WATARU."

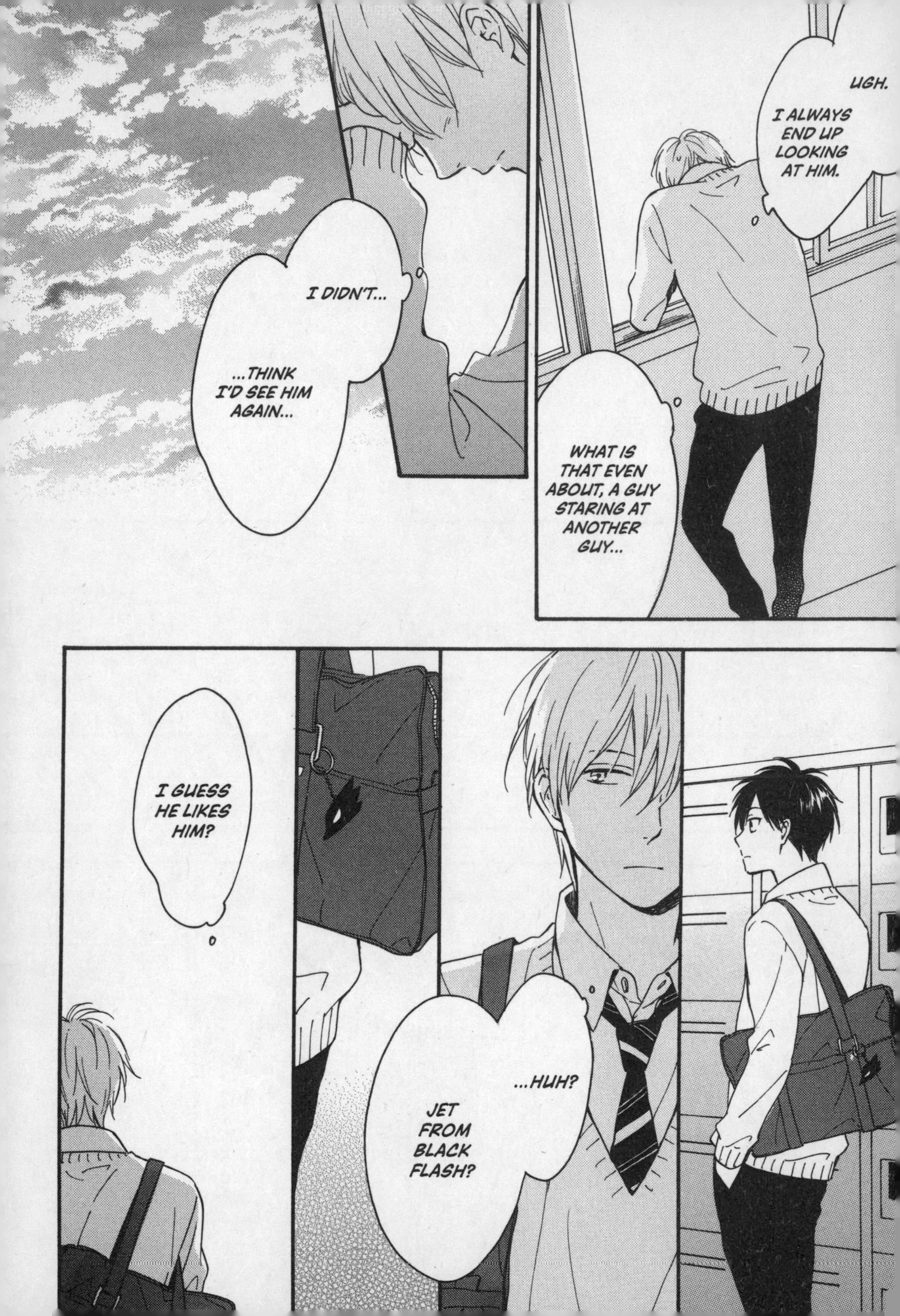
UGH.
I ALWAYS END UP LOOKING AT HIM.
WHAT IS THAT EVEN ABOUT, A GUY STARING AT ANOTHER GUY...
I DIDN'T...
...THINK I'D SEE HIM AGAIN...
...HUH?
JET FROM BLACK FLASH?
I GUESS HE LIKES HIM?

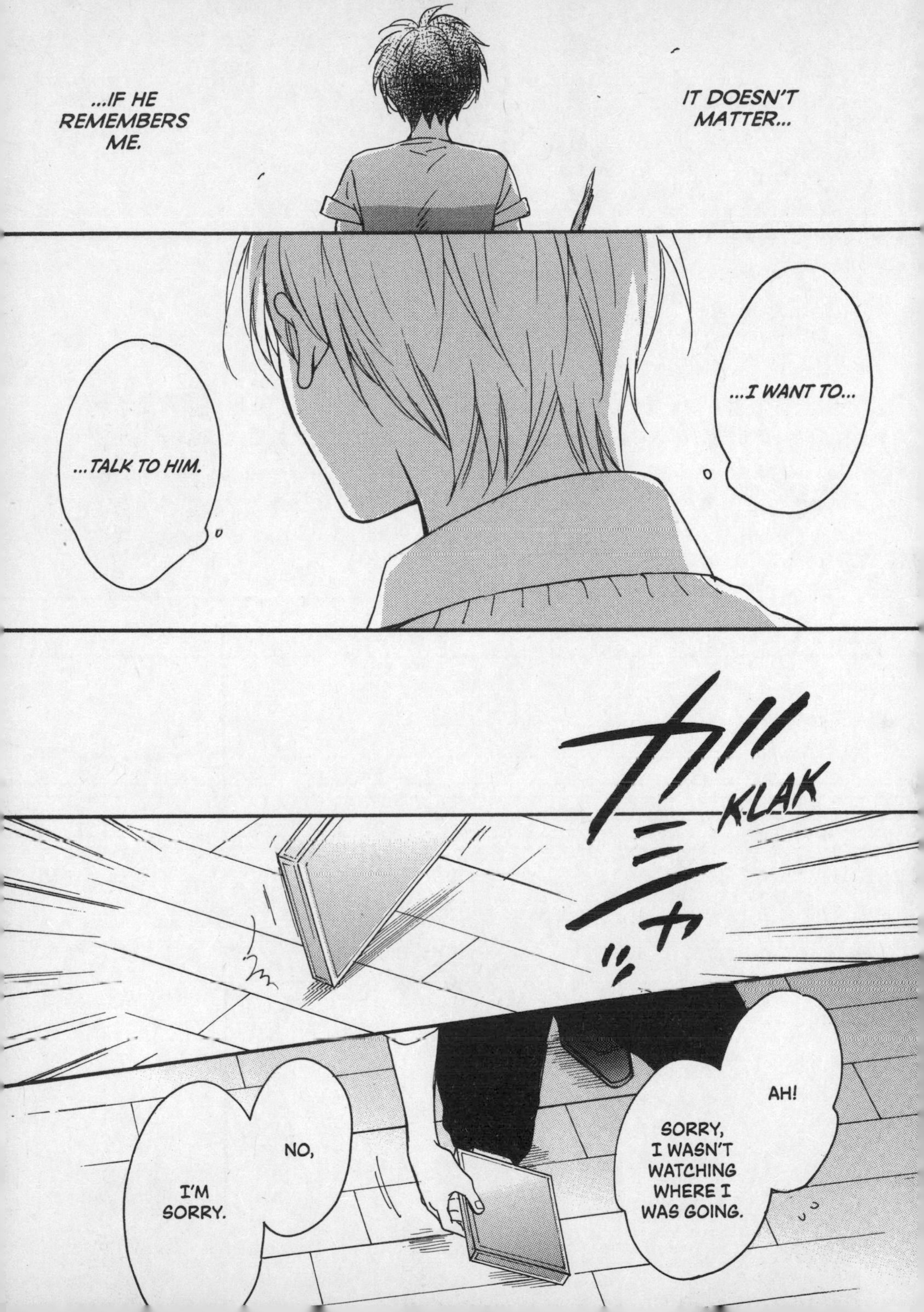
IT DOESN'T MATTER...
...IF HE REMEMBERS ME.
...I WANT TO...
...TALK TO HIM.
KLAK
AH!
SORRY, I WASN'T WATCHING WHERE I WAS GOING.
NO, I'M SORRY.

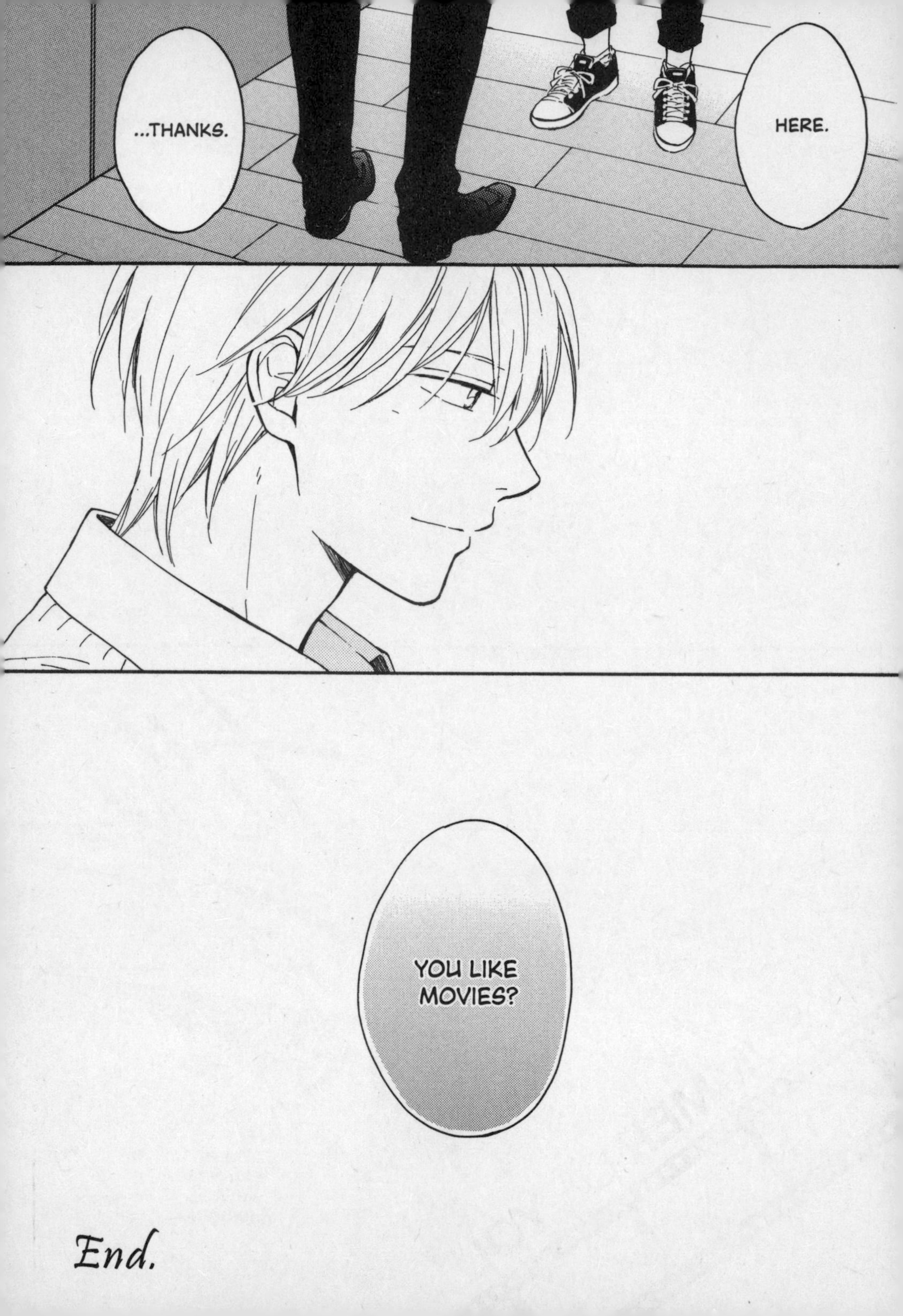
HERE.
...THANKS.
YOU LIKE MOVIES?
End.

MY SUMMER OF YOU

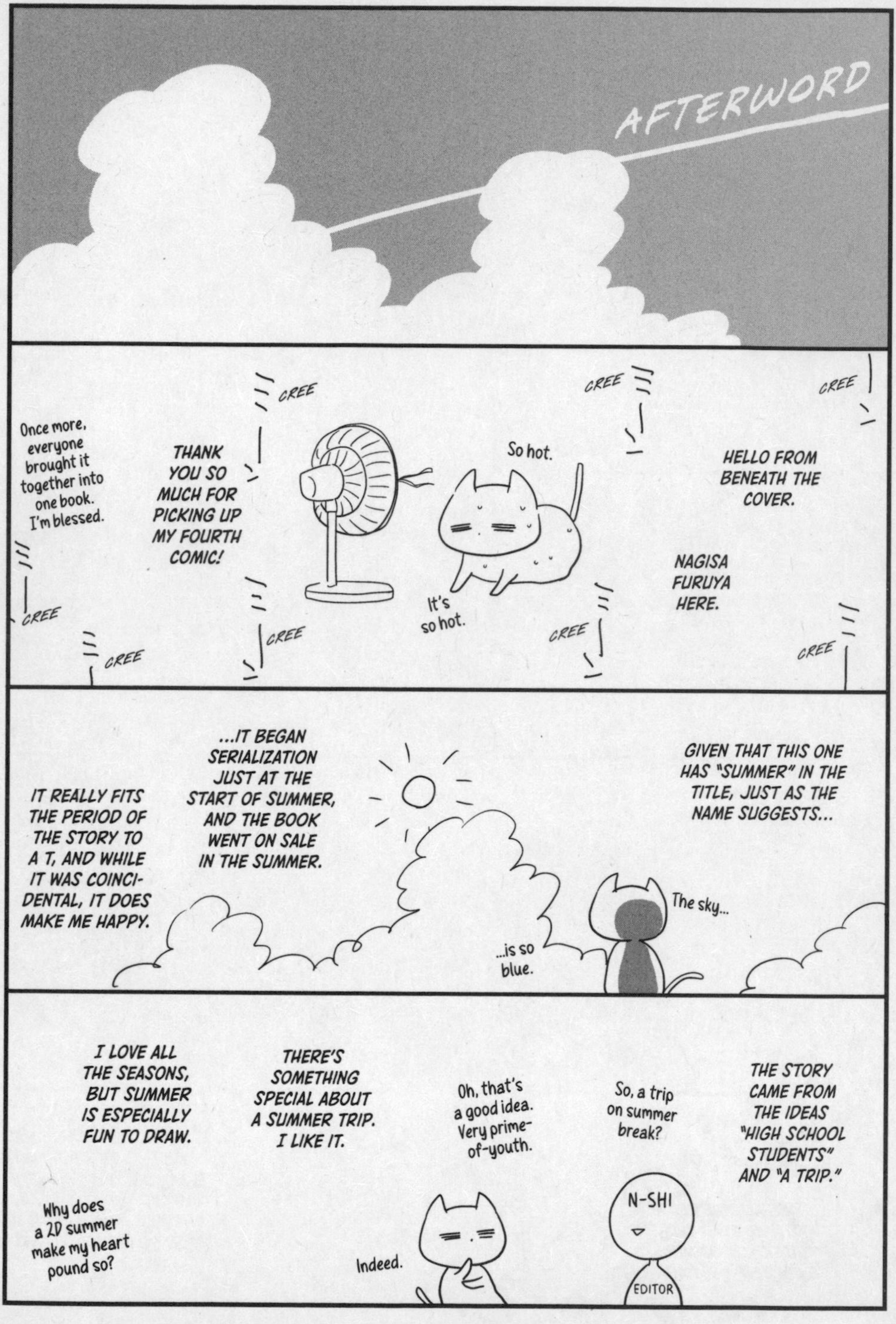
AFTERWORD
CREE
HELLO FROM BENEATH THE COVER.
NAGISA FURUYA HERE.
CREE
CREE
So hot.
It's so hot.
CREE
CREE
THANK YOU SO MUCH FOR PICKING UP MY FOURTH COMIC!
CREE
Once more, everyone brought it together into one book. I'm blessed.
CREE
CREE
GIVEN THAT THIS ONE HAS "SUMMER" IN THE TITLE, JUST AS THE NAME SUGGESTS...
The sky...
...is so blue.
...IT BEGAN SERIALIZATION JUST AT THE START OF SUMMER, AND THE BOOK WENT ON SALE IN THE SUMMER.
IT REALLY FITS THE PERIOD OF THE STORY TO A T, AND WHILE IT WAS COINCI-DENTAL, IT DOES MAKE ME HAPPY.
THE STORY CAME FROM THE IDEAS "HIGH SCHOOL STUDENTS" AND "A TRIP."
So, a trip on summer break?
N-SHI
EDITOR
Oh, that's a good idea. Very prime-of-youth.
Indeed.
THERE'S SOMETHING SPECIAL ABOUT A SUMMER TRIP. I LIKE IT.
I LOVE ALL THE SEASONS, BUT SUMMER IS ESPECIALLY FUN TO DRAW.
Why does a 2D summer make my heart pound so?

THERE WAS ALSO THE PILGRIMAGE, AND I HAD FUN DRAWING SCENES THAT I DON'T NORMALLY GET TO.
SO EVEN THOUGH THEY'RE IN HIGH SCHOOL, THEY'RE NOT AT SCHOOL TOO MUCH, WHICH FEELS STRANGELY FRESH.
The station is fun! The river is fun! The woods are fun!
The beach is fun...
...Huh? They're basically never at school?
THEY'RE BOTH MOVIE LOVERS, AND THEY HAVE THEIR OWN FAVORITE GENRES...
...BUT THEY'LL BASICALLY GO AND SEE ANYTHING, WHATEVER THE GENRE.
Wataru
Action
Comedy
Adventure
Epic series stuff
Saeki
Suspense
Mystery
Science fiction
Tense dramas
They just like movies themselves.
We'll watch anything.
THEY GO ALL OVER THE PLACE TOGETHER, AND WHEN I LOOKED AT THE DIALOGUE WHILE THE WORK WAS IN PROGRESS, WITHOUT THE IMAGES YET, IT WAS TOTALLY LIKE THEY WERE GOING OUT.
AND THEN I WOULD THINK, OH, RIGHT! THEY'RE NOT ACTUALLY DATING YET... THIS HAPPENED A LOT.
Leave us alone.
What? No way... You're not dating? What?
Shut up!
LOOKING AT IT ALL TOGETHER, THERE'S A SENSE OF DISTANCE BETWEEN THEM, BUT I'M SURE THEY'LL GET OVER THAT.
I believe in you!
BY THE WAY, I HAD PLANNED TO HAVE WATARU SWITCH FROM CALLING SAEKI "SAEKI" TO CALLING HIM "CHIHARU" AT SOME POINT, BUT I TOTALLY COULDN'T FIND A PLACE TO FIT IT IN...
It's too bad, huh, Saeking?
King?
WHILE THERE WERE OTHER THINGS I DIDN'T MANAGE TO GET TO, THESE TWO WERE A LOT OF FUN FOR ME TO DRAW.
That's a good one!
I HOPE THIS VOLUME MADE YOU FEEL THEIR SUMMER, EVEN JUST THE TINIEST BIT. TO MY EDITOR, THE DESIGNER, THE PUBLISHER, K-SHI, WHO HELPED ME WITH SCREENTONES...
GRATITUDE
...AND ALL THE READERS WHO HAVE READ THIS FAR, THANK YOU SO MUCH. I HOPE WE MEET AGAIN!

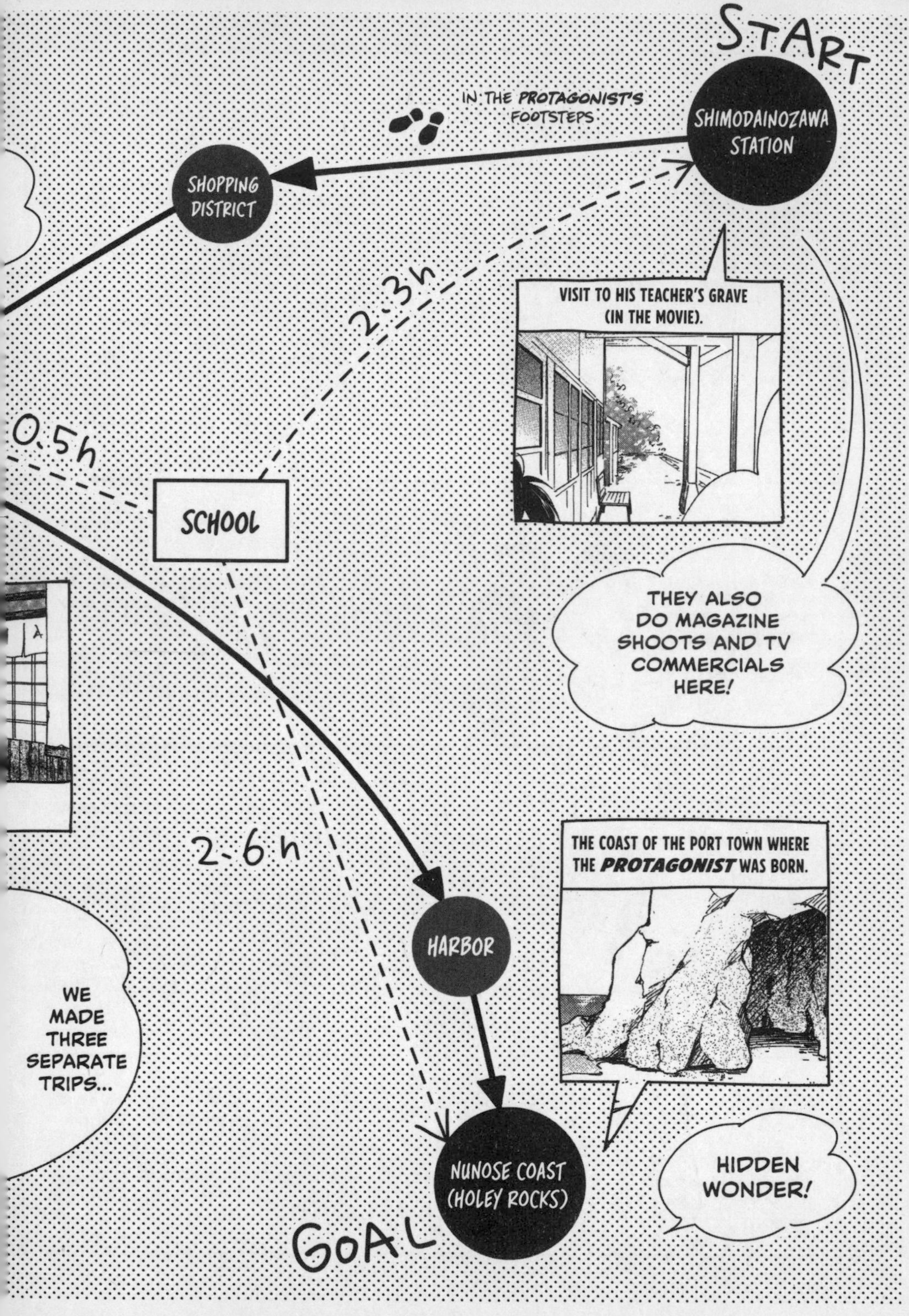
START
IN THE PROTAGONIST'S FOOTSTEPS
SHIMODAINOZAWA STATION
SHOPPING DISTRICT
2.3h
VISIT TO HIS TEACHER'S GRAVE (IN THE MOVIE).
0.5h
SCHOOL
THEY ALSO DO MAGAZINE SHOOTS AND TV COMMERCIALS HERE!
2.6h
THE COAST OF THE PORT TOWN WHERE THE PROTAGONIST WAS BORN.
HARBOR
WE MADE THREE SEPARATE TRIPS...
NUNOSE COAST (HOLEY ROCKS)
HIDDEN WONDER!
GOAL

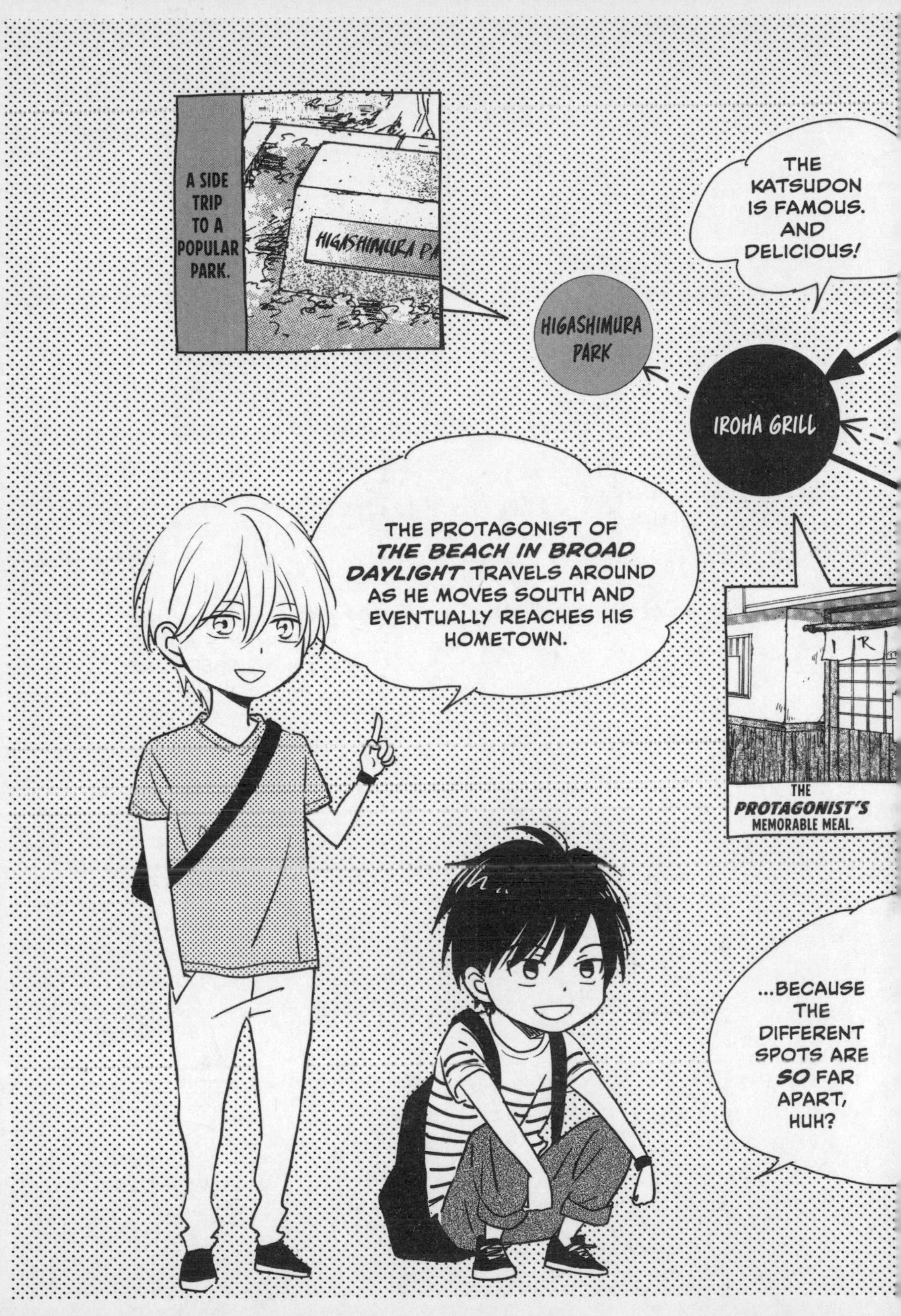
THE KATSUDON IS FAMOUS. AND DELICIOUS!
IROHA GRILL
HIGASHIMURA PARK
A SIDE TRIP TO A POPULAR PARK.
THE ***PROTAGONIST'S*** MEMORABLE MEAL.
THE PROTAGONIST OF ***THE BEACH IN BROAD DAYLIGHT*** TRAVELS AROUND AS HE MOVES SOUTH AND EVENTUALLY REACHES HIS HOMETOWN.
...BECAUSE THE DIFFERENT SPOTS ARE ***SO*** FAR APART, HUH?

Nagisa Furuya

I like drawing summer stories.

TRANSLATION NOTES

2-C, page 6
In Japanese schools, students are assigned to a homeroom where they spend most of the school day, and it's the teachers, not the students, who move from room to room be tween periods. These homerooms are designated with a combination of a number, representing the class year, and a letter. So 2-C, for example, would be second-year, class C.

-kun, page 6
-kun is an honorific often attached to the names of boys or younger men.

Senpai, page 37
Senpai (sometimes romanized as *sempai*; literally "a fellow who has gone before") is a term of respect for someone who is ahead of you in a particular discipline or social group. In the context of school, it typically means an upperclassman. It can be used as a noun or form of address on its own, or attached to a person's name like any other honorific (as we see here with Wataru calling Sekiguchi "Sekiguchi-senpai"). The opposite of senpai is *kouhai* (literally "a fellow who comes after").

Garigari-kun and PaXXko, page 37
Sekiguchi is referring to Garigari-kun popsicles, a popular brand of cheap popsicles widely available in Japanese convenience stores, and known for its classic soda flavor. PaXXko isn't referring to a specific, real-life snack (the middle character is obscured in the original Japanese), but in the context of this scene, it is likely a candy or other type of snack.

Katsudon, Page 67
Katsudon is a Japanese rice bowl (*donburi*) dish consisting of slices of pork cutlet (*katsu*), eggs, and vegetables (often scallions) served over a bowl of rice.

-chan, page 144
-chan is an honorific used to express endearment, and is often used between close friends. *-chan* often implies a sense of childish cuteness and is mostly used toward girls, but can also be used to address little children, pets, and anything considered cute.

Shinkansen, page 196
The Shinkansen, or bullet train, is the fastest train line in Japan, and is used to travel to major cities across the country.

USJ, page 197
USJ is short for Universal Studios Japan, a popular theme park in Osaka.

"Hello from beneath the cover," page 240
In the Japanese edition of *My Summer of You*, the bonus comics on pages 240 and 241 originally appeared on the inside cover of the paperback, hidden beneath the book's dust jacket.

Young characters and steampunk setting, like *Howl's Moving Castle* and *Battle Angel Alita*

Beyond the Clouds © 2018 Nicke / Ki-oon

A boy with a talent for machines and a mysterious girl whose wings he's fixed will take you beyond the clouds! In the tradition of the high-flying, resonant adventure stories of Studio Ghibli comes a gorgeous tale about the longing of young hearts for adventure and friendship!

A SMART, NEW ROMANTIC COMEDY FOR FANS OF *SHORTCAKE CAKE* AND *TERRACE HOUSE*!

A romance manga starring high school girl Meeko, who learns to live on her own in a boarding house whose living room is home to the odd (but handsome) Matsunaga-san. She begins to adjust to her new life away from her parents, but Meeko soon learns that no matter how far away from home she is, she's still a young girl at heart — especially when she finds herself falling for Matsunaga-san.

PERFECT WORLD

Rie Aruga

A TOUCHING NEW SERIES ABOUT LOVE AND COPING WITH DISABILITY

An office party reunites Tsugumi with her high school crush Itsuki. He's realized his dream of becoming an architect, but along the way, he experienced a spinal injury that put him in a wheelchair. Now Tsugumi's rekindled feelings will butt up against prejudices she never considered — and Itsuki will have to decide if he's ready to let someone into his heart...

"Depicts with great delicacy and courage the difficulties some with disabilities experience getting involved in romantic relationships... Rie Aruga refuses to romanticize, pushing her heroine to face the reality of disability. She invites her readers to the same tasks of empathy, knowledge and recognition."
—Slate.fr

"An important entry [in manga romance]... The emotional core of both plot and characters indicates thoughtfulness... [Aruga's] research is readily apparent in the text and artwork, making this feel like a real story."
—Anime News Network

KC KODANSHA COMICS

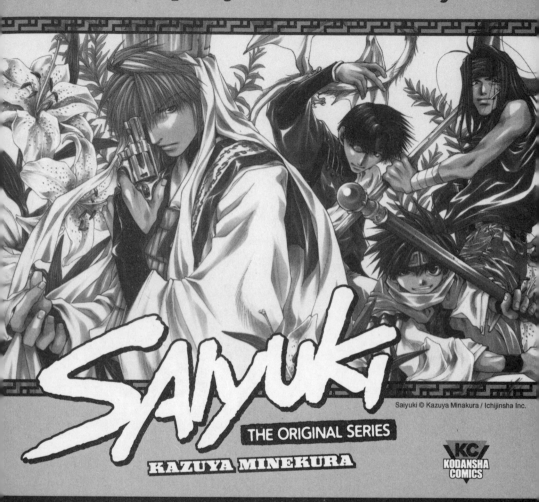

The adorable new odd-couple cat comedy manga from the creator of the beloved *Chi's Sweet Home*, in full color!

Praise for Chi's Sweet Home

"Nearly impossible to turn away... a true all-ages title that anyone, young or old, cat lover or not, will enjoy. The stories will bring a smile to your face and warm your heart."

—School Library Journal

Sue & Tai-chan

Konami Kanata

Sue is an aging housecat who's looking forward to living out her life in peace... but her plans change when the mischievous black tomcat Tai-chan enters the picture! Hey! Sue never signed up to be a catsitter! *Sue & Tai-chan* is the latest from the reigning meow-narch of cute kitty comics, Konami Kanata.

KC KODANSHA COMICS

THE SWEET SCENT OF LOVE IS IN THE AIR! FOR FANS OF OFFBEAT ROMANCES LIKE *WOTAKOI*

Sweat and Soap © Kintetsu Yamada / Kodansha Ltd.

In an office romance, there's a fine line between sexy and awkward... and that line is where Asako — a woman who sweats copiously — meets Koutarou — a perfume developer who can't get enough of Asako's, er, scent. Don't miss a romcom manga like no other!

One of CLAMP's biggest hits returns in this definitive, premium, hardcover 20th anniversary collector's edition!

Chobits © CLAMP·ShigatsuTsuitachi CO.,LTD./Kodansha Ltd.

"A wonderfully entertaining story that would be a great installment in anybody's manga collection."
— Anime News Network

"CLAMP is an all-female manga-creating team whose feminine touch shows in this entertaining, sci-fi soap opera."
— Publishers Weekly

Poor college student Hideki is down on his luck. All he wants is a good job, a girlfriend, and his very own "persocom"—the latest and greatest in humanoid computer technology. Hideki's luck changes one night when he finds Chi—a persocom thrown out in a pile of trash. But Hideki soon discovers that there's much more to his cute new persocom than meets the eye.

KC
KODANSHA
COMICS

CARDCAPTOR SAKURA
COLLECTOR'S EDITION
CLAMP

DELUXE · EDITION

Cardcaptor Sakura
CLAMP

Ten-year-old Sakura Kinomoto
lives a pretty normal life with
her older brother, Tōya, and
widowed father, Fujitaka—
until the day she discovers a
strange book in her father's
library, and her life takes a
magical turn...

- A deluxe large-format
  hardcover edition
  of CLAMP's shojo
  manga classic
- All-new foil-stamped cover
  art on each volume
- Comes with exclusive
  collectible art card

KC
KODANSHA
COMICS

The art-deco cyberpunk classic from the creators of *xxxHOLiC* and *Cardcaptor Sakura*!

"Starred Review. This experimental sci-fi work from CLAMP reads like a romantic version of *AKIRA*."
—Publishers Weekly

CLOVER © CLAMP·ShigatsuTsuitachi CO.,LTD./Kodansha Ltd.

Su was born into a bleak future, where the government keeps tight control over children with magical powers—codenamed "Clovers." With Su being the only "four-leaf" Clover in the world, she has been kept isolated nearly her whole life. Can ex-military agent Kazuhiko deliver her to the happiness she seeks? Experience the complete series in this hardcover edition, which also includes over twenty pages of ravishing color art!

KC KODANSHA COMICS

MAGIC KNIGHT RAYEARTH

25TH ANNIVERSARY EDITION

CLAMP

A BELOVED CLASSIC MAKES ITS STUNNING RETURN IN THIS GORGEOUS, LIMITED EDITION BOX SET!

MAGIC KNIGHT RAYEARTH
CLAMP
MAGIC KNIGHT RAYEARTH
MAGIC KNIGHT RAYEARTH
CLAMP
MAGIC KNIGHT RAYEARTH
CLAMP

MAGIC KNIGHT RAYEARTH
CLAMP
KC KODANSHA CLASSICS
MAGIC KNIGHT RAYEARTH
KC KODANSHA CLASSICS
MAGIC KNIGHT RAYEARTH
KC KODANSHA CLASSICS
MAGIC KNIGHT RAYEARTH

This tale of three Tokyo teenagers who cross through a magical portal and become the champions of another world is a modern manga classic. The box set includes three volumes of manga covering the entire first series of *Magic Knight Rayearth*, plus the series's super-rare full-color art book companion, all printed at a larger size than ever before on premium paper, featuring a newly-revised translation and lettering, and exquisite foil-stamped covers. A strictly limited edition, this will be gone in a flash!

KC KODANSHA COMICS

The beloved characters from *Cardcaptor Sakura* return in a brand new, reimagined fantasy adventure!

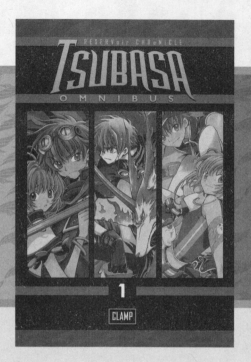

"[*Tsubasa*] takes readers on a fantastic ride that only gets more exhilarating with each successive chapter." —Anime News Network

In the Kingdom of Clow, an archaeological dig unleashes an incredible power, causing Princess Sakura to lose her memories. To save her, her childhood friend Syaoran must follow the orders of the Dimension Witch and travel alongside Kurogane, an unrivaled warrior; Fai, a powerful magician; and Mokona, a curiously strange creature, to retrieve Sakura's dispersed memories!

Beautifully seductive artwork and uniquely Japanese depictions of the supernatural will hypnotize CLAMP fans!

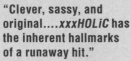

xxxHOLiC © CLAMP-ShigatsuTsuitachi CO.,LTD./Kodansha Ltd.
xxxHOLiC Rei © CLAMP-ShigatsuTsuitachi CO.,LTD./Kodansha Ltd.

Kimihiro Watanuki is haunted by visions of ghosts and spirits. He seeks help from a mysterious woman named Yuko, who claims she can help. However, Watanuki must work for Yuko in order to pay for her aid. Soon Watanuki finds himself employed in Yuko's shop, where he sees things and meets customers that are stranger than anything he could have ever imagined.

KC
KODANSHA COMICS

A BL romance between a good boy who didn't know he was waiting for a hero, and a bad boy who comes to his rescue!

Masahiro Setagawa doesn't believe in heroes, but wishes he could: He's found himself in a gang of small-time street bullies, and with no prospects for a real future. But when high school teacher (and scourge of the streets) Kousuke Ohshiba comes to his rescue, he finds he may need to start believing after all... in heroes, and in his budding feelings, too.

Hitorijime My Hero

Memeco Arii

KC KODANSHA COMICS

A Kodansha Comics Trade Paperback Original
My Summer of You Vol. 1: The Summer of You copyright © 2021 Nagisa Furuya
English translation copyright © 2021 Nagisa Furuya

All rights reserved.

Published in the United States by Kodansha Comics, an imprint of
Kodansha USA Publishing, LLC, New York.

Publication rights for this English edition arranged through
Kodansha Ltd., Tokyo.

First published in Japan in 2017 by Ichijinsha Inc., Tokyo
as *Kimi wa natsu no naka.*

ISBN 978-1-64651-204-1

Printed in the United States of America.

www.kodansha.us

9 8 7 6 5 4 3 2
Translation: Jocelyne Allen
Lettering: Nicole Roderick
Editing: Tiff Joshua TJ Ferentini
Kodansha Comics edition cover design by Adam Del Re

Publisher: Kiichiro Sugawara

Director of publishing services: Ben Applegate
Associate director of operations: Stephen Pakula
Publishing services managing editor: Noelle Webster
Assistant production manager: Emi Lotto, Angela Zurlo
Logo and character art ©Kodansha USA Publishing, LLC